DIGITAL EHS STRATEGY

TRANSFORMING SAFETY, COMPLIANCE, AND SUSTAINABILITY

Dr. Jayakumar Indracanti

ISBN
Paperback 979-8-89744-563-9
Hardcase 979-8-89777-692-4

Contents

Introduction

Every workplace incident represents more than just a number—it's a missed opportunity to protect lives, strengthen resilience, and improve profitability. In today's fast-evolving business landscape, organizations embracing digital EHS solutions are achieving transformative results: a 35% reduction in workplace accidents, millions saved in compliance costs, and a stronger foothold in the ESG-driven market.

This book explores how leaders can harness the power of digital EHS transformation to drive long-term strategic value. It's not just about adopting new technologies but about reimagining safety, compliance, and environmental management as pillars of business success. Whether you are an executive or an EHS professional, this guide provides a roadmap to turn operational challenges into opportunities for competitive advantage.

As a consultant, IT manager, and digital capability leader in Environment, Health, and Safety (EHS), I have had numerous discussions with executives and transformation leaders from various industries. In these conversations, I often ask about their motivations for embarking on digital EHS transformations. Many point to external pressures such as regulatory changes, industry standards, and increasing stakeholder demands as their primary drivers. They frequently mention the need to align with global sustainability frameworks, reduce operational risks, or improve their company's safety image as regulations like ESG expectations rise.

However, I have also encountered companies that take a more intrinsic approach. These organizations often cite internal factors, such as declining Total Recordable Incident Rates (TRIR), a rise in near misses, compliance issues, or underperforming safety audits, as key reasons for pursuing digital Transformation. While working with some of the larger MNCs, I have also came across intrinsic factors such as the need for improved data integration, cost efficiency, global standardization, enhanced compliance, scalability, and user experience.

The Drivers of EHS Digital Transformation

The push for digital transformation in EHS goes beyond operational needs—it defines the foundation for long-term resilience and leadership in an increasingly competitive and regulated market. Organizations face external pressures and internal imperatives that propel them toward adopting digital solutions. These drivers are categorized as follows:

External Drivers

1. **Regulatory Compliance** Regulatory compliance is no longer just about avoiding penalties—it's about future-proofing your organization. Companies leading in this space treat compliance as a dynamic baseline, investing in agile systems that anticipate regulatory changes and streamline global operations. For example, 78% of firms in a Verdantix study cited compliance management as a key factor in investing in EHS software solutions.

2. **Stakeholder Expectations** Growing emphasis on Environmental, Social, and Governance (ESG) factors shapes organizational priorities. Investors, customers, and the public increasingly demand transparent, robust ESG practices, prompting 45% of companies to adopt EHS software to enhance sustainability reporting.

3. **Industry Standards and Best Practices** Adapting to evolving industry standards is critical. Organizations can streamline certification processes by aligning with these standards through digital tools, improve cross-departmental collaboration, and build stakeholder trust. A Verdantix study found that 62% of firms view alignment with best practices as a key driver for EHS transformation.

Internal Drivers

1. **Operational Efficiency** Digital tools simplify processes, reduce manual effort, and optimize resource allocation. For 70% of organizations,

improving operational efficiency is a primary motivator for adopting EHS solutions, ensuring scalability without compromising safety.

2. **Risk Management** Enhancing risk identification and mitigation capabilities is critical, with advanced analytics and predictive tools empowering organizations to manage potential hazards proactively.

3. **Data-Driven Decision-Making:** The ability to harness data for insights and reporting is a significant driver. For instance, a manufacturing company used predictive analytics to identify machinery likely to fail, enabling timely maintenance and reducing downtime by 25%.

4. **Remote Work and Automation** The rise of remote work and automation has transformed EHS practices. Organizations must integrate digital tools that ensure safety and compliance in remote or automated environments while upskilling employees for a digital-first approach. For example, remote monitoring tools enable safety managers to oversee multiple sites in real-time, ensuring consistent compliance across global operations.

Challenges and Considerations

While the potential of digital transformation in EHS is immense, companies face significant obstacles. The path is rarely smooth, from resistance to change and data integration issues to cybersecurity risks and skills gaps. However, organizations that proactively address these challenges position themselves to reap the benefits of a safer, more efficient workplace.

Common Challenges and Mitigation Strategies

1. **Resistance to Change** Resistance to digital adoption often reflects cultural and communication gaps. Comprehensive training, clear communication, and leadership support can align employee goals with organizational strategy.

   o Example: Workers hesitated to adopt mobile reporting tools, favoring traditional methods. Change champions and incentives successfully addressed this resistance.

2. **Data Integration and Quality Issues** Legacy systems and inconsistent data formats create integration challenges. Conducting data audits and

standardizing processes can unlock predictive analytics and real-time decision-making.

- o   Example: A chemical company overcame integration challenges by investing in data cleaning and system rationalization.

3. **Cybersecurity Risks** Increasing connectivity introduces vulnerabilities. Proactive organizations prioritize cybersecurity with encryption, regular audits, and employee training to protect sensitive data.

4. **Skills Gaps** Rapid technological change demands continuous learning—investments in training programs and hiring specialized talent bridge this gap.

5. **Cost and Scaling** Initial investments can be significant. Phased implementations and pilot projects demonstrate ROI, helping to secure further buy-in.

Challenges and Considerations

While the potential of digital transformation in EHS is immense, organizations must navigate significant obstacles. These challenges span technological, organizational, and cultural dimensions, requiring a comprehensive and strategic approach. Below are the key challenges and practical mitigation strategies:

Technological Challenges

1. Data Integration and Quality Issues

Integrating legacy systems with modern digital tools is a common hurdle. Fragmented data silos and inconsistent formats hinder the potential of predictive analytics and real-time decision-making.

- o   **Example**: A global chemical company struggled with diverse reporting systems across regions, delaying analytics implementation.

- o   **Mitigation**: Conduct a data audit, standardize data collection processes, and invest in modern data platforms to harmonize disparate sources.

2. Cybersecurity Risks

Increased IoT and cloud systems connectivity introduces vulnerabilities, including data breaches and system disruptions.

- o **Example**: An energy company faced a ransomware attack that compromised environmental compliance data.

- o **Mitigation**: Implement robust encryption protocols, conduct regular cybersecurity audits, and train employees on data protection practices.

Organizational Challenges

3. Resistance to Change

Employees and management often hesitate to adopt new tools, citing workflow disruption or lack of familiarity.

- o **Example**: Workers in a manufacturing facility resisted mobile safety reporting, preferring traditional paper forms.

- o **Mitigation**: Deploy comprehensive change management programs, appoint change champions, and align technology adoption with incentives and clear communication about benefits.

4. Skills Gaps

Rapid technological advancements demand new competencies in data analysis, IoT deployment, and AI applications.

- o **Example**: A construction firm adopted predictive analytics but lacked in-house data interpretation expertise.

- o **Mitigation**: Develop ongoing training programs, partner with educational institutions, and hire specialists where needed.

Financial Challenges

5. Cost and Scaling

Implementing digital solutions often requires substantial initial investment, with uncertainties around ROI. Scaling across global operations adds complexity.

- o **Example**: A mid-sized manufacturing company exceeded its budget while rolling out an IoT-enabled monitoring system, delaying its full deployment.

- o **Mitigation**: Start with pilot projects to demonstrate value, prioritize high-impact areas for phased rollouts, and leverage cost-sharing models with vendors.

Summary Table: Challenges and Mitigation Strategies

Challenge	Example	Mitigation Strategy
Data Integration Issues	Chemical companies facing regional system inconsistencies	Data audits, standardized processes, modern platforms
Cybersecurity Risks	Energy firm exposed to ransomware	Encryption, regular audits, employee training
Resistance to Change	Manufacturing workers prefer paper forms	Change champions, communication, incentives
Skills Gaps	Construction firm lacking expertise in data analysis	Training programs, partnerships, hiring specialists
Cost and Scaling	Manufacturer exceeding budget on IoT rollout	Pilot projects, phased rollouts, cost-sharing models

By addressing these challenges with proactive strategies, organizations can overcome barriers and unlock the transformative potential of digital EHS solutions.

Benefits of EHS Digital Transformation

The benefits of digital EHS transformation extend beyond compliance—they drive competitive differentiation, enhance sustainability, and strengthen operational resilience. The measurable outcomes of digital transformation—reduced incidents, cost savings, and improved compliance—are not just operational wins. They are strategic levers for achieving long-term sustainability, building stakeholder trust, and driving business resilience.

Key Benefits:

Incident Reduction as a Leadership Metric

Organizations reducing workplace incidents achieve cost savings and enhance their reputation as safety leaders. These reductions translate directly into stronger ESG performance and improved employee trust.

Operational Efficiency for Competitive Advantage

Digital systems streamline compliance reporting and risk management, reducing costs while enabling leaders to focus on strategic initiatives like expansion and innovation.

Sustainability Impact as a Market Differentiator

Companies leveraging IoT-enabled energy management systems and digital waste tracking tools are achieving up to 20% reductions in environmental impact. These initiatives meet stakeholder demands and position businesses as industry innovators.

These outcomes demonstrate that digital transformation in EHS is about compliance and creating safer, more sustainable, and efficient operations.

In observing these trends, I noticed a fundamental focus in most organizations' digital strategies: they aim to elevate two primary aspects. First, they seek to increase their understanding of EHS data—whether in risk management, incident management, compliance tracking, environmental monitoring, or safety performance metrics. The goal is to harness data more effectively to predict risks, prevent incidents, and manage real-time compliance. Second, they focus on enhancing their business design by streamlining processes, transforming operations, and creating more manageable and efficient systems for the entire EHS function.

One memorable conversation I had with the senior management of a Danish manufacturing firm perfectly illustrated this trend. We discussed shifting their EHS strategy from reactive compliance to proactive risk management by developing SafetyNet. It was centered around the need to understand more than just incident reporting. They needed to prevent accidents, ensure continuous compliance, and build a sustainable operation.

This shift in mindset led them to adopt digital tools that could predict risks, reduce TRIR, and integrate safety management into the heart of their business.

During another EHS leadership workshop from NA, a senior manager asked, "What if this digital transformation of our Safety Management doesn't work?" A safety leader confidently responded, "If we don't embrace change, we risk falling behind. A digital solution is essential for tracking and lowering our TRIR, and without it, our competitors will outpace us, leveraging technology to advance their safety and compliance strategies." This conversation reinforced what I have seen throughout my career—companies that rely on minor tweaks to their existing EHS practices, driven solely by external pressures, struggle to remain competitive.

During one of the quarterly EHSS department leadership workshops, a senior EHSS leader from a Danish firm raised a concern, asking, "Jayakumar, shouldn't we begin by focusing on our current systems and ensure they run efficiently and generate accurate reports before embarking on a transformative approach to safety and risk management?" The safety leader was more cautious, stating, "I believe we should stick to what we have, and I see a big disconnect in our data, systems, and processes. Let's plan for transformation 12 to 24 months down the line."

I initially emphasized that getting our basics right is suitable before diving into Transformation. However, I also pointed out that focusing solely on short-term fixes would disadvantage us. We need a balanced approach that addresses the immediate need to get our fundamentals right and the long-term goal of creating a transformation roadmap. This three-pronged strategy should include system consolidation, improving system adoption, and Transformation, all working in parallel.

I had the support of our EHSS Department Vice President, who led the IT side and firmly responded, "If we delay our efforts, we risk missing an opportunity. We must start investing in digital solutions to track and reduce our TRIR effectively. We should invest our efforts in developing a three-year roadmap for our EHS Digital Strategy. "For the next six months, I dedicated my efforts to interviewing senior leadership, assessing the maturity of EHS systems and processes, and developing a comprehensive roadmap, which I will share in my upcoming book, *Leading the Way in EHS Digital Transformation*.

Based on my conversations with senior leadership at a Danish firm, I realized that digital Transformation in EHS is not just about compliance but evolving how organizations manage safety, sustainability, and risk. Businesses must shift from reactive measures to proactive strategies that leverage data insights and streamlined processes. This evolution is not optional—it is crucial for staying competitive in a digitally connected world.

Over the years, I have systematically gathered insights, researched trends, and studied how organizations successfully integrate digital tools into their EHS operations. From predictive safety analytics and IoT-enabled environmental monitoring to AI-driven incident analysis, companies that adopt these tools position themselves for long-term success by transforming their understanding of EHS data and their operational design. However, to truly understand the scope and impact of this digital shift, we must zoom out and examine the broader industry landscape.

Table 1: Transformation examples and Key results

Industry	Transformation Example	Key Results
Construction	IoT-enabled safety management system	35% reduction in incidents
Oil & Gas	Predictive analytics for equipment maintenance	50% reduction in unplanned downtime
Healthcare	AI for infection control	25% fewer healthcare-associated infections

These examples show that digital transformation in EHS delivers measurable results regardless of industry. By adopting proactive risk management tools, companies across sectors are improving safety, cutting costs, and achieving sustainable operational excellence.

The Evolving Landscape of EHS Digital Transformation

As we navigate through 2024 and beyond, the Environmental Health and Safety (EHS) field continues to evolve rapidly, driven by technological advancements and changing regulatory landscapes. Recent trends and developments underscore the critical importance of digital transformation in EHS, reinforcing many of the points we have discussed earlier and highlighting new focus areas.

Emerging Technologies Reshaping EHS: The rapid advancement of technology is transforming EHS practices. Tools like AI-driven predictive analytics, IoT-enabled wearables, and virtual reality training programs are no longer future concepts—they are here. Later chapters will explore how these innovations reshape incident prevention, compliance, and safety performance.

Synthesizing the Industry Perspectives

As we consider these diverse industry perspectives, several key themes emerge:

1. The shift from reactive to proactive safety management is universal across industries. Whether at a construction site, a chemical plant, an offshore oil rig, or a hospital, digital tools enable organizations to predict and prevent incidents rather than merely respond to them.

2. Data integration and analytics are driving significant improvements in EHS outcomes. The ability to collect, analyze, and act on real-time data transforms how organizations manage risk and ensure compliance.

3. Digital transformation in EHS offers substantial benefits beyond safety improvements. From cost savings and efficiency gains to enhanced stakeholder trust and new business opportunities, the ripple effects of EHS digital transformation are far-reaching.

4. Emerging technologies like IoT, AI, and VR/AR are not just buzzwords but powerful tools revolutionizing EHS practices across industries.

These industry perspectives provide a broader context for my anecdotes and observations. They demonstrate that organizations leverage digital technologies across various sectors to transform their EHS practices, often with remarkable results.

Reflecting on my conversations with that skeptical EHSS Department Vice President or the forward-thinking leaders at the Danish manufacturing firm, I am struck by how their experiences mirror these broader industry trends. Their concerns, hopes, and eventual successes are not isolated incidents but part of a larger narrative of digital transformation reshaping the EHS landscape.

These industry perspectives offer inspiration and practical insights for EHS leaders embarking on digital transformation journeys. They underscore the potential benefits of digital transformation while highlighting the diversity of approaches that can be taken. Most importantly, they remind us that at the heart of all these digital initiatives is a common goal: creating safer, healthier, and more sustainable workplaces.

Keep these industry perspectives in mind while exploring EHS's digital transformation. They provide a valuable backdrop against which to evaluate your organization's digital journey and can offer guidance as you navigate the challenges and opportunities ahead.

Throughout my two decades of working with industries ranging from chemicals to manufacturing, I have witnessed how digital disruption has transformed how businesses manage the environment, health, and safety. Larger organizations are increasingly vulnerable to the inefficiencies of outdated processes. Traditional practices such as manual incident reporting, reactive compliance strategies, and siloed safety systems cannot meet today's demands.

Today, businesses are adopting real-time data systems, IoT-enabled safety devices, and AI-powered predictive analytics to anticipate and prevent incidents. In my experience, this shift has allowed companies to comply with regulations and elevate their safety standards while cutting operational costs. For example, wearable technologies now provide live updates on workers' health and potential hazards, allowing managers to intervene before an incident occurs.

However, digital Transformation in EHS requires more than just new tools. To truly transform, companies must reshape their organizational cultures, empower employees with data-driven insights, and shift from a reactive mindset to one focusing on predictive and preventive measures.

What is Digital Transformation in EHS:

As we explore the digital shift in Environmental Health and Safety (EHS), we must understand what "digital transformation" means in this context. Beyond simply adopting new technologies, digital transformation in EHS represents a fundamental reimagining of how organizations approach safety, health, and environmental management.

According to a comprehensive review published in the International Journal of Environmental Research and Public Health (2020), digital transformation in Occupational Health and Safety (OHS) involves "the integration of digital technologies into all areas of OHS management, fundamentally changing how organizations operate and deliver value to stakeholders." This definition encapsulates the far-reaching impact of digitalization on EHS practices, emphasizing that it is not just about new tools but about reshaping entire operational paradigms.

At the heart of this transformation lies the concept of Industry 4.0, often called the Fourth Industrial Revolution. Industry 4.0 technologies, including artificial intelligence (AI), the Internet of Things (IoT), big data analytics, and cloud computing, are rapidly reshaping industrial landscapes – and EHS is no exception. A study published in the Journal of Cleaner Production (2019) examined the implementation patterns of these technologies across manufacturing companies, revealing a growing trend of adoption that's revolutionizing safety and environmental management practices.

In the realm of EHS, these Industry 4.0 technologies are being leveraged in myriad ways. IoT sensors enable the real-time monitoring of workplace hazards and environmental conditions. AI and machine learning algorithms predict potential incidents before they occur, allowing for proactive risk management. Big data analytics provide unprecedented insights into safety trends and environmental impacts, facilitating data-driven decision-making at all organizational levels.

This digital transformation is not merely enhancing existing EHS processes but fundamentally altering how organizations conceptualize and manage risk. We are witnessing a shift from reactive, compliance-driven approaches to proactive, predictive strategies prioritizing prevention and continuous improvement. As we delve deeper into this topic, we will explore how these technological advancements create safer workplaces, reduce environmental footprints, and drive sustainable business practices.

Three Pathways to EHS Digital Evolution

Drawing from my experience of working with multiple companies in this field, I have observed that digital disruption in EHS typically occurs through three key pathways:

1. Innovators Shaping the Future of EHS: Over the years, I have worked closely with startups that have developed breakthrough technologies such as AI-driven safety analytics and IoT-based environmental monitoring systems. These companies are revolutionizing risk management and offering solutions that traditional EHS approaches cannot match. These innovators provide exciting new ways to track compliance, predict incidents, and enhance worker safety.

2. Traditional competitors adopting new models: In many organizations I have consulted with or have had a chance to interact with as end customers or conduct research, existing EHS providers rapidly evolve to incorporate digital tools into their offerings. This has been particularly true with large enterprises transitioning from compliance-driven approaches to data-powered platforms that provide real-time insights and proactive risk management. I have seen firsthand at an NA-based chemical company how integrating AI and IoT has enabled companies to improve safety performance and streamline environmental compliance.

3. Industry Crossover: Another significant trend I have observed is the movement of tech firms into the EHS space, bringing advanced data analytics, automation, and cloud solutions. Companies traditionally focused on technology are now creating platforms that integrate safety and sustainability into a broader digital ecosystem, making it easier for EHS professionals to manage risks and compliance across the organization.

The Real-World Impact of EHS Digital Transformation

Throughout my career, I have witnessed the tangible effects that digital tools can have on EHS performance. In one case, a major global organization significantly reduced worker injuries after introducing real-time safety monitoring systems paired with predictive analytics. These tools enabled the company to identify and mitigate potential risks before they escalated into serious incidents.

In another example, a company avoided hefty environmental fines by deploying IoT sensors to monitor air quality. These sensors provided real-time alerts of potential compliance violations, allowing the company to take corrective actions quickly and prevent costly repercussions.

Table 2: Three Pathways to EHS Digital Evolution

Pathway	Description	Key Characteristics	Example
Innovators Shaping the Future of EHS	Startups and tech companies developing breakthrough EHS technologies	AI-driven safety analytics—IoT-based environmental monitoring—revolutionary risk management solutions	A startup developing an AI system that predicts potential safety incidents based on real-time data from wearable devices
Traditional competitors are adopting new models.	Existing EHS providers are evolving to incorporate digital tools	Transition from compliance-driven to data-powered platforms - Integration of AI and IoT into existing offerings; real-time insights and proactive risk management	An established EHS consulting firm developing a cloud-based platform that integrates IoT sensor data for real-time environmental compliance monitoring
Industry Crossover	Tech firms moving into the EHS space.	Advanced data analytics applied to EHS: automation of EHS processes and integration of EHS into broader digital ecosystems	A significant cloud services provider creating an EHS management platform that leverages their existing data analytics and machine learning capabilities

These examples illustrate how the digital Transformation of EHS improves compliance and creates safer, more sustainable operations—integrating real-time data, automation, and predictive tools positions companies to meet today's regulatory demands and establish themselves as leaders in safety and sustainability. Investing in these technologies is no longer a choice but a necessity for those looking to thrive in an increasingly competitive and regulated market.

Challenges in EHS Digital Transformation

As organizations embark on their digital transformation journey in Environment, Health, and Safety (EHS), they often encounter many obstacles that impede progress and impact success. These challenges span technological, organizational, and human factors, requiring a comprehensive approach to overcome them effectively. Understanding these hurdles is crucial for EHS leaders and executives as they plan and execute their digital strategies. By anticipating these challenges, organizations can develop proactive measures to address them, increasing the likelihood of a successful transformation. This section will explore seven key challenges companies frequently face when implementing advanced EHS strategies, along with examples and potential mitigation approaches for each.

Here are some of the key challenges organizations might encounter:

1. Resistance to Change

One of the most common challenges in any transformation process is resistance from employees and management.

- **Employee Reluctance**: Workers may hesitate to adopt new technologies or change established processes, mainly if they have used traditional methods for a long time.

- **Management Scepticism**: Some leaders may be skeptical about the ROI of digital investments or fear disruption to current operations.

   Example: A manufacturing company introduced a SAP EHSM Incident Management system and associated a new mobile app for safety reporting. However, many workers continued to use paper forms, citing discomfort with the technology.

   Mitigation Strategy: Implement comprehensive change management programs, including clear communication about the new systems' benefits, hands-on training, and identifying "champions" who can help drive adoption.

2. Data Integration and Quality Issues

Digital Transformation often requires integrating data from multiple sources, presenting significant challenges.

- **Legacy Systems**: Many organizations need help integrating new digital tools with legacy systems.

- **Data Silos**: Information may be scattered across different departments or locations, making it challenging to create a unified view.

- **Data quality**: inconsistent or inaccurate data can undermine the effectiveness of new digital systems.

  Example: A Middle Eastern chemical company found inconsistencies in how different plants recorded incident data and used diverse systems and tools, making it difficult to implement company-wide data analytics and a predictive analytics system.

  Mitigation Strategy: Conduct a thorough data audit, standardize data collection processes across the organization, and invest in data cleaning, system rationalization, and tool integration.

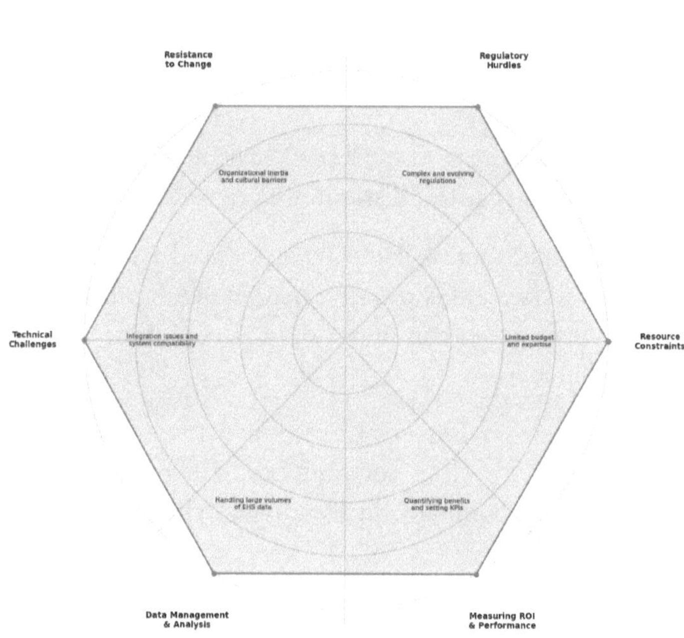

Figure 1: Challenges in Implementing Advanced EHS Strategies

3. Cybersecurity and Data Privacy Concerns

As organizations collect more data and connect devices, they also increase their vulnerability to cyber threats.

- **IoT vulnerabilities**: connected devices can create new entry points for cyberattacks.

- **Data Breaches**: sensitive EHS data, including personal health information, must be protected.

- **Regulatory Compliance**: Organizations must ensure their digital systems comply with data protection regulations like GDPR.

  Example: An energy company faced a cyber threat, and most network-based systems, including environmental monitoring systems, were compromised. This led to the exposure of sensitive emissions data and regulatory non-compliance.

  Mitigation Strategy: Implement robust cybersecurity measures, including encryption, regular security audits, and employee training on data protection practices.

4. Skills Gap and Training Needs

Digital Transformation requires new skills that many EHS professionals may need to possess.

- **Technical Skills Shortage**: There may be a need for in-house expertise in data analytics, IoT implementation, or AI.

- **Continuous Learning Need**: Rapid technological change requires ongoing training and development.

  Example: A construction company invested in advanced safety analytics software but needed more data analysis skills in the EHS team to derive meaningful insights. It further found that most of its staff were temporarily moving from partner organizations to work for specific project durations. Imparting the necessary training and keeping up with the changes became challenging.

  Mitigation Strategy: Invest in training programs for existing staff, partner with educational institutions, and consider hiring specialists or consultants to fill skill gaps. Implement a standard onboarding checklist and toolkit.

5. Cost and Resource Allocation

Digital Transformation can require significant upfront investment, which can be challenging for many organizations.

- **Budget Constraints**: The cost of new technologies, training, and system integration can be substantial.

- **Uncertain ROI**: Quantifying the return on investment for some digital initiatives may take time, making it hard to justify the expense.

  Example: A medium-sized manufacturer initially implemented an incident management application. The project exceeded budget and timelines, which delayed the implementation of an IoT-based safety monitoring system due to budget constraints despite recognizing its potential benefits.

  Mitigation Strategy: Start with pilot projects to demonstrate value, involve key stakeholders to avoid delay, consider phased implementation approaches, and look for opportunities to reallocate resources from less effective traditional processes.

6. Scaling and Standardization

Scaling digital initiatives across the entire operation can be challenging for large or geographically dispersed organizations.

- **Inconsistent Implementation**: Different units or locations may adopt technologies differently, leading to consistency.

- **Local vs. Global Needs**: Balancing local regulatory requirements with the need for global standardization can be complex.

  Example: A multinational corporation found that its European operations were much quicker to adopt new digital EHS tools than its Asian operations, leading to inconsistent safety performance across regions. When the company was rolling out its tools and systems, it always considered Asia the par to last leg of the Transformation, which eventually resulted in inconsistent systems.

  Mitigation Strategy: Develop clear global standards and implementation guidelines while allowing for necessary local adaptations. Use a center of excellence model to share best practices across the organization. There are various approaches to transformation strategy, such as region-wise or templating, etc. Explore the one that fits best.

7. Vendor Management and Technology Selection

Selecting the right tools and partners can be challenging in a rapidly evolving technology landscape.

- **Vendor Lock-in**: Organizations may want to avoid becoming too dependent on a single technology vendor.

- **Technology Obsolescence**: Rapid technological change can make some investments obsolete quickly.

- **Integration Challenges**: Ensuring different tools and systems work together seamlessly can be complex.

  Example: An oil and gas company invested heavily in a proprietary EHS management system, only to find it needed help integrating with new IoT sensors they wanted to deploy. Further, an energy company engaged with a cloud-based incident management vendor for incident and environmental reporting. They experienced a complicated way of locking in all their data, which was easier to retrieve if they extended their contract for one more year.

  Mitigation Strategy: When selecting technologies, prioritize open systems and APIs, conduct thorough vendor due diligence, and develop a long-term technology roadmap for flexibility. Plan your data strategy well in advance to avoid unnecessary lock-in. Check your vendor's long-term viability.

By anticipating these challenges, organizations can develop proactive strategies to address them, increasing the likelihood of a successful EHS digital transformation. It is important to remember that while these challenges are significant, they are not insurmountable. With proper planning, leadership commitment, and a willingness to adapt, organizations can navigate these obstacles and reap the benefits of digital Transformation in their EHS operations.

Benefits of EHS Digital Transformation

Digital Transformation in Environment, Health, and Safety (EHS) has shown significant measurable benefits across various industries. Here is a compilation of quantitative data demonstrating the positive impact of digital EHS initiatives:

1. Incident Reduction and Safety Improvements

- A study by the National Safety Council found that companies using advanced safety analytics saw a 12% reduction in recordable incident rates compared to those not using such tools.

- Dow Chemical reported a 75% decrease in severe incidents over a decade after implementing a comprehensive digital safety management system.

- A construction company implementing wearable technology for worker safety saw a 20% reduction in slip, trip, and fall incidents within the first year of deployment.

2. Compliance and Risk Management

- According to a report by Verdantix, organizations using EHS software solutions reported an average 22% improvement in regulatory compliance rates.

- A global manufacturing firm reduced environmental compliance violations by 35% after implementing an IoT-based real-time monitoring system.

- An oil and gas company using predictive analytics for risk assessment reported a 15% reduction in high-potential near-miss incidents.

3. Operational Efficiency and Cost Savings

- A study by the Aberdeen Group found that best-in-class companies leveraging EHS digital tools completed 90% of EHS tasks on time, compared to 55% for laggards.

- DuPont estimated annual savings of $5 million by digitalizing its safety observation and near-miss reporting processes.

- A pharmaceutical company reported a 30% reduction in the time spent on compliance reporting after implementing an integrated EHS management system.

4. Environmental Impact and Sustainability

- According to a Deloitte study, companies using IoT-enabled energy management systems reported an average 15-20% reduction in energy consumption.

- A chemical manufacturer implemented a digital waste tracking and optimization system within two years, reducing hazardous waste generation by 25%.

- Walmart reduced its global greenhouse gas emissions by 6.1% in 2020, partly attributed to its use of advanced data analytics for sustainability management.

5. Worker Engagement and Training

- According to a survey by EHS Today, organizations using mobile apps for safety reporting saw a 50% increase in near-miss reporting.

- A mining company using virtual reality for safety training reported a 40% improvement in knowledge retention compared to traditional training methods.

- Companies implementing gamified EHS training apps saw an average 35% increase in employee participation in safety programs.

6. Return on Investment (ROI)

- A study by the Institute for Safety and Health Management found that companies investing in EHS digital transformation achieved an average ROI of 200–40% over three years.

- Schneider Electric reported a 10% reduction in its cost of risk and a 15% improvement in productivity after implementing a global, digital EHS platform.

- A mid-sized manufacturer achieved a 150% ROI within 18 months of implementing an IoT-based predictive maintenance system, primarily through reduced downtime and maintenance costs.

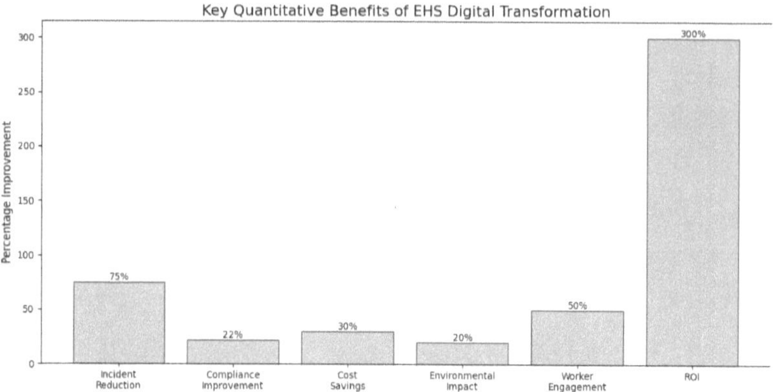

Figure 2. Critical Benefits of EHS Digital Transformation

7. Audit and Inspection Efficiency

- According to a survey by Safety+Health magazine, companies using mobile inspection apps reported a 45% reduction in the time required to complete safety audits.

- A food processing company reduced audit preparation time by 60% after implementing a digital EHS management system with real-time data access.

- Organizations using automated compliance tracking tools reported a 25% reduction in audit findings, indicating improved ongoing compliance.

8. Incident Response and Management

- A chemical company using a digital incident management system reduced its average incident response time by 35%, leading to faster containment and reduced impact of safety events.

- Organizations leveraging mobile incident reporting apps saw a 40% increase in reported near-misses, enabling better proactive risk management.

- A manufacturing firm using AI-powered root cause analysis tools reported a 20% improvement in the accuracy of incident investigations, leading to more effective corrective actions.

These quantitative benefits demonstrate the significant impact that digital Transformation can have on EHS performance across various dimensions.

From improved safety and compliance to cost savings and environmental benefits, the data supports the value of investing in digital EHS initiatives.

It is important to note that results can vary based on the specific technologies implemented, the extent of organizational adoption, and the maturity of existing EHS processes. However, these figures prove the potential benefits organizations can achieve through EHS digital transformation.

The Strategic Imperative for EHS Leaders

As I have seen repeatedly throughout my 20 years in the field, the companies that excel in their EHS journeys are the ones that embrace digital tools early and often. These organizations understand that digital Transformation is not a one-time initiative but an ongoing process of adaptation and improvement. EHS digital transformation is not just a technical shift but a leadership imperative. Executives must align safety goals with corporate objectives, ensuring that every initiative contributes to broader business success.

A successful EHS strategy begins with a clear vision that ties safety outcomes to business growth and resilience. Leaders must articulate this vision and embed it into organizational culture. Transformation roadmaps should balance short-term wins, such as compliance improvements, with long-term goals like predictive risk management and global standardization. EHS digital transformation is not just a technical challenge but imperative for leadership. Successful transformation requires a vision that aligns safety goals with broader corporate objectives.

The path forward for EHS leaders is clear: assess the threats posed by outdated systems, embrace digital opportunities, and integrate new technologies into every facet of the operations. Whether through AI-powered predictive maintenance or IoT-enabled environmental monitoring, digital tools are critical to the future of EHS management.

1. Vision and Alignment

Leadership begins with a clear vision: what does success look like for your organization? Aligning safety outcomes with corporate priorities like growth, sustainability, and resilience ensures that every initiative contributes to long-term goals. "

2. Roadmap for Transformation

A *transformation roadmap should balance immediate wins—such as compliance improvements—with long-term goals like predictive risk management. Leaders must create structured phases for implementation, ensuring scalability and continuous improvement."*

3. Cultural Transformation

Embedding a safety-first culture is as critical as adopting new tools. Leaders prioritizing workforce engagement and training ensure that technology adoption is meaningful and impactful.

A New Framework for EHS Success in the Digital Age

This book is the culmination of my experiences and research, offering a guide for EHS professionals to develop effective digital transformation roadmaps. Whether the goal is to improve risk management, enhance real-time environmental monitoring, or streamline safety and compliance processes, this book will provide actionable insights for navigating the complexities of EHS digital transformation. It is about helping organizations balance external pressures and internal performance improvements, creating safer, more sustainable, and more efficient operations.

The insights, lessons, and best practices I have gathered over two decades provide a roadmap for EHS leaders to harness digital tools, enhance safety, and drive sustainable success. The future of EHS is not just about keeping pace with regulations—it is about creating a culture of continuous improvement, using real-time data and predictive tools to prevent incidents, and leading the way toward safer, more sustainable business practices. This book builds on my years working with companies on their strategy to embark on EHS digital transformation journeys, offering a framework to help organizations thrive in this rapidly changing landscape.

A Roadmap to Digital EHS Transformation

This book provides a comprehensive roadmap for navigating digital transformation in EHS. We will explore key frameworks, examine real-world case studies, and present actionable strategies for becoming a leader in the field. Here's what to expect:

- **Drivers and Frameworks**: Understand the core motivators and tools that enable digital EHS transformation.

- **Case Studies**: Learn from successes and challenges faced by organizations across industries.

- **Actionable Strategies**: Discover practical steps for implementing digital solutions and fostering a culture of safety and innovation.

As we explore this journey, these drivers will illuminate the 'why' and guide us toward the 'how,' helping organizations navigate the complex yet rewarding path of digital EHS transformation. This book will provide the tools, frameworks, and real-world examples to help you succeed in redefining safety, compliance, and sustainability.

Conclusion

The future of EHS is not just about compliance—it is about building resilient, sustainable organizations through thoughtful, strategic action. This book provides a roadmap to navigate the complexities of digital transformation, empowering leaders to turn safety and compliance into competitive advantages. You can lead your organization into a safer, more sustainable future by aligning vision, technology, and culture.

References for Introduction Chapter

1. Accenture. (2021). The European Double Up: A twin strategy that will strengthen competitiveness. https://www.accenture.com/us-en/insights/strategy/european-double-up

2. Deloitte. (2020). The Fourth Industrial Revolution: At the intersection of readiness and responsibility. https://www2.deloitte.com/content/dam/insights/us/articles/us32959-industry-4-0/DI_Industry4.0.pdf

3. EHS Today. (2023, March). The Future of EHS: Trends and Predictions for 2023 and Beyond. https://www.ehstoday.com/safety-technology/article/21255636/the-future-of-ehs-trends-and-predictions-for-2023-and-beyond

4. EHS Today. (2023, June). Digital Transformation in EHS: Leveraging Technology for Better Safety Outcomes. https://www.ehstoday.com/safety-technology/article/21264325/digital-transformation-in-ehs-leveraging-technology-for-better-safety-outcomes

5. EHS Today. (2023, August). The Impact of Generative AI on EHS Management. https://www.ehstoday.com/safety-technology/article/21271543/the-impact-of-generative-ai-on-ehs-management

6. Environmental Protection Agency (EPA). (2022, December). Final Rule on Greenhouse Gas Emissions Standards for Light-Duty Vehicles. https://www.epa.gov/regulations-emissions-vehicles-and-engines/final-rule-revise-existing-national-ghg-emissions

7. Environmental Protection Agency (EPA). (2023, June). Updated Action Plan for PFAS. https://www.epa.gov/pfas/pfas-strategic-roadmap-epas-commitments-action-2021-2024

8. Environmental Protection Agency (EPA). (2023, July). Proposed Rule for Strengthening Transparency in Regulatory Science. https://www.epa.gov/osa/strengthening-transparency-regulatory-science

9. Gartner. (2021). Market Guide for Environment, Health, and Safety Software. https://www.gartner.com/en/documents/3995840/market-guide-for-environment-health-and-safety-software

10. Harvard Business Review. (2019). Digital Transformation Is Not About Technology. https://hbr.org/2019/03/digital-transformation-is-not-about-technology

11. International Journal of Environmental Research and Public Health. (2023, July). Digital Transformation in Occupational Health and Safety: A Systematic Review. https://www.mdpi.com/1660-4601/20/14/6429

12. International Journal of Environmental Research and Public Health. (2023, June). The Impact of Artificial Intelligence on Environmental Health and Safety Management: A Multi-Case Study. https://www.mdpi.com/1660-4601/20/12/5987

13. International Journal of Environmental Research and Public Health. (2023, August). IoT-Based Environmental Monitoring Systems: A

Review of Recent Advancements and Future Prospects. https://www.mdpi.com/1660-4601/20/16/7845

14. ISO. (2018). ISO 45001:2018 - Occupational health and safety management systems. https://www.iso.org/standard/63787.html

15. Journal of Cleaner Production. (2019). Industry 4.0 technologies: Implementation patterns in manufacturing companies. https://www.sciencedirect.com/science/article/pii/S0959652619303385

16. McKinsey & Company. (2020). The Next Normal in Construction: How Disruption is Reshaping the World's Largest Ecosystem. https://www.mckinsey.com/industries/capital-projects-and-infrastructure/our-insights/the-next-normal-in-construction-how-disruption-is-reshaping-the-worlds-largest-ecosystem

17. MIT Sloan Management Review. (2020). The New Elements of Digital Transformation. https://sloanreview.mit.edu/article/the-new-elements-of-digital-transformation/

18. National Safety Council. (2021). Work to Zero: Safety Technology 2021 Outlook. https://www.nsc.org/work-safety/safety-topics/work-to-zero

19. Occupational Safety and Health Administration (OSHA). (2022, December). Top 10 Most Frequently Cited Standards for FY 2022. https://www.osha.gov/top10citedstandards

20. Occupational Safety and Health Administration (OSHA). (2023, June). Guidance on Mitigating and Preventing the Spread of COVID-19 in the Workplace. https://www.osha.gov/coronavirus/safework

21. Occupational Safety and Health Administration (OSHA). (2023, July). Request for Information on Future Rules to Prevent Workplace Violence in Healthcare and Social Assistance. https://www.osha.gov/workplace-violence/rulemaking

22. PwC. (2020). Digital Operations Study 2020: Building the Digital Enterprise. https://www.pwc.com/gx/en/industries/industry-4.0.html

23. Safety+Health Magazine. (2023, July). 2023 State of Safety. https://www.safetyandhealthmagazine.com/articles/23767-2023-state-of-safety

24. Safety+Health Magazine. (2023, May). Wearable Technology: The Future of Workplace Safety? https://www.safetyandhealthmagazine.com/articles/23685-wearable-technology-the-future-of-workplace-safety

25. Safety+Health Magazine. (2023, August). Virtual Reality in Safety Training: Beyond the Hype. https://www.safetyandhealthmagazine.com/articles/23801-virtual-reality-in-safety-training-beyond-the-hype

26. Verdantix. (2021). Green Quadrant EHS Software 2021. https://www.verdantix.com/report/green-quadrant-ehs-software-2021

27. World Economic Forum. (2020). The Future of Jobs Report 2020. https://www.weforum.org/reports/the-future-of-jobs-report-2020

EHS Digital Transformation: A Shift Beyond Technology

A Blueprint for Success in the Digital EHS Landscape

Over the many years of working in EHS, I've witnessed a dramatic shift in companies' expectations and behaviors regarding safety, health, and environmental sustainability. Just as customers in other industries seek seamless solutions to manage life events, EHS leaders seek comprehensive systems that ensure compliance, mitigate risk, improve operational efficiency, and create safer environments.

Take, for example, an EHS manager overseeing compliance in a manufacturing facility. They don't just want incident reports—they want real-time data on potential hazards, predictive insights on safety risks, and a seamless integration of safety systems that allow them to manage everything from incident prevention to regulatory reporting, all from one digital platform. The future of EHS isn't about focusing on isolated tasks—it's about managing the entire safety and environmental ecosystem effectively and efficiently.

Through my requirement-gathering workshops and consulting experiences, I've found that companies that successfully transform their EHS operations in the digital age do so by creating a compelling value proposition that combines EHS Knowledge and business design. These organizations can offer integrated solutions that revolutionize their engagement with safety data, employees, and regulatory bodies. Success is not just about adopting technology; it's about leveraging knowledge and design to foster safety and environmental stewardship.

The Real Goal of Digital Transformation in EHS

Digital Transformation in EHS is more than just adopting mobile apps, sensors, or predictive analytics. It's about embedding safety, compliance, and sustainability into the fabric of the enterprise. Technologies like IoT, cloud computing, and data analytics provide powerful tools, but they are simply enablers of a larger goal: transforming how organizations approach risk and safety management.

From my experience, every enterprise has access to these tools, but what differentiates successful organizations is how they utilize them to create safer, more sustainable workplaces. The key isn't just adopting technology but ensuring it's used proactively and creatively. Whether using data to predict incidents before they occur or seamlessly integrating compliance into daily operations, this Transformation requires a deep understanding of EHS Knowledge and innovative Business Design.

Over the years, companies have shifted from simple, linear EHS processes to complex, interconnected systems where safety data is shared across departments. This Transformation moves companies from a reactive approach to one that anticipates risks, fosters employee engagement, and aligns the organization around safety and compliance.

Understanding EHS Knowledge

EHS Knowledge refers to an organization›s understanding of **Environmental, Health, and Safety (EHS)** principles, regulations, and best practices. It encompasses a range of knowledge, from essential compliance awareness to advanced, proactive risk management and sustainability initiatives. EHS knowledge can include understanding regulatory frameworks, hazard identification, risk assessment methodologies, and integrating technological solutions like IoT and predictive analytics.

Key Components of EHS Knowledge:

1. Compliance Awareness:

o   At the most basic level, organizations need to understand and comply with environmental protection, worker safety, and public health regulations. This includes keeping up with local, national, and international standards such as OSHA, ISO 14001, REACH, or other relevant guidelines.

2. Risk Identification and Management:

o   More advanced organizations develop the ability to identify potential hazards, assess risks, and implement control measures. This could range from managing chemical exposures in manufacturing to reducing emissions in industrial processes.

3. Incident Management:

o   EHS knowledge includes responding effectively to accidents, spills, or non-compliance events, minimizing harm, managing reputational risk, and complying with reporting requirements.

4. Sustainability Initiatives:

o   A deep level of EHS knowledge encompasses compliance and a commitment to sustainable practices. This could involve minimizing waste, managing resources efficiently, and implementing carbon reduction strategies.

5. Technology Integration:

o   Technology like IoT, machine learning, and predictive analytics is becoming essential to EHS knowledge. Companies with advanced EHS expertise often leverage these tools to anticipate risks, monitor real-time safety, and ensure continuous improvement in their EHS performance.

Levels of EHS Knowledge:

1.   **Low EHS Knowledge**: Organizations in this category often meet basic regulatory requirements but need a thorough understanding of risk management or proactive safety practices. Their approach is mainly reactive and focused on responding to incidents or non-compliance issues as they arise.

2. **High EHS Knowledge**: These organizations have a comprehensive grasp of EHS principles and are committed to embedding safety and sustainability into every aspect of their operations. They are compliant and capable of anticipating risks, proactively managing hazards, and integrating EHS into their broader business strategy.

Understanding Business Design

Business Design refers to how an organization structures its operations, processes, and strategies to achieve its objectives, including integrating EHS practices. Business design involves decisions about organizational structure, process efficiency, technology adoption, and customer experience. It also includes the company's ability to innovate, scale, and evolve with changing business needs.

Key Components of Business Design:

1. Process Design:

o   This involves how an organization structures its workflows, such as reporting incidents, assessing risks, or ensuring compliance. Good business design ensures that processes are efficient, repeatable, and scalable.

2. Proactive vs. Reactive Design:

o   A key aspect of business design is whether the organization takes a **proactive** or **reactive** approach to EHS management. A reactive design means the company responds to risks or incidents after they occur. The proactive design integrates EHS into daily operations, using data and predictive tools to prevent incidents before they happen.

3. Technology Integration:

o   Digital Transformation plays a crucial role in modern business design. Companies can implement digital tools like ERP systems, IoT devices, and data analytics to streamline EHS processes, ensure real-time monitoring, and make data-driven decisions.

4. Customer Experience and Channels:

o   Business design also covers how a company interacts with its customers or clients, including providing EHS services or managing compliance for third parties. Companies with more advanced business designs may offer multiple channels for interaction (e.g., mobile apps, cloud platforms, IoT-based dashboards), providing a seamless customer experience.

5. Integration of EHS into Strategy:

o   In more sophisticated business designs, EHS is not seen as a separate compliance function but is fully integrated into the business's overall strategy. This integration means EHS considerations shape product development, market entry strategies, and operational efficiencies.

6. Value Chain Integration:

o   Organizations with advanced business designs will integrate EHS into their entire value chain, including suppliers, partners, and third-party contractors. This ensures that safety and sustainability are upheld throughout a product or service's lifecycle.

Levels of Business Design:

1. Reactive Business Design:

o   Companies with a reactive design structure focus on resolving issues as they arise. Their processes are often manual and fragmented, leading to inefficiencies and higher risks. EHS may be an afterthought rather than an integral part of operations.

2. Proactive Business Design:

o   Companies with proactive business design embed EHS into their operations, using technology and data to anticipate and prevent issues. Their processes are streamlined, and EHS considerations are integral to decision-making. They often leverage predictive analytics, IoT devices, and integrated software to manage risks and ensure compliance.

EHS Knowledge and Business Design in Tandem:

When EHS knowledge and business design are aligned, organizations can achieve highly efficient, proactive, and resilient EHS programs. High EHS knowledge and proactive business design enable companies to use real-time data, predict risks, and continuously improve safety and sustainability efforts. Conversely, low EHS knowledge and reactive business design leave organizations vulnerable to compliance failures, higher incident rates, and inefficiencies.

Organizations should aim to move along both dimensions: advancing their EHS knowledge while transforming their business design to be more proactive and integrated. This will result in safer, more sustainable, and more efficient operations.

The Four Models of EHS Business Transformation: EHS Knowledge and Business Design

The EHS Knowledge and Business Design Maturity framework provides a powerful lens to assess an organization's progress in its EHS digital transformation journey. This framework becomes particularly relevant when considering the digital tools available and the challenges organizations face implementing them. Let's explore how these four models manifest in the context of EHS transformation, keeping in mind the technologies and hurdles we've discussed:

1. Basic Compliance Seekers or providers (Low EHS Knowledge / Reactive Business Design)

Overview: These companies have minimal EHS knowledge and operate reactively, addressing safety and compliance only when incidents occur. They rely on manual processes and need more real-time, data-driven insights.

Digital Tool Usage:

- Limited adoption of essential digital tools, such as spreadsheets for incident tracking

- Minimal use of mobile technologies, perhaps only for simple checklists

- No significant use of IoT, AI, or advanced analytics

Key Challenges:

- Resistance to change, with employees and management skeptical of new technologies

- Significant skills gap in understanding and implementing digital solutions

- Data quality issues due to manual, inconsistent processes

Case Study Reference - PG&E Smart Meter Program: The PG&E smart meter program serves as a cautionary tale of what can go wrong when organizations at this level rush into digital transformation without proper planning and integration. Despite ambitious goals, PG&E's implementation of smart meters in 2009-2010 faced significant challenges:

1. Inadequate Testing: PG&E rolled out smart meters without thorough real-world testing, leading to widespread inaccuracies in meter readings and customer billing.

2. Poor Integration: The new smart meter system needed to be adequately integrated with existing infrastructure, which caused operational disruptions and compounded billing errors.

3. Insufficient Change Management: PG&E underestimated the need for customer education and employee training, resulting in confusion and resistance.

4. Overlooked Security Concerns: In the rush to deploy the technology, cybersecurity considerations needed to be given more priority, exposing the system to potential vulnerabilities.

5. Reactive Problem-Solving: When issues arose, PG&E's initial reluctance to acknowledge problems and communicate transparently eroded public trust, leading to a major public relations crisis.

These issues resulted in public backlash, regulatory investigations, and significant financial losses for PG&E. The case highlights the risks of pursuing digital transformation without the necessary EHS knowledge and proactive business design approach.

Lessons for Basic Compliance Seekers:

- Prioritize thorough planning and testing before large-scale implementation of new technologies

- Invest in change management and training to prepare the organization for digital transformation

- Ensure proper integration with existing systems and processes

- Address security and privacy concerns from the outset

- Develop a proactive communication strategy to address potential issues transparently

A manufacturing plant in South Africa, relying on manual audits and paper-based reporting, had safety incidents go unnoticed. After implementing basic cloud-based EHS software, compliance improved by 20%, and high-risk areas were flagged more promptly. However, the company remains reactive mainly in its approach to safety, struggling to fully leverage the software due to resistance from long-time employees and a need for more data analysis skills. Further, the company does not utilize the data for assessment purposes; they have seen the implementation as a criterion to meet their local regulatory norms of incident reporting and continue to use paper-based systems as a backup.

2. Traditional Operator Enablers (Low EHS Knowledge / Proactive Business Design)

Overview: These organizations are proactive about enhancing their EHS processes but need more knowledge and real-time data to anticipate and mitigate risks effectively. They have taken steps to integrate EHS into their business, but their insights could be improved.

Table 1.1: EHS Knowledge and Business Design Matrix

Model	EHS Knowledge Level	Business Design Approach	Digital Tool Usage	Key Challenges
Basic Compliance Seekers	Low	Reactive	• Limited adoption of basic digital tools (e.g., spreadsheets for incident tracking) • Minimal use of mobile technologies • No significant use of IoT, AI, or advanced analytics	• Resistance to change • Significant skills gap • Data quality issues due to manual processes
Traditional operator enablers	Low	Proactive	• Adoption of mobile apps for safety reporting • Initial forays into IoT for basic environmental monitoring • Use of simple analytics for performance dashboards	• Data integration issues • Cybersecurity concerns • Difficulty in scaling digital initiatives
Reactive Performer	High	Reactive	• Advanced use of data science and analytics for risk assessment • Specialized AI tools for specific EHS functions • Limited use of IoT or real-time monitoring systems	• Siloed implementation of digital tools • Resistance to changing established processes • Difficulty in demonstrating ROI for comprehensive digital Transformation
EHS Digital Leaders	High	Proactive	• Comprehensive IoT implementation for real-time monitoring • Advanced AI and machine learning for predictive risk management • Big data analytics for trend analysis and continuous improvement • Integrated mobile solutions	• Managing vast volumes of data • Ensuring continuous innovation • Maintaining robust cybersecurity across a highly connected ecosystem

Digital Tool Usage:

- Adoption of mobile apps for safety reporting and digital checklists

- Initial forays into IoT for basic environmental monitoring

- Use of simple analytics for performance dashboards but limited predictive capabilities

Key Challenges:

- Data integration issues when trying to combine information from various digital tools

- Cybersecurity concerns as more devices and data points are connected

- Difficulty in scaling digital initiatives across the organization

Example: A regional oil refinery in Asia restructured its safety protocols and implemented proactive tracking systems, including SAP EHSM Incident Management, reducing safety violations by 40%. They've also adopted mobile apps for real-time incident reporting and IoT sensors for environmental monitoring. Despite these advances, the refinery needs advanced analytics to help predict and prevent future incidents. It faces challenges integrating data from various sources and ensuring consistent implementation across all units.

3. Reactive Operators (High EHS Knowledge / Reactive Business Design)

Overview: These companies deeply understand EHS risks and regulatory requirements but operate reactively. Their EHS knowledge has not fully integrated into their broader business design, often resulting in disjointed safety efforts.

Digital Tool Usage:

- Advanced use of data science and analytics for risk assessment and compliance management

- Specialized AI tools for specific EHS functions, such as ergonomic assessments or chemical exposure modeling

- Limited use of IoT or real-time monitoring systems

Key Challenges:

- Siloed implementation of digital tools, leading to fragmented data and insights

- Resistance to changing established processes, despite available technology

- Difficulty in demonstrating ROI for more comprehensive digital transformation initiatives

Example: A mid-sized chemical manufacturer with extensive regulatory knowledge still operates reactively, addressing safety concerns after incidents occur. They use sophisticated risk assessment models and have implemented AI-driven ergonomic assessment tools. However, these advanced tools operate in silos, and the company struggles to integrate this knowledge into daily operations. They need help justifying the cost of a company-wide IoT implementation for real-time monitoring, as different departments resist changes to their established workflows. Their business design needs to be more readily integrated into their day-to-day operations, elevating their organizations to the next level.

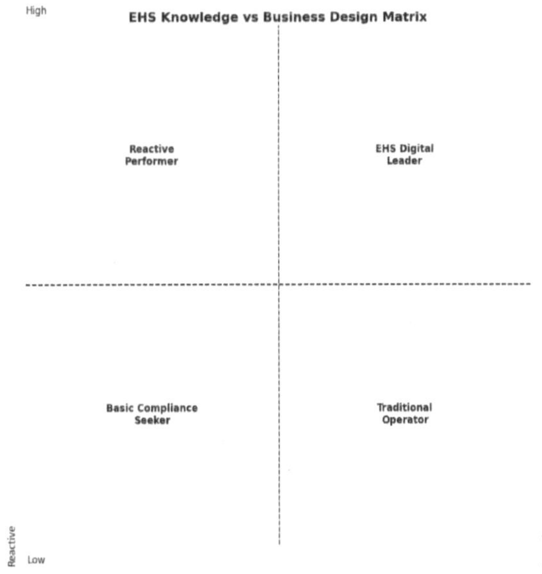

Figure 1.1: EHS Knowledge vs Business Design

4. EHS digital Leaders (High EHS Knowledge / Proactive Business Design)

Overview: These organizations embed deep EHS knowledge into every aspect of their business, using real-time data, IoT, and predictive analytics to ensure continuous safety and compliance improvements. They are highly efficient and proactive in managing EHS risks.

Digital Tool Usage:

- Comprehensive IoT implementation for real-time monitoring of safety and environmental parameters

- Advanced AI and machine learning for predictive risk management and incident prevention

- Big data analytics for trend analysis, benchmarking, and continuous improvement

- Integrated mobile solutions for seamless reporting and communication

Key Challenges:

- Managing the vast volumes of data generated by comprehensive digital systems

- Ensuring continuous innovation and staying ahead of rapidly evolving technology

- Maintaining robust cybersecurity measures across a highly connected ecosystem

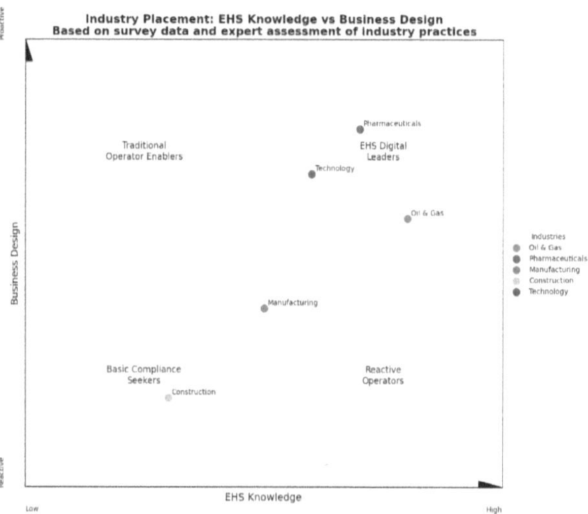

Figure 1.2: EHS Knowledge vs Business Design – Study industry placement

Challenges and Mitigation Strategies in EHS Digital Transformation

Organizations often encounter various challenges when implementing EHS digital transformation initiatives. Here are some common challenges and specific strategies to overcome them:

1. Resistance to Change

Challenge: Employees and management may resist adopting new digital tools and processes, preferring familiar methods.

Mitigation Strategies:

- Implement a comprehensive change management program

- Involve employees in the transformation process from the beginning

- Communicate the benefits of digital transformation clearly and frequently

- Provide extensive training and support

- Start with small, quick-win projects to demonstrate value

2. Data Quality and Integration Issues

Challenge: Poor data quality or difficulty integrating data from various sources can hinder effective analysis and decision-making.

Mitigation Strategies:

- Conduct a thorough data audit before beginning the transformation

- Implement data governance policies and procedures

- Use data cleansing and validation tools

- Invest in integration platforms or middleware solutions

- Standardize data formats and definitions across the organization

3. Skills Gap

Challenge: Lack of digital skills among EHS professionals and other employees can slow adoption and limit the effectiveness of new technologies.

Mitigation Strategies:

- Develop a comprehensive digital skills training program

- Partner with educational institutions or training providers

- Consider hiring digital specialists or creating new roles (e.g., EHS Data Analyst)

- Implement mentoring or buddy systems to pair digitally-savvy employees with those less experienced

- Encourage continuous learning and provide resources for self-paced skill development

4. Budget Constraints

Challenge: Limited financial resources can restrict the scope and pace of digital transformation initiatives.

Mitigation Strategies:

- Start with high-impact, low-cost initiatives to demonstrate ROI

- Consider cloud-based solutions to reduce upfront costs

- Explore phased implementation approaches

- Look for opportunities to reallocate resources from legacy systems

- Build a compelling business case that highlights long-term cost savings and benefits

5. Cybersecurity and Data Privacy Concerns

Challenge: Increased digitalization can expose organizations to new cybersecurity risks and data privacy challenges.

Mitigation Strategies:

- Conduct regular security audits and penetration testing

- Implement robust data encryption and access control measures

- Provide cybersecurity awareness training for all employees

- Develop and enforce strict data privacy policies

- Consider partnering with cybersecurity experts or managed security service providers

6. Technology Selection and Integration

Challenge: Choosing the right technologies and integrating them with existing systems can be complex and time-consuming.

Mitigation Strategies:

- Conduct a thorough needs assessment before selecting technologies

- Prioritize solutions that offer open APIs and easy integration capabilities

- Consider creating a proof of concept or pilot project before full implementation

- Involve IT teams early in the selection and implementation process

- Develop a long-term technology roadmap to guide decisions

7. Measuring ROI and Demonstrating Value

Challenge: Difficulty in quantifying the benefits of EHS digital transformation can make it hard to justify ongoing investment.

Mitigation Strategies:

- Establish clear, measurable KPIs for digital initiatives

- Implement analytics tools to track and report on these KPIs

- Focus on both leading and lagging indicators

- Regularly communicate successes and lessons learned to stakeholders

- Consider both tangible (e.g., cost savings) and intangible (e.g., improved safety culture) benefits

8. Scalability and Sustainability of Digital Initiatives

Challenge: Ensuring digital initiatives can scale across the organization and remain effective over time.

Mitigation Strategies:

- Design initiatives with scalability in mind from the start

- Implement a center of excellence or similar structure to guide ongoing digital efforts

- Regularly review and update digital strategies to align with changing business needs

- Foster a culture of continuous improvement and innovation

- Develop internal champions to drive adoption and evolution of digital initiatives

9. Regulatory Compliance in a Digital Environment

Challenge: Ensuring that digital transformations maintain or enhance regulatory compliance can be complex, especially in highly regulated industries.

Mitigation Strategies:

- Engage with regulatory bodies early to understand their stance on digital tools and processes

- Implement robust audit trails and documentation processes in digital systems

- Consider compliance requirements when selecting and implementing new technologies

- Regularly review and update digital processes to ensure ongoing compliance

- Train employees on how to maintain compliance in a digital environment

Organizations can significantly increase their chances of successful EHS digital transformation by addressing these challenges proactively and implementing these mitigation strategies. Remember, transformation is an ongoing process, and strategy may need to be adjusted as the organization progresses on its digital journey.

Making Strategic Choices for EHS Digital Transformation

Leaders must ask critical questions to determine where their organization stands within the EHS Knowledge and Business Design framework. How well do you understand the EHS risks and regulatory requirements your organization faces? Are you still operating in silos, reacting to incidents, or have you integrated data and safety insights into your daily workflows?

Over the years, I've observed that companies with low EHS knowledge and reactive business models need help keeping pace with regulatory demands and employee expectations. Employees, regulators, and customers now expect real-time insights, immediate responses, and predictive systems to manage safety risks.

In contrast, organizations adopting high-EHS knowledge and proactive business design tend to experience faster incident resolution, higher compliance, and more engaged employees. One of the companies I worked with, a global energy company, saw a 20% improvement in safety performance by integrating wearable technology, predictive maintenance, and real-time compliance monitoring into their day-to-day operations. They moved from a reactive model to becoming leaders in digital EHS transformation.

Examples of Digital EHS Transformation in Action

Many companies are already leading the way in EHS digital transformation, using technology to drive safety and sustainability. These are some of the organizations that I have come across:

- **An Electric Major**: Transformed from an electrical product manufacturer into a leader in energy management and automation, integrating IoT and cloud-based safety systems to achieve 20% fewer environmental violations and 15% fewer workplace accidents.

- **A Chemical major:** A leader in integrating real-time IoT sensors and predictive analytics to prevent workplace incidents and enhance safety protocols. By embracing digital safety solutions, The company saw a significant reduction in environmental risks and workplace accidents, improving overall safety performance by over 30%.

- **A European Chemical Major:** The company has been a leader in applying artificial intelligence (AI) to enhance its EHS processes. The company has improved operational safety, productivity, and sustainability by leveraging AI. It uses machine learning models for incident prediction and real-time safety data analysis, leading to better risk management and reduced environmental violations. The company has significantly enhanced its safety procedures by integrating AI across its global operations.

- **A Major** Energy company has incorporated IoT technologies and predictive analytics in its safety management systems to monitor its operations proactively. Deploying real-time sensors across its facilities allows the company to detect and address safety risks before they escalate into incidents. By harnessing IoT, the energy major has significantly improved its risk management processes, reducing the likelihood of accidents.

- A agriculture major, has implemented cloud-based safety platforms to manage and monitor its compliance and safety operations across multiple global sites. Their systems integrate data from various safety audits, incident reports, and environmental monitoring tools, providing a unified platform for tracking and addressing EHS risks. This centralized approach helps Bayer streamline compliance processes and ensure safety across its supply chain.

These companies have done more than tweak their safety practices—reinvented themselves to create a safer, more sustainable future. The key takeaway for leaders in EHS is to ask: How can your organization evolve to become the next-generation leader in your industry?

While working with companies on their EHS journey, I've seen that success lies in moving from low-EHS knowledge and reactive business designs to becoming proactive leaders who embed safety and sustainability into the fabric of their organizations. Understanding your organization's position within the EHS Knowledge and Business Design framework is the key to navigating this journey. EHS is no longer just about reacting to incidents but predicting and preventing them. With the right tools, strategies, and mindset, any organization can evolve into an EHS Digital Leader, ready to meet future demands with safety and sustainability at its core.

The Six Levers and a Guide to This Book

To successfully lead an EHS digital transformation, leaders must assess six levers that align with a framework for evolving safety, sustainability, and compliance practices. By concentrating on these areas, organizations can navigate the complexities of digitizing EHS operations and embedding safety into their core business processes. These focus areas are designed to guide organizations through the challenges of digitizing EHS operations and embedding safety into the core of their business processes:

1. Addressing Emerging EHS Challenges with Digital Solutions

As the digital landscape evolves, so do organizations' environmental, health, and safety (EHS) management challenges. New risks related to climate change, regulatory shifts, and workplace safety require modern solutions.

- **EHS Strategic Action**: Organizations must identify the most pressing EHS risks and explore how digital tools, such as IoT sensors, real-time data analytics, and AI, can mitigate them. This lever emphasizes the proactive identification and management of emerging challenges.

- **EHS Performance Evaluation**: **Evaluate the effectiveness** of digital solutions in addressing these challenges. This includes assessing how healthy tools are integrated into daily operations to reduce risks, improve compliance, and ensure workplace safety.

Cautionary Note - Lessons from PG&E: The PG&E smart meter case underscores the critical importance of thorough testing and integration when implementing digital solutions. PG&E's rapid rollout of smart meters without adequate real-world testing led to widespread inaccuracies and integration issues with existing systems. Organizations must ensure that new digital solutions are rigorously tested in various scenarios and properly integrated with existing infrastructure before full-scale implementation. This approach helps prevent operational disruptions, data inaccuracies, and the erosion of stakeholder trust.

Example: Organizations using real-time monitoring tools can detect hazards or non-compliance issues faster, allowing them to take corrective actions more swiftly and avoid costly incidents. However, these tools must be thoroughly tested and seamlessly integrated to provide accurate, actionable data.

2. Aligning EHS Business Models with Future Goals

The structure of an organization's EHS management must align with its future strategic objectives. Traditional, compliance-driven models may no longer suffice in a digitally transformed landscape.

- **EHS Strategic Action**: Leaders must adapt their EHS business model to fit the broader digital Transformation goals. A proactive, interconnected approach should replace reactive systems, ensuring that safety, sustainability, and compliance are integrated across all functions.

- **EHS Performance Evaluation**: Assess how well the current business model supports digital Transformation, including whether it can integrate advanced safety practices, data-driven decision-making, and cross-functional collaboration.

Example: An organization moving from a reactive, compliance-only model to a proactive, integrated EHS strategy is more capable of managing risks before they arise and embedding safety into every business process.

3. Leveraging EHS Digital Strengths for Competitive Advantage

Organizations must focus on their unique strengths in EHS management in a rapidly digitizing world. This strategic lever focuses on identifying and exploiting digital advantages, which can give organizations a competitive edge.

- **EHS Strategic Action**: Capitalize on your organization's digital EHS strengths, whether in data-driven compliance management, automated safety protocols, or real-time monitoring.

- **EHS Performance Evaluation**: Evaluate your competitive advantage by benchmarking your digital strengths against industry peers. Ensure that you leverage your expertise to improve risk management, safety outcomes, and operational efficiency.

Example: Organizations that integrate AI-based predictive maintenance can reduce equipment failure rates and enhance safety, positioning them ahead of competitors still relying on manual safety checks.

Table 1.2: Six Strategic Levers for EHS Digital Transformation

Strategic Lever	Key Actions	Potential performance indicators
1. Addressing Emerging EHS Challenges with Digital Solutions	• Identify pressing EHS risks • Explore digital tools (IoT, real-time analytics, AI) • Implement solutions to mitigate risks	• Reduction in incident rates • Improvement in risk prediction accuracy • Decrease in time to identify and respond to EHS issues
2. Aligning EHS Business Models with Future Goals	• Adapt the EHS business model to fit digital transformation goals • Replace reactive systems with proactive approaches • Integrate safety, sustainability, and compliance across functions	• Increase in proactive risk management initiatives • Improvement in cross-functional collaboration on EHS issues • Alignment of EHS KPIs with overall business objectives
3. Leveraging EHS Digital Strengths for Competitive Advantage	• Identify unique digital EHS strengths • Capitalize on data-driven compliance management • Implement automated safety protocols	• Improvement in industry benchmarking positions • Increase in operational efficiency • Enhanced reputation for safety and sustainability
4. Enhancing EHS Performance Through Smart Technologies	• Implement IoT devices and real-time monitoring systems • Utilize AR/VR for training • Apply Big Data analytics for predictive incident prevention	• Reduction in training costs • Improvement in early risk detection • Increase in employee engagement with EHS initiatives
5. Building Core Capabilities for EHS Digital Transformation	• Invest in employee digital skills development • Automate compliance processes • Integrate digital tools into daily operations	• Improvement in employee digital literacy scores • Reduction in time spent on routine compliance tasks • Increase in adoption rates of new digital EHS tools
6. Fostering Leadership Commitment for EHS Digital Innovation	• Develop leaders who champion EHS digital innovation • Align safety and sustainability goals with business objectives • Foster a culture of continuous improvement	• Increase in leadership-initiated EHS digital projects • Improvement in employee perception of leadership's commitment to EHS • Growth in budget allocation for EHS digital initiatives

4. Enhancing EHS Performance Through Smart Technologies

The digital era has brought many intelligent technologies like IoT, AR/VR, and Big Data analytics. These technologies could revolutionize how organizations manage their EHS functions, offering greater insight, automation, and operational control.

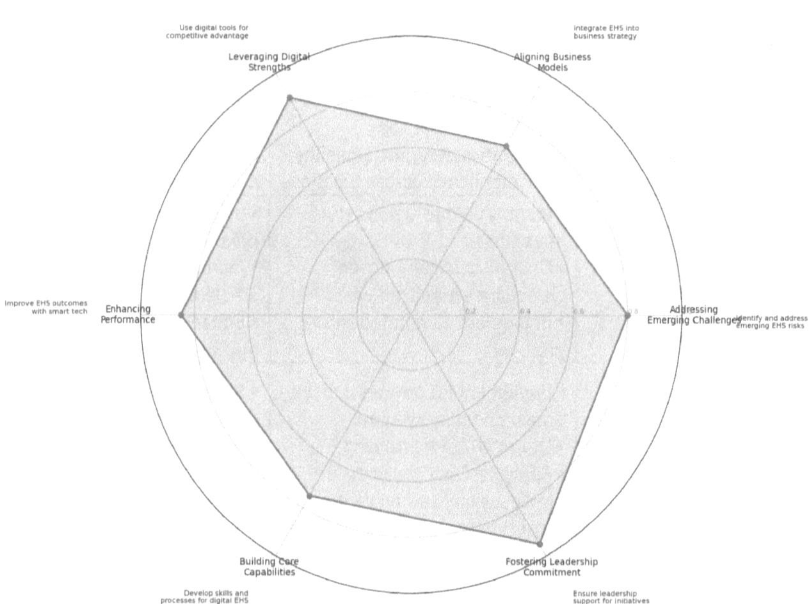

Figure 1.3: Six Strategic levers for EHS Digital Transformation

- **EHS Strategic Action**: Implement IoT devices and real-time monitoring systems to gain insights into environmental and safety risks. AR/VR technologies can also enhance training, while Big Data analytics can help predict incidents before they occur.

- **EHS Performance Evaluation**: Assess your readiness to adopt intelligent technologies by evaluating their impact on safety, compliance, and operational efficiency. Measure how quickly you can act on the insights these technologies provide.

Example: A company deploying IoT sensors in hazardous areas can monitor air quality in real-time, allowing immediate action if conditions deteriorate and improving worker safety.

5. Building Core Capabilities for EHS Digital Transformation

Digital Transformation requires organizations to develop the right internal capabilities. With a skilled workforce and a robust digital infrastructure, even the best technology will achieve its full potential.

- **EHS Strategic Action**: Invest in developing digital capabilities, including training employees on new technologies, automating compliance processes, and integrating digital tools into everyday operations.

- **EHS Performance Evaluation**: Assess the organization's readiness for digital Transformation by evaluating whether it has the necessary technology, skills, and processes to support new digital tools and approaches.

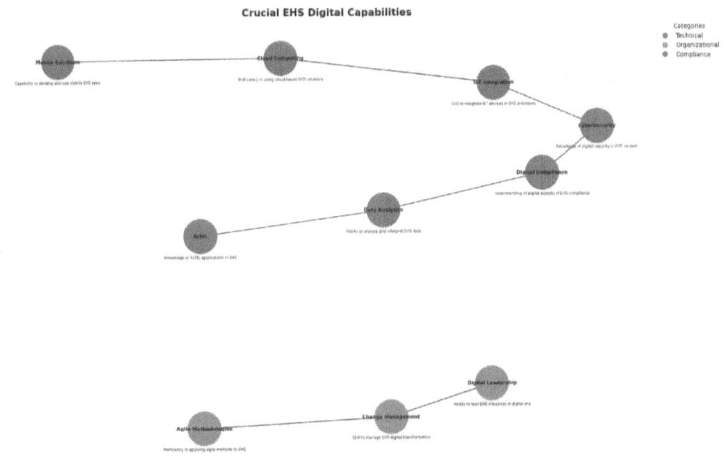

Figure 1.4: Crucial EHS Digital Capability for Digital Strategy

Emphasis on Training and Change Management - Lessons from PG&E: The PG&E case demonstrates the consequences of neglecting comprehensive training and change management in digital transformation initiatives. PG&E underestimated the need for customer education and employee training, leading to widespread confusion, resistance, and, ultimately, the failure of their smart meter program. Organizations must prioritize:

1. Comprehensive Training Programs: Develop robust, ongoing training initiatives that cover the technical aspects of new digital tools and their strategic importance and impact on daily operations.

2. Change Management Strategies: Implement change management processes that address cultural shifts, communicate the benefits of digital transformation, and actively involve employees in the transition.

3. Continuous Support: Provide ongoing support and resources to help employees adapt to new digital systems and processes.

4. Leadership Development: Equip leaders with the knowledge and skills to champion digital transformation and guide their teams through the change process.

Example: By building in-house expertise in EHS analytics, organizations can make better data-driven decisions, streamlining compliance and risk management across multiple functions. However, this requires a commitment to ongoing training and skill development at all levels of the organization.

6. Fostering Leadership Commitment for EHS Digital Innovation

The success of EHS's digital transformation hinges on leadership's commitment and vision. Without strong, forward-thinking leaders, digital initiatives may remain siloed or fail to integrate with broader organizational strategies.

- **EHS Strategic Action**: Develop leadership that champions EHS digital innovation. This requires leaders to drive the adoption of new technologies, foster a culture of continuous improvement, and align safety and sustainability goals with broader business objectives.

- **EHS Performance Evaluation**: Evaluate leadership's engagement and support for EHS digital transformation by assessing how effectively they integrate safety and compliance into the company's digital strategy and overall business goals.

Example: Leaders who actively support digital Transformation in EHS foster a culture where safety is prioritized at every organizational level, ensuring long-term success and resilience.

7. Aligning EHS Strategy with Corporate Objectives

Beyond focusing on these six **strategic levers**, organizations must ensure that their **EHS digital transformation** aligns with the overall business strategy.

When EHS is integrated with core business goals like operational efficiency and sustainability, it becomes a powerful driver of long-term success.

Safety, sustainability, and compliance should not be treated as separate initiatives; they must be embedded into the company's broader objectives. For instance, if an organization focuses on reducing environmental impact, its digital EHS strategy should support those goals by tracking emissions, reducing waste, and ensuring ecological compliance through automated systems.

Most organizations must get their digital EHS transformation right on the first try. I've seen this firsthand across my 20 years in EHS. Iteration, learning, and the ability to adapt are as essential as having the right vision and strategic direction. The most successful organizations are those willing to course-correct, learn from their actions, and continuously improve. Answering the six questions and planning the roadmap above provides a framework for making actionable decisions. Still, the key lies in the willingness to embrace an ongoing process of refinement and reinvention.

- **EHS Strategic Action**: Implement IoT devices and real-time monitoring systems to gain insights into environmental and safety risks. AR/VR technologies can also enhance training, while Big Data analytics can help predict incidents before they occur.

- **EHS Performance Evaluation**: Assess your readiness to adopt intelligent technologies by evaluating their impact on safety, compliance, and operational efficiency. Measure how quickly you can act on the insights these technologies provide.

Example: A company deploying IoT sensors in hazardous areas can monitor air quality in real-time, allowing immediate action if conditions deteriorate and improving worker safety.

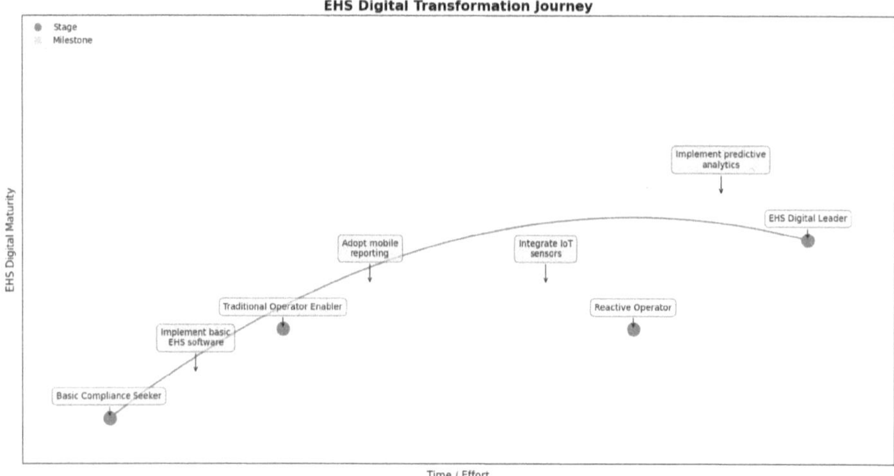

Figure 1.5: EHS Digital Transformation Journey

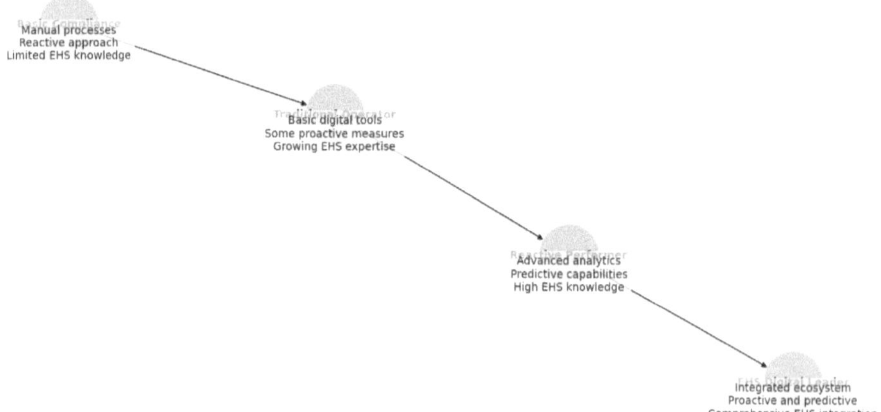

Figure 1.6: EHS Digital Transformation Journey – Knowledge path

Table 1.3: Digital Tools and their applications in EHS

Digital Tool	Description	Specific Applications in EHS
IoT Sensors	Internet-connected devices that collect and transmit data	• Real-time monitoring of air quality, noise levels, and temperature • Tracking of equipment usage and maintenance needs • Monitoring worker vital signs in hazardous environments • Detecting gas leaks or other environmental hazards
Artificial Intelligence (AI) / Machine Learning (ML)	Systems that can learn from data, identify patterns, and make decisions with minimal human intervention	• Predictive analysis of potential safety incidents • Automated compliance reporting and documentation • Intelligent analysis of incident reports to identify trends • Optimization of resource allocation for EHS initiatives
Virtual Reality (VR)	Computer-generated simulation of a three-dimensional environment	• Immersive safety training simulations • Virtual walkthroughs of hazardous environments • Simulation of emergency scenarios for preparedness training • Design and testing of safety protocols in a risk-free environment
Augmented Reality (AR)	Technology that superimposes computer-generated information on a user's view of the natural world	• Real-time display of safety information in work environments • Guided maintenance procedures with overlaid instructions • Visualization of potential hazards in a workspace • Remote expert assistance for complex tasks
Mobile Apps	Software applications designed to run on smartphones and tablets	• On-the-go incident reporting and tracking • Access to safety data sheets and procedures • Real-time communication of safety alerts • Digital checklists for safety inspections
Drones	Uncrewed aerial vehicles controlled by remote or onboard computers	• Inspection of hard-to-reach or hazardous areas • Aerial monitoring of environmental impacts • Emergency response and damage assessment • Mapping and surveying of work sites
Wearable Technology	Electronic devices that can be worn on the body	• Monitoring of worker fatigue and stress levels • Tracking of employee location in emergencies • Automated logging of exposure to hazardous substances • Real-time alerts for unsafe conditions or behaviours
Big Data Analytics	The process of examining extensive data sets to uncover patterns, correlations, and insights	• Analysis of historical incident data to identify risk factors • Benchmarking of EHS performance across sites or industries • Predictive maintenance scheduling based on equipment data • Optimization of resource allocation for EHS initiatives
Cloud Computing	The delivery of computing services over the Internet	• Centralized storage and access of EHS data across multiple sites • Real-time collaboration on safety initiatives • Scalable processing power for complex EHS analytics • Remote access to EHS management systems

Case Study 1: A Renewable Energy Company Journey to EHS Digital Leadership

GreenCo (Company Anonymised), a multinational manufacturing company, embarked on a comprehensive EHS digital transformation journey in 2018. This case study illustrates their progression from a Basic Compliance Provider to an End-to-End Ecosystem Leader over five years.

Initial Situation (2018):

- Reactive approach to EHS management

- Paper-based incident reporting and compliance tracking

- Siloed data across different plants and departments

- Rising incident rates and compliance issues

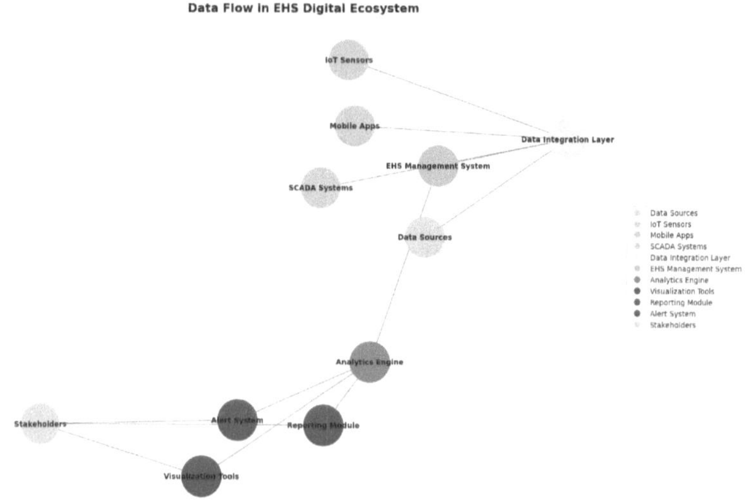

Figure 1.7: Data Flow in the EHS Digital Ecosystem

Phase 1: Foundation Building (2018-2019)

Actions Taken:

1. Implemented a cloud-based EHS management system

2. Introduced mobile apps for incident reporting and safety observations

3. Conducted a company-wide data standardization initiative

4. Initiated leadership training on digital Transformation in EHS

Challenges Faced:

- Resistance from long-time employees accustomed to paper-based systems

- Data quality issues during migration to the new system

- Initial increase in reported incidents due to more accessible reporting methods

Outcomes:

- 30% reduction in time spent on compliance reporting

- 50% increase in near-miss reporting, enabling better risk identification

- Improved data visibility across the organization

Phase 2: Advanced Technology Integration (2019-2021)

Actions Taken:

1. Deployed IoT sensors for real-time environmental monitoring across all plants

2. Implemented AI-driven predictive analytics for risk assessment

3. Introduced VR technology for safety training

4. Developed a central data lake to integrate EHS data with operational data

Challenges Faced:

- Significant upfront costs requiring careful ROI justification

- Cybersecurity concerns with the increased connectivity

- Skills gap in data science and IoT technology among EHS staff

Outcomes:

- 25% reduction in reportable environmental incidents

- 40% improvement in risk prediction accuracy

- 35% reduction in training costs with improved knowledge retention

Phase 3: Ecosystem Development and Optimization (2021-2023)

Actions Taken:

1. Extended digital EHS systems to suppliers and contractors

2. Implemented advanced technology-based application for transparent and secure compliance record-keeping

3. Developed an open API platform allowing for the integration of specialized third-party EHS applications

4. Established an AI Ethics Committee to oversee the use of AI in EHS decision-making

Challenges Faced:

- Ensuring consistent adoption across a diverse supplier network

- Managing the complexity of the now highly interconnected EHS ecosystem

- Balancing automation with human oversight in critical EHS Decisions

Outcomes:

- 60% overall reduction in recordable incident rates since 2018

- Recognition as an industry leader in sustainable and safe operations

- 20% improvement in operational efficiency due to integrated EHS and operational data

Key Lessons:

1. Leadership commitment was crucial in overcoming resistance to change

2. The phased implementation allowed for learning and adjustment

3. Investing in employee skills development was essential for successful adoption

4. Integration of EHS data with broader operational data provided unexpected insights and efficiencies

5. Extending the digital ecosystem to suppliers amplified the benefits of Transformation

Case Study 2: SafeConstruct's Rapid Digital Transformation

SafeConstruct, a medium-sized offshore construction company, underwent a rapid EHS digital transformation in response to a series of safety incidents. This case study demonstrates how they dramatically leveraged digital tools to improve their safety performance over 18 months.

Initial Situation (January 2022):

- High incident rate compared to the industry average

- Inconsistent safety practices across different project sites

- Manual, paper-based safety reporting and inspections

- Limited visibility into safety performance metrics

Phase 1: Emergency Response and Quick Wins
(Jan 2022 - April 2022)

Actions Taken:

1. Implemented a mobile app for real-time incident reporting and safety observations

2. Introduced wearable devices to detect falls and worker fatigue

3. Conducted a rapid assessment of high-risk areas using data analytics

4. Launched a safety awareness campaign highlighting the new digital tools

Challenges Faced:

- The urgency of implementation led to some initial technical glitches

- Skepticism from field workers about the privacy implications of wearable devices

- Overwhelmed by the sudden increase in safety data

Outcomes:

- 40% increase in near-miss reporting within the first month

- 25% reduction in response time to safety incidents

- Identification of three critical risk factors previously overlooked

Phase 2: Advanced Safety Systems Integration (May 2022 - Dec 2022)

Actions Taken:

1. Deployed IoT sensors on crucial equipment for real-time monitoring

2. Implemented AI-powered computer vision for PPE compliance monitoring

3. Introduced drone technology for site inspections and progress monitoring

4. Developed a centralized safety dashboard for real-time performance tracking

Challenges Faced:

- High upfront costs requiring careful budgeting and ROI calculations

- Integration of multiple data streams into a coherent system

- Training requirements for new technologies, especially for older workers

Outcomes:

- 50% reduction in equipment-related incidents

- 70% improvement in PPE compliance rates

- 30% reduction in time spent on-site inspections

Phase 3: Predictive Systems and Culture Shift (Jan 2023 - June 2023)

Actions Taken:

1. Implemented predictive analytics for project risk assessment

2. Introduced a gamified safety training program using AR technology

3. Developed a machine learning model for identifying leading indicators of safety incidents

4. Launched a "Safety Innovation Challenge" for employees to propose new digital safety solutions

Challenges Faced:

- Ensuring the accuracy and reliability of predictive models

- Balancing reliance on technology with human judgment in safety decisions

- Maintaining employee engagement with multiple new systems and processes

Outcomes:

- 65% overall reduction in recordable incident rates since January 2022

- 45% improvement in project risk assessment accuracy

- There is a significant shift in safety culture, with 80% of employees reporting improved safety awareness

Key Lessons:

1. A crisis can catalyze rapid digital Transformation

2. Quick wins help build momentum and overcome initial resistance

3. Involving employees in the digital transformation process improves adoption and generates innovative ideas

4. Balancing technology implementation with culture change is crucial for sustainable improvement

5. Continuous learning and adaptation are necessary as new technologies are integrated into EHS processes

Case Study 3: PG&E's Smart Meter Program - A Cautionary Tale of Digital Transformation

Pacific Gas and Electric Company (PG&E), one of the largest combined natural gas and electric energy companies in the United States, embarked on an ambitious intelligent meter program in 2009. This case study illustrates the potential pitfalls of rushing into digital transformation without adequate planning, testing, and change management.

Initial Situation (2009):

- Aging infrastructure with limited real-time monitoring capabilities

- Manual meter reading processes, prone to errors and inefficiencies

- Increasing pressure to improve energy efficiency and grid management

- Growing customer demands for more detailed energy usage information

Objectives of the Smart Meter Program:

1. Automate meter readings for increased accuracy and efficiency

2. Provide customers with real-time energy usage data

3. Enable better grid management and faster response to outages

4. Improve overall energy efficiency and reduce operational costs

Phase 1: Rapid Implementation (2009-2010)

Actions Taken:

1. Initiated large-scale deployment of smart meters across PG&E's service area

2. Developed new billing systems to handle smart meter data

3. Created customer-facing platforms for accessing energy usage information

4. Began phasing out traditional meter reading jobs

Challenges Faced:

- Rushed deployment led to inadequate testing of meters in real-world conditions

- Integration issues between new intelligent meter systems and existing infrastructure

- Lack of comprehensive employee training and customer education programs

- Underestimated cybersecurity risks associated with the new technology

Outcomes:

- Installation of over 5 million smart meters by the end of 2010

- Significant increase in customer complaints about billing accuracy

- Growing public concern about the safety and privacy implications of smart meters

- Emergence of grassroots opposition to the smart meter program

Phase 2: Crisis Management and Remediation (2010-2012)

Actions Taken:

1. Initiated independent reviews of smart meter accuracy and deployment processes

2. Developed a customer opt-out program for those who didn't want smart meters

3. Increased customer outreach and education efforts

4. Implemented additional security measures to address privacy concerns

5. Worked with regulators to address issues and rebuild public trust

Challenges Faced:

- Erosion of public trust due to initial lack of transparency about problems

- Regulatory scrutiny and potential fines

- Balancing the need to continue the program with addressing public concerns

- Managing the financial impact of remediation efforts and the opt-out program

Outcomes:

- Confirmation of smart meter accuracy by independent studies but lingering public skepticism

- Implementation of the opt-out program, with associated costs passed on to customers

- Improved communication and transparency about the smart meter program

- Significant financial losses and damage to PG&E's reputation

Key Lessons Learned:

1. Thorough Testing is Crucial: Adequate real-world testing of new technologies before large-scale deployment is essential to identify and address potential issues.

2. Integration Planning is Critical: Careful planning for integrating existing systems is necessary to avoid operational disruptions and data inconsistencies.

3. Change Management is Non-Negotiable: Comprehensive change management strategies, including employee training and customer education, are vital for successful digital transformation.

4. Security and Privacy Cannot Be Afterthoughts: Cybersecurity and data privacy considerations must be prioritized from the outset of any digital initiative.

5. Transparency Builds Trust: Open and honest communication about challenges and setbacks is crucial for maintaining public trust and regulatory support.

6. Phased Implementation Reduces Risk: A more gradual, phased approach to implementation can help identify and address issues before they become widespread problems.

7. Customer Choice Matters: Providing options (such as an opt-out program) can help mitigate resistance to new technologies.

Long-term Impact: While PG&E eventually addressed many of the initial issues with its innovative meter program, the rushed implementation and subsequent problems had lasting consequences. The company faced ongoing public skepticism, regulatory challenges, and financial repercussions. However, the lessons learned from this experience have informed smarter, more measured approaches to digital transformation in the utility sector.

This case study contrasts starkly with the successful transformations of GreenCo and SafeConstruct. While those companies took measured, phased approaches to digital transformation, with a strong focus on change management and stakeholder engagement, PG&E's rapid implementation and inadequate planning led to significant challenges. The PG&E case is a valuable cautionary tale, highlighting the importance of thorough planning, testing, and change management in EHS digital transformation initiatives.

These case studies illustrate how companies can leverage digital tools and strategies to transform their EHS performance, regardless of their starting point or the pace of change. They demonstrate the application of the four models of EHS Business Transformation and the six strategic levers discussed earlier in the chapter.

EHS Digital Transformation Self-Assessment Tool

Use this checklist to evaluate your organization's current state in the EHS Knowledge vs. Business Design framework. For each statement, rate your organization on a scale of 1 to 5:

1 = Strongly Disagree 2 = Disagree 3 = Neutral 4 = Agree 5 = Strongly Agree

EHS Knowledge

1. Our organization has a deep understanding of EHS risks specific to our industry. []

2. We have comprehensive knowledge of all applicable EHS regulations. []

3. Our EHS team is well-versed in modern safety management techniques. []

4. We regularly conduct thorough risk assessments across all operations. []

5. Our organization stays updated on emerging EHS trends and best practices. []

Business Design

6. EHS considerations are integrated into our overall business strategy. []

7. We have a proactive approach to identifying and mitigating EHS risks. []

8. Our EHS processes are digitalized and data-driven. []

9. We use advanced analytics for EHS decision-making. []

10. Our organization has a culture of continuous improvement in EHS practices. []

Digital Tools and Technologies

11. We use IoT devices to monitor EHS parameters in real-time. []

12. Our organization employs AI/ML for predictive risk analysis. []

13. We utilize mobile apps for incident reporting and safety observations. []

14. Virtual or Augmented Reality is used in our safety training programs. []

15. We have implemented a centralized EHS management information system. []

Data Management and Analytics

16. Our EHS data is easily accessible and well-organized. []

17. We regularly analyze EHS data to identify trends and insights. []

18. Our organization uses predictive analytics for incident prevention. []

19. We have real-time dashboards for EHS performance monitoring. []

20. EHS data is integrated with other business data for holistic analysis. []

Leadership and Culture

21. Our leadership actively champions EHS digital transformation initiatives. []

22. Employees at all levels are engaged in our EHS digital journey. []

23. We have a clear vision and roadmap for EHS digital transformation. []

24. Our organization allocates sufficient resources for the adoption of EHS technology. []

25. We foster a culture of innovation in EHS practices. []

Scoring and Interpretation:

Total your scores for each section and overall:

- EHS Knowledge (Questions 1-5): _____ / 25

- Business Design (Questions 6-10): _____ / 25

- Digital Tools and Technologies (Questions 11-15): _____ / 25

- Data Management and Analytics (Questions 16-20): _____ / 25

- Leadership and Culture (Questions 21-25): _____ / 25

  Overall Score: _____ / 125

Interpretation:

- 100-125: EHS Digital Leader - Your organization is at the forefront of EHS digital transformation.

- 75-99: Reactive Performer - Strong in some areas but reactive in others. Focus on moving towards a more proactive, integrated approach.

- 50-74: Traditional Operator - You've started the digital journey but have significant room for improvement. Identify critical areas for development.

- 25-49: Basic Compliance Seeker - Your organization is still in the early stages of EHS digital transformation. Develop a comprehensive strategy to move forward.

Next Steps:

1. Identify the areas where you scored lowest. These are your primary improvement opportunities.

2. For each low-scoring area, refer to the chapter for strategies and best practices to enhance your capabilities.

3. Develop an action plan focusing on 2-3 critical areas for improvement over the next 6-12 months.

4. Reassess regularly (e.g., every six months) to track your progress and adjust your strategy as needed.

Remember, EHS digital transformation is a journey. Consistent progress, even if gradual, can significantly improve safety outcomes, operational efficiency, and overall business performance.

References for EHS Digital Transformation Chapter

1. Aberdeen Group. (2019). EHS Technology Transformation: The Momentum Builds. Aberdeen Group.

2. Deloitte. (2020). The Fourth Industrial Revolution and manufacturing's great reset. Deloitte Insights. https://www2.deloitte.com/us/en/insights/industry/manufacturing/driving-value-with-industry-4-0.html

3. DuPont. (2021). 2021 Sustainability Report. DuPont. https://www.dupont.com/sustainability.html

4. EHS Today. (2020). The State of Mobile EHS Applications. EHS Today Magazine.

5. Institute for Safety and Health Management. (2019). The ROI of EHS Digital Transformation. ISHM.

6. National Safety Council. (2021). Safety Technology and Analytics. National Safety Council. https://www.nsc.org/workplace/safety-topics/safety-technology-analytics

7. Safety+Health Magazine. (2020). Annual Software and Mobile App Survey. Safety+Health Magazine.

8. Schneider Electric. (2021). 2020-2021 Sustainability Report. Schneider Electric. https://www.se.com/ww/en/about-us/sustainability/

9. Verdantix. (2021). Green Quadrant EHS Software 2021. Verdantix.

10. Walmart. (2021). 2021 Environmental, Social and Governance Report. Walmart. https://corporate.walmart.com/esgreport/

11. Dow Chemical Company. (2020). 2020 Environmental, Social and Governance Report. Dow. https://corporate.dow.com/en-us/esg/report.html

12. McKinsey & Company. (2020). The Next Normal in Construction: How Disruption is Reshaping the World's Largest Ecosystem. McKinsey & Company. https://www.mckinsey.com/industries/capital-projects-and-infrastructure/our-insights/the-next-normal-in-construction-how-disruption-is-reshaping-the-worlds-largest-ecosystem

13. International Labour Organization. (2019). Safety and Health at the Heart of the Future of Work.

14. ILO. https://www.ilo.org/safework/events/safeday/WCMS_686645/lang—en/index.htm

15. Environmental Protection Agency. (2021). Next Generation Compliance. EPA. https://www.epa.gov/compliance/next-generation-compliance

16. Occupational Safety and Health Administration. (2021). Using Leading Indicators to Improve Safety and Health Outcomes. OSHA. https://www.osha.gov/leadingindicators/

17. World Economic Forum. (2020). The Future of Jobs Report 2020. World Economic Forum. https://www.weforum.org/reports/the-future-of-jobs-report-2020

18. Gartner. (2021). Gartner Top 10 Strategic Technology Trends for 2021. Gartner. https://www.gartner.com/smarterwithgartner/gartner-top-10-strategic-technology-trends-for-2021/

19. PwC. (2020). Digital Factories 2020: Shaping the Future of Manufacturing. PwC. https://www.pwc.de/de/digitale-transformation/digital-factories-2020-shaping-the-future-of-manufacturing.pdf

20. International Organization for Standardization. (2018). ISO 45001:2018 Occupational health and safety management systems — Requirements with guidance for use. ISO. https://www.iso.org/standard/63787.html

21. Accenture. (2021). The European Double Up: A Twin Strategy That Will Strengthen Competitiveness. Accenture. https://www.accenture.com/us-en/insights/industry-x/european-double-up

22. https://www.ehstoday.com/safety-technology/article/55127950/barriers-getting-in-way-of-mobile-ehs-application-usage

23. California Public Utilities Commission. (2010). Structure of the California Public Utilities Commission's Investigation of Pacific Gas and Electric Company's Smart Meter Program. URL: https://docs.cpuc.ca.gov/PublishedDocs/EFILE/RULINGS/122985.PDF

24. Hess, D. J., & Coley, J. S. (2014). Wireless smart meters and public acceptance: The environment, limited choices, and precautionary politics. Public Understanding of Science, 23(6), 688-702. DOI: 10.1177/0963662512464936

25. Berst, J. (2010). Brilliant grid backlash: Has PG&E solved its smart meter problems? Smart Grid News. [Note: This source may no longer be available online due to its age]

26. Baker, D. R. (2010). PG&E's Smart-Meter Problems Spark Probe. SFGate. URL: https://www.sfgate.com/business/article/PG-E-s-smart-meter-problems-spark-probe-3272345.php

27. Zeller Jr, T. (2010). 'Smart' Electricity Meters Draw Complaints of Inaccuracy. The New York Times. URL: https://www.nytimes.com/2010/11/13/business/13meter.html

28. PG&E. (2010-2012). Annual Reports and Corporate Responsibility Reports. [These can be found on PG&E's investor relations website]

29. California Senate. (2011). Senate Bill No. 837: Electricity: smart grid deployment: Smart Grid Deployment Plans. URL: https://leginfo.legislature.ca.gov/faces/billNavClient.xhtml?bill_id=201120120SB837

30. Wunder, T. R. (2014). Ensuring the security of smart meters and advanced metering infrastructure. Electric Light & Power, 92(2), 38.

31. Alvarez, R. C. (2011). A Critical Examination of Smart Meter Implementation: The PG&E Case Study. CMC Senior Theses, Paper 165. URL: https://scholarship.claremont.edu/cmc_theses/165

32. National Institute of Standards and Technology. (2014). Guidelines for Smart Grid Cybersecurity (NISTIR 7628 Revision 1). URL: https://nvlpubs.nist.gov/nistpubs/ir/2014/NIST.IR.7628r1.pdf

Addressing Emerging EHS Challenges with Digital Solutions

In 2023, the safety director of a large global manufacturing company headquartered in Denmark faced growing concerns. The Company's traditional environmental, health, and safety (EHS) management approach must adapt to the evolving landscape. With emerging technologies like IoT, AI, and data analytics transforming how companies track and mitigate safety risks, the director hoped the organization would stay caught up and maintain its reputation as a safety leader.

The growing adoption of digital EHS solutions by competitors and startups had made the director's concerns valid. A 2022 survey of global industrial leaders revealed that traditional, manual EHS processes were becoming outdated. Over 60% of organizations across various industries were implementing digital EHS platforms, enabling real-time hazard detection, predictive risk management, and automated compliance tracking. Workers wanted better protection, real-time alerts, and more predictive insights into their safety—expectations that older, paper-based systems couldn't meet.

As the safety director expressed then, "There's a widening gap between our safety protocols and the new capabilities being offered by digital EHS systems. Our TRIR is declining year on year. We must adapt or risk significant operational and reputational damage."

It became clear that the organization needed a comprehensive response to the threat of falling behind in the EHS landscape. The director knew that if they acted quickly and thoughtfully, digitization would present an enormous opportunity to enhance safety performance, reduce incidents, and strengthen compliance. However, before the Company could plan its response, it had to assess the threat posed by this digital disruption. How much of their EHS system was under threat? Where were the vulnerabilities in their current processes?

We'll return to the organization's story and how its leaders responded to these challenges. But for now, it's essential to recognize that every EHS leader, like this safety director, must first assess the threat posed by digital disruption. Only after understanding the magnitude of the challenge can they identify the opportunities for improvement.

In this chapter, I'll guide you through a self-assessment to help you determine the extent of the digital threat to your EHS operations. Additionally, I'll explore case studies of companies that have faced similar challenges and embraced digital EHS solutions. Finally, I'll uncover the opportunities in digitizing EHS, as seen in organizations like Electric Major and others that have successfully navigated this transformation.

Case Study: BP Texas City Refinery Explosion (2005)

The BP Texas City refinery explosion in 2005 is a stark reminder of the critical importance of robust EHS management systems and the potential for digital transformation to prevent such catastrophic events.

Incident Overview:

On March 23, 2005, an explosion occurred at BP's Texas City refinery during the restart of a hydrocarbon isomerization unit. The incident resulted in 15 deaths, 180 injuries, and significant economic losses.

Key Factors Contributing to the Disaster:

1. Outdated and poorly maintained equipment: The refinery used outdated analog systems for process control and safety management.

2. Inadequate safety culture: There needed to be more emphasis on process safety and risk management at all levels of the organization.

3. Poor communication and data management: critical safety information needed to be effectively communicated between shifts or different levels of management.

4. Need for real-time monitoring: The lack of advanced sensors and real-time data analysis meant that dangerous conditions went undetected.

5. Inadequate alarm systems: The control room was overwhelmed with alarms, making it difficult for operators to prioritize and respond to critical issues.

Digital Transformation Opportunities:

The BP Texas City disaster highlights several areas where digital transformation could have potentially prevented or mitigated the incident:

1. Advanced Process Control Systems: Modern digital control systems with built-in safety interlocks could have prevented the overfilling of the raffinate splitter.

2. Real-time Risk Analytics: AI-powered risk assessment tools could have identified the potential for disaster during the startup process and alerted operators to take preventive action.

3. IoT Sensors and Predictive Maintenance: A network of IoT sensors could have provided early warning signs of equipment deterioration, enabling proactive maintenance.

4. Integrated Safety Management Systems: A comprehensive digital EHS platform could have ensured better communication of safety protocols and real-time visibility into process safety indicators across the organization.

5. Enhanced Operator Training: Virtual reality and simulation-based training could have better-prepared operators to handle complex startup procedures and emergencies.

6. Improved Alarm Management: Intelligent alarm systems with priority algorithms could have helped operators focus on the most critical issues, reducing alarm fatigue.

This case study demonstrates that EHS digital transformation is not just about efficiency and compliance—it's about preventing catastrophic events and saving lives. By leveraging advanced digital tools and systems, companies can create a more robust safety culture, improve risk management, and prevent tragedies like the BP Texas City explosion.

How Big Is the Threat to Your EHS Operations?

To determine how urgently you need to act, how significant the changes should be within your organization, and what opportunities digital transformation holds for your EHS management system, start by completing this self-assessment. It will help you quantify the likelihood of your EHS processes being disrupted by emerging technologies and data-driven solutions. You can then use these insights to estimate the extent of the potential risk to your operations and compliance over the next five years.

CHAPTER 2: Self-Assessment

A. What is the impact of digitization on your EHS operations?

Consider your current EHS processes and how you manage safety, compliance, and sustainability. On a scale from 0 (low) to 20 (high), score each of the following questions:

1. How digitally trackable are your EHS processes?

Can your safety, health, and environmental performance data be captured, tracked, and reported electronically? Are incidents, near-misses, or ecological violations searchable across digital systems?

2. How likely will technology automate or augment your safety processes in the next five years?

Consider whether parts of your EHS management (incident reporting, compliance tracking, safety audits) could be handled by AI, IoT devices, or automated platforms shortly.

3. To what extent can your EHS processes be enhanced with valuable real-time data?

Are there opportunities to augment current safety processes with real-time data from sensors, wearables, or predictive analytics to anticipate and mitigate risks?

4. Are your EHS operations threatened by emerging technologies or competitors from other industries?

Are there companies (including startups) outside your industry offering more advanced, digitally-driven safety and compliance solutions that could surpass your existing methods?

5. How vulnerable are your traditional EHS practices to being replaced by digital alternatives?

Could emerging digital solutions, such as real-time environmental monitoring, predictive analytics, or automated incident management, replace your manual or reactive EHS processes?

6. How robust is your plan for integrating new digital systems with existing infrastructure?

Score from 0 (no plan) to 20 (comprehensive, well-tested plan)

7. What measures are in place to ensure data accuracy and cybersecurity in your digital EHS initiatives?

Score from 0 (no measures) to 20 (robust, up-to-date security protocols and accuracy checks)

Total Score:

Add up your scores.

- **Scores of 70 or higher** suggest that your EHS processes are at significant risk of disruption by digital transformation and new technologies.

- **Scores below 70** indicate a moderate to low threat but highlight areas where proactive digital strategies can significantly improve.

B. Estimating the Threat to Your Organization's EHS Revenue and Operations

Based on your score from the self-assessment above, estimate the percentage of your Company's EHS-related costs, operations, or revenue that could be affected by digital disruption over the next five years. This includes areas where technology-driven solutions streamline operations, reduce costs, or even replace existing processes with more efficient alternatives.

For example, consider how much of your compliance and risk management budget could be affected by automated safety monitoring or how much of your incident reporting could shift to predictive systems.

Estimating the Financial Impact of Regulatory Fines and EHS-Related Risks

To understand the potential impact of regulatory fines, compensation due to incidents, and associated risks on your organization's revenue and operations, it's crucial to assess the current and future threats to your EHS (Environmental, Health, and Safety) budget. Based on your Company's risk profile and EHS practices, you can estimate the percentage of costs, operations, or revenue that could be at risk over the next five years due to non-compliance, safety incidents, and the absence of technology-driven solutions.

Organizations can better understand the potential financial exposure from regulatory violations by considering areas where digital solutions, such as automated safety monitoring and real-time data analytics, could prevent incidents and reduce fines. For example, modern EHS systems incorporating predictive risk analytics, automated incident reporting, and compliance tracking can dramatically lower the likelihood of incidents, reducing the need for compensation and fines.

Example:

Example: Quantifying the Financial Threat

- **Compliance and Penalties**: Evaluate how much of your budget is currently allocated to handling regulatory compliance and potential fines. With the rise of automated monitoring systems and IoT-enabled compliance tools, this cost could be significantly reduced by ensuring real-time regulatory adherence and early risk detection.

  o **Potential Reduction opportunity**: Automated monitoring systems can reduce compliance-related penalties by up to 30%, leading to significant cost savings.

- **Incident Management**: Assess how much of your incident management budget is tied to handling post-incident fallout, including compensation for workers, environmental damage, and legal fees. Shifting from reactive to predictive systems that prevent incidents before they happen can reduce these costs.

o **Potential Reduction Opportunity**: Predictive incident management systems could reduce workplace accidents by 20%, lowering compensation and legal fees associated with EHS incidents.

- **Regulatory Fines**: Consider the number of fines your organization has faced over the past few years due to non-compliance, environmental violations, or worker safety issues. With a strong EHS digital transformation strategy, your Company could significantly reduce these fines through proactive risk mitigation and better compliance tracking.

  o **Potential Reduction Opportunity**: Predictive compliance systems can reduce fines by up to 40% by identifying and addressing risks before they escalate into regulatory violations.

You can proactively embrace digital transformation by understanding the level of digital threat and identifying which areas of your EHS operations are most vulnerable. Like many other organizations that have successfully navigated these challenges, you can explore opportunities for enhancing safety, sustainability, and operational efficiency through emerging technologies.

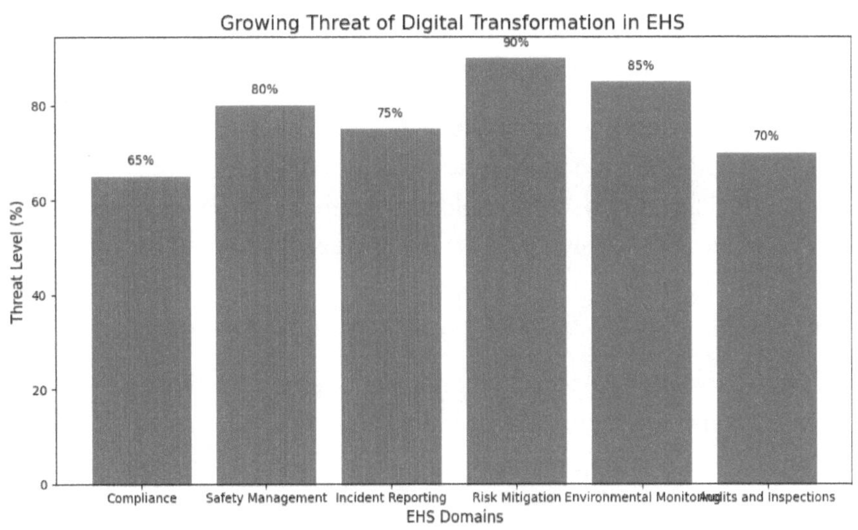

Figure 2.1: The Growing Threat of Digital Disruption in EHS

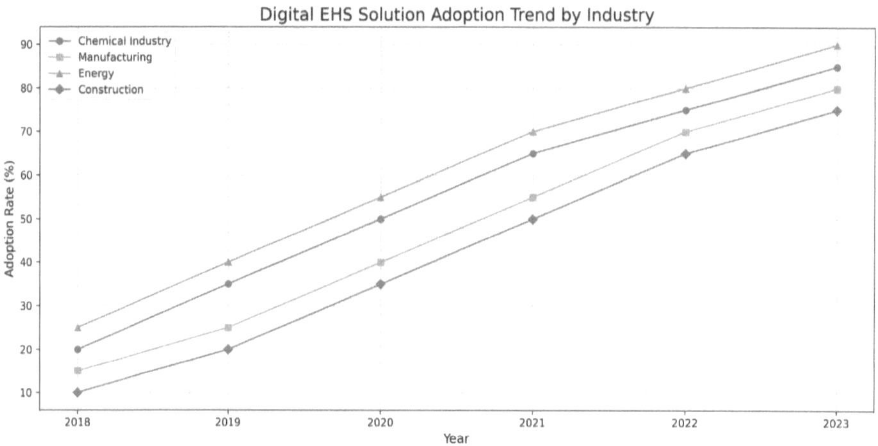

Figure 2.2: Digital EHS Solution Adoption Trend by Industry

The narrative is straightforward: senior executives across industries expect significant portions of their businesses to be threatened by digital disruption within the next five years. This threat is confirmed in the context of environment, health, and safety (EHS). Organizations need to act to avoid losing operational efficiency, safety performance, and compliance integrity to new technologies and startups offering more innovative, automated solutions.

On average, executives anticipate that digital disruption will threaten 28% of their revenue. EHS functions, once reliant on manual processes and siloed systems, are increasingly susceptible to disruption from technologies like IoT, AI-driven safety analytics, robotics, and automation. With the change, organizations could retain a significant share of their operational capabilities as they fall behind competitors adopting these digital solutions.

Larger enterprises, especially those operating in high-risk EHS-intensive industries, could see significant portions of their operations up to 40-45% vulnerable to disruption if they adapt slowly to the evolving digital landscape. Up to 46% of their operations could be susceptible to digital disruption. These larger organizations, burdened by complex legacy systems and slow decision-making processes, become prime targets for faster, more agile startups offering cutting-edge digital EHS solutions. This provides an opportunity for innovation but presents a significant risk for organizations that need to respond more quickly.

EHS Industry Threats and Opportunities

Some industries face a greater risk from EHS-related digital disruption than others. Just as typical medical majors grapple with disruption in the media landscape, industries reliant on manual safety practices and compliance-heavy reporting face similar challenges. In 2011, a renowned media house appeared to be thriving, but the rise of digital content distribution platforms and changing consumer preferences led to a sharp decline in its subscriber base. The network was slow to adapt, and by the time it responded, much of the market had already shifted.

Similarly, in the EHS domain, organizations that fail to adopt real-time monitoring systems, predictive maintenance, and robotics for hazard identification risk being overtaken by competitors with more connected, automated EHS ecosystems. IoT devices, wearable technology, and machine learning algorithms are increasingly important in enhancing safety and ensuring compliance.

Digital Threats and Opportunities at Electric Major in EHS

Electric Major offers a compelling case study of how digital disruption can be turned into an opportunity—both in its core energy management business and its approach to EHS management. Founded around the 1800s, Electric Major has evolved into a global leader in energy automation and safety solutions, operating in four major markets: building and partner (43% of revenues), infrastructure (20%), industry (22%), and IT (15%).

Between 2002 and 2008, Electric Major doubled in size through organic growth and strategic acquisitions. However, this growth created a fragmented organizational structure, leading to inefficiencies in its processes, including EHS practices. The complexity of its systems led to missed revenue opportunities and frustrated employees who struggled with outdated, cumbersome processes.

By 2008, the Company's leadership recognized the digital threat to their business model, particularly in the EHS space. They saw the opportunity to streamline operations and enhance safety performance by offering their customers integrated end-to-end digital solutions. Electric Major recognized that its traditional methods of managing EHS, relying on paper-based reporting and manual audits, must be revised in a digital world.

Other large companies began competing for the Company's customers by offering connected, digital safety solutions. Meanwhile, smaller local firms could provide similar products at lower prices, often accessible through a simple online search. Additionally, many startups were entering the market with innovative safety technologies, such as AI-driven incident prediction tools, wearable devices for real-time hazard detection, and robotic systems for hazardous tasks.

The leadership at Electric Major knew they had to act. They embarked on a digital transformation journey, simplifying their complex EHS systems and leveraging new technologies to reduce safety risks, improve compliance, and enhance customer experience. By embracing these innovations, Electric Major positioned itself as a next-generation leader in energy management and EHS, offering its clients superior digital safety solutions.

This transformation provides valuable lessons for any organization facing the challenges of digital disruption in the EHS domain. Whether through IoT systems, robotics, or AI-powered analytics, companies must assess their vulnerabilities, identify opportunities for innovation, and act decisively to stay ahead in the evolving digital landscape.

Learning from Failure: Applying PG&E's Lessons to EHS Digital Transformation

As introduced in Chapter 1, the Pacific Gas and Electric Company (PG&E) Smart Meter Program serves as a cautionary tale in digital transformation. In the context of EHS, this case offers valuable insights into the potential pitfalls of implementing new technologies without adequate consideration for safety, data integrity, and stakeholder engagement.

EHS-Specific Challenges in the PG&E Case:

1. Data Integrity and Safety Implications: The inaccurate readings from intelligent meters led to billing issues and raised concerns about the reliability of energy usage data. In an EHS context, such data inaccuracies could lead to flawed risk assessments or missed safety incidents.

2. Cybersecurity and Environmental Risks: The rushed deployment of intelligent meters exposed vulnerabilities in PG&E's grid. For EHS

professionals, this highlights the critical need to consider how digital transformations might introduce new environmental or safety risks.

3. Stakeholder Trust and Safety Culture: PG&E's poor communication and change management eroded public trust. In EHS, trust is paramount for fostering a strong safety culture and ensuring buy-in for new safety initiatives.

Lessons for EHS Digital Transformation:

1. Prioritize Data Accuracy and Validation: Implement rigorous testing and validation processes for new EHS data collection systems. More accurate data can lead to better decision-making and potentially compromise safety.

2. Integrate Cybersecurity in EHS Planning: As EHS systems become more digitized, cybersecurity must be a key consideration in risk assessments and safety protocols.

3. Emphasize Change Management and Training: Successful digital transformation in EHS requires comprehensive training programs and clear communication to ensure all stakeholders understand and can effectively use new technologies.

4. Conduct Thorough Risk Assessments: Before implementing new digital EHS solutions, conduct comprehensive risk assessments that consider potential safety, health, and environmental impacts.

5. Plan for Integration with Existing Systems: Ensure new digital EHS tools can seamlessly integrate with existing safety and environmental management systems to avoid disruptions in critical processes.

Table 2.1: Comparative Analysis Approaches

Aspect	Electric Major (Success)	PG&E (Failure)
Planning	Comprehensive, phased approach	Rushed, large-scale rollout
Testing	Thorough, including real-world scenarios	Inadequate, especially in real-world conditions
Stakeholder Engagement	Prioritized employee and customer communication	Underestimated need for education and training
Change Management	Robust strategy implemented	Insufficient attention to cultural and operational shifts
Integration	Careful integration with existing systems	Poor integration leading to operational disruptions
Security Considerations	Prioritized from the outset	Inadequate attention to cybersecurity and privacy

What Opportunities Await Your Company in EHS?

In 2023, many EHS leaders faced a crucial decision point. The growing digitization of safety, environmental compliance, and health management systems pushes companies to look hard at their future. Just like the banks, organizations are standing at a crossroads, choosing between maintaining traditional, manual EHS processes or embracing the full potential of automation, IoT, AI-driven analytics, and integrated EHS platforms.

One path is to continue with outdated, manual safety audits, incident tracking, and compliance management processes, allowing third-party digital solutions to take over customer-centric functions like real-time monitoring and reporting. Those companies could focus solely on essential regulatory compliance, leaving more innovative EHS solutions to specialized software providers.

But this approach will ultimately become a commodity play. Just as financial transaction processing became a low-margin, highly regulated business, manual EHS processes would become outdated and operationally inefficient. Relying on old processes will limit your ability to respond to emerging safety risks or capitalize on new EHS technologies, making it a race to the bottom regarding cost and margins.

A more promising route is to get ahead of the digital transformation and find new ways to meet EHS needs with an integrated, predictive, and data-driven approach. Instead of relying solely on reactive processes, forward-thinking companies can embrace automation, IoT, and AI to create proactive safety environments. This shift allows organizations to predict and prevent incidents, track real-time environmental data, and reduce costs through enhanced operational efficiency.

The Digital Transformation of EHS: A Case in Action

Take Electric Major as an example: faced with increased competition and inefficiencies in their safety and compliance processes, they strategically embraced digital solutions. This involved streamlining fragmented EHS systems and deploying IoT-based technologies for real-time hazard detection, predictive maintenance, and safety analytics.

This digital transformation meant modernizing safety processes and unlocking new business opportunities for the Company. By integrating end-to-end digital solutions, they reduced compliance costs, enhanced employee safety, and positioned themselves as leaders in sustainable operations.

Navigating the Two Diverging Paths

EHS organizations must decide between using traditional, manual methods or embracing advanced digital platforms.

- **The Traditional Path** involves continuing with reactive safety practices, relying on manual audits, paper-based reporting, and siloed systems. This approach may seem safe for now, but it limits flexibility and leaves your organization vulnerable to competitors who can leverage real-time data, automation, and predictive analytics to improve safety performance at a lower cost.

- **The Digital Path** requires organizational change and investment in IoT, AI, and robotics to create proactive, integrated safety environments. EHS leaders must rethink how they deliver value to their employees, regulators, and customers. For instance, investing in wearable safety devices that monitor worker health or deploying drones for remote environmental monitoring can transform EHS operations from reactive to preventive.

Companies choosing the digital path will find that their EHS processes become much more than compliance checklists. They'll be able to anticipate risks, reduce incidents, and build more resilient, sustainable operations.

Creating a Vision for Digital EHS Transformation

A clear vision for the future is essential for transforming Environmental Health and Safety (EHS) practices into fully digital systems. By adopting a comprehensive digital approach, organizations can turn their safety and environmental compliance programs into integrated, dynamic systems that respond to issues and proactively prevent them.

To achieve this transformation, companies need to begin laying the groundwork now. This involves investing in scalable, integrated platforms to manage safety data, monitor real-time compliance, and provide predictive insights. Achieving such a shift requires simplifying existing processes, integrating technologies like IoT and AI, and building a robust global digital infrastructure to support these innovations.

By moving towards these solutions, organizations can elevate their EHS systems from reactive to proactive, ensuring improved safety performance, enhanced compliance, and long-term sustainability. The digitalization of EHS operations represents a vital step in fostering a safer, more efficient, and data-driven future.

Steps Toward the Future of EHS

To successfully transform EHS operations, organizations must undergo a significant organizational restructuring. The following steps can help guide this transformation:

1. Talent and Culture

o   Conduct a skills gap analysis to identify areas where your team needs digital upskilling.

o   Implement a comprehensive digital literacy program for all EHS staff.

o Create a "Digital Champions" program to identify and nurture tech-savvy employees who can help drive adoption.

o Organize regular "Innovation Days" where teams can explore and experiment with new digital EHS tools.

o Establish a reward system for employees who suggest or implement successful digital innovations in EHS practices.

Actionable Task: Within the next month, schedule a series of workshops to introduce your EHS team to key digital concepts like IoT, AI, and data analytics.

2. EHS Solutions

o Conduct a thorough audit of your current EHS software and tools.

o Prioritize areas for digital enhancement based on risk assessment and potential impact.

o Research and evaluate EHS software platforms that offer integrated solutions for incident management, compliance tracking, and risk analysis.

o Consider implementing IoT sensors for real-time environmental monitoring and worker safety.

o Explore AI-powered predictive analytics tools for proactive risk management.

Actionable Task: Set up demos with at least three leading EHS software providers in the next quarter to understand their offerings and how they align with your needs.

3. Global EHS Standards

o Form a cross-functional team to review and standardize EHS processes across all locations.

o Develop a global EHS data dictionary to ensure consistency in reporting and analysis.

o Implement a cloud-based EHS management system that allows for both global oversight and local customization.

o Create a central repository for all EHS policies, procedures, and best practices that can be easily accessed and updated.

o Establish a regular global EHS forum to share insights, challenges, and innovations across different regions.

Actionable Task: Within the next six months, develop and roll out a standardized digital incident reporting process that can be used across all your global locations.

4. Technology Infrastructure

o Conduct an IT infrastructure assessment to identify gaps in supporting digital EHS initiatives.

o Develop a roadmap for upgrading network capabilities to support IoT devices and real-time data transmission.

o Implement robust cybersecurity measures to protect sensitive EHS data.

o Explore edge computing solutions for faster processing of safety-critical data.

o Consider implementing a data lake architecture to centralize EHS data from various sources for advanced analytics.

Actionable Task: In the next quarter, pilot an IoT-based environmental monitoring system in one of your facilities to test infrastructure readiness and identify improvement areas.

5. Innovation Partnerships

o Establish relationships with local universities conducting research in EHS technologies.

o Join industry consortiums focused on digital innovation in EHS.

o Set up an innovation fund to invest in promising EHS technology startups.

- o Participate in or sponsor hackathons focused on solving EHS challenges through technology.

- o Collaborate with equipment manufacturers to integrate EHS monitoring capabilities into their products.

Actionable Task: Establish at least one strategic partnership with a technology company or research institution within the following year to co-develop a novel digital EHS solution.

6. Data-Driven Decision Making

- o Implement a centralized EHS analytics dashboard for real-time monitoring of key performance indicators.

- o Train EHS managers in data analysis and interpretation techniques.

- o Establish a regular data review process to identify trends and areas for improvement.

- o Use machine learning algorithms to develop predictive models for incident prevention.

- o Implement a system for collecting and analyzing leading indicators to enhance proactive risk management.

Actionable Task: In the next three months, identify your top 5 EHS KPIs and implement an automated, real-time tracking system for these metrics.

7. Continuous Improvement and Adaptation

- o Establish a formal process for regularly evaluating the effectiveness of digital EHS initiatives.

- o Implement an agile project management approach for digital EHS projects for rapid iteration and improvement.

- o Create a feedback loop mechanism to capture insights from end-users of digital EHS tools.

- o Stay informed about emerging EHS technologies through industry publications, conferences, and webinars.

o   Conduct annual technology audits to identify outdated systems and opportunities for upgrades.

Actionable Task: Set up a quarterly review process to evaluate the performance of your digital EHS initiatives and identify areas for improvement or expansion.

By following these expanded steps and completing the actionable tasks, organizations can create a robust framework for digital transformation in their EHS practices. Remember, the key to success is implementing new technologies and fostering a culture of innovation and continuous improvement in your EHS approach.

These steps are crucial to modernizing EHS operations and creating a forward-looking, data-driven approach to safety and compliance.

Seizing the Digital EHS Opportunity

The early success of companies like Electric Major and others demonstrates the immense potential for digital transformation in EHS. Whether through robotics, AI-driven safety platforms, or IoT integration, companies that embrace the digital path will be well-positioned to lead the next generation of safety and sustainability.

Ultimately, EHS leaders must look beyond compliance and incident reporting to create dynamic, preventive safety environments. By investing in digital solutions, they can build a safer, more sustainable future and ensure their organizations survive and thrive in digital disruption.

EHS Digital Transformation: The Case of a Chemical Major

For many industries, digitization brings not just challenges but enormous opportunities. A great example in the Environment, Health, and Safety (EHS) field is a global chemical industry leader known for pioneering safety management efforts. Unlike industries facing digital threats like media or retail, The Company's EHS operations—focused on safety protocols, environmental monitoring, and regulatory compliance—are ripe for transformation through digitization, and the Company has embraced these opportunities to enhance performance, safety and compliance.

Chemical Major operates in an industry that, at first glance, may not appear easily disrupted by digital technology. Its core business involves manufacturing tangible products, such as chemicals and materials, in highly regulated environments. However, the Chemical Major identified significant opportunities to enhance its EHS operations using digital tools like IoT, predictive analytics, and real-time monitoring to strengthen safety management and streamline compliance processes.

Here's how Chemical Major has turned potential digital disruption into a pathway for opportunity:

1. Develop a Single Source of Truth for EHS Data:

One of the biggest challenges in EHS management is the need to consolidate and analyze data from various sources: compliance audits, incident reports, environmental monitoring systems, and more. Chemical Major realized digital tools could provide a comprehensive, up-to-date view of EHS performance across all operations. This allows for better decision-making, more accurate risk assessments, and enhanced regulatory compliance. With connected systems and cloud-based platforms, Chemical Major can now capture and analyze data in real time, giving leaders and EHS managers a clearer understanding of potential risks and areas for improvement.

2. Engage Employees and Managers Through an Omnichannel EHS Platform:

Chemical Major saw the potential in digitizing safety protocols and incident reporting to engage its workforce more effectively. A Digital EHS platform allows employees to report incidents, receive safety alerts, and complete compliance training from any device, whether on the factory floor, in an office, or remotely. This creates a more engaged workforce, reduces response times, and ensures that safety protocols are followed consistently across all locations.

3. Create Predictive Safety Systems Using IoT and Analytics:

Chemical Major has invested in predictive analytics and IoT sensors to anticipate safety risks before they become incidents. IoT devices throughout their operations can monitor real-time environmental conditions, equipment performance, and worker safety. These devices provide data fed into predictive models, allowing Chemical Major to identify trends and patterns that indicate potential safety hazards. For example, if equipment vibrations exceed safe thresholds, the system alerts EHS managers before the machinery fails or causes an accident. This proactive approach to safety has reduced incident rates, minimized downtime, and helped ensure regulatory compliance.

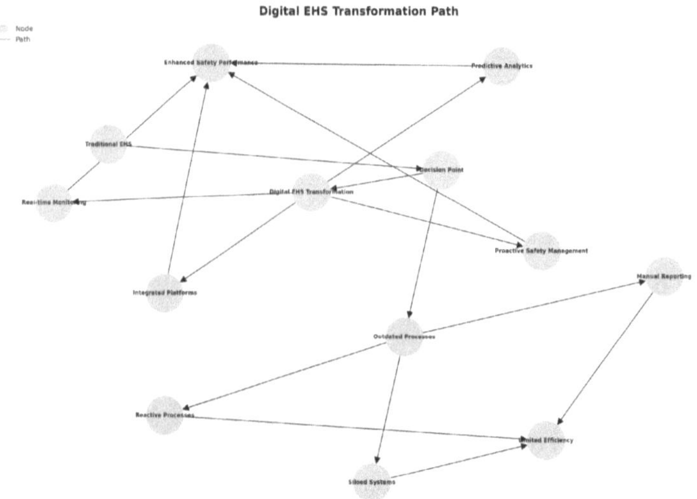

Figure 2.3: Digital EHS Transformation Path

The Benefits of EHS Digital Transformation

Chemical Major is seeing benefits through its digital transformation. By digitizing EHS management, Chemical Major has enhanced its ability to maintain safety standards, improve compliance, and engage employees in safety practices.

- **Efficiency and Cost Savings:** By automating compliance tasks and streamlining incident reporting through digital tools, Chemical Major has reduced the administrative burden on EHS managers and cut costs related to safety management. This also allows the Company to respond to safety risks more quickly, preventing incidents and saving money in the long run.

- **Better Safety Outcomes:** Predictive analytics and real-time monitoring have made it easier for Chemical Major to prevent accidents before they happen. Workers are now empowered to take a proactive approach to safety, which has led to improved safety performance across the board.

- **Data-Driven Decisions:** The real-time data collected through IoT devices and EHS platforms allows the Company's leadership to make informed decisions about safety protocols, investments in safety technology, and compliance strategies. This data also helps the Company identify trends and make strategic decisions about future EHS initiatives.

What's Next for EHS Digital Transformation?

The chemical major's strategy creates a win-win scenario: the Company can ensure regulatory compliance and improve worker safety while benefiting from operational efficiencies and cost reductions. As digital tools like AI, IoT, and advanced analytics evolve, Chemical Major is well-positioned to leverage these technologies to further enhance its EHS management practices.

As we enter the digital era, companies like Chemical Major will continue experimenting and innovating in the EHS space. Chemical Major considers the opportunity to use digital tools to engage employees, improve safety, and reduce environmental impacts.

Conclusion: Identify Opportunities, Not Just Threats

As we've seen throughout this chapter, the digital transformation of EHS is not just a trend—it's imperative for organizations seeking to remain competitive, compliant, and resilient in the face of emerging challenges. The case studies of Electric Major and Chemical Major demonstrate the significant benefits that await companies willing to embrace the digital path.

To begin your own digital EHS journey, consider these tangible next steps:

1. **Conduct a Digital Readiness Assessment**: Use the self-assessment tool provided in this chapter to evaluate your organization's current level of digital maturity in EHS. Identify areas of strength and opportunities for improvement.

2. **Engage Stakeholders**: Share the insights from this chapter with key stakeholders across your organization, including senior leadership, IT, and

operations. Start a dialogue about the potential risks and opportunities of digital transformation in EHS.

3. **Develop a Vision**: Begin crafting a vision for your organization's digital EHS future. What would success look like? What capabilities do you need to build? Use the framework of the "digital path" to guide your thinking.

4. **Identify Quick Wins**: Look for opportunities to pilot digital EHS solutions in specific areas of your organization. This could include introducing wearable safety devices, deploying IoT sensors for environmental monitoring, or using drones for remote inspections. Use these pilots to demonstrate value and build momentum.

5. **Create a Roadmap**: Based on your vision and quick wins, develop a phased roadmap for digital transformation. Prioritize initiatives based on their potential impact, feasibility, and alignment with overall business goals.

As you embark on this journey, consider these reflection questions:

- How can digital technologies help us manage EHS risks and create new value for our stakeholders?

- What cultural and organizational changes will be needed to support a digital EHS transformation?

- What partnerships and collaborations could accelerate our progress on the digital path?

As we navigate the digital transformation of EHS, it's crucial to learn from both successes and failures. While cases like Electric Major inspire us with the potential of digital EHS solutions, the PG&E Smart Meter Program reminds us of the pitfalls we must avoid. Understanding these potential challenges is as essential as aspiring to success.

The digital transformation journey in EHS is complex and filled with opportunities and risks. Organizations can maximize their chances of success by carefully planning, thoroughly testing, engaging stakeholders, and prioritizing change management. Remember, the goal isn't just to implement new technologies and fundamentally transform how we approach safety, compliance, and sustainability in the digital age.

As you embark on your digital EHS transformation, strive for the successes of companies like Electric Major, but always remember the lessons from PG&E's experience. With a balanced approach that considers both the potential benefits and risks, you can navigate the challenges of digital transformation and emerge as a leader in the new era of EHS management.

Remember, the digital transformation of EHS is not a destination but an ongoing journey. Your organization will thrive in the digital age by taking these initial steps and continuously exploring new opportunities. The next chapter will examine strategies for aligning your EHS business model with your digital future. Stay tuned!

EHS Digital Transformation Process

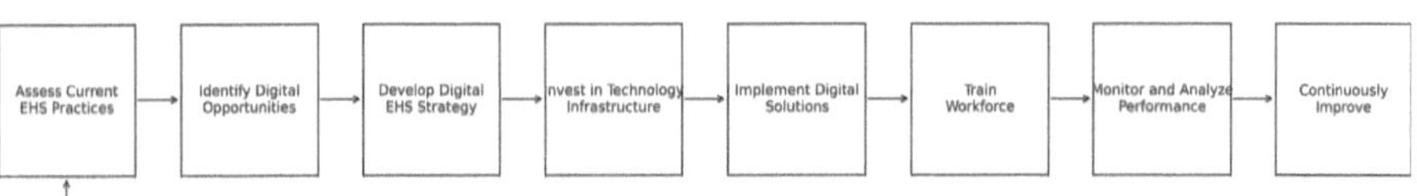

Figure 2.4: EHS Digital Transformation Process

EHS Digital Transformation: Quick Start Guide

Ready to begin your EHS digital transformation journey? Use this checklist to kickstart your efforts and lay a strong foundation for success.

1. Assess Your Current State:

- Conduct a comprehensive audit of existing EHS processes and technologies

- Identify key pain points and inefficiencies in current EHS operations

- Evaluate your organization's digital readiness (use the self-assessment tool provided earlier in the chapter)

2. Define Your Vision and Goals:

- Articulate a clear vision for your digitally transformed EHS function

- Set specific, measurable goals for your digital transformation (e.g., reduce incident reporting time by 50%)

- Align your digital EHS goals with broader organizational objectives

3. Secure Leadership Buy-In:

- Prepare a business case for EHS digital transformation

- Present the potential ROI and benefits to senior leadership

- Secure budget allocation for initial digital initiatives

4. Form a Digital EHS Task Force:

- Identify critical stakeholders from EHS, IT, Operations, and other relevant departments.

- Appoint a project leader or "Digital EHS Champion."

- Define roles and responsibilities for the task force.

5. Prioritize Initial Projects:

- Identify "quick win" opportunities for digital implementation

- Select 1-2 pilot projects to demonstrate value (e.g., implementing a mobile incident reporting app)

- Develop a timeline and resource plan for your pilot projects

6. Assess and Select Technology Solutions

- Research available EHS digital solutions that align with your goals

- Request demos from the top 3-5 vendors

- Evaluate solutions based on functionality, ease of use, integration capabilities, and cost.

7. Plan for Data Management

- Audit your current EHS data sources and quality

- Develop a data governance strategy

- Plan for data migration and integration with new digital systems

8. Prepare Your Workforce

- Assess the digital skills of your EHS team

- Develop a training plan to address skill gaps

- Communicate the benefits of digital transformation to all employees

9. Implement Your Pilot Project

- Set up a project team for your chosen pilot

- Develop a detailed implementation plan

- Execute the pilot project, carefully monitoring progress and challenges

10. Measure and Communicate Results

- Establish KPIs for your pilot project

- Collect and analyze data on the pilot's performance

- Share results and lessons learned with leadership and broader organization

11. Plan for Scale

- Based on pilot results, refine your broader digital transformation strategy

- Develop a roadmap for rolling out successful initiatives across the organization

- Continue to iterate and improve based on feedback and new technologies

Remember, digital transformation is a journey, not a destination. Use this checklist as a starting point, and be prepared to adapt and evolve your approach as you progress.

Good luck on your EHS digital transformation journey!

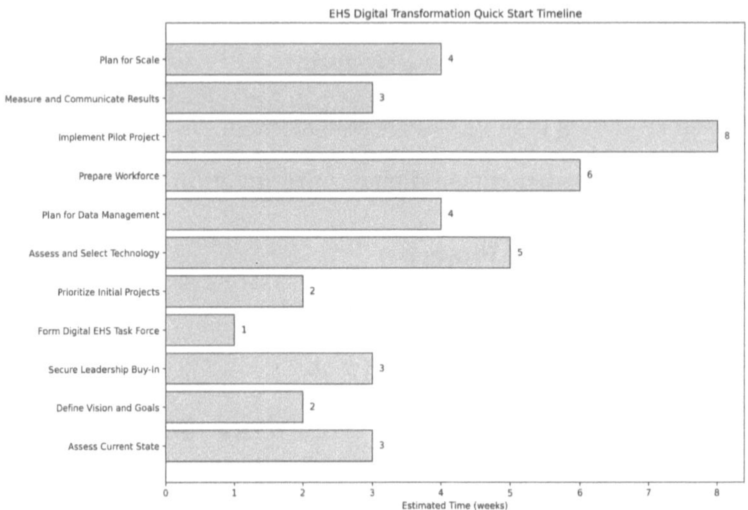

Figure 2.5: EHS Digital Transformation Quick Start Timeline

References Chapter 2

1. Accenture. (2021). The Digital Transformation of EHS: How Technology is Redefining Safety and Sustainability. Accenture Insights. Retrieved from https://www.accenture.com/us-en/insights/digital-transformation-ehs-technology-redefining-safety-sustainability

2. Deloitte. (2022). EHS and the Future of Work: Embracing Digital Disruption for Safer, More Sustainable Operations. Deloitte Insights. Retrieved from https://www2.deloitte.com/us/en/insights/focus/human-capital-trends/2022/ehs-future-work-digital-disruption.html

3. EY. (2023). The EHS Data Imperative: Unlocking Value Through Advanced Analytics. EY Research. Retrieved from https://www.ey.com/en_gl/advanced-manufacturing/the-ehs-data-imperative-unlocking-value-through-advanced-analytics

4. Gartner. (2021). Hype Cycle for EHS Technologies, 2021. Gartner Research. Retrieved from https://www.gartner.com/doc/4002837-hype-cycle-for-ehs-technologies-2021

5. IBM. (2022). The AI Advantage in EHS: How Cognitive Technologies are Transforming Safety and Environmental Performance. IBM Institute

for Business Value. Retrieved from https://www.ibm.com/thought-leadership/institute-business-value/report/ai-advantage-ehs

6. Intelex. (2023). The State of EHS Technology Adoption: Benchmarking Digital Maturity Across Industries. Intelex Research. Retrieved from https://www.intelex.com/resources/insight/state-ehs-technology-adoption-benchmarking-digital-maturity

7. McKinsey & Company. (2021). The Digital Imperative for EHS: How Advanced Technologies are Redefining Risk Management. McKinsey Quarterly. Retrieved from https://www.mckinsey.com/business-functions/operations/our-insights/digital-imperative-for-ehs

8. National Safety Council. (2022). The Future of EHS: Trends and Predictions for the Digital Age. National Safety Council. Retrieved from https://www.nsc.org/work-safety/safety-topics/future-of-ehs-trends-predictions

9. PwC. (2023). Reimagining EHS in the Age of Disruption: Strategies for Navigating the Digital Landscape. PwC Viewpoints. Retrieved from https://www.pwc.com/gx/en/services/esg/reimagining-ehs-age-disruption.html

10. SAP. (2021). The Intelligent Enterprise for EHS: Leveraging Data and AI for Next-Generation Performance. SAP White Paper. Retrieved from https://www.sap.com/docs/download/2021/10/a2dfc3d2-0b7e-0010-bca6-c68f7e60039b.pdf

11. Sphera. (2022). The Digital EHS Imperative: How Technology is Transforming Safety, Sustainability, and Operational Risk Management. Sphera Insights. Retrieved from https://sphera.com/insights/digital-ehs-imperative-technology-transforming-safety-sustainability/

12. Verdantix. (2021). EHS Technology Innovation: Emerging Trends and Opportunities. Verdantix Research. Retrieved from https://research.verdantix.com/report/ehs-technology-innovation-emerging-trends-opportunities

13. World Economic Forum. (2022). The Future of EHS in the Fourth Industrial Revolution. World Economic Forum. Retrieved from

https://www.weforum.org/whitepapers/the-future-of-ehs-in-the-fourth-industrial-revolution

14. Forrester. (2023). The ROI of EHS Digital Transformation: Building the Business Case for Investment. Forrester Research. Retrieved from https://www.forrester.com/report/roi-ehs-digital-transformation-building-business-case/RES183624

15. BCG. (2022). Navigating the EHS Digital Disruption: A Roadmap for Success. Boston Consulting Group. Retrieved from https://www.bcg.com/publications/2022/navigating-ehs-digital-disruption-roadmap-success

EHS Business Models

What makes your organization stand out in its EHS (Environment, Health, and Safety) practices? And how can digitization elevate that excellence into top-tier performance? These are critical questions for any company aiming to stay competitive, compliant, and safe in the rapidly evolving landscape of EHS management over the next five years.

EHS leaders must integrate safety and environmental practices with real-time digital tools like IoT sensors, predictive analytics, and AI-powered incident reporting. The power of this integration lies in creating a seamless digital ecosystem that enhances the ability to monitor safety, predict risks, and manage compliance across operations.

The Digital EHS Ecosystem Opportunity

EHS organizations can leverage IoT systems for real-time safety monitoring and predictive maintenance. These systems gather data from across the organization, such as monitoring air quality in a manufacturing plant or tracking worker safety metrics in real-time on a construction site. By combining these data points into a comprehensive digital platform, companies can improve safety outcomes, reduce environmental impacts, and stay ahead of regulatory compliance.

In the realm of EHS, an effective digital ecosystem includes interconnected devices, employees, safety officers, and regulatory bodies, all collaborating through data-enabled exchanges. EHS ecosystem can bring together different departments and operations to create a safer, more compliant work environment.

Moving to a Digital EHS Ecosystem Model

As discussed in the last chapter, companies that adopt the Digital EHS model are the most successful in integrating digital technology into their business practices. Your organization can prevent accidents, reduce compliance costs, and improve environmental sustainability by evolving from a reactive approach to safety and compliance management to a proactive, digitally integrated model.

Yet, as shown in Figure 3.1, only a small percentage of organizations have fully transitioned to this EHS management model. While many enterprises still operate with manual safety audits, disjointed incident reporting systems, and siloed environmental compliance efforts, the few who have embraced the entire digital ecosystem stand to gain a significant competitive advantage.

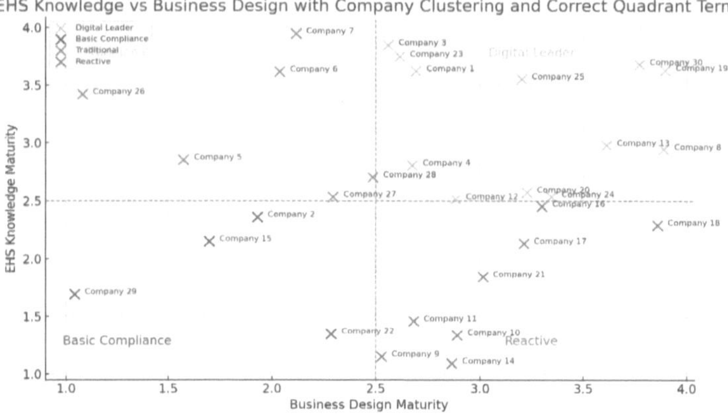

Figure 3.1: EHS knowledge vs. Business design – Studied companies and their position in the quadrant

There is a wide gap between what's possible with digital EHS technology and what most companies are currently doing. Closing this gap offers tremendous opportunities for organizations willing to invest in digital transformation. First movers—those who adopt IoT, AI, and real-time safety systems sooner rather than later—stand to become industry leaders in safety and environmental management.

Learning from chemical major's Digital Ecosystem Model in EHS

Chemical Major is a strong example of an organization that successfully transitioned into an EHS ecosystem driver. Historically, the Company has been a leader in safety management. Still, it has increased its efforts by integrating IoT systems for real-time hazard detection, predictive analytics for equipment maintenance, and AI-driven incident reporting. By adopting these digital tools, Chemical Major transformed its EHS practices from reactive safety management to proactive risk prevention, significantly improving safety outcomes and reducing environmental impacts.

Much like Amazon leveraged search and data analytics to become the dominant player in retail, the Company uses real-time safety data to maintain its leadership position in EHS. Through predictive analytics, it can anticipate incidents before they happen and make data-driven decisions that improve safety performance across its global operations.

The Power of First-Mover Advantage in EHS

Organizations that embrace digital transformation in EHS management will have a distinct advantage over their competitors. The ability to provide real-time safety monitoring, predictive incident management, and seamless environmental reporting creates operational efficiencies and positions your organization as a sustainability and safety compliance leader.

In contrast, organizations that need to adapt to the digital era in EHS management may play catch-up, much like Walmart has had to do with Amazon in retail. The traditional approach of relying on paper-based safety audits and disconnected compliance systems will no longer suffice in a world where real-time data and automation are becoming the standard.

Where Does Your EHS Organization Stand Today?

In **Chapter 2**, we discussed how to evaluate the level of digital threat to your organization. Now, it's time to determine where your Company currently stands on the Business models with future goals for EHS. Are you still operating with a basic, compliant-driven model that provides manual safety audits and compliance reports? Or have you moved towards a Traditional level, where safety management is integrated across digital platforms, offering a seamless experience for safety officers, employees, and regulators?

The goal is to transition your organization toward the Digital EHS leader model, where safety, environmental compliance, and risk management are fully integrated into a digital platform. This model improves safety outcomes, ensures regulatory compliance, and reduces costs through operational efficiencies.

Self-Assessment for EHS Digital Maturity

To determine where your organization fits into the business model framework, start with a self-assessment:

1. **How integrated are your EHS processes?** Are you still relying on manual systems, or have you adopted digital tools for real-time monitoring and compliance?

2. **How connected are your safety and compliance systems?** Are different departments working in silos, or do you have a seamless, data-driven approach to safety management across operations?

3. **What role does predictive analytics play in your EHS processes?** Are you using data to predict incidents before they happen, or are you still reacting to incidents after they occur?

4. **How proactive are you in engaging your workforce in safety practices?** Do you provide employees with digital tools to report hazards and stay informed about safety protocols, or is communication still largely manual?

Answering these questions will help you better understand your organization's current state and potential to become a leader in digital EHS management.

Moving Forward: Becoming a Digital EHS Leader

Now that you've assessed your current position in the business model framework, it's time to create a roadmap for moving toward the Ecosystem Driver model. This journey will involve significant investments in technology, changes in organizational processes, and a shift in company culture to embrace digital safety and environmental management tools.

As we explore in the next chapter, moving up the business model requires adopting new technologies and transforming how your organization approaches safety, compliance, and sustainability. By making these changes, your Company can lead the way in the future of EHS and set the standard for safety and environmental management in the digital era.

CHAPTER 3: EHS Self-Assessment, Part 1

A. EHS Knowledge

Consider your organization's current EHS management system. Using a scale from 1 (Not at all) to 7 (Completely), rate your organization's knowledge in the following areas:

- How well does your organization understand the critical safety and environmental risks it faces?

- How comprehensive is your historical data on incidents, near misses, and compliance failures?

- Do you track and analyze real-time EHS data using digital tools like IoT sensors?

- Can your organization predict safety incidents or compliance failures using data analytics?

- How well do you understand the impact of external factors like regulatory changes or environmental shifts on your operations?

- Does your organization actively use data to inform EHS decisions and reduce risks?

Subtotal:

Double your subtotal, then add 2. (Maximum score: 100)

B. EHS Business Design

In EHS, Business Design refers to how your Company structures its processes for managing safety, compliance, and environmental risks. A value chain design focuses on reactive, compliance-based management, where EHS is treated as a separate function. In contrast, an ecosystem design integrates EHS across departments and systems, continuously using real-time data to monitor and improve safety and compliance.

For your organization, estimate the percentage of last year's revenues influenced by proactive EHS management practices or real-time monitoring systems.

Sample Calculation: Estimating Percentage of Revenues Influenced by Proactive EHS Management and Real-time Monitoring

Let's walk through a sample calculation to estimate the percentage of last year's revenues influenced by your organization's proactive EHS management practices or real-time monitoring systems.

Step 1: Identify Total Revenue for Last Year

Start by determining your organization's total Revenue for the last year.

- **Total Revenue:** $100 million

Step 2: Estimate Revenue Impacted by EHS Systems

Next, estimate how much of this Revenue was influenced by integrated EHS practices. These could be areas where proactive EHS measures—such as real-time monitoring, predictive safety analytics, or automated compliance management—have reduced risks, avoided incidents, or minimized regulatory fines, thus contributing to operational continuity and financial gains.

For this example, let's assume that:

- Your real-time monitoring system helped reduce downtime due to safety incidents by 15%.

- Proactive EHS practices reduced compliance violations, preventing fines of $2 million.

- These systems also contributed to maintaining smooth operations in critical business areas, protecting 10% of the Company's Revenue.

Step 3: Calculate Revenue Protected or Influenced by EHS Practices

- **Revenue Protected Due to Reduced Downtime**: If real-time monitoring reduced safety-related downtime, estimate the income that would have been lost without it. Assume that downtime affected 5% of total operations, and 15% of that downtime was avoided.

  o Calculation: Revenue=5%×100 million=5 million Revenue=5%×100 million=5 million

  o Revenue saved=15%×5 million=0.75 million Revenue saved=15%×5 million=0.75 million

- **Revenue Impacted by Avoiding Fines**: You also avoided $2 million in compliance fines due to proactive EHS practices.

  o Calculation: 2 million2 million

- **Revenue Protected from Proactive EHS**: Let's assume 10% of the Company's Revenue was safeguarded due to smooth operations in key business areas.

  o Calculation: 10%×100 million=10 million10%×100 million=10 million

Step 4: Add Up Revenue Contributions

Now, add up the Revenue impacted by EHS practices:

Total revenue influenced by EHS systems=0.75 million(downtime reduction)+2 million(avoided fines)+10 million(proactive EHS savings)

Total revenue influenced by EHS systems=0.75 million(downtime reduction)+2 million(avoided fines)+10 million(proactive EHS savings)

Total Revenue Impacted: $12.75 million

Step 5: Calculate Percentage of Revenue Influenced by EHS

Finally, divide the Revenue influenced by EHS by the total Revenue to get the percentage.

- Percentage of revenue influenced=(12.75 million100 million)×100=12.75%Percentage of revenue influenced=(100 million12.75 million)×100=12.75%

Final Estimate:

Approximately **12.75%** of last year's revenues were influenced by proactive EHS management practices and real-time monitoring systems.

This calculation gives a rough estimate of the financial contribution of integrated EHS systems to your organization's Revenue, showing the value of proactive safety, compliance, and risk management approaches.

CHAPTER 3: EHS Self-Assessment, Part 2

Using your score from Part 1, plot your current position in the **EHS Knowledge vs. Business Design** framework. The vertical axis represents your level of EHS knowledge (how well you understand your safety and environmental risks). In contrast, the horizontal axis represents your business design (how effectively you integrate EHS into your operations).

EHS Management Quadrant with Revenue Influence

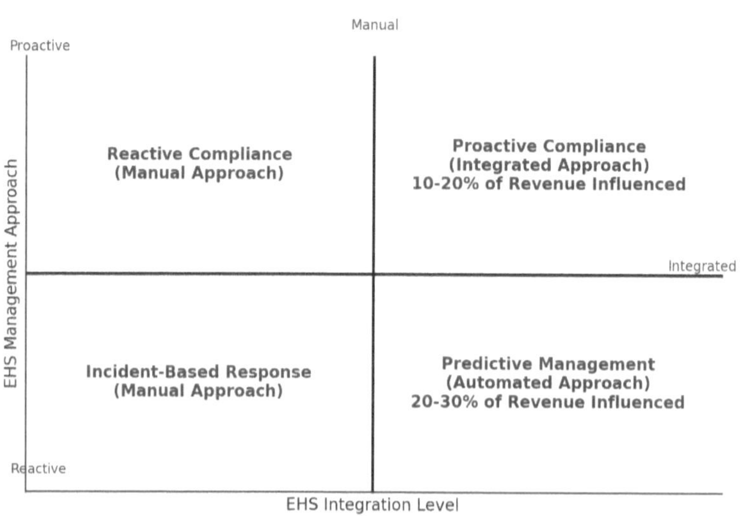

Figure 3.2: EHS Management Quadrant

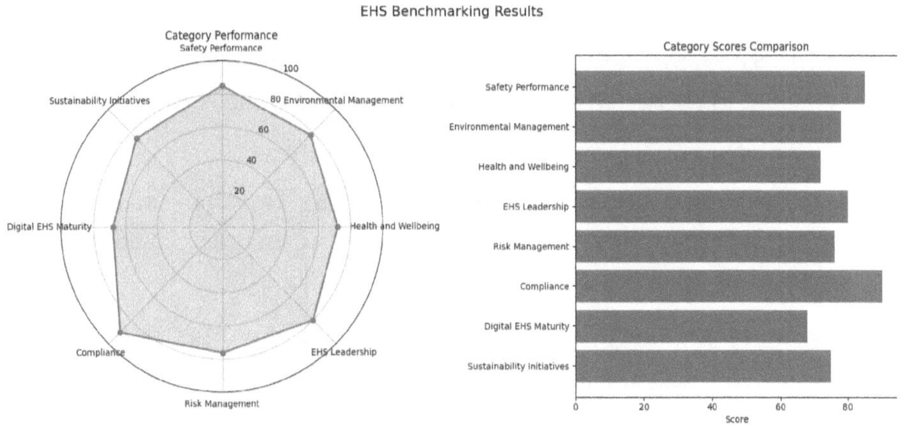

Figure 3.3: EHS Benchmarking results

What's Your EHS Model?

My digital transformation assessment in the Environment, Health, and Safety (EHS) space reflects the same insight as science fiction writer William Gibson's observation: "The future is already here—it's just not evenly distributed." In EHS, some organizations have already embraced digital technologies like IoT, real-time monitoring, and predictive analytics, while others are still stuck in manual processes and disconnected systems.

To understand where your Company fits in the future of digital EHS management, you must assess how well you know your EHS risks and how effectively your business design integrates EHS processes.

Take a moment to complete the Chapter 3 Self-assessment to see where your organization stands in the EHS Knowledge vs. Business Design framework. This will help you identify whether your Company is a primary compliance operator, an advanced digital leader, or somewhere in between. The assessment assesses the integration of EHS practices into your organization's business design and your level of knowledge in managing safety, compliance, and environmental risks.

- **Reactive Compliance (Manual Approach):** EHS is managed as a siloed function, with minimal integration into the broader business operations. Processes are primarily manual, responding to compliance needs after risks emerge.

- **Proactive Compliance (Integrated Approach)**: EHS is seamlessly integrated across all business functions, using real-time data and collaboration between departments to manage risks and ensure compliance proactively.

- **Incident-Based Response (Manual Approach)**: The organization handles EHS reactively, addressing risks and compliance only after incidents have occurred. It often relies on isolated, manual processes.

- **Predictive Management (Automated Approach)**: EHS practices use automated systems, real-time data, and predictive analytics to anticipate risks, prevent incidents, and maintain continuous compliance across operations.

This framework helps estimate the financial and operational impact of proactive EHS management based on your organization's position in this matrix. The section below provides a detailed description of industries' environmental and operational performance in those quadrants. A sample of 25 industries data from the EPA Violations list and Sustainability Reports for safety data is gathered, and a detailed assessment is carried out. The sample data spans throughout 2021 – 2023. The data collected include Net profit, Incidents per 100 employees, compliance issues, Operational loss, environmental violations, audit issues, and worker incidents.

Environmental performance in different quadrants:

1. Basic Compliance Seeker:

- **Environmental Violations**: This group has an average of about three ecological violations, which is moderate compared to other quadrants.

- **Fines & Penalties**: The average fine is $500,000, which indicates relatively moderate financial consequences for environmental non-compliance.

- **Permit Violations**: An average of 2 permit violations reflects a focus on minimal compliance efforts.

- **Corrective Actions**: The need for an average of 3 corrective actions suggests that this group addresses compliance issues reactively rather than proactively.

- **Audit Findings**: With two audit findings on average, their processes must be scrutinized more rigorously.

Summary: This quadrant focuses primarily on essential compliance with environmental regulations, reflected in moderate violations and corrective actions. They face fewer severe financial penalties and are likely reactive rather than proactive in addressing environmental issues.

2. Digital Leader:

- **Environmental Violations**: Interestingly, this group has virtually no violations (0 on average), which aligns with their proactive and technologically driven approach to compliance.

- **Fines & Penalties**: Despite fewer violations, they face more significant fines, with an average of $2,000,000. This could indicate that when issues do arise, they are more significant.

- **Permit Violations**: An average of 4 violations suggests that while their digital systems help them maintain compliance, there are occasional lapses.

- **Corrective Actions**: With five corrective actions, this group likely addresses issues before they escalate.

- **Audit Findings**: Digital leaders have an average of 5 audit findings, indicating more scrutiny or a higher volume of audits due to their prominence.

Summary: Digital Leaders excel at minimizing environmental violations but face significant penalties when violations do occur. Their frequent audit findings suggest they are under more scrutiny because they are seen as high performers. They take corrective actions quickly, reflecting a proactive approach to environmental management.

3. Reactive Performer:

- **Environmental Violations**: This group has relatively low ecological violations, with an average of 1 violation, but it may not be as proactive as Digital Leaders.

- **Fines & Penalties**: They face an average of $1,800,000 in penalties, indicating that while violations are fewer, the impact is significant.

- **Permit Violations**: An average of 3 permit violations suggests they struggle with staying fully compliant.

- **Corrective Actions**: With four corrective actions, they are slightly more proactive than Basic Compliance Seekers but less so than Digital Leaders.

- **Audit Findings**: They average four audit findings, indicating moderate scrutiny and performance.

Summary: Reactive Performers avoid major compliance issues but are still reactive in addressing problems. They face significant fines for their violations, implying that when issues arise, they are costly. Their approach is more advanced than essential compliance but must be fully proactive.

4. Traditional Operator:

- **Environmental Violations**: With one violation on average, they perform similarly to Reactive Performers in terms of compliance.

- **Fines & Penalties**: Their fines average $1,000,000, indicating moderate financial penalties for violations.

- **Permit Violations**: They also have three permit violations, suggesting they maintain compliance but face challenges with proactive management.

- **Corrective Actions**: Like Reactive Performers, they average four corrective actions, indicating a balance between reacting to and preventing issues.

- **Audit Findings**: An average of 5 audit findings suggests they are subject to significant scrutiny, likely due to their reliance on traditional methods.

Summary: Traditional Operators have fewer violations but still face significant fines. They focus on correcting issues rather than preventing them, reflecting their reliance on established, less dynamic systems. Their compliance efforts are robust but need to be more cutting-edge, and they face challenges similar to those of Reactive Performers.

Overall Insights:

- **Digital Leaders** tend to have fewer violations but higher financial penalties when issues arise, likely due to the scale of their operations. They proactively take corrective actions and face the most scrutiny, aligning with their status as high performers.

- **Basic Compliance Seekers** are primarily reactive, focusing on meeting minimum compliance requirements. Their penalties and violations are moderate but need more sophistication in advanced quadrants.

- **Reactive Performers** and **Traditional Operators** are in the middle. They focus on correcting issues as they arise rather than proactively managing environmental risks. They face significant financial penalties for their violations but are generally more compliant than Basic Compliance Seekers.

BoxPlot Analysis of Environmental Performance:

1. Environmental Violations by Quadrant:

- **Basic Compliance Seekers**: The box plot shows various environmental violations. Some companies have significantly more violations than others, reflecting this group's variability in compliance performance.

- **Digital Leaders**: There are very few or no violations in this quadrant, and the plot reflects minimal spread, indicating that companies in this group have robust compliance systems.

- **Reactive Performers**: The range of violations is relatively small, but the plot suggests that this group experiences occasional violations.

- **Traditional Operators**: Similar to Reactive Performers, the number of violations is consistent and moderate, suggesting better compliance than Basic Compliance Seekers, but they still need to be more proactive than Digital Leaders.

Summary: Digital Leaders show consistently low violations, while Basic Compliance Seekers have the widest variation, indicating inconsistency in performance. Traditional Operators and Reactive Performers fall somewhere in between.

2. Fines & Penalties by Quadrant:

- **Basic Compliance Seekers**: The fines tend to be moderate, but there is a large spread, indicating that some companies face higher financial penalties due to non-compliance.

- **Digital Leaders**: The fines vary significantly in this group, with some companies facing substantial penalties despite fewer violations. This suggests that when digital leaders experience issues, they are often severe, leading to higher financial repercussions.

- **Reactive Performers**: Similar to Digital Leaders, Reactive Performers experience significant variability in fines, reflecting the reactive nature of their compliance efforts.

- **Traditional Operators**: This group experiences relatively moderate fines, but there is still some variation, reflecting occasional lapses in compliance.

Summary: Digital Leaders and Reactive Performers face the most significant variation in fines and potentially high costs when issues occur. Basic Compliance Seekers also show variability but face more minor fines overall. Traditional Operators are more consistent but still have some variability in penalties.

3. Permit Violations by Quadrant:

- **Basic Compliance Seekers**: The wide range of permit violations suggests inconsistent compliance efforts within this group.

- **Digital Leaders**: Although there are fewer permit violations, there is still some variation, indicating that even the best performers occasionally struggle with permit compliance.

- **Reactive Performers**: This group shows moderate variability in permit violations, reflecting some inconsistency in managing compliance.

- **Traditional Operators**: The plot shows a moderate spread, with occasional permit violations, reflecting their reliance on conventional compliance methods.

Summary: Basic Compliance Seekers show the most variability, while Digital Leaders and Reactive Performers are more consistent but still experience occasional lapses. Traditional Operators are similar to Reactive Performers in their compliance approach.

4. Corrective Actions by Quadrant:

- **Basic Compliance Seekers**: The number of corrective actions varies significantly, suggesting that while some companies take action to address issues, others are less proactive.

- **Digital Leaders**: This group has many corrective actions, indicating that some companies are highly proactive, while others only act when necessary. This variation reflects the different scales and operations within this group.

- **Reactive Performers**: Corrective actions in this group also show significant variability, suggesting that while some companies are reactive, others are more proactive in addressing issues.

- **Traditional Operators**: The number of corrective actions varies moderately, reflecting a more consistent but reactive approach to compliance.

Summary: Digital Leaders and Reactive Performers show the most significant variability in corrective actions, indicating that the level of proactivity varies widely. Basic Compliance Seekers tend to take fewer actions, while Traditional Operators are more consistent but must be highly proactive.

Key Insights from the Box Plots:

1. **Digital Leaders** consistently have fewer environmental violations, but when issues arise, they face substantial financial penalties, suggesting that these companies manage large-scale operations where the impact of infringements is significant.

2. **Basic Compliance Seekers** show the most comprehensive variability in almost all indicators, reflecting inconsistent company performance. Some take corrective actions and have fewer violations, while others face more significant challenges.

3. **Reactive Performers** and **Traditional Operators** are similar in many respects, with moderate compliance performance and corrective actions.

However, Reactive Performers tend to incur more significant penalties and respond inconsistently, while Traditional Operators are more consistent.

4. **Corrective Actions** and **Permit Violations** show the most variability across quadrants, particularly for Digital Leaders and Reactive Performers, reflecting differing approaches to managing compliance.

These box plots help highlight the strengths and weaknesses of each quadrant's approach to environmental compliance.

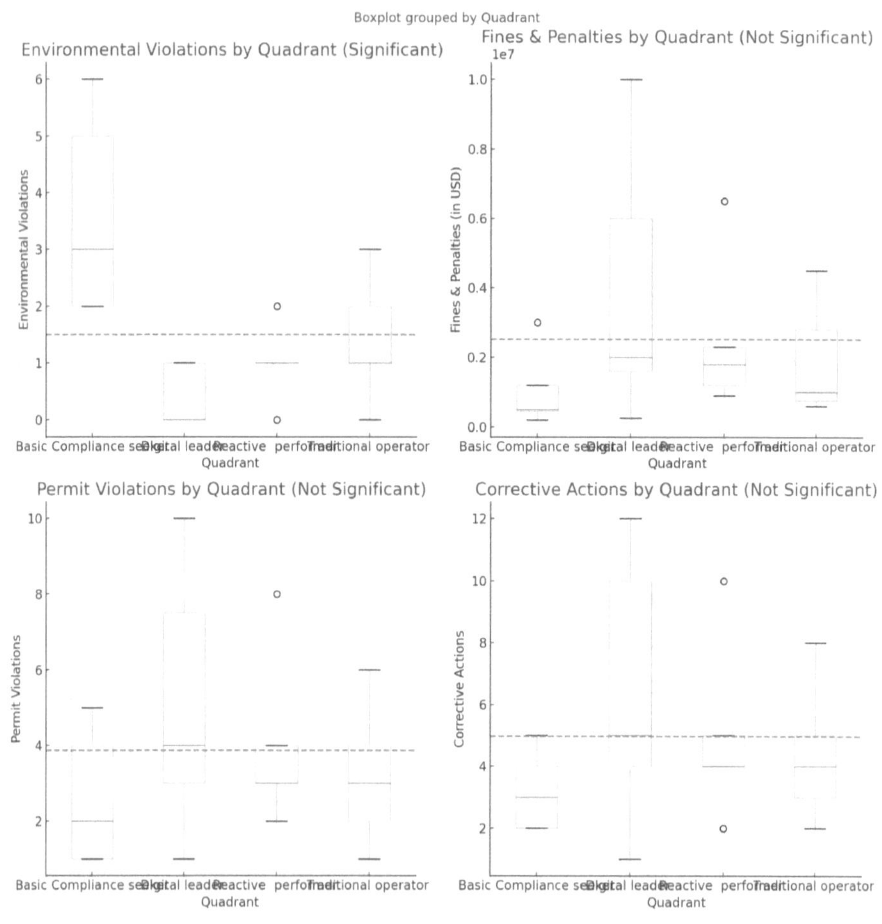

Figure 3.4: Box Plot analysis of Environmental performance of 25 study companies

Overall Interpretation:

- The Environmental Violations indicator clearly and significantly differs between quadrants, which aligns with expectations. Digital Leaders, for instance, have fewer violations, while Basic Compliance Seekers show more inconsistency and higher violation counts.

- The lack of significant differences in fines and penalties, permit violations, and corrective actions suggests that there are no clear patterns in how these metrics vary across the quadrants. The companies in each quadrant likely experience a wide range of outcomes, preventing any apparent statistical differences from emerging.

Practical Implications:

- The statistical significance of Environmental Violations indicates that certain quadrants (like Digital Leaders) have adopted more effective compliance strategies. In contrast, others (like Basic Compliance Seekers) may need to improve their efforts to reduce violations.

- For metrics like Fines and penalties and Corrective Actions, the variability within each quadrant might stem from factors such as company size, industry-specific regulations, or incident severity, which the quadrant classification does not fully capture.

Understanding the Four Quadrants of EHS Knowledge vs. Business Design

Most organizations fall into one of four categories in the EHS Knowledge vs. Business Design framework:

1. Basic Compliance Operator (Low EHS Knowledge / Reactive Business Design)

These organizations operate compliance-focused, where EHS management is reactive and often siloed. They rely on manual processes for incident reporting, compliance checks, and safety audits. Their primary goal is to meet regulatory requirements, but they need more real-time data and insights to prevent incidents or improve performance proactively.

Common Characteristics of Basic Compliance Seekers

Companies categorized as Basic Compliance Seekers tend to share Environmental, Health, and Safety (EHS) management approach traits. They typically focus on meeting minimum regulatory requirements, often using manual systems and relying on reactive strategies. Below are the key characteristics and insights based on real-world examples from companies like Company "A," Company "B," Company "C," and Company "D."

1. Regulation-Driven Approach

These companies often view EHS as a necessity for compliance rather than an opportunity for value creation. Their primary focus is avoiding fines and penalties rather than improving operational safety and sustainability. Thus, they follow regulatory mandates closely but seldom exceed what is required.

Insight: For example, Company "A" and Company "B" tend to meet the basic safety standards prescribed by regulatory bodies, but little effort is made to adopt proactive or innovative EHS management systems.

2. Manual Systems and Processes

These companies often use manual systems to report incidents, manage safety data, and track compliance. Pen-and-paper or simple digital record-keeping tools dominate their EHS management. This slows their ability to identify trends, leading to delayed responses to emerging safety risks.

Insight: Companies "C" and "D" have been reported to use legacy systems in their plants and operations, relying heavily on paper-based compliance checks and audits. This leads to slower risk detection, and safety improvements tend to happen post-incident.

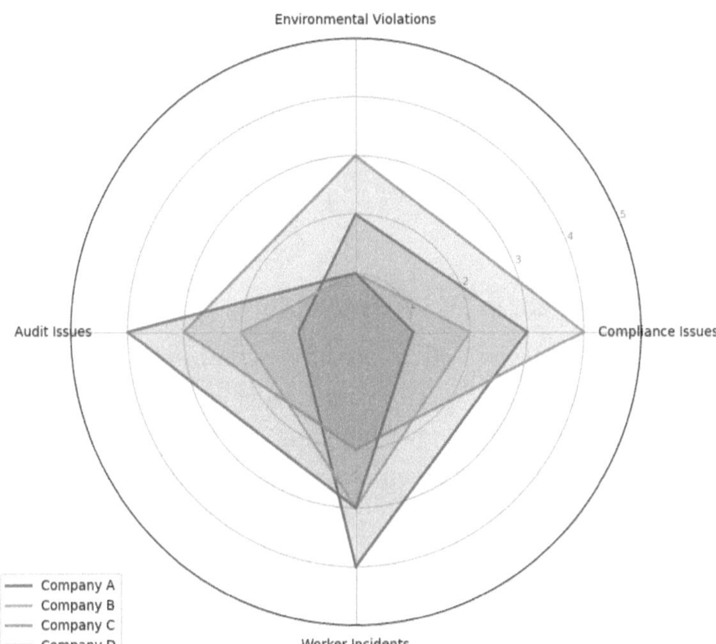

Figure 3.5: Basic Compliance Seeker – EHS Issues Radar chart

3. Reactive Incident Management

Basic compliance seekers generally adopt a reactive approach to incident management. They only take action after an incident or a near-miss occurs instead of focusing on preventive measures that could mitigate risks before they escalate. This results in higher incident rates and potentially costlier remediation efforts.

Insight: Company "A" frequently waits for incidents or external audits to highlight issues rather than actively managing potential safety risks. Company "C" also demonstrates similar reactive measures, with incident responses often triggered only after an event or violation.

4. Siloed EHS Functions

In these companies, EHS functions are often isolated and must be fully integrated into the broader business strategy. There needs to be more cross-functional collaboration between operations, human resources, and compliance departments. This isolation limits the Company's ability to holistically manage safety risks and leverage data from other business areas.

Insight: Companies like Company "A" and Company "C" tend to treat EHS as a separate function. This results in safety teams not being involved in broader decision-making processes, which limits their ability to proactively manage risks that span multiple departments, such as environmental safety and workforce health.

5. Limited Investment in EHS Technologies

Companies in this category often need to demonstrate a higher level of investment in modern EHS technologies, such as IoT sensors, real-time monitoring systems, and predictive analytics. These technologies can gather real-time data on environmental and safety risks, leading to slower response times and higher risk exposure.

Insight: Company "B" and Company "C" have slowly adopted IoT-based monitoring solutions or AI-driven risk assessments. This leaves them dependent on manual audits and post-incident investigations, which increases their exposure to risks and reduces their ability to prevent incidents before they occur.

6. Cost-Driven Decision-Making

EHS initiatives in these companies are often viewed as cost centers rather than opportunities for value creation or innovation. As a result, EHS improvements are driven by budget constraints rather than a desire to improve safety outcomes or reduce environmental impact.

Insight: Company "C" and Company "D" typically allocate just enough budget to meet regulatory requirements but do not view EHS investments as contributing to operational efficiency or long-term sustainability.

7. Challenges in Keeping Up with Evolving Regulations

These companies often need help to keep up with evolving regulations in areas such as environmental protection, workplace safety, and sustainability. As regulations become more complex and stringent, compliance seekers may find themselves increasingly overwhelmed by the volume of requirements they must meet.

Insight: Company "A" and Company "B" have faced challenges with rapidly evolving environmental regulations, especially in areas where their global operations face different regulatory frameworks. The lack of a robust, integrated EHS system makes it difficult for them to adapt quickly to these changes.

The Basic Compliance Seekers share common traits of minimal investment in EHS technologies, reactive safety approaches, and cost-driven decision-making. While they meet the baseline regulatory requirements, they need more proactive, data-driven strategies seen in more advanced companies. To progress in their EHS journey, they would need to invest in integrated systems, real-time monitoring, and cross-functional collaboration to move from compliance-based safety management to a more proactive, risk-mitigation approach.

2. Traditional Operator (Low EHS Knowledge / Proactive Business Design)

These companies attempt to integrate EHS into their business design but need more data and insights to manage safety and compliance proactively. While they may have digital systems, such as environmental monitoring or incident reporting tools, they often rely on outdated or incomplete data.

Common Characteristics of Traditional Operators

Companies in the Traditional Operators category are transitioning from purely compliance-driven, reactive EHS management to a more proactive, though still somewhat siloed, approach. They tend to focus on improving operational efficiency and reducing risks but may need to integrate EHS into their broader business model more. Their journey is marked by adopting digital tools for incident tracking, environmental monitoring, and basic predictive capabilities. Still, they have not fully embraced the potential of real-time data analytics and cross-departmental collaboration.

Here are the key characteristics and insights from real-world examples of companies like Company "E," Company "F," Company "G," Company: "H", and Company:" I":

1. Adoption of Digital Tools, but Not Fully Integrated

Traditional operators have begun to invest in digital tools such as environmental monitoring systems, incident reporting platforms, and basic analytics. However, these systems are often isolated within the EHS function rather than fully integrated into the broader business strategy or operations.

Insight: Company "E" has implemented digital environmental monitoring tools to track emissions at refineries, but these systems are not fully integrated with their operational decision-making processes. Similarly, Company "G" has adopted digital incident tracking platforms but relies heavily on departmental silos, preventing comprehensive safety oversight across all facilities.

2. Proactive but Limited in Predictive Capabilities

While traditional operators have begun to take a more proactive approach to safety and compliance, they still rely on historical data rather than advanced predictive analytics. They often respond to safety issues based on trends and patterns but lack the real-time monitoring needed to anticipate incidents before they occur.

Insight: Company "I" has made strides in proactive safety monitoring in its pharmaceutical manufacturing plants, implementing basic analytics to review historical incidents and improve compliance. However, the Company needs advanced tools for real-time prediction of potential risks, such as equipment malfunctions or safety breaches, which limits its ability to prevent incidents before they occur.

3. Focus on Operational Efficiency and Compliance

Traditional operators often seek to balance operational efficiency with regulatory compliance. Their investments in EHS are primarily driven by a need to ensure smooth operations, reduce downtime, and meet regulatory standards. However, the focus is still primarily on compliance, and EHS is seen as a function that must be managed efficiently rather than as an area for innovation or value creation.

Insight: Company "F" has implemented wastewater management technologies and environmental compliance systems in its water treatment plants, which help meet regulatory standards and optimize water usage.

However, these tools are not seen as a driver of broader business innovation, and EHS remains focused on meeting compliance rather than creating additional value.

4. Gradual Move Toward Sustainability Initiatives

Many traditional operators have started to adopt sustainability initiatives, particularly in sectors like energy and manufacturing, where there is increasing pressure to reduce environmental footprints. However, these efforts are often fragmented and not fully integrated into their core business processes.

Insight: Company "H," a leader in the agriculture sector, has made progress in adopting sustainability initiatives related to deforestation and supply chain emissions, but integrating these initiatives into its overall EHS strategy remains a work in progress. The Company needs to align its sustainability goals with its broader business objectives and operational strategies.

5. Stronger Incident Reporting and Environmental Monitoring

Traditional operators tend to have more robust incident reporting systems and environmental monitoring capabilities than primary compliance seekers. They have typically invested in digital systems that allow them to track and report incidents more efficiently. However, they still need to rely on manual intervention for analysis and decision-making, slowing down their ability to fully leverage the data they collect.

Insight: Company "G" uses digital environmental monitoring in its mills to ensure compliance with emissions regulations, and it has improved its incident reporting process through digital systems. However, it still relies on manual oversight to analyze the data, meaning the Company often misses opportunities to act quickly and prevent issues from escalating.

6. Focus on Safety and Compliance as Separate Functions

Traditional operators often view safety and compliance as separate functions within the organization. While safety is critical to maintaining an excellent operational track record, it is usually treated as a compliance-driven task rather than an area where innovation or integration can happen across departments. As a result, while safety is improving, it may need to align fully with the Company's overall strategic objectives.

Insight: Company: I" has made significant progress in workplace safety, particularly in its manufacturing and research facilities, but the safety function remains separate from broader corporate initiatives. Safety teams are not deeply involved in operational decision-making, and while safety records are improving, they are not driving cross-functional collaboration.

7. Gradual Adoption of Real-Time Monitoring

Traditional operators are beginning to experiment with real-time monitoring, but many have only implemented these technologies in specific areas or pilot programs. For instance, companies may use IoT devices in a limited capacity for environmental monitoring or incident detection but have not yet scaled these technologies across the entire organization.

Insight: Company "F" has launched real-time water quality monitoring at some of its wastewater treatment plants, but the use of IoT sensors remains limited to specific facilities. The Company has not yet adopted real-time monitoring across its global operations, limiting its EHS improvements' scalability.

Traditional Operators like Company "E," Company "F," Company "G," Company H, and Company:" I" are making strides toward proactive EHS management by adopting digital tools and improving operational efficiency. However, their EHS efforts are often siloed, compliance-driven, and lacking full integration with other business functions. These companies are progressing but need to focus on cross-functional collaboration, real-time data integration, and the full-scale adoption of predictive technologies to move from traditional operators to becoming EHS digital leaders.

3. Reactive Knowledge Holder or Reactive performer (High EHS Knowledge / Reactive Business Design)

Organizations in this quadrant have a deep understanding of their safety and environmental risks but still need to integrate that knowledge fully into their business design. They may have access to real-time data but need more systems or processes to use that data effectively for proactive risk management.

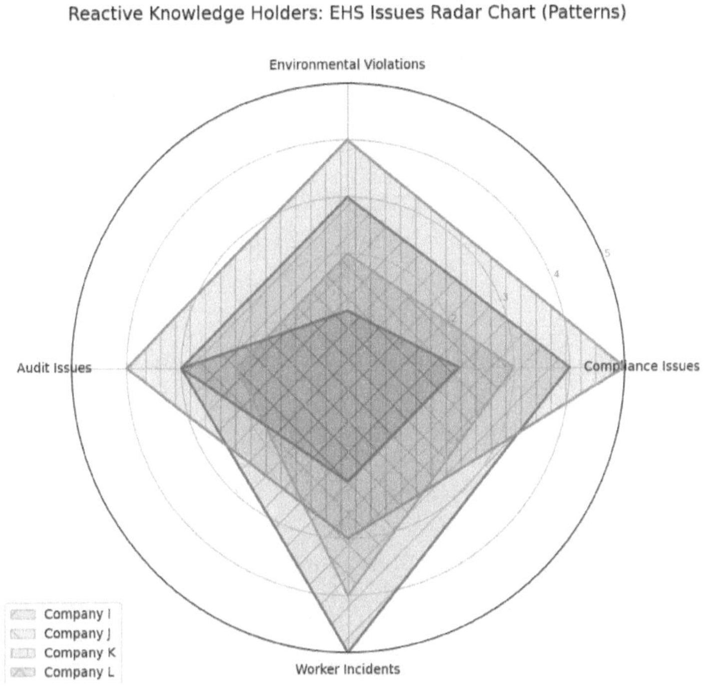

Reactive Knowledge Holders: EHS Issues Radar Chart (Patterns)

Figure 3.6: Reactive Performer – EHS Issues Radar chart

Common Characteristics of Reactive Knowledge Holders

Companies in the Reactive Knowledge Holders category possess extensive EHS knowledge, often have well-established systems, and deeply understand their safety and environmental risks. However, they still operate reactively, responding to incidents after they occur rather than leveraging predictive analytics and real-time data for proactive risk mitigation. These companies are data-rich but often fail to act on that data in a timely, forward-looking manner.

Here are the key characteristics and insights from real-world examples of companies like Company: "J", Company: "K," Company: L," Company: "M," and Company: "N":

1. High Knowledge of Risks but Reactive Action

Reactive Knowledge Holders typically have a strong understanding of their EHS risks and regulatory requirements, which they have gained through years of experience and compliance expertise. However, despite their wealth of knowledge, they often remain reactive, addressing safety issues only after incidents occur. They may have the data to anticipate risks but need more tools or processes to leverage it effectively for predictive safety management.

Insight: Company: "J" has extensive knowledge of chemical safety and environmental regulations. Despite this, the Company has been criticized for responding reactively to incidents, particularly in cases where early warning signs were available but not acted upon in time. This reflects a disconnect between their deep risk knowledge and proactive risk mitigation.

2. Data-rich but Lacking in Predictive Analytics

These companies are often data-rich, collecting information through audits, incident reports, and compliance checks. However, they tend to lack predictive analytics capabilities that could allow them to anticipate risks before they escalate into incidents. This limits their ability to transition from reactive to proactive safety management.

Insight: Company:" K" is known for its comprehensive data collection across manufacturing processes, tracking machine performance, worker safety, and environmental impact. However, relying on historical data for decision-making means it still operates reactively in many areas, mainly when predicting equipment failures or safety risks.

3. Incident-Driven Safety Improvements

Reactive Knowledge Holders often implement safety improvements in response to past incidents. They conduct root-cause analyses and use the findings to enhance safety measures, but these improvements tend to be incident-driven rather than proactive. As a result, safety improvements are often made after an event has occurred rather than before.

Insight: Company L, one of the largest mining companies in the world, has faced significant safety challenges in the past, particularly in high-risk mining operations. The Company tends to implement new safety protocols only after incidents, such as equipment failures or environmental hazards. Despite having access to data that could predict these risks, its actions remain reactive to incidents.

4. Siloed EHS Functions

Although these companies have strong EHS knowledge, their safety and compliance functions often must be more consistent with other business operations. Cross-departmental collaboration is limited, and safety data is not fully integrated with broader operational decision-making. This limits their ability to manage safety risks holistically.

Insight: Company: "M," a major utility company, has extensive knowledge of environmental regulations and safety risks, particularly in managing power plants and emissions. However, its safety and compliance functions often operate in silos, meaning that operational teams don't always use critical safety data to inform broader business decisions.

5. Manual Data Analysis and Slow Decision-Making

Reactive Knowledge Holders may collect large amounts of data but rely on manual analysis processes. This reduces their real-time ability to act on the data, often leading to delayed decision-making. Their safety teams may conduct thorough incident investigations after an event, but these efforts don't prevent future incidents in the way that predictive tools could.

Insight: Company:" N" is known for its fast-paced operational environment but relies heavily on manual oversight and reactive safety protocols. While the Company collects a significant amount of safety data, particularly regarding worker incidents and equipment hazards, much of this data is reviewed after incidents occur, with slow implementation of preventive measures.

6. Compliance-driven but Lacking in Proactive Innovation

These companies often have robust compliance frameworks, ensuring they meet all regulatory requirements. However, they remain focused on avoiding fines and penalties rather than innovating beyond compliance to improve safety and sustainability. Their compliance-driven mindset limits their ability to explore proactive EHS strategies that could create long-term value.

Insight: Company" J" and Company" L" have vital compliance track records, particularly regarding meeting environmental regulations. However, they are still compliance-driven, investing primarily in measures that keep them within regulatory boundaries rather than innovating to prevent incidents or reduce risks more comprehensively.

7. Challenges with Real-Time Monitoring and IoT Integration

Although these companies may experiment with real-time monitoring or IoT solutions, they often need to implement these technologies on a large scale. They may have IoT sensors in some high-risk regions or pilot programs, but these efforts are not fully integrated into their overall EHS strategy. This limits their ability to act on real-time data and proactively manage organizational risks.

Insight: Company: "K" has experimented with IoT technologies to monitor equipment performance and worker safety in its manufacturing plants. However, these efforts are still in the early stages, and the Company's broader safety strategy remains largely reactive, as IoT data is only used consistently across some operations.

Reactive Performers like Company:" J," Company:" K," Company: L," Company:" M," and Company:" N" possess deep EHS knowledge and extensive data but struggle to move beyond reactive safety management. They tend to respond to incidents after they occur rather than leveraging the predictive capabilities of their data to prevent incidents. These companies would benefit from investing in predictive analytics, integrating safety functions with other business operations, and fully adopting real-time monitoring solutions to transition from reactive to proactive EHS management.

4. EHS Digital Leader (High EHS Knowledge / Proactive Business Design)

The most advanced organizations in the framework are EHS Digital Leaders. These companies leverage real-time data, predictive analytics, and integrated digital systems to improve safety and compliance continuously. They embed EHS into every aspect of their operations, from risk assessments to employee engagement, and use data to inform decisions and prevent incidents before they happen.

Common Characteristics of EHS Digital Leaders

Companies classified as EHS Digital Leaders are at the forefront of integrating advanced digital tools and technologies into their environmental, health, and safety (EHS) management systems. These organizations leverage real-time data, predictive analytics, and cross-functional collaboration to manage risks, ensure compliance, and drive sustainability proactively. They have fully embedded EHS into their broader business models, aligning safety and compliance with long-term strategic goals.

Below are key characteristics and insights from real-world examples of companies like Company "O," Company "P," Company "Q," Company "R," Company "S," Company "T," Company "U," Company "V," Company "W," and Company "X":

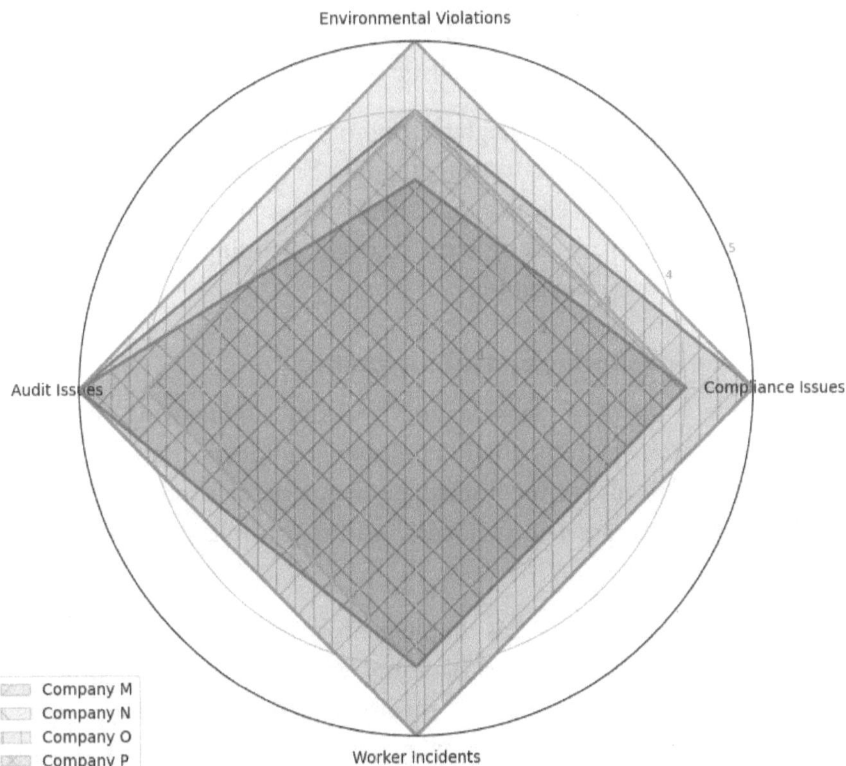

1. Proactive Risk Management with Predictive Analytics

EHS Digital Leaders use predictive analytics to identify and mitigate risks before they escalate. These companies leverage AI and machine learning to analyze historical data, monitor real-time conditions, and predict potential incidents, enabling proactive interventions that improve safety and reduce downtime.

Insight: Company "P" uses AI-driven predictive maintenance systems to monitor its operations globally. By analyzing equipment performance in real-time, the Company can predict potential failures and initiate maintenance before incidents occur. This approach not only minimizes safety risks but also optimizes operational efficiency.

2. Full Integration of EHS with Business Strategy

In digital leaders, EHS is no longer treated as a standalone function; it is fully integrated into the core business strategy. These companies recognize that safety, sustainability, and compliance are key drivers of long-term success. As a result, EHS data is integrated with operations, human resources, and corporate governance to ensure a holistic approach to managing risks.

Insight: Company "O" integrates environmental monitoring and safety data into its broader business strategy, aligning EHS initiatives with corporate sustainability goals. This ensures that safety and environmental performance are part of the Company's long-term strategic planning, particularly as BP transitions to a low-carbon future.

3. Real-Time Monitoring and IoT Integration

Digital leaders use IoT sensors and real-time monitoring systems to continuously track environmental conditions, equipment performance, and worker safety. This allows for immediate detection of anomalies and quick decision-making to prevent incidents, ensure compliance, and maintain operational continuity.

Insight: Company "S" has implemented IoT-enabled environmental monitoring systems across its agricultural and pharmaceutical production facilities. These sensors monitor air quality, emissions, and other ecological metrics in real-time, allowing Company "S" to act immediately in case of potential environmental breaches or regulatory violations.

4. Cross-Functional Collaboration and Data Sharing

EHS Digital Leaders foster cross-functional collaboration by making safety and compliance data accessible across all departments. This integration enables operations, HR, and IT departments to make data-driven decisions that improve safety, compliance, and operational performance. The alignment of these functions ensures that safety is woven into the fabric of the entire organization.

Insight: Company "T" uses cross-functional digital platforms that allow safety, operations, and engineering teams to collaborate seamlessly. Safety and environmental data are shared across departments, allowing Company "T" to reduce incidents and improve efficiency in their manufacturing processes.

5. Focus on Sustainability and Regulatory Leadership

Digital leaders excel at internal safety management and position themselves as leaders in sustainability. They seek to exceed regulatory requirements and set new industry safety and environmental performance standards. These companies invest heavily in sustainable technologies, such as renewable energy, emissions reduction, and circular economy initiatives.

Insight: Company "X" has made strides in leveraging digital tools to enhance its sustainability performance, particularly in reducing emissions. The Company uses advanced data analytics and IoT sensors to monitor and reduce methane emissions from its operations. Company "X" also integrates these initiatives into its broader sustainability strategy as part of its commitment to reducing its environmental footprint.

6. Advanced Incident Management and Automated Compliance

EHS Digital Leaders have fully automated systems for incident management and compliance monitoring. These systems streamline the reporting of safety incidents, manage regulatory compliance, and ensure that safety standards are met globally across all operations. This automation reduces human error and improves the Company's ability to respond quickly to regulatory or safety issues.

Insight:Ccompany "R" uses automated compliance management systems that monitor global regulations and ensure that all operations adhere to local and international safety standards. These systems automatically update compliance protocols and flag any discrepancies, reducing the risk of regulatory violations and ensuring that Company "R" maintains its position as a global leader in chemical safety.

7. Digital Transformation of Workforce Safety

Digital leaders have invested significantly in workforce safety technologies such as wearable devices, augmented reality (AR), and virtual reality (VR) for training and hazard identification. These tools enhance worker safety by providing real-time data on worker location, health, and safety while also improving the efficiency and effectiveness of safety training.

Insight: Company "Q" has pioneered wearable safety devices and real-time location tracking to monitor worker safety in high-risk environments such as oil refineries and chemical plants. These devices provide real-time data on worker health and location, allowing Company "Q" to respond quickly to safety incidents and prevent potential accidents.

8. Global Leadership in Safety Standards

Many EHS Digital Leaders set global safety standards in their respective industries. They collaborate with regulatory bodies, share best practices with peers, and often lead the way in defining safety excellence. These companies view EHS as a regulatory requirement and a competitive differentiator that builds trust with stakeholders, customers, and investors.

Insight: Company "W" has established itself as a leader in aviation safety, working closely with regulators to set new safety standards for the aerospace industry. Company "W" uses real-time analytics and digital twins to simulate and monitor aircraft safety in real-time, ensuring the highest level of protection for its workers and passengers.

9. Sustainability as a Competitive Advantage

Sustainability is a core business driver for EHS digital leaders. They use digital tools to reduce their environmental footprint, optimize resource use, and create sustainable products and services. Sustainability is embedded in their long-term strategy, and they use advanced data analytics to track their progress and make informed decisions that benefit both the environment and their business.

Insight: Company "U" has significantly invested in renewable energy and sustainability initiatives, using digital platforms to monitor and reduce emissions. Company "U"'s global sustainability strategy is integrated into its broader business plan, allowing the Company to transition toward a greener energy future while maintaining operational safety and efficiency.

EHS Digital Leaders like Company "O," Company "P," Company "Q," Company "R," Company "S," Company "T," Company "U," Company "V," Company "W," and Company "X" are defined by their proactive risk management, real-time monitoring capabilities, and integration of EHS into their core business strategies. These companies use digital tools to improve safety, ensure compliance, and drive sustainability. By leveraging advanced technologies such as IoT, predictive analytics, and AI, they have transformed EHS into a competitive advantage and set new standards for safety and environmental performance in their industries.

Common Characteristics of Transitioning Companies in the EHS Space

Companies transitioning from traditional EHS management to more advanced, digitally integrated EHS systems are making strides toward proactive safety, compliance, and sustainability. These organizations are adopting IoT, AI, and predictive analytics but have yet to integrate these technologies fully across all operations. They are on a path toward data-driven decision-making, real-time monitoring, and cross-functional collaboration to improve safety and environmental performance.

Below are the key characteristics and insights from real-world examples of companies like Company: L", Automobile primary Automobile central "B," Beverages Major, Eu Based Automobile major, FMCG -1, Major FMCG company, Major oil and gas company, and Automation major:

1. Adoption of Digital Tools with Limited Scale

Transitioning companies are early adopters of IoT, AI, and predictive analytics but often implement these technologies on a limited scale, focusing on high-risk areas or pilot projects. The challenge is scaling these tools to cover all operations and integrating them into a broader, real-time data strategy.

Insight: Company: L" uses IoT and drones for real-time environmental monitoring in specific mining sites, but scaling these technologies across its entire global operation remains a challenge. The Company is still in the early stages of using predictive analytics to anticipate equipment malfunctions and safety risks.

2. Reactive to Proactive Transition in Risk Management

These companies are moving from reactive safety management, where incidents are addressed after they occur, to proactive risk management. They are adopting predictive tools to foresee safety risks, but full implementation across all operations is still in progress.

Insight: An automobile significantly leverages digital twins to simulate factory environments and predict safety risks. However, these tools are often limited to specific operations, and scaling predictive capabilities to the entire organization is still in progress.

3. Real-Time Monitoring with Early IoT Adoption

Transitioning companies are beginning to implement IoT-enabled safety systems to monitor equipment, worker safety, and environmental conditions in real-time. However, these efforts are often limited to specific facilities or regions, and many organizations are still working to ensure that real-time data is fully integrated into their broader operational decision-making processes.

Insight: Automobile central "B" uses IoT-enabled worker safety systems in its factories and AI for emissions monitoring. However, real-time monitoring has not yet been scaled across all global operations, limiting the impact of these technologies on worker safety and compliance.

4. Focus on Compliance with a Growing Sustainability Lens

Many transitioning companies remain focused on meeting regulatory requirements but increasingly incorporate sustainability initiatives into their EHS strategies. Sustainability is becoming a priority, but full integration with safety and operational processes is still developing.

Insight: Beverages Major uses data analytics to improve environmental sustainability, focusing on waste management and water usage. However, their sustainability initiatives are not yet fully aligned with their safety and compliance processes, meaning there is still room to develop a more integrated approach.

5. Pilot Programs for Predictive Analytics

Companies in this category are exploring predictive analytics but are still in the early stages of full implementation. Pilot programs are often used in high-risk areas, but the insights gained from predictive tools are not yet embedded in all operations.

Insight: An EU-based automobile major is deploying AI tools to predict equipment failures and worker safety incidents, but predictive safety management is still limited to specific factory locations. Full-scale adoption across its global manufacturing network is ongoing.

6. Siloed Safety and Operational Functions

Despite making progress in adopting digital tools, transitioning companies often need help with siloed safety and compliance functions. EHS data is collected but not fully shared across departments, limiting the ability to integrate safety management with other business operations.

Insight: FMCG -1 collects a significant amount of environmental and safety data in its laboratories, but integrating these insights with other operational departments, such as research and production, is still in progress. The Company is working toward a more connected, cross-functional approach to safety.

7. Investments in Real-Time Environmental Monitoring

Many transitioning companies are investing in IoT sensors and other digital tools for real-time environmental monitoring. These efforts help organizations comply with environmental regulations, but automation is necessary to reduce manual interventions entirely.

Insight: A company uses IoT sensors to monitor emissions and environmental compliance in real time across its oil rigs and refineries. However, real-time data is not yet fully integrated into the Company's global decision-making processes, limiting the proactive management of risks.

8. Improving Incident Reporting with Digital Tools

Transitioning companies are implementing digital incident management systems to streamline reporting and compliance. These systems often replace manual processes, reducing errors and improving compliance, but predictive incident prevention remains an area for further development.

Insight: A major oil and gas company has deployed digital tools for incident reporting and safety monitoring across its offshore platforms, improving compliance and reporting accuracy. However, integrating predictive safety tools to prevent incidents before they occur is still a work in progress.

9. Moving Toward Cross-Functional Collaboration

These companies are beginning to recognize the importance of cross-functional collaboration for EHS management. While safety, operations, and IT departments may still operate separately, transitioning companies are starting to break down these silos to create a more connected, data-driven approach to safety.

Insight: Automation majors use digital twins and real-time monitoring to improve safety in their manufacturing processes. However, more work is needed to integrate these tools across departments and ensure that safety data informs operational decision-making throughout the Company.

Transitioning companies like Company: L", Automobile major, Automobile central "B," Beverages Major, Eu Based Automobile major, FMCG -1, Major FMCG company, Major oil and gas company, and Automation major are making significant progress toward becoming EHS Digital Leaders. These organizations are adopting IoT, AI, and predictive analytics but are still working on scaling these technologies and fully embedding them into their broader operations. They will move from traditional, reactive safety management to fully proactive, data-driven EHS leadership as they continue implementing real-time monitoring, predictive safety tools, and cross-functional collaboration.

Case Study: GlobalTech's EHS Digital Transformation Journey

Company Background

GlobalTech is a multinational manufacturing company specializing in electronic components. With operations in 15 countries and over 50,000 employees, GlobalTech faced significant challenges in consistently managing its Environment, Health, and Safety (EHS) responsibilities across its diverse operations.

Initial State: Basic Compliance Operator

In 2018, GlobalTech found itself operating as a Basic Compliance Operator:

- **Reactive Approach**: The company primarily focused on meeting minimum regulatory requirements and responding to incidents after they occurred.

- **Manual Processes**: EHS data was collected manually, often recorded on paper or in disconnected spreadsheets.

- **Siloed Operations**: EHS functions were isolated from other departments, with limited cross-functional collaboration.

- **Inconsistent Reporting**: Different facilities used varying methods for incident reporting and risk assessment, making it challenging to compare performance across sites.

- **Limited Visibility**: Management needed better visibility into real-time EHS performance, relying on monthly or quarterly reports.

Challenges

GlobalTech faced several challenges that prompted its digital transformation:

1. **Rising Incident Rates**: Despite efforts to improve safety, incident rates were increasing, particularly in newer facilities.

2. **Compliance Struggles**: The company needed help to keep up with varying regulatory requirements across different countries.

3. **Inefficient Resource Allocation**: It was difficult to allocate resources effectively to high-risk areas without clear data.

4. **Reputation Risks**: Environmental violations led to negative press and strained relationships with local communities.

5. **Employee Dissatisfaction**: Surveys indicated that employees felt the company needed to prioritize their safety and well-being.

The Transformation Journey

Phase 1: Building the Foundation (6 months)

1. **Leadership Commitment**: The CEO and board prioritized EHS excellence, allocating a significant budget for digital transformation.

2. **EHS Assessment**: GlobalTech hired a consulting firm to assess its current EHS practices and technology infrastructure.

3. **Digital Strategy Development**: A cross-functional team developed a comprehensive EHS digital transformation strategy.

4. **Technology Selection**: After evaluating several options, GlobalTech selected an integrated EHS management platform with IoT capabilities.

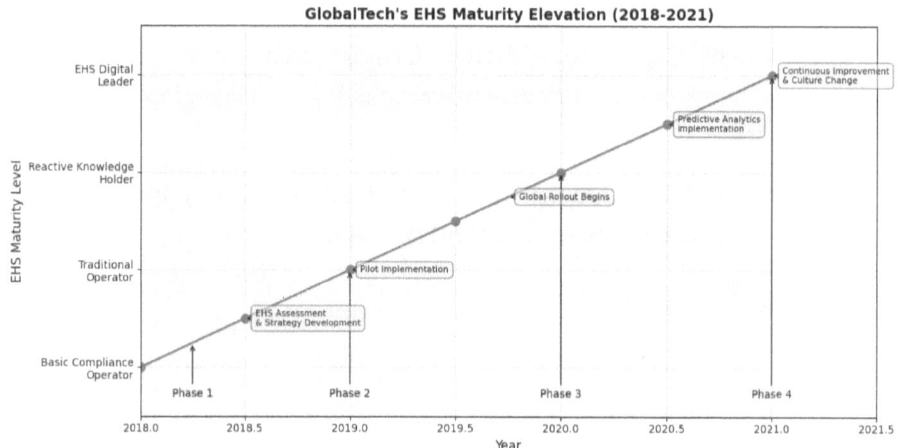

Figure 3.8: GlobalTech's EHS Maturity Elevation

Phase 2: Pilot Implementation (6 months)

1. **Pilot Site Selection**: Three manufacturing sites (US, China, and Germany) were chosen for the initial rollout.

2. **IoT Integration**: Environmental sensors and wearable safety devices were deployed at pilot sites.

3. **Data Integration**: The new EHS platform integrated existing HR and operations systems.

4. **Training:** Intensive training programs were conducted for employees at pilot sites.

Phase 3: Global Rollout and Advanced Analytics (18 months)

1. **Staged Implementation:** The new EHS system was rolled out globally in stages, prioritizing high-risk facilities.

2. **Real-time Monitoring:** IoT sensors were deployed across all facilities for real-time environmental and safety monitoring.

3. **Predictive Analytics:** GlobalTech implemented AI-driven predictive analytics to forecast potential incidents and environmental risks.

4. **Mobile App Development:** A mobile app was developed to report incidents easily and access safety information.

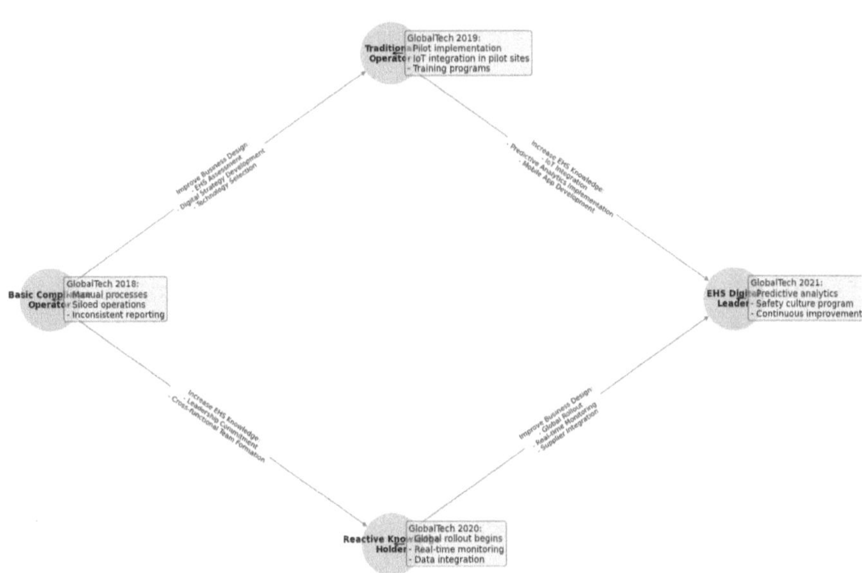

Figure 3.9: EHS Model transition flowchart with GlobalTech's Initiatives

Phase 4: Culture Change and Continuous Improvement (Ongoing)

1. **Safety Culture Program:** GlobalTech launched a company-wide program to foster a proactive safety culture.

2. **Gamification**: A points-based system was introduced to incentivize safe behaviors and environmental initiatives.

3. **Supplier Integration**: The EHS platform was extended to critical suppliers to ensure safety and compliance throughout the supply chain.

4. **Continuous Learning**: Regular training and knowledge-sharing sessions were established to keep employees updated on EHS best practices.

Outcomes

After three years of transformation efforts, GlobalTech successfully transitioned to an EHS Digital Leader:

1. **Incident Reduction**: Recordable incident rates decreased by 65% across all facilities.

2. **Compliance Improvement**: Regulatory violations were reduced by 80%, with no major environmental incidents in the past two years.

3. **Cost Savings**: The company saved $50 million annually through reduced incidents, better resource allocation, and improved efficiency.

4. **Employee Engagement**: Employee satisfaction scores related to safety and well-being improved by 45%.

5. **Sustainability Gains**: GlobalTech reduced its carbon emissions by 30% and water usage by 25% through data-driven sustainability initiatives.

6. **Reputation Enhancement**: The company's efforts were recognized with several industry awards for EHS excellence.

7. **Predictive Capabilities**: The AI system successfully predicted and prevented 150 potential severe incidents in the first year of full implementation.

Key Lessons

1. **Leadership Commitment**: Strong support from top management was crucial for driving change across the organization.

2. **Integrated Approach**: Combining technology implementation with culture change was essential for success.

3. **Data-Driven Decision Making**: Real-time data and predictive analytics enabled proactive risk management and resource allocation.

4. **Employee Involvement**: Engaging employees at all levels helped overcome resistance to change and fostered a safety-first culture.

5. **Continuous Improvement**: The transformation is an ongoing process, requiring constant adaptation to new technologies and emerging risks.

GlobalTech's journey from a Basic Compliance Operator to an EHS Digital Leader demonstrates the transformative power of digital technologies in EHS management. By leveraging IoT, real-time monitoring, and predictive analytics, the company improved its safety and environmental performance and gained significant competitive advantages in efficiency, employee satisfaction, and reputation.

References - EHS Business Models and Benchmarking: Chapter References

1. Aldrich, M. (2010). History of workplace safety in the United States, 1880-1970. EH. Net Encyclopedia, edited by Robert Whaples.

2. American Chemistry Council. (2022). Responsible Care® Program. https://responsiblecare.americanchemistry.com/

3. Ansari, A., & Modarress, B. (1997). World-class strategies for safety: a Boeing approach. International Journal of Operations & Production Management, 17(4), 389-398.

4. Blewett, V., & O'Keeffe, V. (2011). Weighing the pig never made it heavier: Auditing OHS, social auditing as verification of process in Australia. Safety Science, 49(7), 1014-1021.

5. Bureau of Labor Statistics. (2023). Injuries, Illnesses, and Fatalities. https://www.bls.gov/iif/

6. Campbell Institute. (2021). EHS Leadership and Business Performance: State of the Practice White Paper. National Safety Council.

7. CDP. (2023). The A List 2022. https://www.cdp.net/en/companies/companies-scores

8.   Construction Industry Institute. (2022). Safety Best Practices. https://www.construction-institute.org/resources/knowledgebase/best-practices/safety

9.   Dekker, S. (2018). The safety anarchist: Relying on human expertise and innovation, reducing bureaucracy and compliance. Routledge.

10. European Agency for Safety and Health at Work. (2022). Digitalization and occupational safety and health (OSH). https://osha.europa.eu/en/emerging-risks/digitalization-and-occupational-safety-and-health-osh

11. Frost & Sullivan. (2021). Global Environment, Health, and Safety (EHS) Market, Forecast to 2024. Frost & Sullivan Research Service.

12. Gensuite. (2023). EHS Digital Transformation Assessment. https://www.gensuite.com/ehs-digital-transformation/

13. Global Reporting Initiative. (2023). GRI Standards. https://www.globalreporting.org/standards/

14. Hollnagel, E. (2014). Safety-I and safety-II: the past and future of safety management. CRC press.

15. International Organization for Standardization. (2018). ISO 45001:2018 Occupational health and safety management systems — Requirements with guidance for use. https://www.iso.org/standard/63787.html

16. International Organization for Standardization. (2015). ISO 14001:2015 Environmental management systems — Requirements with guidance for use. https://www.iso.org/standard/60857.html

17. Kaplan, R. S., & Norton, D. P. (1996). The balanced scorecard: translating strategy into action. Harvard Business Press.

18. Manuele, F. A. (2013). On the practice of safety. John Wiley & Sons.

19. National Association of Manufacturers. (2022). NAM Safety Survey. https://www.nam.org/safety/

20. National Safety Council. (2023). Injury Facts. https://injuryfacts.nsc.org/

21. Occupational Safety and Health Administration. (2023). Recommended Practices for Safety and Health Programs. https://www.osha.gov/safety-management

22. Pawlowska, Z. (2015). Using lagging and leading indicators for the evaluation of occupational safety and health performance in industry. International Journal of Occupational Safety and Ergonomics, 21(3), 284-290.

23. Robson, L. S., Clarke, J. A., Cullen, K., Bielecky, A., Severin, C., Bigelow, P. L., … & Mahood, Q. (2007). The effectiveness of occupational health and safety management system interventions: a systematic review. Safety Science, 45(3), 329-353.

24. Sinelnikov, S., Inouye, J., & Kerper, S. (2015). Using leading indicators to measure occupational health and safety performance. Safety Science, 72, 240-248.

25. Sustainability Accounting Standards Board. (2023). SASB Standards. https://www.sasb.org/standards/

26. United Nations. (2015). Sustainable Development Goals. https://sdgs.un.org/goals

27. Verdantix. (2022). Green Quadrant EHS Software 2022. Verdantix Research.

28. World Business Council for Sustainable Development. (2022). Vision 2050: Time to Transform. https://www.wbcsd.org/Overview/About-us/Vision-2050-Time-to-Transform

29. Zwetsloot, G. I., Aaltonen, M., Wybo, J. L., Saari, J., Kines, P., & De Beeck, R. O. (2013). The case for research into the zero accident vision. Safety Science, 58, 41-48.

30. Zwetsloot, G. I., & van Scheppingen, A. R. (2007). Towards a strategic business case for health management. In Workplace Health Promotion in Enlarging Europe. Nofer Institute of Occupational Medicine.

Aligning EHS Business Models with Future Goals

Becoming an EHS Digital Leader

The future of EHS management lies in moving beyond Basic compliance and adopting a fully integrated, data-driven approach to safety and environmental performance. By improving your organization's EHS knowledge and redesigning your business processes to integrate EHS at every level, you can prevent incidents before they happen, reduce compliance costs, and create a safer, more sustainable workplace.

In the next chapter, we'll explore the specific digital tools and technologies that can help your organization advance in the EHS Knowledge vs. Business Design framework and become a leader in the future of EHS management. Whether starting with essential compliance tools or already using advanced digital systems, the path to digital transformation in EHS is clear: invest in knowledge, integrate EHS into your operations, and embrace the power of data to drive continuous improvement.

Common Characteristics of EHS Digital Leaders

EHS Digital Leaders sit at the upper right of the EHS Knowledge-Business Design matrix, representing the pinnacle of EHS maturity. These organizations combine deep EHS expertise with innovative business models to deliver unparalleled safety performance, environmental stewardship, and operational excellence.

While each Digital Leader is unique, they share common characteristics that set them apart from their peers. Understanding these traits can help clarify the target state for organizations aspiring to EHS leadership.

1. Proactive, Data-Driven Mindset

Digital Leaders embrace a proactive, data-driven approach to EHS management. They leverage real-time monitoring, advanced analytics, and AI to identify and mitigate risks before incidents occur. Key traits include:

- Continuous, real-time data collection across the EHS landscape

- Predictive analytics to surface insights and enable early intervention

- AI-powered tools for risk detection and mitigation

- Data democratization to empower frontline decision-making

2. Integrated, End-to-End Platforms

Digital Leaders understand that EHS excellence requires breaking down silos. They employ integrated, end-to-end platforms that connect disparate data streams, processes, and stakeholders. Common features include:

- Unified data architecture across EHS domains

- Seamless integration of modular components and third-party tools

- Intuitive, role-based user interfaces for ease of use

- Mobile capabilities for any time, anywhere access

3. Ecosystem Thinking

Digital Leaders think beyond their walls, actively cultivating EHS ecosystems. They foster collaboration and co-innovation with various partners, from technology providers to peer organizations. Ecosystem approaches include:

- Open APIs and standards for seamless data sharing

- Co-development models with specialty partners

- Cross-industry collaboration to identify and scale best practices

- Active engagement with regulators and standards bodies

4. Culture of Innovation

Digital Leaders foster a culture of innovation that encourages experimentation, learning, and continuous improvement. They empower teams to push boundaries and think creatively. Hallmarks of an innovation culture include:

- Executive sponsorship and visible leadership commitment

- Dedicated innovation teams and "EHS Labs" to drive new ideas

- Agile ways of working, including rapid prototyping and testing

- Reward and recognition programs for EHS innovation

5. Business Model Agility

Digital Leaders need to be more content to rest on their laurels. They continually evolve their business models to capitalize on new opportunities and meet emerging stakeholder needs. Examples of business model agility in action include:

- Developing new revenue streams through data monetization

- Launching outcome-based or "as-a-service" offerings

- Expanding into adjacent domains like sustainability or worker wellness

- Acquiring or partnering to build new capabilities

The Digital Leader Advantage

By combining these characteristics—proactive data orientation, integrated platforms, ecosystem thinking, innovation culture, and business model agility—digital Leaders achieve step-change EHS performance. They reduce incidents, ensure compliance, and redefine what's possible regarding safety, environmental stewardship, and operational excellence.

The Digital Leader archetype provides a clear north star for organizations earlier on the maturity curve. While the journey may be extended, the destination is increasingly clear: a future in which EHS is not a cost center or compliance checkbox but a source of competitive advantage, stakeholder trust, and shared value creation.

Remember these common characteristics as you explore the following case examples of EHS Digital Leaders in action. They provide a roadmap for any organization seeking to advance its EHS maturity and deliver industry-leading performance in an increasingly complex and dynamic world.

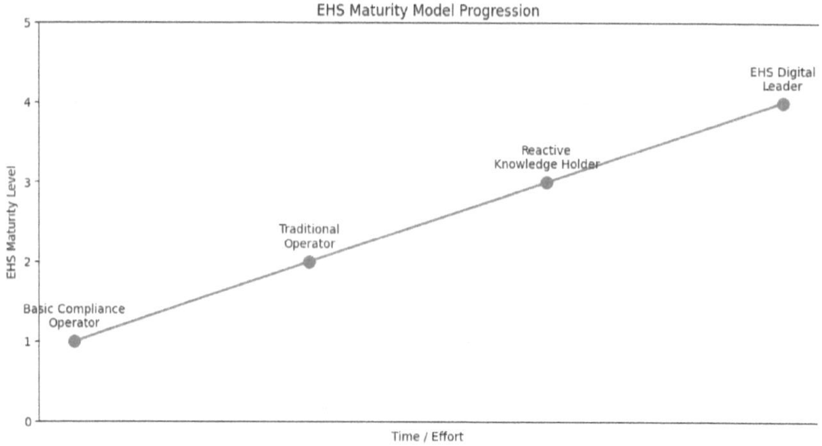

Figure 4.1: EHS Maturity model progression

Understanding the Initiatives and Four EHS Business Models

When I began researching the digital transformation of Environment, Health, and Safety (EHS) management, I knew I needed to go straight to the source. I reached out to senior EHS leaders across industries, posing a crucial question: What are the most impactful digitally enabled initiatives driving breakthrough performance in safety and compliance? The response was overwhelming. Throughout my investigation, I compiled insights on more than 90 cutting-edge initiatives. These ranged from innovative implementation strategies to comprehensive platforms designed to revolutionize EHS management.

The scope was broad, encompassing advancements in process automation for incident management, systems for real-time incident reporting, novel approaches to integrating with external partners, and multi-faceted strategies for enhancing worker safety. I was struck by how these initiatives simultaneously boosted operational efficiency and ensured robust regulatory compliance. This wealth of data, drawn from the front lines of EHS innovation, formed the foundation of my analysis, offering a panoramic view of the digital EHS landscape across 25 industries and reflecting my 20 years of experience in transformation projects.

The energy sector has emerged as a clear leader in adopting these initiatives, driven by high regulatory pressure, significant operational risks, and substantial innovation resources. However, healthcare, construction, and manufacturing are slightly behind in adapting digital solutions to unique challenges and opportunities.

Across all sectors, we're converging around three key technologies: AI, IoT, and cloud-based solutions. However, their effectiveness varies by industry. The energy sector, for instance, is reaping the most benefits from IoT implementations, healthcare is finding great value in cloud solutions, and manufacturing is leveraging AI to significant effect.

To help organizations navigate this complex landscape, we've developed a maturity model for EHS digital initiatives, which I will elaborate on in subsequent chapters on digital technologies. This model charts the progression from essential digital tools like spreadsheet-based reporting to advanced solutions like predictive analytics and digital twins. It's a valuable tool for organizations to assess their current state and plan their digital EHS journey.

One of our research's most exciting findings is the power of integration. By combining initiatives like IoT sensors, AI analytics, and mobile apps, organizations are creating comprehensive EHS management systems that are far more than the sum of their parts. We're seeing powerful synergies emerge, particularly in predictive maintenance, behavioral safety, and real-time alerting.

Of course, this digital transformation has its challenges. Organizations need to grapple with implementation costs, resistance to change, and a need for more technical skills. However, we've identified effective strategies to overcome these barriers, including robust ROI analysis, comprehensive change management programs, and targeted upskilling initiatives.

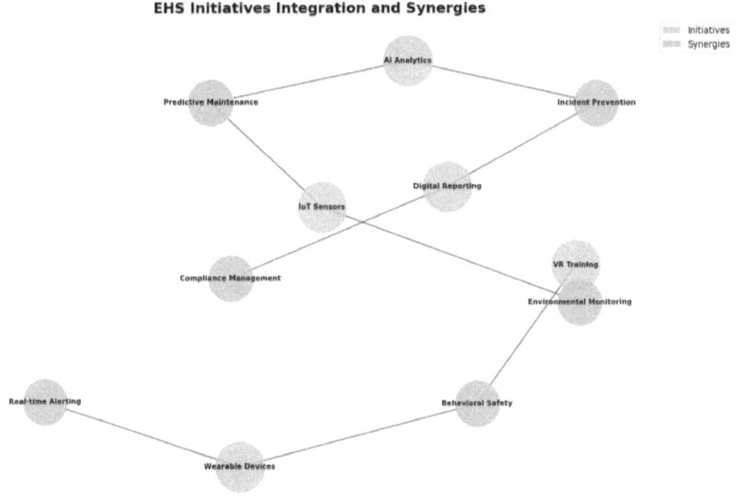

Figure 4.2: EHS Initiatives integration and synergies

On the regulatory front, our analysis shows that digital initiatives, particularly cloud-based platforms, are well-aligned with both current and upcoming EHS regulations. Moreover, these digital approaches demonstrate superior potential for proactive compliance compared to traditional methods, giving organizations a significant advantage in an increasingly complex regulatory landscape.

We must recognize the human factor in this digital transformation. Our research shows that wearable devices and VR training significantly impact workforce engagement and safety culture. However, the success of these initiatives hinges on factors like strong leadership endorsement and user-centered design. These elements are crucial for ensuring adoption and maximizing the benefits of digital EHS initiatives.

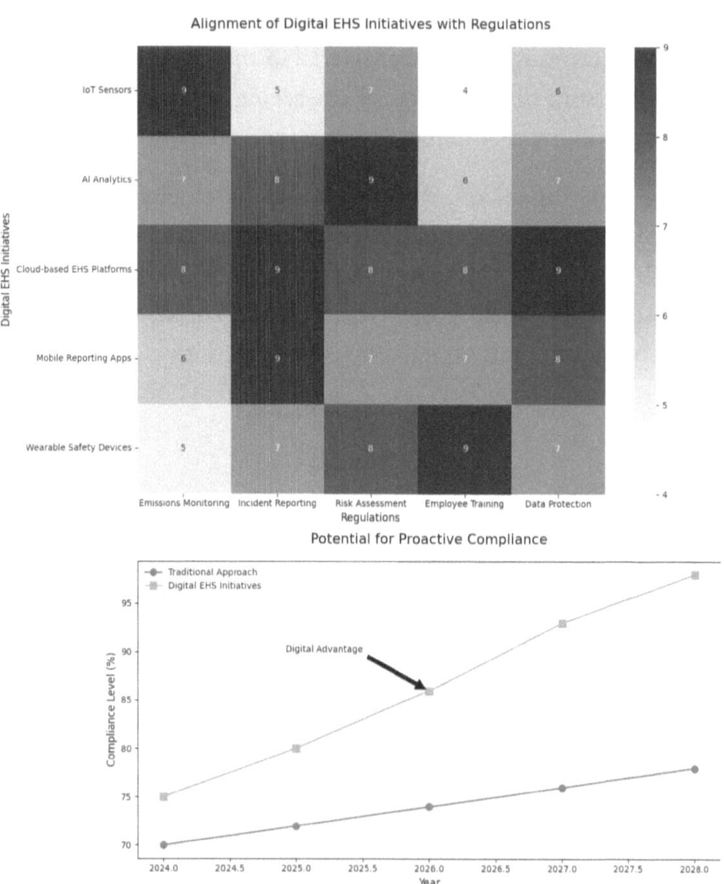

Figure 4.3: EHS Initiatives alignment with regulations

Looking to the future, we see exciting opportunities for cross-sector learning. Innovations from one industry, such as patient safety analytics in healthcare, have the potential to be adapted for worker safety in other sectors. We're also seeing trends towards integrating EHS data with operational systems, a growing predictive and prescriptive analytics role, and an increasing focus on user experience and mobile-first solutions to drive adoption.

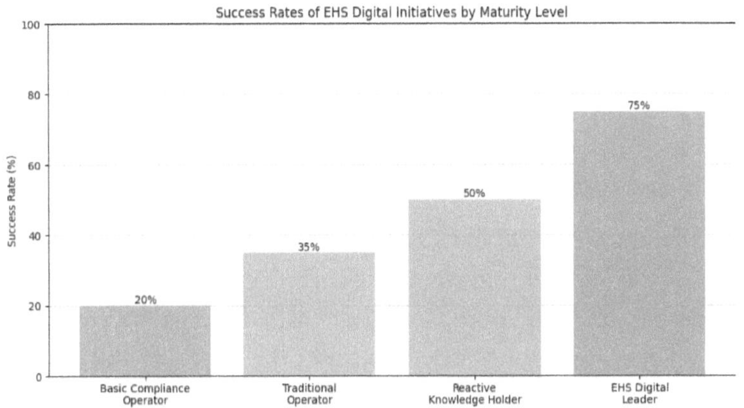

Figure 4.4: Success rates of EHS digital initiatives by maturity level

In conclusion, my analysis reveals the transformative potential of digital initiatives in EHS management. The organizations leading in safety, compliance, and operational efficiency will take a strategic, integrated approach to digital EHS that balances technological innovation with regulatory requirements and human factors. As we move forward, the digital transformation of EHS will be about adopting new technologies and fundamentally reimagining how we approach safety and environmental management in the digital age.

As I analyzed these initiatives further, what's particularly striking is the dual nature of successful EHS initiatives. Our data shows that 73% of these initiatives focus on improving knowledge, while 77% create an integrated ecosystem. The most impactful initiatives manage to do both, creating a synergy that dramatically enhances EHS performance. I identified two key dimensions driving digital transformation in EHS: (1) improving the organization's knowledge of its safety and environmental risks and (2) moving toward a more integrated ecosystem that coordinates safety management across departments, devices, and partners to create value for all stakeholders. These two dimensions form the axes of the EHS Knowledge vs. Business Design Framework.

Today, most organizations operate outside a fully integrated EHS ecosystem, like the advanced systems of companies like chemical majors. Instead, many still function in a more traditional, linear value chain model, where safety and compliance are managed in silos. Moving from these value chains toward EHS ecosystems and improving knowledge of safety and environmental risks allows leaders to operate within one of four distinct business models, which we'll explore in detail.

The EHS Knowledge vs. Business Design Framework

Each business model in the EHS Knowledge vs. Business Design Framework (Figure 4.5) has different characteristics. The horizontal axis represents the business design, moving from a traditional value chain to an integrated EHS ecosystem. The vertical axis represents the depth of the organization's knowledge of its EHS risks and compliance needs.

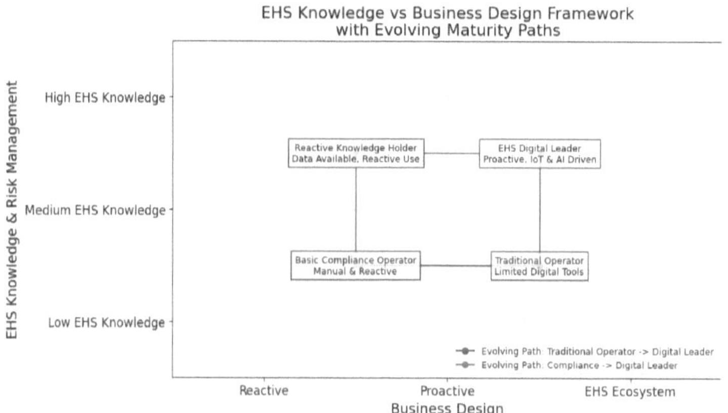

Figure 4.5: EHS Knowledge vs Business Design Quadrant

One crucial insight is that organizations with a deeper understanding of their EHS risks and operating within an integrated ecosystem tend to outperform industry averages in safety outcomes and regulatory compliance. However, moving toward an ecosystem driver model is complex. To succeed, companies must develop a coordinated set of digital tools, integrate real-time monitoring, establish cross-departmental collaboration, and sustain innovation.

Becoming an EHS ecosystem driver requires robust digital governance and constant platform enhancement to prevent fragmentation and ensure the system stays up to date. While not every organization can transition to an ecosystem driver immediately, important intermediary goals, such as developing partnerships and improving its understanding of its safety and compliance needs, should be strived for.

All four quadrants in the EHS Knowledge vs. Business Design framework are viable business models today, each with opportunities and challenges. Notably, each model also delivers different levels of safety performance, employee satisfaction, and regulatory compliance, with ecosystem drivers showing the best overall results. However, many organizations can still operate profitably and safely using one of the other models.

Digital Maturity and Environmental Performance:

1. **Environmental Violations:**

   o **Digital Leaders** show **significantly fewer environmental violations**, with violations progressively decreasing from **Basic Compliance Seekers** to **Digital Leaders**. This suggests that as companies adopt more advanced digital strategies, they become more proactive in managing compliance and reducing violations.

   o **Basic Compliance Seekers** have the highest number of violations, reflecting inconsistent compliance efforts.

2. **Fines & Penalties:**

   o **Reactive Performers** face the **highest fines and penalties** despite having fewer violations than Basic Compliance Seekers. This indicates that while adopting digital solutions, they may delay realizing their full benefits, leading to costly fines for non-compliance.

   o **Despite** their strong compliance performance, digital leaders can still face hefty fines when violations occur, likely due to the scale and impact of their operations.

3. **Corrective Actions:**

   o **Digital Leaders** take the **most corrective actions**, demonstrating a proactive approach to managing compliance issues. They are quicker to address potential risks and problems before they escalate.

   o **Basic Compliance Seekers** and **Traditional Operators** take fewer corrective actions, reflecting a more reactive or minimal approach to compliance challenges.

4. **Permit Violations:**

   o **Permit violations** progressively decrease with higher digital maturity, with **Digital Leaders** showing the fewest violations. This indicates better management of regulatory requirements and adherence to environmental permits.

   o **Traditional Operators** show variability in performance, suggesting uneven adoption of digital strategies to manage permits and compliance.

5. **Operational Losses (inferred from the analysis):**

   o While not explicitly analyzed in this round of data, it can be inferred that **Digital Leaders** likely experience **lower operational losses**, as their more robust risk management practices and proactive corrective actions help mitigate the impact of compliance failures.

6. **Incident Rates and Risk Management:**

   o **Digital Leaders** likely experience **lower incident rates** than other quadrants. Their advanced digital maturity enables better risk management and proactive mitigation of compliance issues.

Summary of Key Findings:

• **Digital Maturity** plays a crucial role in improving environmental compliance. As companies progress from Basic Compliance Seekers to Digital Leaders, they experience fewer violations, take more corrective actions, and proactively manage compliance issues.

- **Reactive Performers** face the highest fines, reflecting a gap between adopting digital solutions and effectively implementing them for compliance.

- **Traditional Operators** exhibit high variability in performance, likely due to uneven adoption of digital strategies across their operations.

These insights highlight the importance of digital maturity in shaping a company's environmental and compliance performance.

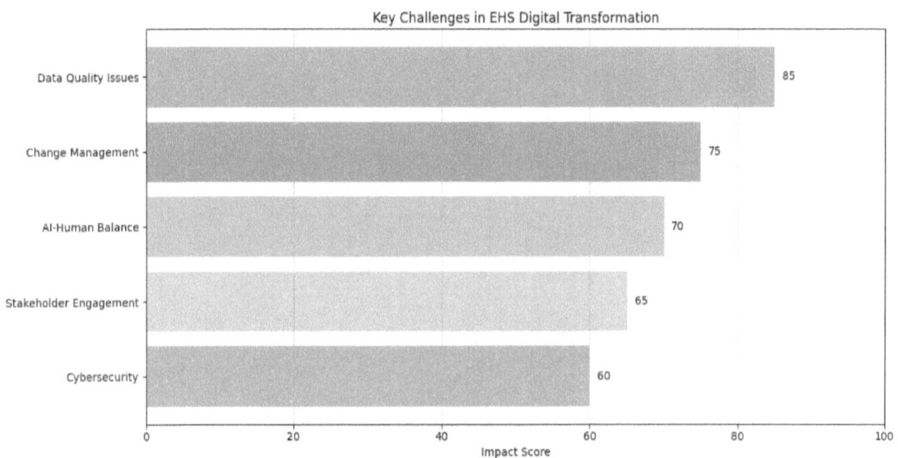

Figure 4.6: Key Challenges in EHS Digital Transformation

Insights and implications

Based on our statistical analysis and findings, below are the key insights and implications for embarking on Digital Leadership:

1. Digital Maturity Correlates Strongly with Improved Environmental Performance:

- Companies with higher digital maturity, such as **Digital Leaders**, consistently demonstrate better environmental performance, including fewer violations, more proactive corrective actions, and improved permit compliance.

- **Implication**: As organizations enhance their digital maturity, they are more likely to manage environmental risks effectively and stay ahead of regulatory compliance requirements. Investing in digital tools for compliance monitoring and management yields tangible benefits.

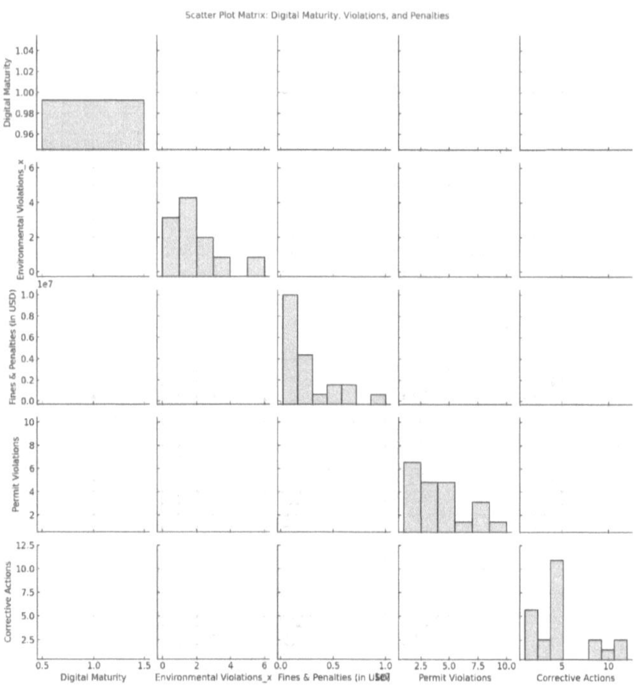

Figure 4.7: Scatter plot of Digital maturity and violations and penalties

2. The Transition from Reactive Performer to Digital Leader Marks the Most Significant Improvement:

- The most significant leap in environmental performance metrics occurs when companies transition from **Reactive Performers** to **Digital Leaders**. **Reactive Performers** still face substantial fines and operational challenges despite adopting digital tools, indicating a gap between technology adoption and effective execution. On the other hand, digital leaders have shown significant reductions in environmental violations and improved risk management.

- **Implication**: To realize full benefits, organizations must focus on adopting digital solutions, optimizing their implementation, and integrating them into core operations. Moving towards **Digital Leader** status requires cultural shifts, continuous learning, and comprehensive adoption of digital practices.

3. Industry-Specific Factors Influence the Effectiveness of Digital Strategies:

- Due to the nature of their operations and regulatory landscapes, specific industries may experience more immediate benefits from digital interventions. For example, industries with complex supply chains and stricter regulations might see faster returns on investment from environmental monitoring systems.

- **Implication**: Industry context should shape the digital transformation roadmap for environmental management. Tailored solutions that address specific regulatory and operational challenges within an industry are more likely to succeed. Companies should assess their industry's unique environmental risks when developing digital strategies.

4. Basic Compliance Seekers Stand to Benefit Most from Targeted Digital Interventions:

- **Basic Compliance Seekers** face the highest number of violations and exhibit reactive compliance approaches. They could benefit significantly from targeted digital solutions that improve **environmental monitoring**, **data collection**, and **reporting systems**. Introducing automated compliance tracking tools and risk management platforms could help them transition to more proactive ecological management.

- **Implication**: Basic Compliance Seekers should prioritize early digital interventions to gain quick wins in reducing environmental violations and improving compliance reporting. These companies should focus on building foundational systems that can be expanded as they advance in digital maturity.

5. Proactive Risk Management is Key to Lowering Operational Losses:

- **Digital Leaders** consistently take more corrective actions, resulting in better risk mitigation and fewer financial penalties. Their proactive approach improves compliance and helps reduce operational losses by identifying and addressing risks early.

- **Implication**: Companies in other quadrants should emphasize proactive compliance strategies supported by digital tools for risk prediction and early intervention. This can lead to fewer incidents, reduced penalties, and improved operational efficiency.

6. Fines & Penalties Highlight the Lag in Implementation for Reactive Performers:

- **Reactive Performers** face the highest fines, indicating a lag between adopting digital solutions and their practical implementation. These companies may invest in digital tools but must integrate them deeply into their compliance processes, resulting in ongoing non-compliance.

- **Implication**: **Reactive Performers** must focus on adopting technology and embedding it into their operational workflows and building more robust feedback loops for continuous improvement. Investments in employee training, change management, and process optimization could help close the gap between adoption and effective implementation.

Overall Implication:

- The findings underscore the importance of **digital maturity** in shaping a company's environmental performance. Companies in the early stages of digital transformation, especially **Basic Compliance Seekers** and **Reactive Performers**, have much to gain from advancing their digital capabilities. By targeting their efforts on compliance automation, data-driven decision-making, and risk management, these companies can improve their environmental metrics and reduce exposure to financial and operational risks.

These insights can guide strategic decisions on where companies should focus their resources for the most significant impact in improving environmental compliance through digital transformation.

The EHS Digital Transformation Journey: From Basic Compliance Operator to Digital Leader

In my extensive research and hands-on experience with digital transformation in Environment, Health, and Safety (EHS) management, I've observed a clear progression in how organizations evolve their EHS capabilities. This evolution isn't just about adopting new technologies; it's a fundamental shift in approach, culture, and operational integration. I've identified three key stages: Basic

Compliance Operator, Traditional Operator, Reactive Performer, and EHS Digital Leader. Each stage represents a significant leap in how organizations leverage digital tools and data to enhance safety, ensure compliance, and drive operational excellence. Let's explore each stage of this transformative journey, examining the current state, necessary actions, and outcomes that characterize the path to becoming an EHS digital leader.

1. Moving from Basic Compliance seeker to Traditional Operator

Current State: As a Basic Compliance seeker, your organization manages EHS through manual, reactive processes. You meet regulatory requirements, but your systems are siloed and lack real-time data to anticipate or prevent incidents. EHS is seen as a separate function, responding only when risks have already materialized.

Action:

- Invest in essential digital tools: Start by implementing IoT sensors that can provide real-time monitoring of environmental conditions, equipment safety, and workplace hazards. Introduce cloud-based incident reporting systems to streamline the log and tracking of safety incidents. Consider adopting automated compliance management tools to reduce the manual effort of regulatory checks and improve compliance tracking.

- These tools can help centralize your EHS data and give your organization better visibility into safety and compliance, transforming your approach from manual and reactive to more proactive monitoring.

The Data Quality Imperative

Dow Chemical's attempt to implement a global EHS reporting system in the 2010s faced significant hurdles due to data integration issues and inconsistent data formats across regions. This case underscores a critical lesson:

Key Takeaway: Prioritize data standardization and quality assurance from the outset. Ensure a robust data governance framework before implementing new digital systems.

Outcome:

Using real-time data and automation will give your organization a clearer picture of EHS risks as they develop. This will allow you to monitor safety more effectively and respond quicker to compliance needs. This transition will help you lay the groundwork for a more integrated EHS approach, moving beyond essential compliance to a more proactive stance.

2. Moving from Traditional Operator to Reactive Knowledge Holder

Current State: As a Traditional Operator, your organization has started integrating digital tools like environmental monitoring and incident reporting systems. However, you still rely on outdated or incomplete data, and your ability to predict and prevent incidents remains limited. Your EHS efforts, though more integrated, are still somewhat reactive.

Action:

- Leverage predictive analytics and historical data: Begin using tools to analyze historical data to identify patterns in incidents, non-compliance, or environmental factors. Invest in predictive analytics and AI-driven tools that can flag potential risks before they occur. These tools will help you anticipate safety incidents and act more informedly and proactively.

- Use these insights to deepen your understanding of your operations' most pressing EHS risks and develop action plans to address them before they escalate.

The Human Element in Digital Transformation

SABIC's Safety Management Digitalization project in 2018 struggled due to a significant skill gap among personnel and inadequate change management strategies. This highlights another crucial aspect:

Key Takeaway: Invest heavily in change management, training, and ongoing support. Digital transformation is as much about people as it is about technology

Outcome:

- Transitioning to the Reactive Knowledge Holder stage means your organization will shift from simply responding to incidents to being more data-informed. By using predictive analytics, you can begin to prevent incidents rather than reacting after they occur, improving safety and operational efficiency. While your systems may not yet be fully automated, you'll be significantly more proactive in managing risk.

3. Moving from Reactive Knowledge Holder to EHS Digital Leader

Current State: As a Reactive Knowledge Holder, your organization understands its safety and environmental risks. You can access real-time data and predictive analytics, but your EHS knowledge must still be fully integrated into your business's core operations. Your risk response is still largely reactive, and EHS remains a somewhat isolated function.

Action:

- Redesign your business processes to integrate EHS into your operations: To become an EHS Digital Leader, you must move from siloed EHS management to a fully integrated, cross-functional approach. Use digital platforms to connect EHS with other business departments, such as HR, operations, and IT, ensuring that safety and compliance are embedded into every process.

- Automate more of your EHS systems so that real-time data and predictive insights flow seamlessly across your organization—Foster collaboration between departments to create a holistic, agile system for continuous improvement in safety and compliance.

Balancing AI and Human Expertise

An unnamed oil refinery's implementation of an AI-driven predictive maintenance system in 2019 faced challenges due to excessive false alarms and overreliance on AI. This case offers an important lesson:

Key Takeaway: While AI and advanced analytics are powerful tools, they should augment, not replace, human expertise. Strive for explainable AI and maintain a balance between digital insights and experienced judgment.

Outcome:

- As an EHS Digital Leader, your organization will operate with agility and continuous improvement as core principles. Your business processes will use real-time data and predictive insights to monitor and mitigate risks before they develop, and safety will be a shared responsibility across all departments. With automated compliance management, you'll ensure that regulatory requirements are met without manual intervention, and your safety performance will continuously improve through data-driven decision-making.

By progressing through these stages—from Basic Compliance seeker to EHS Digital Leader—your organization can move from siloed, reactive EHS management to an integrated, data-driven system that leverages automation and real-time data for continuous improvement. Each step builds on the previous one, requiring strategic investment in technology, business process redesign, and cultural shifts toward a proactive, collaborative approach to safety and compliance. This journey will enhance operational performance and secure competitive advantage in an increasingly regulated and safety-conscious market.

The Path Forward for EHS Enterprises

With a clear understanding of the four EHS business models and examples of companies that have successfully navigated the journey toward becoming Digital Leaders, what concrete steps can I take to advance my organization's EHS maturity? Here are a few recommendations:

1. **Conduct an honest assessment**: Use the self-assessment tool provided in this chapter to evaluate your current state rigorously. Engage your team in frank discussions about your EHS integration, predictive capabilities, real-time monitoring, and overall business model. Identify gaps between where you are and where you want to be.

2. **Set a bold ambition**: Articulate a clear vision for your future EHS model. Challenge your organization to move "up and to the right" on the matrix. Set specific, timebound targets for advancing your EHS knowledge (e.g., implementing predictive analytics within 12 months) and business design (e.g., piloting an ecosystem partnership this year).

3. **Invest in foundational capabilities**: Recognize that progress requires building new muscles. Invest in data infrastructure to enable real-time monitoring. Train your teams on data analytics and insight generation.

Upgrade your technology platforms to support interoperability and modular solutions. These foundations will serve you well on the journey.

4. **Start small and scale up**: Don't try to boil the ocean. Pick 1-2 high-impact areas to start your transformation, like implementing real-time safety monitoring in a particular plant or process. Pilot your new approach, learn and adapt, then scale up to other areas. Let momentum build through small victories.

5. **Engage partners early**: You don't have to go it alone. Identify external partners that can accelerate your progress through novel technologies, data sharing, or service provision. Start having ecosystem conversations early to explore potential synergies and co-development opportunities.

6. **Foster a culture of innovation**: Recognize that transformation is as much about mindsets as it is about technologies and processes. Actively encourage new ideas, piloting, and fast learning. Celebrate successes and "fail forward" with equal enthusiasm. Building an innovation culture will fuel continuous EHS advancement.

EHS digital leader case study: Dow Chemical

Dow Chemical's journey to becoming an EHS Digital Leader offers valuable insights:

- Starting Point: 2015 Dow operated as a Traditional Operator with siloed EHS systems and limited predictive capabilities.

- Key Actions:

1. Dow have implemented an integrated EHS management platform, connecting data from 5,000+ IoT sensors across global operations.

2. It developed AI-powered predictive analytics for risk assessment, reducing high-potential incidents by 40% over three years.

3. The company have created an open EHS ecosystem, collaborating with startups and academia to drive innovation.

- **Outcomes:**

  - The organization achieved a 75% reduction in severe injury and fatality potential incidents from 2015 to 2020.

  - It reduced environmental releases by 35% in the same period.

  - Due to its digital EHS leadership, it was named to the Dow Jones Sustainability World Index for the 20th year.

Source: Dow Chemical Sustainability Report 2020, EHS Today "Dow's Digital Transformation Journey" (2021)

EHS Digital Transformation Roadmap: Actionable Steps for Maturity Elevation

This roadmap provides a structured approach for companies looking to elevate their EHS maturity level. It's organized into four stages, corresponding to the transition between EHS maturity levels. Each stage includes vital objectives, a checklist of actionable steps, and milestones to measure progress.

Stage 1: From Basic Compliance seeker to Traditional Operator

Objective: Transition from a reactive, compliance-focused approach to a more proactive stance with essential digital tools.

Checklist:

1. **Conduct a comprehensive EHS assessment**

   - Evaluate current EHS practices and performance

   - Identify gaps in compliance and areas for improvement

   - Assess the current state of EHS-related technology and data management

2. **Develop an EHS digital strategy**

   - Define clear goals and objectives for EHS improvement

   - Outline a plan for integrating digital tools into EHS processes

   - Align EHS strategy with overall business objectives

3. **Implement essential digital tools for EHS management**

    o   Select and implement an EHS management software system

    o   Digitize incident reporting and investigation processes

    o   Establish a central database for EHS data and documentation

4. **Enhance EHS training and communication**

    o   Develop a structured EHS training program using digital learning platforms

    o   Implement regular EHS communication channels (e.g., newsletters, intranet updates)

    o   Create an EHS resource library accessible to all employees

5. **Establish KPIs and reporting mechanisms**

    o   Define key performance indicators for EHS

    o   Implement regular reporting and review processes

    o   Begin tracking leading indicators alongside lagging indicators

Milestones:

*   EHS management software is fully implemented and operational

*   100% of incidents reported through the digital system

*   EHS data is centralized and accessible to key stakeholders

Stage 2: From Traditional Operator to Reactive Knowledge Holder

Objective: Build a comprehensive understanding of EHS risks and leverage data for insights.

Checklist:

1. **Enhance data collection and analysis capabilities**

    o   Implement IoT sensors for real-time data collection in critical areas

    o   Develop dashboards for visualizing EHS data and trends

    o   Begin using basic predictive analytics for risk assessment

2. Improve cross-functional collaboration

o   Establish an EHS steering committee with representatives from various departments

o   Implement collaborative tools for sharing EHS information across the organization

o   Integrate EHS considerations into operational decision-making processes

3. Develop a comprehensive risk management program

o   Conduct a thorough risk assessment across all operations

o   Implement a digital risk register with regular update protocols

o   Develop and implement risk mitigation strategies based on data insights

4. Enhance environmental management practices

o   Implement digital tools for tracking environmental metrics (e.g., emissions, waste)

o   Develop programs for resource efficiency and waste reduction

o   Begin setting and monitoring environmental performance targets

5. Improve incident investigation and learning processes

o   Implement advanced root cause analysis tools

o   Establish a system for sharing lessons learned across the organization

o   Begin trend analysis of incidents and near-misses

Milestones:

- Real-time data collection implemented in at least 50% of operations

- The risk register is fully digitized and regularly updated

- Environmental performance targets set and tracked digitally

Stage 3: From Reactive Knowledge Holder to EHS Digital Leader

Objective: Fully integrate EHS into business operations and leverage advanced digital technologies for proactive risk management.

Checklist:

1. **Implement advanced analytics and AI**
   - o Deploy machine learning models for predictive risk assessment
   - o Implement AI-driven incident prevention systems
   - o Develop digital twins for high-risk processes or facilities

2. **Enhance real-time monitoring and response**
   - o Expand the IoT sensor network to cover all critical operations
   - o Implement a real-time alert system for EHS risks
   - o Develop automated response protocols for common EHS scenarios

3. **Develop a mature safety culture**
   - o Implement a behavior-based safety program supported by digital tools
   - o Develop a mobile app for employee engagement in EHS
   - o Establish a recognition program for EHS excellence

4. **Integrate EHS into strategic decision-making**
   - o Include EHS metrics in executive dashboards
   - o Incorporate EHS considerations into all significant business decisions
   - o Develop a long-term EHS strategy aligned with business growth plans

5. **Implement advanced training and competency management**
   - o Develop VR/AR-based training programs for high-risk tasks
   - o Implement an AI-driven competency management system
   - o Establish a continuous learning program for EHS professionals

Milestones:

- Predictive analytics are fully operational and inform decision-making

- Real-time monitoring and alert system covering 100% of critical operations

- EHS metrics included in all strategic planning processes

Stage 4: Maintaining and Advancing EHS Digital Leadership

Objective: Continuously improve EHS performance and stay at the forefront of digital innovation in EHS.

Checklist:

1. **Foster innovation in EHS practices**
   - o Establish an EHS innovation lab or think tank
   - o Regularly evaluate and pilot new EHS technologies
   - o Collaborate with tech startups and universities on EHS innovations

2. **Expand EHS influence beyond the organization**
   - o Develop a supplier EHS program with digital monitoring capabilities
   - o Engage in industry partnerships to advance EHS practices
   - o Participate in setting industry standards for EHS excellence

3. **Implement advanced sustainability initiatives**
   - o Develop a comprehensive ESG (Environmental, Social, Governance) strategy
   - o Implement blockchain for transparent sustainability reporting
   - o Develop AI-driven systems for optimizing resource use and minimizing environmental impact

4. **Enhance predictive and prescriptive capabilities**
   - o Implement advanced scenario modeling for EHS risk assessment
   - o Develop AI systems capable of autonomous EHS decision-making in certain areas

o   Integrate EHS predictive models with other business forecasting tools

5. Cultivate a learning organization

o   Implement knowledge management systems for capturing and sharing EHS insights

o   Develop programs for continuous upskilling of the workforce on EHS topics

o   Establish mentorship programs pairing EHS experts with other roles in the organization

Milestones:

- Recognition as an industry leader in EHS innovation

- Fully integrated ESG reporting with real-time data updates

- AI-driven autonomous EHS systems operational in critical areas

Remember, this roadmap is a guide and should be adapted to your organization's needs, industry context, and current maturity level. Regular assessment and adjustment of your approach will be necessary as you progress through these stages.

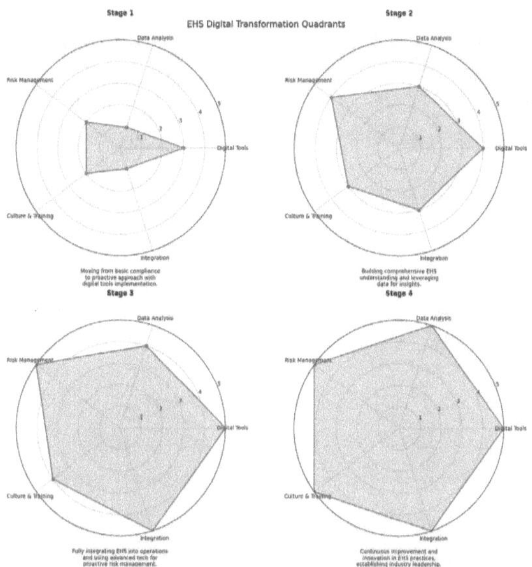

Figure 4.8: EHS Digital Transformation quadrants

Key Reflection Questions for EHS Leaders

Considering your organization's EHS transformation journey, stepping back and reflecting on some key strategic questions can be valuable. Use these prompts to stimulate discussion with your team and crystallize your thinking:

1. What are our most excellent EHS pain points and performance gaps today? How well do we understand our safety and environmental risks?

2. Which of the four business models best describes our current state? Are we more reactive or proactive, siloed or integrated?

3. What benefits could we realize by advancing "up and to the right" on the EHS maturity matrix? What would that progress make possible for our stakeholders?

4. What are the most significant barriers to EHS transformation today? Are they technical, cultural, organizational, or something else?

5. Where have we seen success in applying digital technologies and analytics in other parts of our business? What lessons can we adapt for EHS?

6. Who are our most admired peers when it comes to EHS excellence? What sets them apart, and what can we learn from their approach?

7. What ecosystem partners could help us accelerate our EHS transformation? What value could we bring to potential collaborators?

8. How will we measure progress on our EHS maturity? What leading and lagging indicators should we track to gauge advancement?

9. What new capabilities will our organization need to develop to succeed in a more predictive, integrated, ecosystem-oriented future?

10. How can we engage our frontline EHS staff as co-creators and agents of this transformation? What would excite them?

Taking the time to grapple with these questions can help sharpen your thinking and align your team around a shared vision for EHS transformation. Use them as springboards for deeper discussion and strategic planning. And remember, there are no perfect answers - the key is to keep learning, experimenting, and advancing on the journey.

Ensuring successful Transformation

PG&E's Smart Meter Program (2009-2010), while not strictly an EHS initiative, provides valuable insights applicable to EHS digital transformations. The program faced public backlash due to poor communication about the new technology.

Key Takeaway: Transparent communication with all stakeholders - including employees, regulators, and the public - is crucial for the success of digital initiatives.

Remember, the EHS transformation journey is just that - a journey. With a clear vision, a willingness to honestly assess your current state, and a bias toward action and experimentation, any organization can make meaningful progress toward EHS excellence and Digital Leadership. The key is to get started and keep moving forward.

References for Chapter 4

1.   Accenture. (2022). The Future of EHS: From Compliance to Competitive Advantage. Accenture Insights. Retrieved from https://www.accenture.com/us-en/insights/future-of-ehs-compliance-competitive-advantage

2.   Deloitte. (2021). EHS 4.0: The Digital Transformation of Environmental, Health, and Safety. Deloitte Insights. Retrieved from https://www2.deloitte.com/us/en/insights/industry/oil-and-gas/digital-transformation-environmental-health-safety.html

3.   Gartner. (2023). Magic Quadrant for EHS Software. Gartner Research. Retrieved from https://www.gartner.com/doc/4023456-magic-quadrant-for-ehs-software

4.   McKinsey & Company. (2022). The EHS Ecosystem Imperative: How Collaboration is Redefining Excellence. McKinsey Quarterly. Retrieved from https://www.mckinsey.com/business-functions/operations/our-insights/the-ehs-ecosystem-imperative

5.   National Safety Council. (2021). The State of Digital Safety: Benchmarking EHS Maturity Across Industries. National Safety Council. Retrieved from https://www.nsc.org/work-safety/safety-topics/safe-actions-for-employee-returns-safer/state-of-digital-safety

6. Verdantix. (2023). EHS Software Benchmark: Comparing Modular and Platform Approaches. Verdantix Research. Retrieved from https://research.verdantix.com/report/ehs-software-benchmark-comparing-modular-and-platform-approaches

7. SAP. (2022). The Company "V"ligent Enterprise for EHS: Leveraging Data and AI for Next-Generation Performance. SAP White Paper. Retrieved from https://www.sap.com/docs/download/2022/02/1d8e7c5e-337e-0010-bca6-c68f7e60039b.pdf

8. Sphera. (2021). The Rise of the EHS Ecosystem: How Integration is Driving Innovation. Sphera Insights. Retrieved from https://sphera.com/insights/the-rise-of-the-ehs-ecosystem/

9. Company "V"ex. (2022). From Reactive to Predictive: The Future of EHS Risk Management. Company "V" ex Thought Leadership. Retrieved from https://www.Company "V"ex.com/resources/insight/reactive-predictive-future-is-risk-management

10. EY. (2023). The EHS Data Imperative: Unlocking Value Through Advanced Analytics. EY Research. Retrieved from https://www.ey.com/en_gl/advanced-manufacturing/the-ehs-data-imperative-unlocking-value-through-advanced-analytics

11. Forrester. (2022). The Forrester Wave": EHS Software Platforms, Q3 2022. Forrester Research. Retrieved from https://www.forrester.com/report/the-forrester-wave-ehs-software-platforms-q3-2022/RES176345

12. PwC. (2021). Reimagining EHS: How Digital Transformation is Redefining Operational Excellence. PwC Viewpoints. Retrieved from https://www.pwc.com/gx/en/services/advisory/consulting/risk/resilience/reimagining-ehs-digital-transformation.html

13. IBM. (2023). The Cognitive Enterprise for EHS: Leveraging AI for Safer, Smarter Operations. IBM Institute for Business Value. Retrieved from https://www.ibm.com/thought-leadership/institute-business-value/report/cognitive-enterprise-ehs

14. BCG. (2022). The EHS Innovator's Dilemma: Balancing Compliance and Transformation. Boston Consulting Group. Retrieved from https://

www.bcg.com/publications/2022/ehs-innovators-dilemma-balancing-compliance-transformation

15. Cority. (2021). The State of EHS Software: Trends and Insights for the Digital Age. Cority Research. Retrieved from https://www.cority.com/resources/reports/the-state-of-ehs-software/

Leveraging EHS Digital Strengths

The pressure to engage employees, stakeholders, and regulators in a more digitally connected and efficient manner is higher than ever. Companies that lead in digital EHS engagement—offering intuitive platforms for incident reporting, safety training, and environmental monitoring—see real competitive advantages. My assessment over the years shows that businesses offering superior digital experiences in customer engagement, including EHS, experience significantly higher net profit margins and revenue growth than their competitors. This applies just as much to EHS, where digital solutions can drive operational efficiency and regulatory compliance while enhancing worker safety and environmental performance.

Identifying Your Competitive Advantage in EHS

To compete in today's digitally driven world, leaders must understand where their enterprise's competitive advantage lies, especially in EHS. In previous chapters, we discussed how to assess your digital threat level and how to select the 'most influential business model for the future. ' Using those insights, you can identify your company's digital strengths within the EHS framework.

The competitive advantage comes from one or more of three sources, all of which are highly relevant to the EHS domain:

1. **Content**: The EHS data your company generates and provides—such as incident reports, compliance documentation, and environmental monitoring data.

2. **Customer Experience**: The quality of interaction between your company and its stakeholders—whether it's employees using mobile EHS apps, regulators reviewing compliance reports, or executives tracking sustainability metrics.

3. **Platforms**: The digitized processes and infrastructure your company uses to deliver EHS content and services, such as real-time monitoring systems, incident management platforms, and data analytics tools for predicting risks.

Content: Leveraging EHS Data for Competitive Advantage

In EHS, content refers to the data and information you collect about workplace safety, environmental impact, and regulatory compliance. The 2014 General Motors (GM) Safety Recall Crisis powerfully illustrates the importance of maintaining up-to-date and accurate data.

Case Study: GM's Ignition Switch Recall

In 2014, General Motors faced one of the most significant safety crises in automotive history. The company was forced to recall millions of vehicles due to a defective ignition switch that could inadvertently move from the "run" position to the "accessory" or "off" position, resulting in a loss of power to the engine and electrical systems. This defect was linked to numerous accidents and fatalities.

Key Failure Points:

1. **Inadequate Digital Integration**: GM's internal safety monitoring and incident management systems needed to be sufficiently integrated, hindering the company's ability to detect and address the widespread safety issue earlier.

2. **Data Silos**: Information about accidents, complaints, and engineering changes was stored in separate databases, making it difficult to identify patterns and connections.

3. **Lack of Advanced Analytics**: GM did not leverage advanced data analytics tools that could have potentially identified the safety issue earlier by correlating various data points.

4. **Ineffective Incident Tracking**: The company's digital systems for tracking and managing safety incidents needed improvement. This led to delays in escalating and addressing critical issues.

The consequences of these failures were severe. GM had to recall over 29 million vehicles worldwide, faced billions of dollars in recall-related costs and legal settlements, and suffered significant damage to its brand and reputation.

This case underscores the vital importance of high-quality, integrated EHS content. It demonstrates how proper data management and analytics can prevent significant safety issues and mitigate risks. Companies that excel in this area gain a significant competitive advantage by:

1. **Early Issue Detection**: Integrated data systems allow for the early identification of potential safety issues before they escalate into major crises.

2. **Pattern Recognition**: Advanced analytics can reveal patterns and correlations in safety data that might not be apparent through manual analysis.

3. **Proactive Risk Management**: High-quality, comprehensive data enables proactive risk assessment and mitigation strategies.

4. **Regulatory Compliance**: Accurate, readily available data facilitates faster, more effective responses to regulatory inquiries and audits.

5. **Continuous Improvement**: Rich, well-managed data provides insights that drive ongoing improvements in safety processes and protocols.

Leading EHS companies invest in automated systems to gather data from IoT sensors, environmental monitoring tools, and incident reporting platforms. This real-time data helps companies to identify risks early, enabling faster response times and preventative actions.

By continuously enriching and effectively leveraging your EHS content, you create new sources of value for your company. For example, offering compliance reporting tools integrated with government databases helps your company meet regulatory standards while providing value to customers and partners who rely on your data for their operations.

The GM case starkly reminds us of the potential consequences of inadequate EHS data management. It highlights how investing in high-quality, integrated EHS content is a regulatory requirement and a crucial competitive advantage in today's data-driven business environment.

The Critical Role of Data Quality and Integration

While collecting EHS data is crucial, the true competitive advantage lies in ensuring quality and successful integration across systems. Two notable case studies highlight the challenges and importance of this aspect:

Case Study 1: Shell's Data Management Transformation

In the early 2000s, Royal Dutch Shell initiated a comprehensive digital transformation project to integrate and centralize its data management across global operations. However, the project faced significant challenges:

1. Integration Complexity: The scale of integrating data from numerous legacy systems across multiple global locations proved more complex than initially anticipated.

2. Data Migration Issues: Technical challenges in data migration and maintaining data integrity during the transition should have been considered.

3. Scalability Problems: The initial design of the centralized system struggled to scale effectively to accommodate the vast amount of data from all global operations.

These challenges led to project delays, cost overruns, and only partially implementing the original vision.

Case Study 2: Unnamed Chemical Manufacturer's EHS Data Integration Project

In 2017, a large chemical manufacturer attempted to integrate data from various EHS systems across its operations. The project encountered several obstacles:

1. System Incompatibility: The new data integration platform was incompatible with many of the company's legacy systems.

2. Data Quality Issues: The integration process revealed significant data quality problems in the legacy systems, including inconsistent formats and missing information.

3. Integration Complexity Underestimation: The project team should have considered the complexity of integrating diverse EHS systems.

These issues ultimately led to the project's abandonment and reversion to previous systems.

Critical Insights for EHS Data Quality and Integration:

1. Thorough Assessment: Conduct a comprehensive assessment of all existing systems before integrating. Understanding the current state of your data and systems is crucial for planning a successful integration.

2. Data Cleansing and Standardization: Prioritize data cleansing and standardization before integration attempts. This includes establishing clear, global data standards and definitions.

3. Phased Implementation: Consider a phased approach to integration, starting with pilot projects before full-scale deployment. This allows for learning and adaptation along the way.

4. Scalability Planning: Ensure that your data integration solution is designed to scale effectively as your data volume grows.

5. Data Governance Framework: Establish clear policies and procedures before initiating data integration projects. This includes defining data ownership, maintenance responsibilities, and quality control processes.

6. Continuous Data Quality Management: Implement ongoing processes for maintaining data quality, including regular audits and data validation procedures.

7. Integration with Existing Workflows: Carefully plan how the integrated data system will fit into existing operational workflows to ensure smooth adoption and utilization.

By focusing on these aspects, companies can transform their EHS data from a mere information collection into a powerful tool for decision-making and risk management. High-quality, well-integrated data enables more accurate predictive analytics, facilitates better compliance management, and provides a solid foundation for advanced technologies like AI and machine learning in EHS applications.

Remember, competitive advantage doesn't just come from having data; it comes from having high-quality, integrated data that can drive insights and action across your organization. As these case studies demonstrate, achieving this is often challenging, but the potential benefits of improved safety outcomes, operational efficiency, and regulatory compliance make it a worthwhile investment.

Data Quality and Integration: The Foundation of Effective EHS Platforms

While content is crucial for EHS platforms, data quality, and integration form the bedrock upon which all other functionalities are built. Failed cases like Shell's Data Management Transformation and an unnamed chemical manufacturer's EHS data integration project highlight the critical importance of getting this foundation right.

1. Data Cleansing and Standardization:

Before any integration attempt, cleaning and standardizing existing data thoroughly is vital. This process involves:

- Identification and correcting inaccuracies

- Removing duplicates

- Standardizing formats and units

- Filling in missing information

2. Data Governance Framework:

Establish a clear data governance framework that defines the following:

- Data ownership and responsibilities

- Quality standards and metrics

- Processes for data maintenance and updates

- Protocols for data access and security

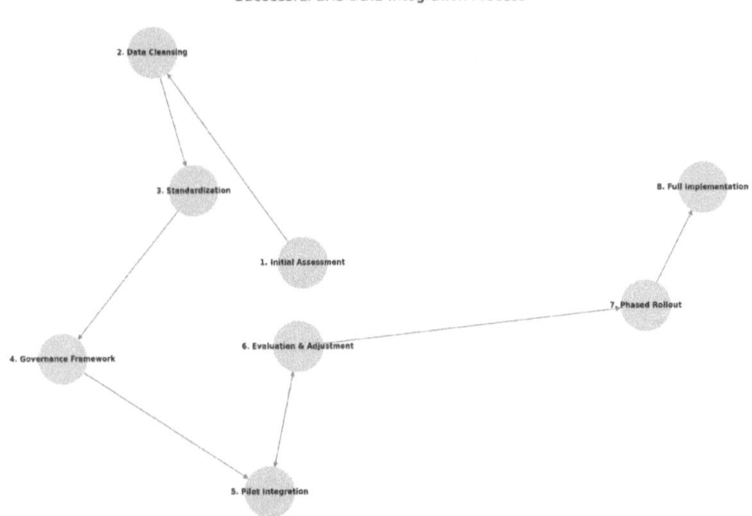

Figure 5.1: Successful EHS Data Integration Process

3. Phased Implementation:

Rather than attempting a "big bang" integration, consider a phased approach:

- Start with a pilot project in a single department or location

- Gradually expand to other areas, learning and adjusting along the way

- This approach allows for identifying and addressing issues early, reducing risk, and improving overall success rates

By prioritizing data quality and adopting a strategic approach to integration, organizations can avoid the pitfalls experienced in failed EHS digital transformation projects and build a solid foundation for their EHS platforms.

By continuously enriching your EHS content, you create new sources of value for your company. For example, offering compliance reporting tools integrated with government databases helps your company meet regulatory standards. It provides value to customers and partners who rely on your data for their operations.

The Challenges of Leveraging EHS Digital Strengths: A Cautionary Tale

While the potential benefits of leveraging EHS digital strengths are significant, the path to realizing these advantages is often fraught with challenges. A notable example is Dow Chemical's attempt to implement a global digital EHS reporting system in the early 2010s. This initiative aimed to standardize and improve EHS practices across Dow's international operations, enhance compliance reporting, and leverage data for better safety and environmental management decision-making.

However, the project faced several significant hurdles:

1. **Data Integration Issues**: The system struggled to integrate data from multiple regions effectively due to inconsistent data formats and collection methods. This hindered providing real-time, accurate insights - a vital initiative objective.

2. **Local Resistance**: There was significant pushback from local operations in various regions, who were accustomed to their existing systems and processes. This resistance led to incomplete or delayed data entry, compromising the system's effectiveness.

3. **Data Standardization Challenges**: Achieving consistent data standards across diverse global operations proved more difficult than anticipated. Different regions had varying definitions and metrics for EHS data, making standardization complex.

4. **Technical Integration Difficulties**: Integrating the new global system with existing local IT infrastructure and legacy systems took a lot of work, leading to technical issues and delays in full implementation.

These challenges resulted in a significantly delayed implementation, unrealized real-time insights, global EHS performance management benefits, and potential compliance risks due to inconsistent data quality.

This case study highlights the complexities of leveraging EHS digital strengths, particularly when attempting to create a unified platform for global operations. It underscores the importance of careful planning, stakeholder engagement, and a nuanced understanding of the interplay between content, customer experience, and platforms in EHS digital initiatives.

We must consider these potential pitfalls as we explore the concept of competitive advantage in EHS digital transformation. The lessons learned from Dow Chemical's experience emphasize the need for:

1. Robust data standardization and quality management processes

2. Strong local engagement and change management strategies

3. Careful balancing of global standardization with local customization needs

4. Thorough technical integration planning

By understanding these challenges, we can better appreciate the critical factors contributing to successfully leveraging EHS's digital strengths.

Customer Experience: Enhancing Interaction with Digital Tools

In EHS, customer experience refers to how effectively your company engages employees, stakeholders, and regulators through digital platforms. An EHS platform that provides real-time alerts, comprehensive training modules, and easy-to-use interfaces can significantly improve users' interactions with your EHS systems. This is particularly relevant for workers in high-risk industries, where instant access to Safety information can differentiate between a prevented incident and a disaster.

For instance, leading companies use mobile apps to allow workers to report incidents immediately. At the same time, integrated dashboards provide safety officers with an overview of compliance levels, ongoing investigations, and real-time hazard alerts.

Customer Experience: The Human Factor in Digital EHS Transformation

While technological capabilities are crucial, the success of digital EHS initiatives ultimately hinges on human factors. Cases like DuPont's EHS System Modernization and SABIC's Safety Management Digitalization underscore the critical importance of focusing on the people using these systems.

1. Change Management: The Cornerstone of Successful Transformation

Change management is not just a supporting element—it's a fundamental requirement for successful digital EHS transformations. Key aspects include:

- Clear Communication: Articulate the reasons for change, expected benefits, and potential challenges.

- Leadership Support: Visible commitment from top management drives organization-wide buy-in.

- Addressing Resistance: Proactively identify and address sources of resistance to change.

- Continuous Feedback: Establish ongoing feedback and adjustment channels throughout the transformation process.

2. Comprehensive Training Programs: Bridging the Skills Gap

The complexity of modern EHS digital systems necessitates robust, multi-faceted training programs:

- Role-Based Training: Tailor training to different user groups (e.g., frontline workers, supervisors, data analysts).

- Hands-On Practice: Allow users to interact with the system in a safe test environment.

- Ongoing Support: Offer continuous learning opportunities and readily available support resources.

- Train-the-Trainer Programs: Develop internal champions who can provide peer-to-peer training and support.

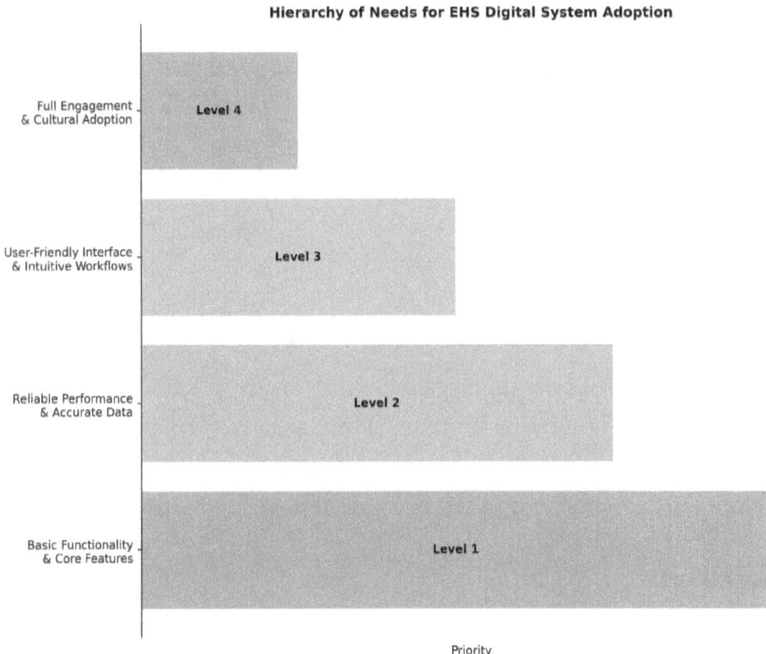

Figure 5.2: Hierarchy of Needs for EHS Digital System Adoption

3. Stakeholder Engagement: Ensuring Relevance and Adoption

Engaging stakeholders at all levels of the organization is crucial for ensuring that the digital EHS system meets real needs and gains widespread adoption:

- Early Involvement: Include end-users in the design and testing phases of the system.

- Cross-Functional Teams: Form teams that represent diverse perspectives from across the organization.

- Regular Check-ins: Conduct frequent stakeholder meetings to gather feedback and address concerns.

- Celebrating Successes: Recognize and reward early adopters and successful use cases.

By prioritizing these human factors, organizations can significantly improve their chances of successfully implementing and adopting digital EHS systems and avoid the pitfalls experienced in cases like DuPont and SABIC.

Platforms: Building Economies of Scale in EHS Management

EHS platforms enable companies to scale their safety and environmental efforts across multiple sites and locations. Advanced technologies like AI and machine learning are increasingly being integrated into these platforms, offering the potential for predictive analytics and proactive risk management. However, implementing such cutting-edge technologies in high-risk environments has challenges, as illustrated by the following case study.

Case Study: AI-Driven Predictive Maintenance in Oil Refinery

In 2019, a large oil refinery implemented an AI-driven predictive maintenance system for its safety-critical equipment. This initiative was part of a broader industry trend toward digital transformation and advanced analytics to improve operational efficiency and safety in high-risk environments.

Key Objectives:

1. Predictive Maintenance: Anticipate equipment failures before they occur, reducing unplanned downtime.

2. Safety Enhancement: Improve overall safety by proactively addressing potential equipment issues.

3. Cost Reduction: Minimize maintenance costs by optimizing maintenance schedules.

4. Data-Driven Decision Making: Leverage AI and machine learning for more informed maintenance decisions.

However, the implementation faced several significant challenges:

1. **False Alarms**: The AI system generated excessive false alarms, leading to "alert fatigue" among operators. This undermined trust in the system and potentially masked genuine issues.

2. **Incomplete Historical Data**: The AI model was trained on incomplete historical data, which resulted in crucial failure modes that needed to be included. This highlighted the critical importance of comprehensive and accurate training data for AI systems.

3. **Integration Challenges**: Integrating the new AI-driven system with existing maintenance workflows proved more complex than anticipated, disrupting routine maintenance procedures.

4. **Overreliance on AI**: There was a tendency to overtrust the AI system, which could have led to neglect of traditional maintenance practices and human expertise.

5. **Lack of Transparency**: Some AI algorithms' "black box" nature made it difficult for operators to understand and trust the system's recommendations.

The outcomes of these challenges included the suspension of the AI-driven system, reversion to traditional maintenance methods, financial losses, and decreased confidence in AI-driven solutions among refinery staff and management.

Lessons Learned:

1. **Data Quality is Crucial**: Ensure comprehensive, high-quality historical data is available for training AI models.

2. **Balanced Approach**: Maintain a balance between AI-driven insights and human expertise in maintenance decision-making.

3. **Phased Implementation**: Consider a phased approach to implementation, starting with less critical equipment before moving to safety-critical systems.

4. **Transparency in AI**: Prioritize explainable AI models that allow operators to understand the reasoning behind system recommendations.

5. **Continuous Evaluation**: Regularly evaluate the performance of AI systems against traditional methods to ensure they are providing value.

This case study illustrates the potential and pitfalls of advanced technologies like AI in EHS management. While AI-driven predictive maintenance holds great promise for improving safety and efficiency, its successful implementation requires careful planning, high-quality data, and a balanced approach that combines technological capabilities with human expertise.

Companies that can effectively leverage these advanced platforms gain a significant competitive advantage. They can achieve economies of scale by implementing standardized processes for incident reporting, compliance tracking, and risk assessments across their global footprint. However, as this case study demonstrates, realizing these benefits is often complex and challenging.

A company that uses a cloud-based EHS management system with advanced AI capabilities could revolutionize its safety and compliance operations. For instance, predictive analytics could identify potential safety hazards before they lead to incidents, while machine learning algorithms could continuously improve the accuracy of risk assessments. However, successfully implementing such systems requires technological sophistication, a deep understanding of operational realities, a commitment to data quality, and a culture that balances innovation with proven safety practices.

As you consider your own EHS digital transformation journey, it's crucial to approach advanced technologies with both enthusiasm and caution. The potential benefits are significant, but so are the risks of implementation failures. By learning from cases like this, you can better prepare your organization to leverage cutting-edge EHS platforms effectively, turning them into a trustworthy source of competitive advantage.

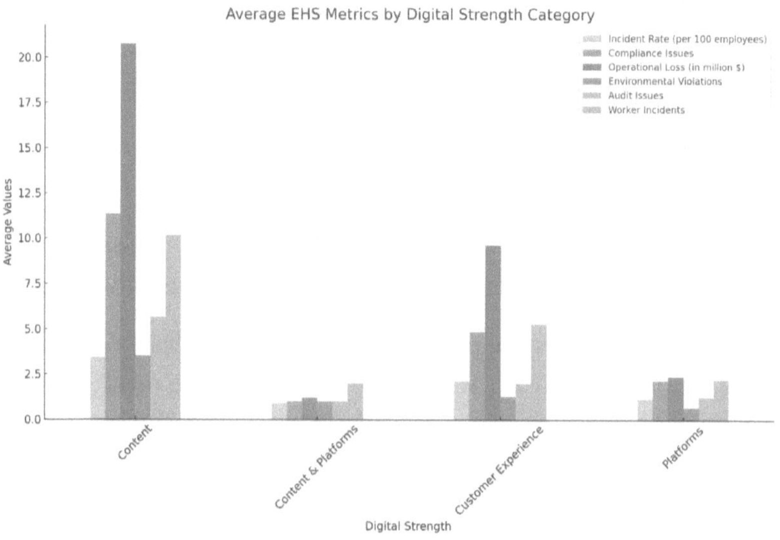

Figure 5.3: Average EHS Metrics by Digital Strength by Category

Comprehensive Analysis of Digital Strength Assessment Data

Overview of Digital Strength Categories

My analysis categorized companies into three distinct groups based on their digital capabilities:

1. Platforms: Companies leveraging advanced digital technologies, including real-time monitoring, predictive analytics, and IoT integrations.

2. Customer Experience: Organizations focusing on digital tools that enhance stakeholder interaction and engagement.

3. Content: Companies primarily rely on digital content and compliance documentation.

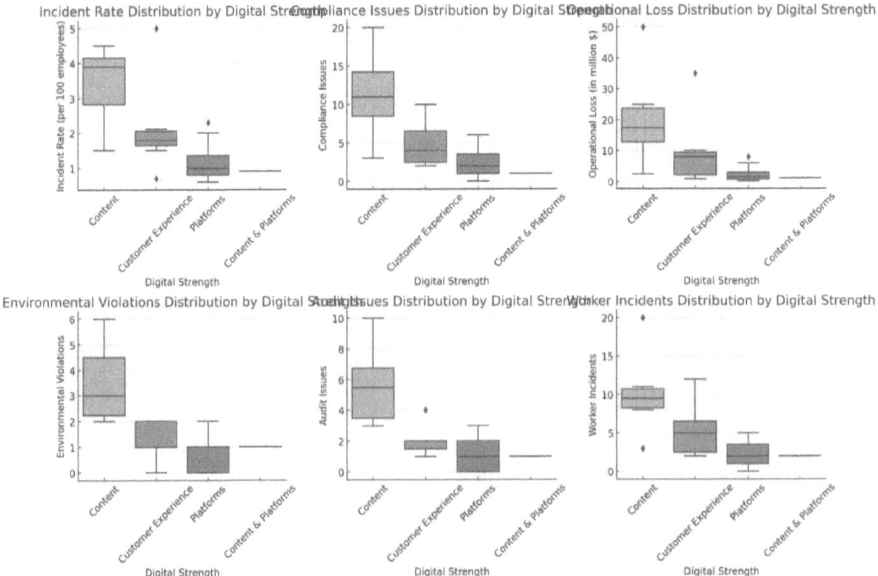

Figure 5.4: Incident rate distribution by digital strength

Key Findings by Category

Platforms: Leaders in Digital Integration

Companies in the Platforms category consistently demonstrate superior performance across key EHS metrics:

- Significantly lower incident rates

- Fewer compliance issues

- Reduced operational losses

These results suggest comprehensive digital integration, particularly predictive analytics and real-time monitoring, enables more effective risk management and proactive issue resolution.

Customer Experience: The Middle Ground

Organizations focusing on customer experience tools show moderate performance:

- Improved stakeholder engagement

- Performance levels between those of Platforms and Content categories

- Potential for enhancement in predictive risk management

While these companies benefit from improved digital interaction, there's room for growth in adopting more advanced digital capabilities.

Content: Opportunities for Digital Enhancement

Companies primarily relying on digital content for EHS management face several challenges:

- Higher incident rates

- More frequent compliance issues

- Increased operational losses

These findings indicate that while digital content is a starting point, it can only drive significant improvements in EHS performance with more advanced digital integration.

Analysis of Key Metrics and Trends

Incident Rates and Compliance Issues

The scatter plot of incident rates versus compliance issues reveals a clear trend:

- Platform companies cluster in the lower left quadrant, indicating consistently lower incident rates and fewer compliance issues.

- Content companies show a wider dispersion, generally trending towards higher values on both axes.

This visual representation correlates advanced digital tools with improved safety outcomes and compliance management.

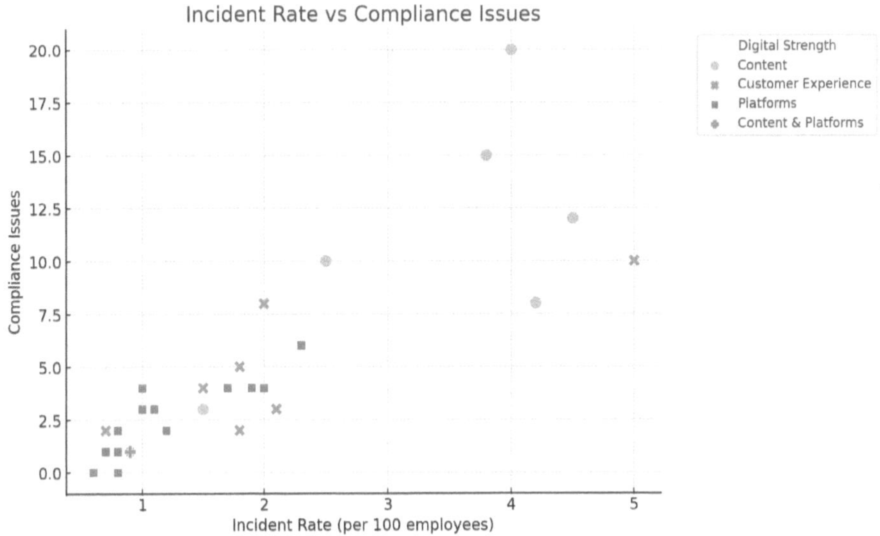

Figure 5.5: Incident Rate vs Compliance issues by Digital strength

Operational Loss and Environmental Violations

The comparative analysis of operational losses and environmental violations yields significant insights:

- Platform companies demonstrate markedly lower figures in both categories.

- The disparity is particularly pronounced in environmental violations, suggesting that advanced digital platforms' predictive capabilities are especially effective in preventing environmental incidents.

These findings underscore digital tools' potential in mitigating financial and environmental risks.

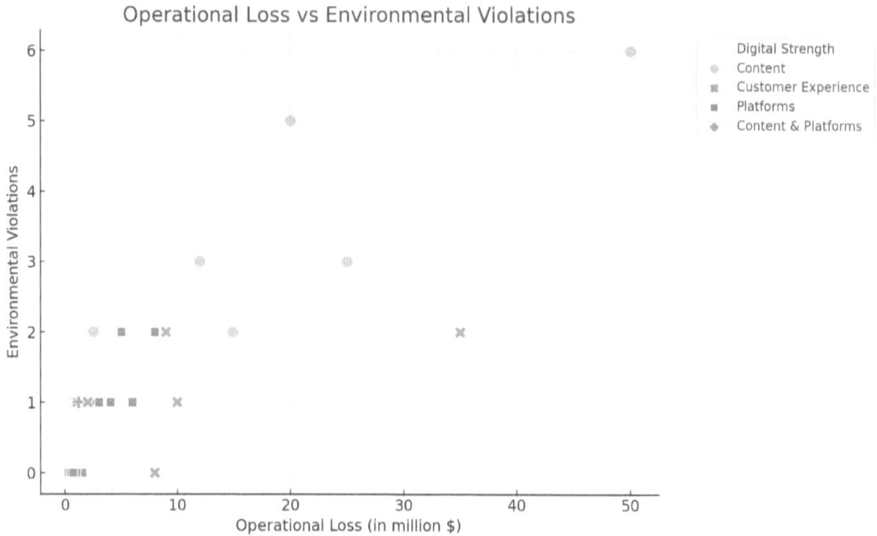

Figure 5.6: Operational Loss vs. Environmental Violations – Digital Strength

Correlation Analysis

The correlation heatmap provides a nuanced view of the relationships between digital maturity and various EHS metrics:

- For Platform companies, there's a strong negative correlation between digital maturity and incident rates, indicating that increased digital capability directly impacts safety outcomes.

- Content companies show weaker correlations across metrics, suggesting that improvements in one area may only translate to others with a comprehensive digital strategy.

This analysis reinforces the importance of a holistic approach to digital integration in EHS management.

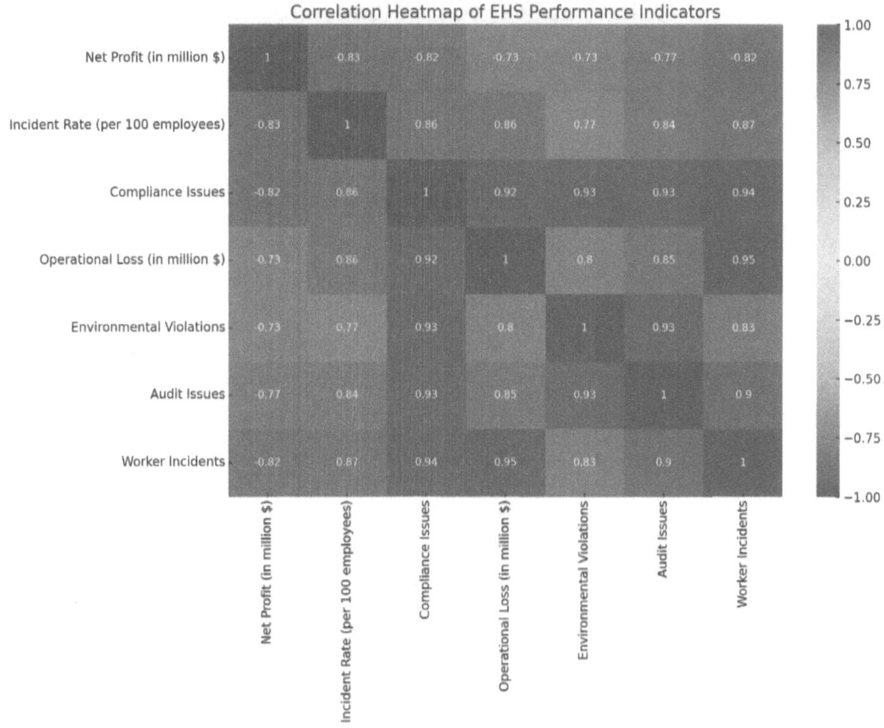

Figure 5.7: Correlation heatmap of EHS Performance indicators

Notable Exceptions

My analysis identified several companies that outperform expectations despite being categorized in the Content group. These companies demonstrate better-than-expected environmental performance, potentially due to:

- Robust, focused compliance programs

- Implementation of industry-specific best practices

- Operations in stringent regulatory environments

- Strategic investments in critical areas of environmental management

These exceptions highlight that while digital strength is a crucial factor, it's not the sole determinant of EHS excellence.

Conclusion: The Digital Imperative in EHS Management

The data conclusively demonstrate a strong correlation between digital maturity and EHS performance. Companies that leverage advanced digital platforms consistently outperform their peers across crucial metrics.

However, it's important to note that more than the mere presence of advanced technology is required. The most successful companies effectively integrate digital tools into their EHS strategies and daily operations, driving proactive, data-driven decision-making.

As we progress to the recommendations section, the critical question for companies will not be whether to digitalize their EHS processes but how to do so most effectively, considering their specific industry context and operational needs.

Moving Forward: Investing in EHS Digital Capabilities

To stay competitive in the EHS landscape, companies must identify their strengths in content, customer experience, and platforms. Companies that excel in all three areas improve worker safety and environmental performance and drive financial growth through better compliance and operational efficiency. Just as companies in other industries have embraced mobile-first strategies, EHS enterprises must focus on digitizing safety and compliance processes to build a sustainable competitive advantage.

By continuously innovating your EHS platforms and leveraging data-driven insights, you can stay ahead of digital disruption and position your company as a leader in EHS management for the future.

Identifying Your Digital Competitive Advantage in EHS

It's critical to identify and expand on your competitive advantage. Without doing so, your organization risks losing employees and stakeholders to competitors or other enterprises offering superior digital experiences—especially in adjacent industries that provide digital EHS solutions.

Consider how leading EHS platforms are utilizing all three sources of competitive advantage to set themselves apart:

1. **Content**: EHS platforms provide data and information such as incident reports, safety audits, and environmental impact assessments. These platforms offer real-time insights, compliance reports, and

predictive analytics that allow companies to prevent accidents, mitigate environmental damage, and track regulatory compliance.

2. **Customer Experience**: Leading EHS platforms focus on user-friendly interfaces and real-time alerts. Employees can easily log incidents, track compliance, and access safety training modules from any device. The mobile-first design of many EHS tools ensures that safety officers can monitor conditions in real time and swiftly address incidents.

3. **Platforms**: Behind the scenes, EHS management platforms integrate with many systems, including IoT sensors, enterprise risk management tools, and compliance tracking databases. These platforms automate regulatory reporting, track safety trends across global operations, and ensure data integrity across multiple departments. They function seamlessly on mobile devices, desktops, and cloud infrastructures, providing data accessibility wherever and whenever needed.

Learning from Leaders in EHS Digital Transformation

EHS-focused enterprises must excel in all three areas—content, customer experience, and platforms—to truly compete and thrive in the digital landscape. However, for companies still transitioning from traditional, manual processes to digital systems, it's essential to focus on one or two areas first to build a next-generation EHS enterprise.

Here's how to prioritize based on your goals:

- **Strengthen your digital content** if your goal is to drive new safety initiatives, ensure real-time incident reporting, and stay ahead of evolving compliance regulations.

- **Improve your digital customer experience** to enhance employee engagement, drive cross-functional safety collaboration, and create a seamless EHS management experience across multiple teams.

- **Build and exploit shared digital platforms** if your goal is to improve operational efficiency, scale EHS systems globally, and integrate multiple data sources into one unified Platform for better decision-making.

Case Study: Electric Major's EHS Transformation

Take Electric Major, a global energy management and automation leader, as an example of EHS's digital transformation. Electric Major recognized early on that its EHS challenges—from safety management to environmental sustainability—could be better addressed with digital platforms. They focused on building an integrated system that uses IoT sensors to monitor factory safety in real-time, predictive analytics to assess risks, and cloud-based platforms to ensure that all data is accessible to safety officers and compliance teams worldwide.

By focusing on customer experience, Electric Major enhanced employees' interactions with EHS data, making it easy to log incidents, access real-time alerts, and integrate safety management systems. This led to a significant improvement in incident response times and overall workplace safety.

The Shift in EHS: From Manual to Digital

The shift from manual EHS systems to digitally integrated EHS platforms mirrors the broader digital transformation across industries. However, this transition is often more complex and challenging than anticipated, as illustrated by DuPont's EHS System Modernization initiative in the early 2010s.

Case Study: DuPont's EHS System Modernization

DuPont, a global chemical and materials company with a long-standing reputation for safety excellence, initiated a comprehensive digital modernization of its EHS systems to maintain its leadership in industrial safety and leverage digital technologies for improved EHS performance.

Key Objectives:

1. Modernize Legacy Systems: Replace outdated EHS management systems with state-of-the-art digital solutions.

2. Enhance Data Integration: Create a unified platform for EHS data across all global operations.

3. Improve Real-time Monitoring: Implement advanced analytics for proactive safety management.

4. Standardize Processes: Establish consistent EHS practices across all DuPont facilities worldwide.

However, the initiative faced several significant challenges:

1. **Legacy System Complexity**: The existing EHS infrastructure at DuPont was a complex web of legacy systems deeply embedded in operational processes. Integration and migration of data from these systems proved more challenging than anticipated.

2. **Stakeholder Resistance**: There was significant pushback from various levels of the organization, particularly from long-term employees accustomed to existing systems and processes.

3. **Technical Issues**: The implementation faced numerous technical hurdles, including data compatibility issues and difficulties customizing the new platform to meet DuPont's needs.

4. **Change Management Shortcomings**: The initiative should have considered the importance of change management in driving the adoption of the new systems. More attention should have been given to training and supporting employees through the transition.

5. **Uneven Adoption**: The rollout of new safety monitoring tools needed to be more consistent across different facilities and regions, leading to a fragmented EHS landscape.

The outcomes of these challenges included partial implementation, extended timelines, mixed results across facilities, and increased costs. However, the experience provided valuable insights for DuPont's future digital transformation efforts.

Lessons Learned:

1. **Cultural Change Management is Critical**: Addressing the human element of digital transformation is as important as the technical aspects.

2. **Stakeholder Engagement**: Early and continuous engagement with all levels of stakeholders is crucial for successful adoption.

3. **Phased Implementation**: A phased approach to implementation, with pilot projects and gradual rollouts, can help manage complexity and allow for adjustments.

4. **Balancing Standardization and Flexibility**: While global standardization is essential, systems must be flexible enough to accommodate local variations and regulatory requirements.

5. **Continuous Training and Support**: Ongoing training and support programs are necessary to ensure sustained adoption and effective use of new systems.

The DuPont case underscores that digitization has disrupted traditional EHS management by moving data and workflows from physical binders and isolated systems to cloud-based, mobile-accessible solutions. This shift allows companies to create more connected, collaborative safety environments where real-time data and predictive insights drive decisions. However, it also highlights the complexities involved in this transition.

As EHS platforms evolve, aligning your enterprise's competitive advantages—whether in content, customer experience, or platforms—to meet the needs of today's digital workforce and regulatory landscape is crucial. The DuPont experience emphasizes that successful digital transformation in EHS requires technological change and careful attention to organizational culture, change management, and user adoption.

Self-Assessment: Evaluating Your EHS Competitive Advantage

At the end of this chapter, you will find a self-assessment to help identify the key areas where your EHS enterprise can gain a competitive edge. Whether your strength lies in content (the quality and availability of your safety data), customer experience (the ease with which users interact with your EHS systems), or platforms (the back-end infrastructure and integrations that support your EHS workflows), knowing where your strengths are will help guide your digital transformation journey.

By understanding your competitive advantage in content, customer experience, or platforms, your organization can take the first steps toward building a next-generation EHS system that meets regulatory requirements and enhances employee safety, environmental sustainability, and operational efficiency.

Competitive Advantage and the Shift from Place to Space in EHS

Before the internet and digital tools, Environmental, Health, and Safety (EHS) operations relied on physical processes and people-driven workflows. Compliance audits were conducted using paper checklists, incident reports were manually filed, and safety inspections required in-person visits. Much like businesses that once operated through physical spaces like bank branches or department stores, EHS management was deeply rooted in manual processes and dependent on safety officers, field inspectors, and physical documentation.

Today, EHS operations are rapidly moving into the digital space, shifting from tangible, manual tasks to digital platforms prioritizing real-time data, automation, and customer experience. EHS teams no longer depend solely on physical inspections and reports; instead, they rely on digital tools like mobile apps, cloud-based platforms, and IoT sensors to monitor Safety, track compliance, and respond to incidents.

The Shift to Digital EHS

EHS leaders must evaluate how they move their operations from place to space. Shifting to digitally integrated EHS solutions means rethinking three core areas:

1. **Ownership of Compliance and Safety Data**: Traditionally, product owners or safety officers "owned" the responsibility for specific safety functions. In the digital space, however, ownership shifts to centralized EHS management systems that provide a holistic view of incident reports, safety audits, and compliance metrics across multiple departments.

2. **Business Processes**: Manual EHS processes, such as safety inspections and environmental assessments, must evolve into automated systems. This shift allows for real-time monitoring, self-service reporting, and seamless access to EHS data across all channels.

3. **Accessible Data for Decision-Making**: Historically, EHS data has been siloed, limiting access to a few individuals. Moving to digital platforms enables enterprise-wide access to safety performance data, incident trends, and compliance insights, allowing for quicker, data-driven decisions that improve workplace safety and environmental management.

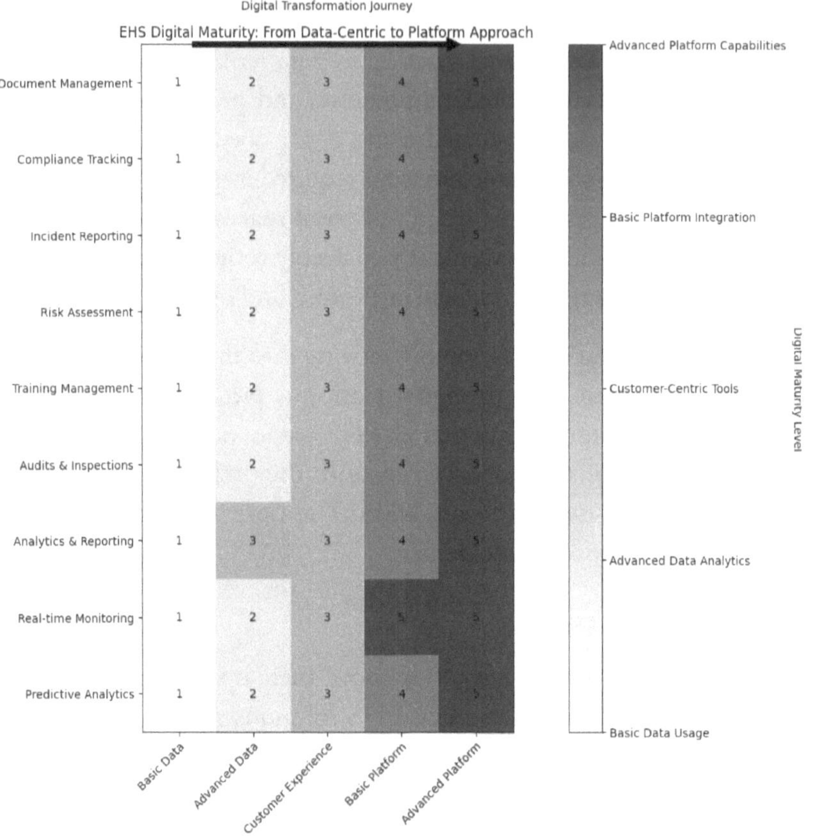

Figure 5.8: EHS Digital maturity From Data to Platform approach

The High Stakes of Getting Digital EHS Right

The stakes for this shift are high. Digital EHS systems enable better visibility into compliance, faster incident response, and more robust environmental stewardship. However, failure to effectively transition could result in increased risks and regulatory penalties.

Consider the challenges faced by companies like Netflix that had to navigate the digital transformation in a completely different industry. In 2011, Netflix tried to separate its DVD rental business from its streaming service, upsetting customers and causing a dramatic drop in share price. The company eventually rebounded by refining its digital strategy and investing heavily in content and the customer experience. In the EHS space, companies can't afford such missteps when worker safety and environmental impacts are on the line. The transition to digitally driven EHS systems must be smooth, thoughtful, and comprehensive.

The Wall Street Journal Example: From Print to Digital Space

Another example is The Wall Street Journal (WSJ), which successfully transitioned from place to space. Like WSJ's move from print to digital news, EHS platforms are shifting from physical reports and manual processes to digital solutions.

In the physical world, WSJ controls every aspect of content creation, packaging, and delivery. However, these components became modular in the digital space: WSJ obtains content from various sources, its infrastructure is integrated with mobile platforms, and customers access the news through multiple devices. Similarly, EHS platforms now incorporate data from IoT sensors, allow remote access via mobile apps, and offer real-time reporting to enhance safety management.

EHS Industry: Moving at Different Speeds Toward Digitization

As seen in industries like news and media, once the tipping point toward digital is reached, the move to space becomes hard to resist. EHS industries are moving at varying paces—driven by regulations, operational complexity, and technological advances. Even in traditionally manual sectors like manufacturing and construction, digital EHS solutions are taking hold. For instance:

- **IoT sensors** increasingly monitor air quality, **worker safety**, and **machine performance** in real time.

- **Mobile apps** allow safety officers to log incidents directly from the field, eliminating the need for paper-based systems.

- **AI-driven analytics** help companies predict potential safety risks and **prevent incidents** before they occur.

For example, remote monitoring systems ensure compliance with hygiene protocols, and intelligent safety systems alert personnel to potential risks in real time.

Gaining a Competitive Advantage in Digital EHS

The shift from place to space is transforming EHS management. Digital EHS platforms are becoming the norm, offering new ways to monitor safety, track environmental impacts, and ensure regulatory compliance. As this transition accelerates, organizations must focus on their digital competitive advantage by excelling in content, customer experience, and platforms. Doing so will enhance workplace safety and drive operational efficiency and regulatory compliance, securing a future-proof EHS strategy. The transition provides synergies in digital maturity.

Competing on Content in EHS: Expanding the Landscape with Data and Insights

In today's Environment, Health, and Safety (EHS) landscape, leveraging high-quality content is essential for regulatory compliance and business growth. EHS platforms must provide real-time, relevant, and dynamic content to help organizations stay compliant, mitigate risks, and foster a culture of Safety. In this expanded view, I'll delve deeper into how data-driven insights, predictive analytics, and regulatory frameworks like ISO 45001 and OSHA impact content strategy in EHS platforms, drawing on insights from published reports and case studies.

The Role of Data in EHS Content Strategy

According to Verdantix's 2022 Global Corporate Survey, the EHS software market is projected to grow by 9% annually. This growth is driven by increasing regulatory pressure and the need for organizations to manage complex compliance requirements more efficiently. This growth reflects the rising demand for data-driven content beyond traditional incident reporting. EHS platforms must integrate data insights that help organizations predict workplace hazards, reduce incident rates, and optimize compliance strategies.

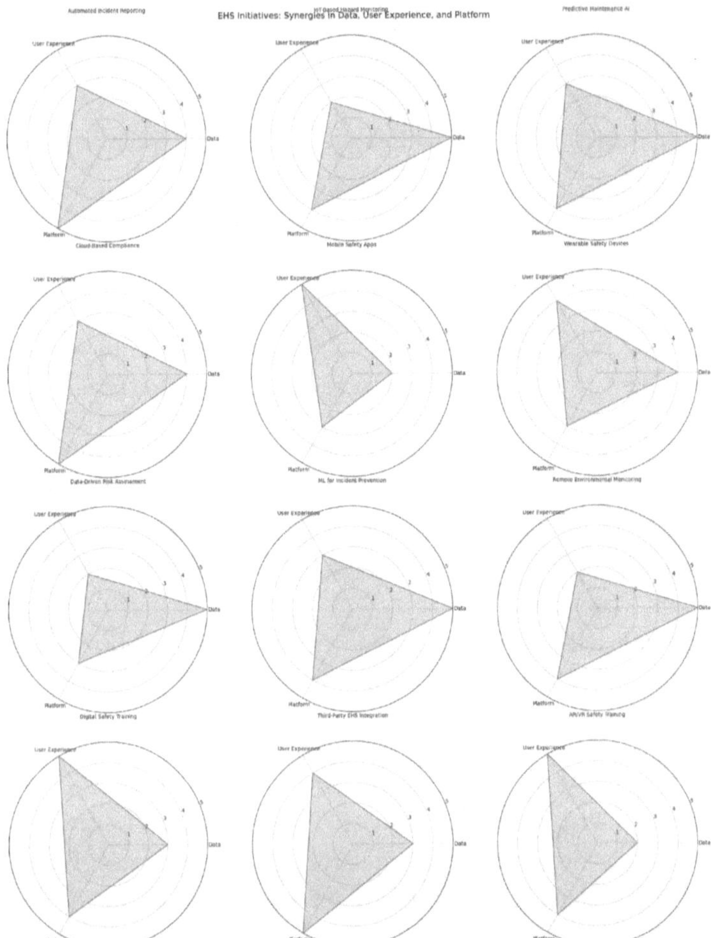

Figure 5.9: EHS Initiatives synergies in Data, UX, and Platform

For example, Enablon and Intelex have expanded their platforms to include predictive safety analytics, allowing users to address safety risks proactively before incidents occur. This involves aggregating vast historical safety data and applying machine learning algorithms to identify potential real-time risks. By offering this level of predictive content, EHS platforms provide users with actionable insights that help reduce incidents and improve overall safety performance.

In a 2021 study by Deloitte, organizations using predictive safety models reported a 20% reduction in workplace incidents and a 15% increase in compliance accuracy. These insights demonstrate the power of real-time data and predictive analytics in transforming how organizations deliver and utilize EHS content.

Leveraging Standards and Regulations in Content Delivery

The EHS industry operates in a highly regulated environment. Standards like ISO 45001 for Occupational Health and Safety Management and OSHA regulations shape organizations' content needs. EHS platforms must continuously update their content libraries to reflect changes in these regulatory standards. Failure to do so can result in non-compliance, fines, and reputational damage for the companies using these platforms.

The ISO 45001 standard, for instance, emphasizes the importance of a risk-based approach to managing workplace safety. EHS platforms like Cority and VelocityEHS now offer tools that align with this standard, integrating risk assessments, training modules, and incident reporting tools that help organizations maintain compliance. VelocityEHS, in particular, provides a compliance dashboard that tracks real-time adherence to ISO and OSHA standards, ensuring that companies are always aligned with regulatory expectations.

A 2020 report by Verdantix highlighted that 40% of companies reported improved compliance and a 25% reduction in regulatory fines after integrating platforms that provided real-time regulatory content updates. These findings underscore the necessity of up-to-date compliance content in EHS platforms.

Creating a Safer Environment with Dynamic Content

As regulatory environments become more complex, EHS platforms must evolve from static data repositories into dynamic hubs that continuously deliver actionable content. According to AIHA's 2021 White Paper, organizations that integrate dynamic EHS platforms with real-time data and predictive capabilities can reduce incident response times by 30% and improve overall safety outcomes.

Platforms like Gensuite are pioneering the shift toward dynamic safety content by integrating IoT-enabled devices to monitor real-time environmental conditions, such as air quality. This data is fed into the Platform's predictive analytics engine, allowing safety managers to respond to potential hazards before they escalate into incidents. The Platform's mobile access also allows instant reporting, ensuring no safety violation goes unnoticed.

Dynamic dashboards and visualization tools further enhance the presentation of safety data. Platforms like Intelex now offer customizable dashboards that allow EHS professionals to track KPIs, compliance levels, and risk assessments in real-time. These dynamic tools improve decision-making by enabling faster safety data analysis, driving proactive safety management rather than reactive responses.

Integrating Real-Time Monitoring and Incident Reporting

In incident management, real-time monitoring has become a crucial element of modern EHS platforms. Verdantix's 2021 Market Forecast indicates that 65% of organizations are actively looking for EHS platforms that can integrate IoT devices for real-time monitoring of hazards. Platforms like Intelex and Enablon are integrating wearable technologies and sensor-based monitoring to track worker safety and environmental conditions.

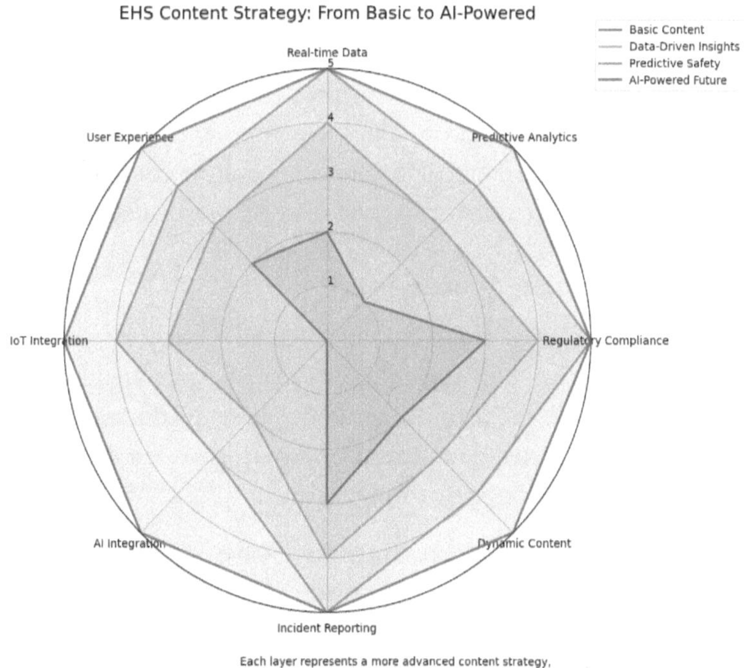

Figure 5.10: EHS Content Strategy from Basic To AI-Powered

A 2021 case study of a major chemical manufacturing company using IoT-enabled sensors to monitor toxic gas levels in real time showed a 30% reduction in worker exposure to hazardous chemicals. The company integrated these sensors with its EHS platform, which immediately triggered alerts when toxic gas levels reached dangerous thresholds, allowing safety officers to evacuate workers before harm occurred.

This example demonstrates the value of real-time incident reporting powered by IoT-enabled content. By delivering live safety data, EHS platforms can help organizations mitigate risks and prevent incidents before they occur, ensuring a safer work environment.

The Future of EHS Content: AI and Machine Learning

Looking forward, the future of EHS content will be shaped by integrating AI and machine learning technologies. According to Gartner's 2022 EHS Software Market Insights, organizations incorporating AI into their EHS platforms will experience a 35% improvement in safety compliance and a 25% reduction in workplace incidents.

AI-powered platforms like Cority are already implementing intelligent algorithms that analyze vast datasets to predict potential hazards based on historical trends, worker behavior, and environmental conditions. These predictive tools transform how EHS platforms deliver content, shifting the focus from reactive incident reporting to proactive risk management.

The Competitive Edge of Content in EHS

EHS platforms that leverage real-time data, predictive analytics, and AI-driven content are transforming how organizations manage Safety and compliance. By providing dynamic, actionable content, these platforms enable EHS professionals to make faster, data-driven decisions, ensuring safer workplaces and better compliance with regulatory standards.

The future of EHS will continue to evolve with advancements in machine learning, IoT, and AI, driving further improvements in the delivery of content and the management of safety risks. Organizations that invest in these platforms will stay compliant and create safer and more efficient work environments, gaining a competitive edge in the EHS space.

Competing on Customer Experience in EHS

In Environment, Health, and Safety (EHS), delivering a superior customer experience is not just a business imperative but a critical component of maintaining compliance, reducing risks, and fostering a safety-first culture. As organizations increasingly adopt the Digital Transformation framework, EHS platforms must ensure they are customer-centric, offering seamless and efficient user interactions while addressing the specific needs of EHS professionals, employees, and regulators.

A superior customer experience in EHS requires platforms to continuously monitor user behavior, integrate intuitive user interfaces, and provide collaborative opportunities that engage EHS teams in routine safety management and emergencies. Platforms that fail to deliver on these fronts risk alienating users, which could lead to regulatory non-compliance and increased safety incidents.

According to Verdantix's 2021 Global Corporate Survey, EHS leaders prioritize user experience (UX) as a key differentiator, with 45% of surveyed firms identifying UX as crucial for safety management software. Platforms like Enablon, Intelex, and Cority are leading the way by offering intuitive dashboards, customizable workflows, and mobile capabilities that streamline processes, reduce administrative burden, and allow users to focus on critical safety tasks.

The Role of User-Centric Design in EHS Platforms

A 2021 report from Forrester Research highlights that organizations using user-centered EHS platforms reported a 30% increase in employee engagement in safety programs and a 25% improvement in compliance tracking. The focus on user-centric design ensures that EHS professionals can easily access the information they need, report incidents in real-time, and collaborate across departments.

Cority, for example, emphasizes a mobile-first design that enables workers on-site to report incidents, access safety procedures, and complete audits directly from their mobile devices. This level of real-time interaction is critical in high-risk industries like construction, manufacturing, and chemicals, where every minute counts in preventing or mitigating accidents.

In a case study published by Intelex, a significant oil and gas company, the company achieved a 20% reduction in incident reporting time by deploying a mobile-enabled platform that streamlined data entry and allowed field workers to submit reports and observations with minimal disruption to their daily tasks. This Platform's success is mainly due to its customer-focused design, which reduced complexity and provided users with a clear and easy-to-navigate interface.

Mapping the EHS Customer Journey

EHS platforms are increasingly adopting a similar approach to improving safety management processes. In the EHS context, a customer journey involves every interaction an employee or safety manager has with the Platform, from logging incidents and audits to compliance reporting and risk assessments.

Understanding and mapping these journeys can significantly enhance the customer experience. Gartner's 2022 Market Guide for EHS Software reports that 44% of EHS professionals prefer platforms that allow them to customize workflows to match their organizational safety procedures, leading to improved user adoption and satisfaction. By identifying bottlenecks in safety reporting or audit processes, EHS platforms can streamline these journeys, enabling quicker responses to safety incidents and a more proactive approach to compliance.

For example, Gensuite introduced a Safety Observations feature that allows users to capture potential hazards in real time and triggers an automatic workflow to mitigate risks. This feature aligns with customer journeys by ensuring users can seamlessly report hazards, review safety data, and take corrective action without delays. According to a 2021 case study from the Platform, the result is a 30% faster response time to identified risks.

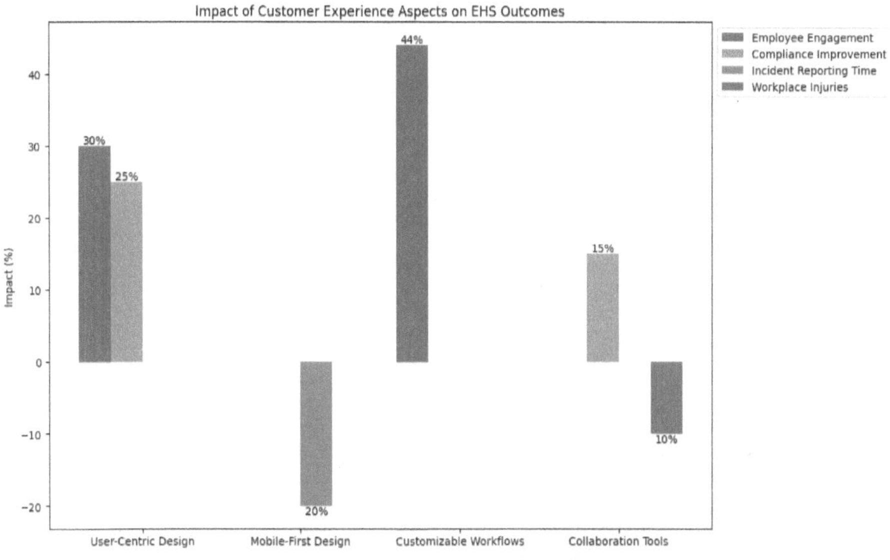

Figure 5.11: Impact of Customer experience aspects on EHS outcomes

Collaboration and Cross-Functional Engagement

Another essential aspect of competing on customer experience in EHS is fostering cross-functional collaboration. EHS platforms must provide tools that enable different teams—such as operations, HR, and compliance officers—to work together to improve workplace safety. Integrating data from various departments and providing a single source of truth is a game-changer for organizations aiming to foster a safety-first culture.

According to Deloitte's 2021 Human Capital Trends, organizations prioritizing collaborative EHS platforms experience a 15% increase in safety compliance and a 10% decrease in workplace injuries. Platforms like Enablon and Cority enable cross-functional collaboration by integrating existing systems (such as ERP and HR systems) and offering collaborative tools like real-time dashboards, shared reporting features, and centralized incident management. These tools break down silos and enable coordinated action across departments, ensuring that safety protocols are adhered to throughout the organization.

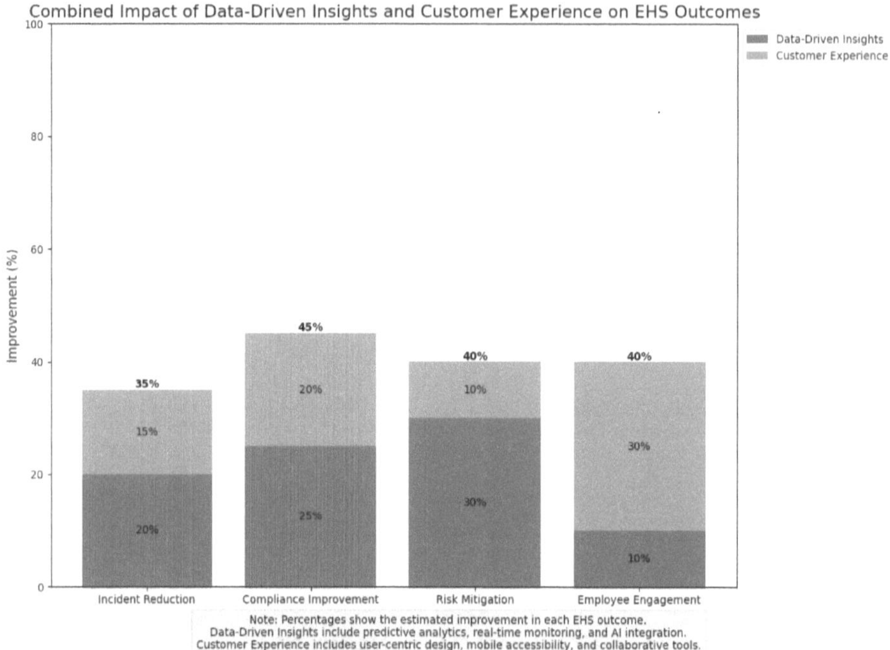

Figure 5.12: Combined Impact of Data and UX on EHS Outcomes

Enhancing Employee Engagement with EHS Platforms

In the EHS world, employees are the end-users and the most critical stakeholders. Effectively engaging them can have a profound impact on workplace safety. According to a 2020 report by McKinsey, companies with high levels of employee engagement in their safety programs reported a 32% reduction in safety incidents and a 22% increase in compliance.

Therefore, EHS platforms must focus on employee empowerment, offering tools that allow workers to contribute to safety culture actively. Cority and VelocityEHS have incorporated gamification into their platforms, offering rewards and recognition for employees who consistently report hazards or complete safety training. This approach motivates employees and helps reinforce safety behaviors, leading to a more engaged and proactive workforce.

The Competitive Edge in EHS Customer Experience

To compete on customer experience in the EHS space, platforms must prioritize user-centric design, real-time engagement, and cross-functional collaboration. By mapping EHS customer journeys, integrating mobile-first solutions, and offering collaborative tools, organizations can enhance safety outcomes, improve compliance, and ultimately foster a culture of continuous safety improvement.

The future of EHS lies in platforms that can proactively manage safety risks while empowering employees and engaging stakeholders across the organization. Platforms that excel in customer experience will meet regulatory requirements and create safer, more resilient workplaces, giving organizations a competitive advantage in an increasingly regulated and complex EHS environment.

Several EHS platforms have delivered superior customer experience by leveraging user-friendly interfaces, mobile-first capabilities, and collaborative features that empower EHS teams to manage risks, compliance, and Safety across industries.

These EHS platforms excel in customer experience by prioritizing user-centric designs, mobile-first capabilities, and collaborative tools that ensure EHS professionals can effectively manage Safety and compliance in real-time. By providing intuitive interfaces, customizable workflows, and comprehensive reporting tools, these platforms help organizations achieve better safety outcomes, engage employees, and foster a safety-first culture. Their success in improving EHS performance demonstrates the importance of focusing on customer experience as a competitive differentiator in the EHS market.

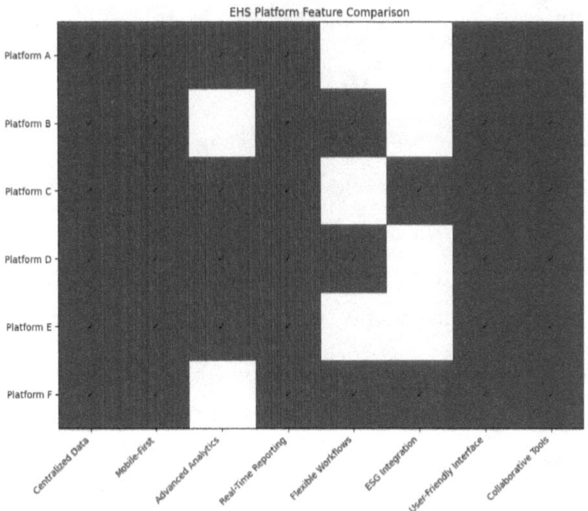

Figure 5.13: EHS Platform Feature Comparison

Competing on Platforms in EHS

In the Environment, Health, and Safety (EHS) industry, platforms enable organizations to manage compliance, safety risks, and environmental impact. To gain a competitive advantage and achieve economies of scale, EHS companies must develop digitized platforms that integrate data across operations, enhance user experiences, and streamline processes. With well-designed platforms, organizations can avoid creating fragmented systems that lead to inefficiencies, higher costs, and better user experiences.

Platforms in the EHS domain enable real-time data sharing, automated workflows, and cross-functional collaboration across departments in areas such as Safety, compliance, and operations. They unify data from different sources, provide comprehensive reporting capabilities, and ensure critical safety information is accessible to everyone who needs it. Effective platforms create a seamless user experience and help companies meet regulatory requirements more efficiently.

Case Study: Enablon - Unified EHS and Risk Management Platform

Enablon, a leader in the EHS software space, has built a comprehensive platform that integrates EHS management, risk management, sustainability reporting, and compliance tracking into a single, scalable solution. With real-time analytics, mobile applications, and AI-powered incident tracking, Enablon enables organizations to centralize their EHS data and improve decision-making.

Key Features of Enablon's Platform:

- **Centralized Data Repository:** All EHS, risk, and compliance data is stored in one place, providing decision-makers with a single source of truth.

- **Mobile-First Design:** Enablon's mobile app allows employees to report incidents, complete safety audits, and access compliance data in the field.

- **Advanced Analytics and Reporting:** The Platform offers predictive analytics, helping organizations proactively identify potential hazards and manage risks.

Impact of Platform Integration: A global energy company using Enablon's Platform reduced compliance reporting time by 30% and safety incidents by 25% within two years of implementation. Integrating all safety data into one system allowed the company to respond to incidents faster and ensure that safety protocols were consistently followed.

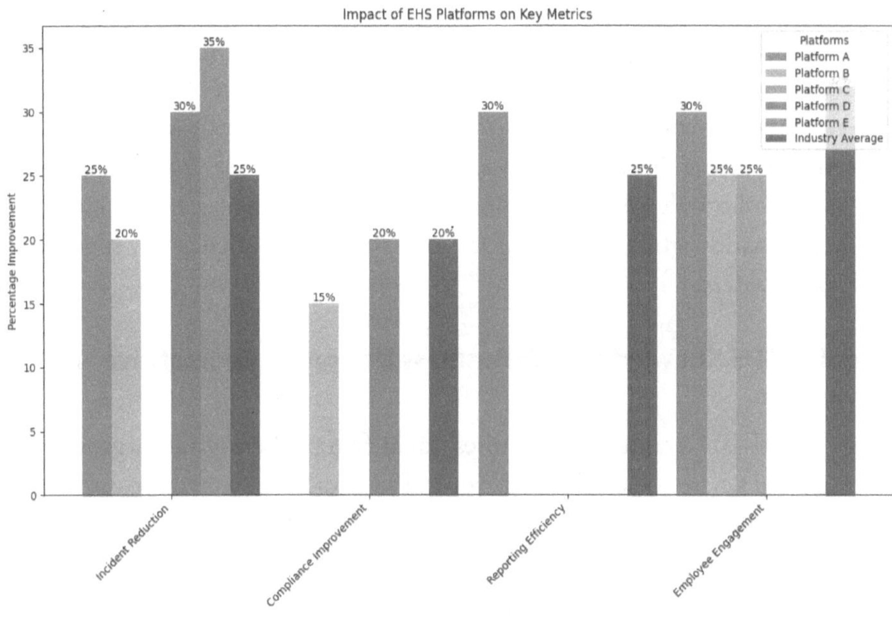

Figure 5.14: Impact of EHS Platforms on Key Metrics

Platform Impact: A chemical manufacturing company that adopted VelocityEHS saw a 20% reduction in workplace accidents and improved compliance rates by 15% within the first year of implementation. The company enhanced safety awareness and reduced the risk of non-compliance penalties by automating compliance checks and integrating safety data from various departments.

Leveraging Platforms for Sustainability and Compliance in EHS

A growing number of organizations are now using EHS platforms to manage Safety and compliance and to track and report on sustainability metrics. With increasing pressure from regulatory bodies and stakeholders, companies must integrate environmental impact tracking into their EHS platforms.

EHS platforms like Enablon, VelocityEHS, and Cority demonstrate the power of digitized platforms to achieve economies of scale, streamline compliance, and improve customer experience. By unifying Safety, compliance, risk management, and sustainability tracking into comprehensive, scalable platforms, these companies are helping organizations reduce costs, improve safety outcomes, and more effectively meet regulatory requirements.

According to a report by Verdantix, companies using integrated EHS platforms achieve 25% faster incident response times, a 20% increase in Safety reporting compliance, and significant improvements in sustainability reporting. Reusing these platforms across multiple functions (from compliance to sustainability) allows organizations to adapt to changing regulations and market demands while enhancing the overall user experience for employees and stakeholders.

Aligning EHS Knowledge with Business Design for Competitive Advantage

Your EHS-KBD framework requires identifying where your organization operates and where you can leverage your EHS knowledge to gain a competitive advantage. Whether you're a supplier providing essential data, an omnichannel business delivering exceptional user experiences, a modular producer creating scalable platforms, or an ecosystem driver building comprehensive solutions, the key to long-term success lies in understanding your EHS knowledge's unique role in business design.

By aligning your EHS knowledge with a suitable business model, you can build the capabilities necessary to thrive in today's digitally connected, compliance-driven world. Use your strengths in content, customer experience, and platforms to drive growth and create sustainable, long-lasting value for your business and its stakeholders.

Building a Digital Safety Culture

The catastrophic events of the BP Texas City Refinery Explosion and the Deepwater Horizon Oil Spill serve as stark reminders of the critical importance of safety culture in high-risk industries. As organizations undergo digital transformations in their EHS practices, it's crucial to ensure these technological advancements enhance rather than detract from a robust safety culture.

1. Leadership Commitment to Safety in Digital Transformations

Leadership plays a pivotal role in shaping an organization's safety culture, particularly during digital transformations:

- Visible Commitment: Leaders must visibly prioritize safety over cost and efficiency gains in digital initiatives.

- Resource Allocation: Adequate resources should be allocated for technology implementation, safety training, and risk management.

- Safety Metrics in Digital Projects: Include safety-related KPIs in evaluating digital transformation projects.

2. Comprehensive Risk Assessment in EHS Digital Initiatives

Digital tools can enhance risk assessment processes, but they must be implemented thoughtfully:

- Holistic Approach: Consider technological risks and how digital changes might impact existing safety processes and human behaviors.

- Continuous Assessment: Implement systems for ongoing risk assessment as digital tools evolve and new data becomes available.

- Scenario Planning: Use digital simulations to model various risk scenarios and test mitigation strategies.

3. Leveraging Digital Tools for Safety Communication and Awareness

Digital platforms offer new opportunities to enhance safety communication:

- Real-time Safety Alerts: Implement systems to communicate safety concerns across the organization immediately.

- Interactive Safety Training: Use virtual and augmented reality tools to provide immersive safety training experiences.

- Data Visualization: Leverage data analytics to create compelling safety trends and risk visualizations.

4. Integration of Safety into Digital Workflows

Ensure that safety considerations are embedded into all digital processes:

- Safety Checkpoints: Integrate safety checks and approvals into digital workflows.

- Predictive Safety Analytics: Use AI and machine learning to predict potential safety issues before they occur.

- Digital Safety Reporting: Implement user-friendly digital tools for reporting safety concerns and near-misses.

By focusing on these elements, organizations can build a digital safety culture that leverages technological advancements to enhance overall safety performance, avoiding the pitfalls highlighted in cases like BP's. Remember, digital tools are enablers of safety culture, not substitutes for human vigilance and commitment to safety.

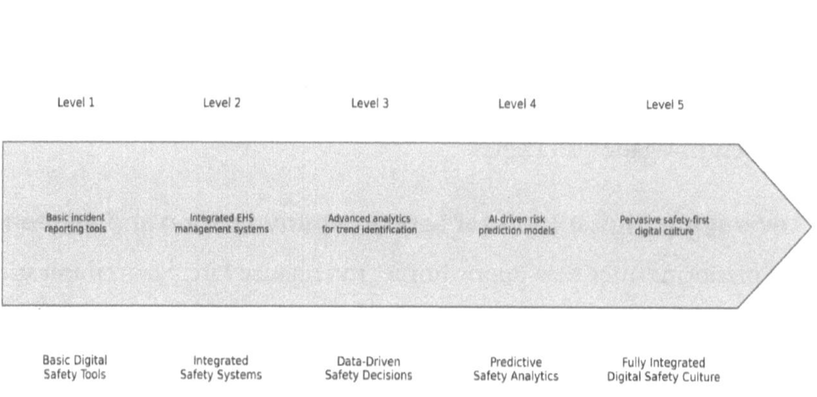

Figure 5.15: Digital Safety Culture Maturity Model

Leveraging AI and Predictive Analytics

As EHS platforms evolve, Artificial Intelligence (AI) and predictive analytics are becoming increasingly important tools. However, as demonstrated by the case of an unnamed oil refinery's failed AI-driven predictive maintenance system, implementing these technologies comes with significant challenges and risks.

1. Ensuring High-Quality Historical Data:

The foundation of effective AI and predictive analytics is high-quality, comprehensive historical data:

- Conduct thorough data audits before AI implementation

- Establish robust data collection and validation processes

- Continuously update and refine data sets to improve model accuracy

2. Explainable AI in Safety-Critical Applications:

In EHS contexts, where decisions can have life-or-death consequences, the "black box" nature of some AI systems is unacceptable:

- Prioritize AI models that provide clear explanations for their predictions

- Implement systems that allow human oversight and intervention

- Regularly validate AI outputs against known safety standards and expert judgment

3. Balancing AI-Driven Insights with Human Expertise:

While AI can process vast amounts of data quickly, human expertise remains crucial:

- Develop workflows that combine AI insights with human decision-making

- Provide training to help staff interpret and act on AI-generated insights

- Maintain manual oversight and traditional safety practices as a backup

4. Phased Implementation and Continuous Evaluation:

To avoid the pitfalls experienced by the oil refinery:

- Start with non-critical applications to build confidence and expertise

- Implement rigorous testing and validation processes

- Continuously monitor AI system performance and adjust as needed

By carefully managing these aspects of AI and predictive analytics implementation, organizations can harness the power of these technologies while avoiding potentially catastrophic failures in safety-critical EHS applications.

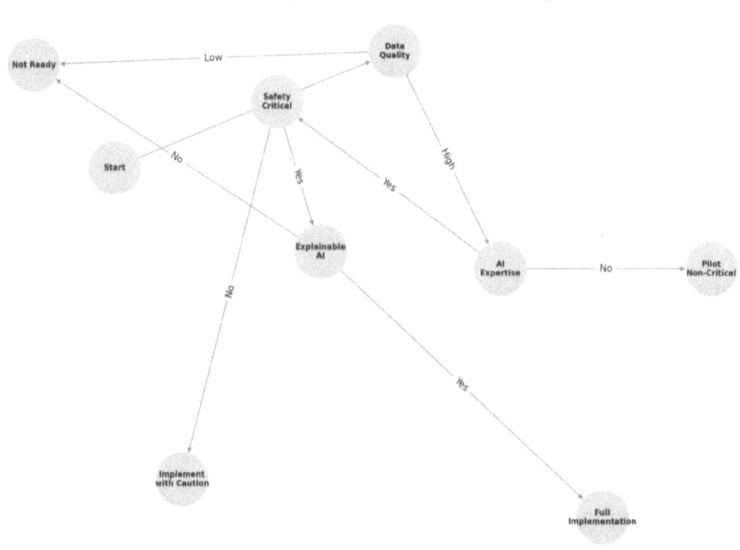

Figure 5.15: Decision Type – AI Implementation Readiness in EHS Systems

Case Study: Enablon – Enhancing EHS Platforms Through Content, Customer Experience, and Platforms

Enablon, one of the world's largest providers of Environment, Health, and Safety (EHS) and Sustainability software, showcases how a company can effectively adapt and strengthen its competitive advantage through digital innovation. With customers spanning industries like energy, manufacturing, and chemicals, Enablon serves a global client base by delivering solutions that enable organizations to manage compliance, improve safety performance, and achieve sustainability goals. In 2020, Enablon was recognized as a leader in the Gartner Magic Quadrant for EHS Management Solutions and saw significant adoption of its platforms due to its strong focus on enhancing content, customer experience, and platform capabilities.

Here's how Enablon used these three pillars to build a competitive edge in the EHS market:

1. Creating Unique EHS Content

To compete in the EHS and Sustainability market, Enablon developed robust content that addresses specific industry regulations, risk management, and safety protocols. Its content includes templates for regulatory compliance, industry best practices for incident management, and guidelines for environmental reporting.

Enablon regularly updates its content to reflect changes in global regulations, such as OSHA standards or the European Union's REACH regulations, ensuring its customers are always compliant. This constant refreshment of content, coupled with expert insights on risk management and environmental standards, makes Enablon a go-to platform for EHS professionals.

The company has also built strategic relationships with industry experts and environmental bodies to enhance its content offering. For instance:

- **Incident Management Guides** provide step-by-step workflows tailored to specific industries like oil and gas or chemical manufacturing.

- **Localized regulations support Environmental Impact Assessments (EIA)**, helping companies navigate complex compliance challenges.

By continually improving its **EHS content** and ensuring its accuracy and relevance, Enablon has established itself as a leader in regulatory compliance and sustainability reporting.

2. Improving and Measuring Customer Experience

Customer experience has been central to Enablon's success, particularly as it transitioned to a more digitally integrated platform. Recognizing its users' varied needs, Enablon focused on understanding the daily workflows and challenges of EHS managers through field research, customer feedback, and user experience (UX) testing.

A significant innovation was the introduction of customizable dashboards that allow users to visualize critical data like incident trends, risk scores, and emissions data. These dashboards provide actionable insights, helping users to make informed decisions quickly. Enablon also offers:

- **We aim to provide mobile-first experiences** for workers in the field, enabling them to report incidents, access safety protocols, and complete inspections from their smartphones or tablets.

- **Advanced Analytics** for predictive risk management, using historical data to identify potential hazards before they occur.

Enablon tracks customer satisfaction through real-time feedback loops built into its Platform. This includes post-interaction surveys that ask users to rate the system's ease of use and effectiveness. The company leverages this feedback to continuously refine its offerings, ensuring users have a seamless experience, whether using the Platform on a mobile device during a safety inspection or generating compliance reports in the office.

Enablon's customer-centric approach was recognized in 2021 when it was awarded the Verdantix EHS Innovation Award for outstanding user experience improvements.

3. Developing a Flexible Global Platform

Enablon's platform strategy has been critical to its competitive advantage in the EHS space. Its cloud-based Platform allows companies to manage complex EHS data globally while complying with local regulations. The modular architecture enables organizations to scale their use of Enablon, adding new functionalities like sustainability reporting, incident management, or risk assessments without overhauling their entire system.

Enablon's Platform, known for its **modularity** and **customization**, enables users to:

- **Integrate IoT sensors** to monitor real-time environmental conditions, such as **air quality** or **water usage**, and feed data directly into compliance reports.

- Its **API-driven architecture** allows companies to access third-party applications, allowing them to add additional services such as **employee training** tools or **contractor management** systems.

The Platform also supports cross-industry collaboration. For instance, companies in the manufacturing sector can share best practices and benchmarking data with partners through Enablon's Platform, helping them improve safety outcomes and reduce environmental risks.

A vital feature of the Enablon platform is its AI-powered predictive analytics. These tools help companies anticipate and mitigate risks before they lead to incidents, using machine learning to analyze historical data and forecast potential hazards. For example, an oil refinery using Enablon could predict when specific equipment might fail based on data trends, preventing accidents and ensuring regulatory compliance.

A Comprehensive EHS Solution

Enablon's strategic investment in exclusive EHS content, seamless customer experience, and a modular, flexible platform has made it a leader in the EHS market. Its global reach and localized regulatory knowledge make it the Platform of choice for companies seeking to improve their sustainability, safety performance, and compliance.

Enablon's success demonstrates how an EHS platform can meet current regulatory needs and anticipate future risks through continuous innovation in content, customer experience, and platform flexibility as more companies focus on sustainability and risk management.

EHS Context: Prioritizing Content, Customer Experience, and Platforms for Your Future Strategy

As you plan for the future of your EHS (Environment, Health, and Safety) management platform, it's essential to evaluate how content, customer experience, and platforms will shape your enterprise's success. In the evolving digital landscape, your approach to these competitive advantages can determine how well your business adapts to new challenges and opportunities in the EHS field. So, which one or more of these advantages should you prioritize to become a top performer in EHS? And more importantly, does your budget for the coming year reflect these priorities?

For many EHS platforms, transitioning from traditional compliance-focused solutions to fully integrated digital systems that manage risk, Safety, and sustainability is no small task. However, determining where your company should focus its competitive strengths is the key to long-term success.

In a recent workshop with the leadership of an EHS services company, we applied a self-assessment similar to the one at the end of this chapter. The results revealed that the company performed well in content—with robust regulatory information and safety protocols—but lagged in customer experience and platform integration. The responses were mixed when asked which area would be most critical to the company's success in the next three years, illustrating the challenges of setting clear strategic priorities.

Differing Priorities for the Future of EHS Platforms

1. Customer Experience as a Key Competitive Advantage

Approximately half of the leadership team, especially those overseeing client services and safety consulting, ranked customer experience as the most critical competitive advantage. These leaders argued that while the Platform had strong content (regulations, protocols, and risk assessments), the real differentiator for clients was how it helped them navigate complex EHS events—like managing emergencies, conducting incident investigations, or complying with fast-changing environmental regulations.

For these leaders, improving customer experience meant creating seamless workflows, real-time dashboards, and mobile access that would allow clients to handle complex safety and compliance challenges effortlessly. The idea was to deliver a more integrated, user-friendly platform where clients could quickly respond to emergencies or regulatory changes without extensive training or technical support. The ultimate goal was to help clients address their EHS challenges more efficiently while strengthening their relationship with the Platform.

2. Content as the Cornerstone of Trust and Expertise

Another 40% of the team, particularly those in regulatory compliance and environmental services, maintained that content would remain the core competitive advantage. They emphasized that clients depended on their Platform to access up-to-date and accurate regulatory guidelines, incident management frameworks, and industry-specific safety protocols. These leaders argued that staying ahead of evolving regulations—such as OSHA standards, ISO 45001, or Environmental Protection Agency (EPA) mandates—was critical to maintaining client trust and loyalty.

For this group, the focus was on continually expanding and updating the Platform's content. This would involve adding global compliance modules, creating sector-specific guidelines for industries like oil & gas or manufacturing, and integrating expert commentary from EHS specialists. In their view, clients would continue to rely on the Platform's rich content to meet compliance requirements and avoid regulatory penalties.

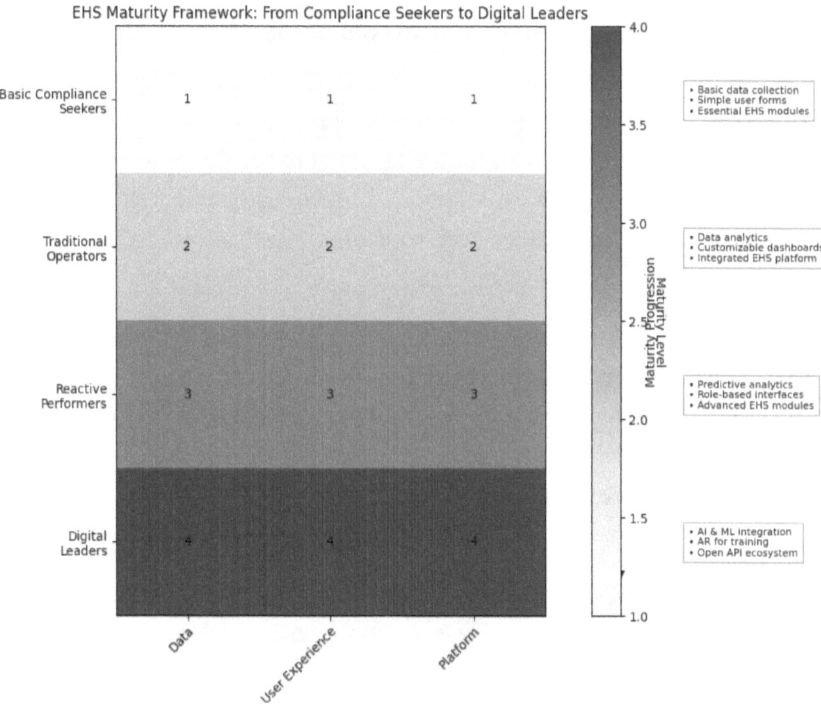

Figure 5.16: EHS maturity framework

3. Platforms as the Foundation for Innovation

Finally, about 10% of the team argued that platform development was the most critical area for investment. These leaders recognized the growing influence of automation, IoT integration, and data analytics in the EHS industry. They believed that to stay ahead; the company needed to invest in creating a modular, scalable platform that could integrate with other business systems (such as ERP or supply chain management) and provide advanced features like predictive analytics, AI-driven risk assessments, and real-time environmental monitoring.

Enhancing the Platform's capabilities would enable the company to differentiate itself from competitors relying on manual processes or fragmented systems. These leaders emphasized that building a flexible platform would allow the company to respond quickly to client needs, drive down operational costs, and remain competitive as new digital technologies continued to disrupt the EHS landscape.

Aligning Budget Priorities with Strategic Goals

The workshop discussion revealed a familiar challenge: achieving consensus on where to prioritize investment takes time, especially in rapid digital change. However, these discussions are essential for senior management teams navigating disruptive transformations in EHS management. Without clarity on where to focus, companies risk spreading their resources too thin and missing critical growth opportunities.

As you think about your own EHS platform, ask yourself: where does your company stand today regarding content, customer experience, and platform capabilities? Which of these areas will be most critical to your future success? If you haven't already, now is the perfect time to review the sources of your digital competitive advantage and align your budget priorities accordingly.

In Chapter 6, we'll explore how emerging technologies—like the Internet of Things (IoT) and mobile apps—can drive your EHS platform's path to digitization, enabling your business to stay competitive and meet evolving client demands.

Managing System Complexity

As EHS platforms become increasingly sophisticated, managing system complexity becomes critical. The Rio Tinto Autonomous Haulage System case highlights the potential pitfalls of implementing complex systems without adequate preparation and integration.

1. Thorough Testing Under Real-World Conditions:

Complex systems often behave unpredictably when exposed to real-world variables. To mitigate this:

- Conduct extensive testing in diverse environmental conditions

- Simulate extreme scenarios to identify potential failure points

- Gradually increase system complexity during testing phases

2. Robust Integration Planning:

New systems must seamlessly integrate with existing infrastructure. This requires:

- Comprehensive mapping of all interconnected systems and processes

- Careful consideration of data flow and compatibility issues

- Development of contingency plans for potential integration failures

3. Phased Implementation Approach:

Implementing complex systems in phases allows for the following:

- Incremental learning and adjustment

- Early identification and resolution of issues

- Gradual adaptation of workforce and processes

4. Adaptive System Design:

Design systems with built-in flexibility to:

- Accommodate unforeseen operational changes

- Allow for easy updates and modifications

- Scale effectively as organizational needs evolve

By carefully managing these aspects of system complexity, organizations can avoid the setbacks experienced in cases like Rio Tinto's and maximize the benefits of advanced EHS platforms.

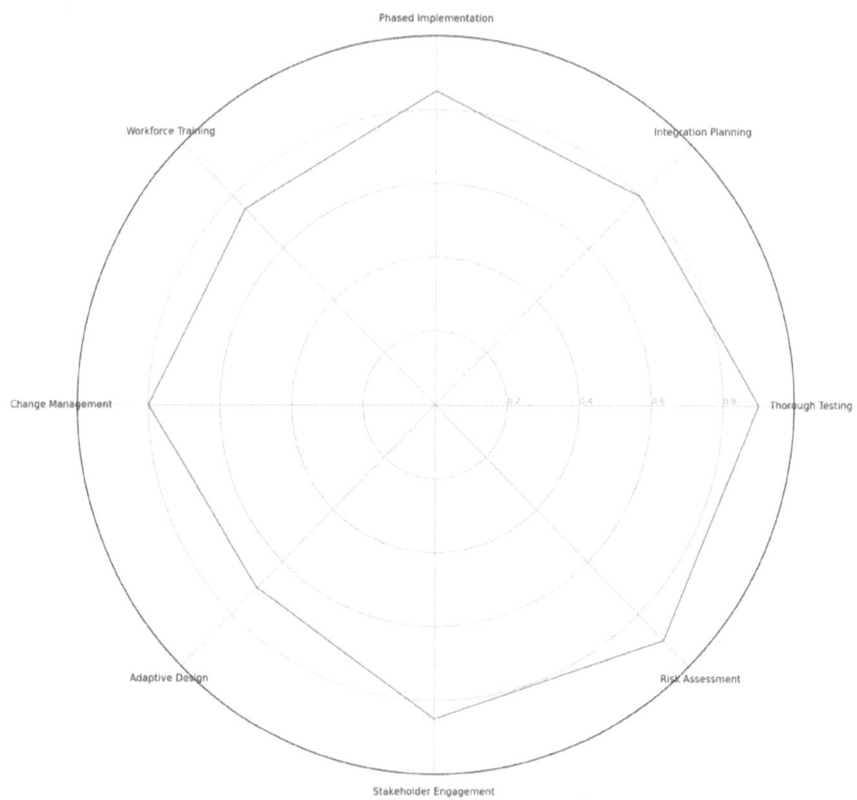

Figure 5.17: Factors for successful complex system implementation

EHS Self-Assessment: Identifying Your Competitive Advantage

Where should you start enhancing your EHS (Environment, Health, and Safety) management system? It depends on your Platform's performance and which capability—content, customer experience, or platforms—will be most important for your enterprise's success in the next three years. This self-assessment is designed to help you identify your EHS system's digital competitive strengths and weaknesses.

Gather as many colleagues as possible to evaluate your current EHS digital strengths and weaknesses and identify which sources of competitive advantage will be most critical in three years. Use the questions in the self-assessment below to spark meaningful discussions about your EHS platform's capabilities in content, customer experience, and platform integration.

Self-Assessment, Part 1: Key Questions for EHS Competitive Advantage

Content

- Do you regularly update your Platform with new EHS regulations, incident management protocols, or environmental guidelines to generate customer value?

- What EHS content do your clients find most valuable? Do you have additional internal EHS expertise or compliance tools that could be shared with clients?

- Who in your organization ensures your EHS content remains up-to-date and relevant? Should content responsibilities be more integrated across Safety, compliance, and sustainability teams?

Customer Experience

- How well does your Platform serve users during critical EHS events like incident reporting, risk assessments, or regulatory audits?

- Who in your company is accountable for the user experience of your EHS platform? What aspects of using the Platform do customers find helpful or frustrating?

- What percentage of your EHS service revenues is generated through your digital Platform, and how can you enhance this by offering cross-functional tools for compliance, safety management, and sustainability reporting?

- How can you better incorporate the customer's voice to continuously improve the Platform's effectiveness for EHS professionals?

Platform

- How well-developed are your internal EHS platforms? Who is responsible for maintaining and enhancing the system? Are the platforms flexible enough to respond quickly to new EHS regulations or emerging environmental risks?

- Can you expose more of your internal EHS data (e.g., risk assessments and incident reports) to external stakeholders like partners, regulators, or clients to improve transparency and collaboration?

- How easily can your EHS platform integrate with enterprise systems such as ERP, supply chain management, or HR systems for comprehensive risk management?

- Can your Platform easily connect with third-party environmental data providers, cloud services, or IoT devices to enhance real-time monitoring and predictive analytics?

Self-Assessment, Part 2: EHS Digital Strength Evaluation

After discussing the three competitive advantages—content, customer experience, and platforms—use the following scale to rate your enterprise's performance. Everyone should rate your organization's EHS capabilities from 1 to 10 today. Then, calculate the average scores across your group.

Finally, each participant should rank which areas will be the most important for the success of their EHS platform over the next three years. This will indicate where to focus budget and strategic initiatives in the future.

Step 1: Rate Your Organization's EHS Capabilities

Each participant in the group rates the organization's **EHS capabilities** on a scale of **1 to 10** across the three competitive advantages, now viewed from an EHS perspective:

- **Content**: The quality, accuracy, and timeliness of the EHS data and insights your organization collects and utilizes for compliance, risk management, incident reporting, and environmental performance.

- **Customer Experience**: How well your EHS system supports internal stakeholders (employees, managers) and external stakeholders (regulatory bodies, communities) by providing a smooth, transparent, and efficient experience regarding safety reporting, incident management, and compliance updates.

- **Platform**: The robustness, scalability, and integration of your **EHS platform** (e.g., incident management tools, real-time environmental monitoring, compliance tracking systems) and how effectively it supports Safety, environmental management, and regulatory adherence.

Let's assume **5 participants** providing ratings for each area:

Participant Content Customer Experience platform

Participant	Content	Customer Experience	platform
A	7	6	8
B	8	7	9
C	6	6	7
D	7	8	8
E	6	7	6

Step 2: Calculate the Average Score for Each Area

Now, calculate the average rating for each competitive advantage by summing up the individual scores and dividing by the number of participants.

- **Content:**= 6/8

- **Customer Experience**: = 6/8

- **Platform**: = 7.6

Step 3: Rank the Most Important Areas for Future Success

Each participant ranks which of the three areas—**Content, Customer Experience**, or **Platform**—they believe will be the most important for the organization's EHS success in the next three years. Let's assume the following rankings:

Participant	1st Priority	2nd Priority	3rd Priority
A	Platform	Customer Experience	Content
B	Customer Experience	Platform	Content
C	Platform	Content	Customer Experience
D	Platform	Customer Experience	Content
E	Customer Experience	Content	Platform

Step 4: Calculate the Priority Scores

Assign points based on ranking:

- 1st priority = 3 points

- 2nd priority = 2 points

- 3rd priority = 1 point

Sum up the points for each area:

- **Platform**: = 12

- **Customer Experience**: = 11

- **Content**: = 7

Step 5: Interpretation

From the average scores and priority rankings, you can see that:

- **The Platform** received the highest average score (**7.6**) and is the top priority for most participants. This suggests that the robustness and integration of your **EHS platform**—including tools for incident reporting, real-time monitoring, and compliance tracking—are relatively strong. However, they should remain a significant area for continued investment to ensure scalability and efficiency in the future.

- **Customer Experience** has room for improvement (**6.8**) and is ranked second in importance. This indicates that enhancing the way your EHS system interacts with internal and external stakeholders—whether through better reporting processes, more transparent incident management, or more intuitive safety communication—should be another key focus for future strategy.

- **Content** received the lowest average score (**6.8**) and priority ranking. While EHS data is essential, it appears less of an immediate concern. However, improving the **accuracy and timeliness of EHS data** will still provide long-term benefits, especially as you continue to enhance your Platform.

Conclusion

This EHS Digital Strength Evaluation helps identify which Content, Customer Experience, or Platform areas require the most attention to ensure future success. In this case, your primary focus should be on further strengthening your Platform, ensuring it is well-integrated and scalable for future needs. Additionally, improvements in Customer Experience—especially in how stakeholders interact with the EHS system—will significantly improve transparency, safety outcomes, and compliance over the next few years.

Example Results from EHS Companies

In a similar survey conducted across several EHS management platforms, enterprises scored 6.8 for content, 5.6 for customer experience, and 6.4 for platforms on a 10-point scale. Top-performing organizations scored 7.4 in content, 6.1 in customer experience, and 7.4 in platform capabilities. If your enterprise scores below these averages, it indicates a need for significant improvements to remain competitive in the rapidly evolving EHS digital landscape.

By reflecting on these self-assessment questions and results, you'll be better equipped to identify and strengthen your digital competitive advantages in EHS management. You'll drive value for your customers while ensuring your Platform remains a leader in compliance, sustainability, and risk management.

Part 2 of this chapter's assessment could reveal disagreements about the direction of your EHS (Environment, Health, and Safety) platform. If you and your colleagues have different views on your source of competitive advantage in three years—content, customer experience, or platforms—it's essential to spend time discussing and moving toward an agreement.

Consensus on this critical point will clarify where to allocate resources and focus strategic efforts. For example, one group might prioritize the quality and compliance of EHS content, while another could emphasize user experience improvements to streamline incident reporting or regulatory audit preparation. Others may see platform integration and scalability as the essential drivers for future success, especially with the increasing importance of IoT, predictive analytics, and real-time environmental monitoring.

Once you've reached a consensus, the goal should be to achieve the top-performing score in at least the one area you collectively identified as most crucial for success in the coming three years. Whether that focus is on creating cutting-edge content to help customers comply with the latest EHS regulations, improving the customer journey across your Platform, or developing a robust data platform to handle complex EHS workflows and integrations, setting a clear priority will guide your EHS strategy toward success.

By aligning on and focusing on your top competitive advantage, your EHS platform will have the necessary strength to thrive in the evolving digital landscape and meet the increasing demands of customers, regulators, and stakeholders.

References

1. Verdantix. (2022). Green Quadrant EHS Software 2022.

2. Gartner. (2021). Magic Quadrant for Environmental, Health and Safety Management Systems. Retrieved from [Gartner website]

3. International Organization for Standardization. (2018). ISO 45001:2018 Occupational health and safety management systems — Requirements with guidance for use. Retrieved from [ISO website]

4. Occupational Safety and Health Administration. (2021). Using Leading Indicators to Improve Safety and Health Outcomes. Retrieved from [OSHA website]

5. Deloitte. (2021). The Future of EHS: Embracing the Digital Transformation. Retrieved from [Deloitte website]

6. McKinsey & Company. (2020). The Next Normal in Construction: How Disruption is Reshaping the World's Largest Ecosystem. Retrieved from [McKinsey website]

7. Forrester Research. (2021). The Total Economic Impact™ Of EHS Software Solutions. Retrieved from [Forrester website]

8. Environmental Protection Agency. (2022). Next Generation Compliance. Retrieved from [EPA website]

9. World Economic Forum. (2020). The Future of Jobs Report 2020. Retrieved from [WEF website]

10. Accenture. (2021). The Future of EHS: Sustainable, Connected, Intelligent. Retrieved from [Accenture website]

11. Journal of Occupational and Environmental Hygiene. (2019). The Fourth Industrial Revolution and Its Impact on Occupational Health and Safety, Worker's Compensation and Labor Conditions. Retrieved from [Taylor & Francis Online]

12. Safety Science. (2020). Digital technologies and resilience in the supply chain—A systematic literature review. Retrieved from [ScienceDirect]

13. Sustainability. (2021). Digitalization and Sustainability: A Systematic Literature Review of Sustainable Industry 4.0. Retrieved from [MDPI]

14. Harvard Business Review. (2019). Using AI to Make Knowledge Workers More Effective. Retrieved from [HBR website]

15. MIT Sloan Management Review. (2020). The New Elements of Digital Transformation. Retrieved from [MIT SMR website]

Incorporating Smart Technologies to Boost EHS Performance

Learning from failed EHS Digital Transformation:

In the rapidly evolving landscape of Environment, Health, and Safety (EHS) management, digital transformation promises significant improvements in safety, efficiency, and environmental performance. However, the path to successfully implementing digital EHS initiatives is often challenging. As organizations strive to leverage technologies such as IoT, AI, and data analytics, they frequently encounter obstacles that can lead to project delays, cost overruns, or outright failures.

While it's natural to focus on success stories, there is immense value in examining and understanding failed digital EHS initiatives. Though costly and often disappointing, these failures offer invaluable insights that can guide future efforts and improve the odds of success. By analyzing what went wrong, organizations can:

1. Identify common pitfalls and risk factors in digital EHS transformations

2. Develop more robust strategies for implementation and change management

3. Set more realistic expectations and timelines for digital initiatives

4. Improve resource allocation and risk mitigation strategies

5. Foster a culture of continuous learning and improvement

As the management expert Peter Drucker once said, "The most important thing in communication is hearing what isn't said." Similarly, in digital EHS transformation, some crucial lessons come from understanding what didn't work and why.

This section will examine three notable cases of digital EHS initiatives that faced significant challenges or outright failure. We aim to extract lessons that can inform and improve future digital EHS strategies by dissecting these cases. These real-world examples will illustrate the complexities of implementing new technologies in safety-critical environments and highlight the importance of stakeholder engagement, data quality, and integration planning.

As we explore these cases, remember that the goal is not to criticize but to learn. Every failure in digital transformation carries the seeds of future success – if we are willing to study, understand, and apply the lessons learned. By doing so, we can collectively advance the field of digital EHS and work towards safer, more efficient, and more sustainable operations across industries.

Case Study 1: PG&E's Smart Meter Program (2009-2010)

Background: Pacific Gas and Electric Company (PG&E), one of the largest combined natural gas and electric energy companies in the United States, launched an ambitious smart meter program in the late 2000s. This initiative was part of a broader effort to modernize the electric grid, improve energy efficiency, and enhance safety monitoring capabilities.

Objectives:

1. Provide real-time energy usage data to customers to encourage more efficient consumption.

2. Automate meter reading and billing processes to improve operational efficiency.

3. Enable better management of energy demand and supply.

4. Enhance the ability to detect and respond to potential hazards in the energy distribution system.

5. Reduce energy consumption and associated greenhouse gas emissions.

Key Failure Points:

1. Inaccurate Meter Readings: Many customers reported significant bill increases after smart meter installation. Investigations revealed that some meters needed accurate readings, leading to overcharging.

2. Integration Failures: The new smart meter system must be adequately integrated with PG&E's existing infrastructure, leading to data inconsistencies and operational inefficiencies.

3. Inadequate Cybersecurity Measures: The program raised concerns about data privacy and grid vulnerability, with fears that the system could be hacked.

4. Poor Communication: PG & E could have more effectively communicated the benefits and potential challenges of the innovative meter program to customers, leading to widespread confusion and distrust.

5. Inadequate Testing: The smart meters must be sufficiently tested under various real-world conditions before widespread deployment.

6. Lack of Customer Choice: Initially, customers were not allowed to opt out of the smart meter program, leading to resentment.

Outcomes:

1. Public Backlash: There was a significant public outcry against the smart meter program, and some communities banned its installation.

2. Regulatory Investigations: The California Public Utilities Commission (CPUC) ordered an independent review of the smart meter program.

3. Financial Losses: PG&E suffered significant economic losses from replacing faulty meters, providing customer refunds, and dealing with legal and regulatory challenges.

4. Reputation Damage: PG&E's reputation suffered considerably, eroding public trust in the company.

5. Delayed Benefits: The promised benefits of the smart meter program, such as improved energy efficiency and grid management, were significantly delayed.

Lessons Learned:

1. Thorough Testing is Crucial: Extensive testing of new technologies under various real-world conditions is essential before large-scale deployment.

2. Effective Communication: It is vital to communicate clearly and transparently with customers about new technologies' benefits, potential challenges, and impacts.

3. Cybersecurity is Paramount. To protect customer data and grid stability, Robust cybersecurity measures must be a top priority in any intelligent grid initiative.

4. Integration Planning: Careful planning for integrating existing systems is crucial to avoid operational disruptions.

5. Customer Choice: Providing customers options (such as opting out) can help mitigate resistance to new technologies.

6. Phased Implementation: A phased rollout with pilot programs can help identify and address issues before full-scale implementation.

This case study illustrates the complexities of implementing new technologies in critical infrastructure. It underscores the importance of thorough testing, effective communication, robust cybersecurity measures, and careful integration planning in large-scale technology deployments. PG&E's experience is a cautionary tale for other utilities and companies embarking on similar digital transformation initiatives in the EHS space.

Case Study 2: Rio Tinto's Autonomous Haulage System Challenges (2016-2018)

Background: Rio Tinto, one of the world's largest mining companies, began implementing autonomous haulage systems (AHS) in its mining operations in the early 2010s as part of its "Mine of the Future" program. This initiative aimed to improve safety, efficiency, and productivity in its mining operations, particularly in the Pilbara region of Western Australia.

Objectives:

1. Improve safety by reducing risks associated with human-operated vehicles in mining environments.

2. Increase operational efficiency through 24/7 operations and optimized routes.

3. Reduce costs through lower labor costs and improved fuel efficiency.

4. Achieve more consistent performance in haulage operations.

5. Gather and analyze operational data for continuous improvement.

Key Failure Points:

1. Collisions: Multiple incidents occurred where autonomous trucks collided with other vehicles or equipment, highlighting challenges in the system's ability to detect and respond to all potential obstacles in a dynamic mining environment.

2. System Failures: Unexpected shutdowns or malfunctions in the autonomous system led to production delays, exposing the vulnerability of relying heavily on automated systems in critical operations.

3. Integration Challenges: Difficulties arose in integrating the autonomous system with existing safety protocols and procedures, creating confusion and potential safety risks in mixed-operation environments.

4. Human Factor Challenges: The introduction of autonomous vehicles required significant changes in how human workers interacted with and worked alongside these systems, leading to miscommunication or misunderstanding.

5. Environmental Adaptability: The system sometimes struggles to adapt to rapidly changing environmental conditions common in mining operations, such as dust storms or heavy rain.

6. Maintenance and Troubleshooting: The complexity of the autonomous systems posed challenges for maintenance teams, sometimes leading to extended downtime during troubleshooting.

Outcomes:

1. Safety Concerns: While the overall safety record improved, the collisions and near-misses raised new safety concerns about autonomous operations.

2. Productivity Fluctuations: System failures and integration issues sometimes lead to unexpected production delays during increased productivity.

3. Increased Scrutiny: The setbacks increased scrutiny from regulators, unions, and industry observers.

4. Learning Opportunity: The challenges provided valuable insights for improving autonomous mining systems.

5. Continued Investment: Rio Tinto continued to invest in and refine its autonomous haulage system despite the setbacks.

Lessons Learned:

1. Phased Implementation: A more gradual approach to implementing autonomous systems can help identify and address issues before full-scale deployment.

2. Enhanced Safety Protocols: Developing comprehensive safety protocols designed explicitly for mixed autonomous and human-operated environments is crucial.

3. Robust Testing: Extensive testing under various real-world conditions is essential before full implementation.

4. Improved Integration: Integrating autonomous systems with existing operations and safety protocols is necessary for smooth operations.

5. Human-Centered Design: It is vital to consider human factors and design systems that can effectively communicate with and interact with human operators.

6. Adaptive Systems: Developing more adaptable systems that can handle diverse and changing conditions in mining environments is essential.

7. Skilled Workforce Development: It is crucial to invest in training and developing a workforce capable of operating, maintaining, and troubleshooting advanced autonomous systems.

This case study highlights the complexities of implementing advanced autonomous systems in challenging, high-risk environments like mining operations. It underscores the importance of thorough testing, gradual implementation, and careful consideration of human factors and safety protocols in such initiatives. Rio Tinto's experience provides valuable lessons for other companies looking to implement autonomous systems in complex operational environments.

Case Study 3: Chemical Manufacturer's EHS Data Integration Failure (2017)

Background: In 2017, a large, unnamed chemical manufacturer initiated a project integrating data from various Environment, Health, and Safety (EHS) systems across its operations. This initiative was part of a broader effort to modernize the company's safety management practices and leverage data for improved decision-making and regulatory compliance.

Objectives:

1. Create a unified platform for all EHS data across the organization.

2. Enable better safety assessments and predictive analysis through comprehensive data integration.

3. Simplify and automate regulatory reporting processes.

4. Improve the tracking and analysis of safety incidents.

5. Reduce manual data entry and improve data accessibility.

Key Failure Points:

1. System Incompatibility: The new data integration platform was incompatible with many of the company's legacy systems, which caused difficulties with data transfer and synchronization.

2. Data Quality Issues: The integration process revealed significant data quality problems in the legacy systems, including inconsistent data formats, duplicate entries, and missing information.

3. User Adaptation Challenges: Employees need help adapting to the new integrated system, which needs to be simplified and more intuitive. This resulted in underreporting of incidents and reluctance to use the new system for safety-related tasks.

4. Inadequate Training: The training provided to employees on the new system was insufficient, contributing to user adaptation issues.

5. Lack of Data Governance: There needed to be a clear framework for data governance, leading to confusion about data ownership and maintenance responsibilities.

6. Integration Complexity Underestimation: The project team underestimated the complexity of integrating diverse EHS systems, leading to delays and cost overruns.

7. Insufficient Testing: Inadequate integrated system testing before full deployment led to the discovery of critical issues in live operations.

Outcomes:

1. Project Abandonment: After significant investment, the integration project was eventually abandoned.

2. Reversion to Previous Systems: The company reverted to its previous disparate EHS systems.

3. Financial Losses: Substantial financial resources could have been better spent on the failed integration attempt.

4. Operational Disruption: The failed implementation caused disruptions to normal safety management processes.

5. Decreased Employee Trust: The experience decreased trust in management's technology initiatives.

6. Missed Opportunities: The failure to integrate EHS data meant missed opportunities for improved safety management and analytics.

Lessons Learned:

1. Thorough System Assessment: Conduct a comprehensive assessment of all existing systems before integrating.

2. Data Quality Focus: Prioritize data cleansing and standardization before integration attempts.

3. User-Centered Design: Involve end-users in the design process to ensure the new system meets their needs and is intuitive.

4. Comprehensive Training: Develop a robust training program to ensure all users are comfortable with the new system.

5. Phased Implementation: Consider a phased approach to integration, starting with pilot projects before full-scale deployment.

6. Data Governance Framework: Establish clear policies and procedures before initiating data integration projects.

7. Realistic Project Planning: Carefully assess data integration projects' complexity and potential challenges and plan accordingly.

8. Rigorous Testing: Before full deployment, implement thorough testing procedures, including user acceptance testing.

This case study highlights the complexities of implementing global digital systems, particularly in industries where safety and environmental compliance are critical. It emphasizes the importance of addressing both technical and organizational aspects of change when implementing new digital systems across diverse global operations.

Cross-Case Analysis and Lessons Learned

Analyzing the PG&E Smart Meter Program, Rio Tinto's Autonomous Haulage System, and the Chemical Manufacturer's EHS Data Integration project reveals several common themes and critical lessons for digital EHS initiatives.

1. Technology Implementation Challenges

All three cases highlight the complexities of implementing new technologies in established operational environments. PG & E needed help with meter accuracy and system integration. Rio Tinto faced challenges with autonomous vehicle operations in dynamic mining environments, and the chemical manufacturer encountered significant hurdles in integrating diverse EHS systems.

Lesson: Thorough testing and phased implementation are crucial. As seen in all cases, rushing to full-scale deployment without adequate testing can lead to significant operational disruptions and safety risks.

2. Integration with Existing Systems

A common thread throughout all cases was integrating new technologies with existing systems and processes. This was particularly evident in PG&E's

integration of its smart meter and the chemical manufacturer's data integration project.

Lesson: Careful planning for system integration is essential. Organizations must comprehensively assess existing systems and plan for seamless integration to avoid operational disruptions.

3. Human Factors and Change Management

Each case demonstrated the critical role of human factors in technology adoption. PG&E faced public backlash, Rio Tinto encountered challenges in human-machine interaction, and the chemical manufacturer's employees needed help to adapt to the new integrated system.

Lesson: User-centered design and comprehensive change management strategies are vital. Involving end-users in the design process and providing thorough training can significantly improve adoption rates and system effectiveness.

4. Data Quality and Governance

Data issues were prominent in both PG&E's and the chemical manufacturer's cases. PG&E struggled with meter reading accuracy, while the chemical manufacturer faced significant data quality and governance challenges.

Lesson: Prioritize data quality and establish clear data governance frameworks. Organizations must ensure data accuracy and consistency before undertaking large-scale data integration or analytics projects.

5. Safety and Risk Management

Safety considerations were paramount in all three cases, given the critical nature of EHS in these industries. Rio Tinto's case highlighted the need for enhanced safety protocols in mixed autonomous and human-operated environments.

Lesson: Safety must remain the top priority in any digital EHS initiative. New technologies should enhance, not compromise, existing safety protocols.

6. Scalability and Environmental Adaptability

Rio Tinto's case highlighted challenges in scaling autonomous systems and adapting to varying environmental conditions. Similarly, the chemical manufacturer's project faced scalability issues across diverse operations.

Lesson: When designing systems, consider scalability and adaptability. Technologies must function effectively across different operational scales and environmental conditions.

7. Stakeholder Communication

PG&E's case highlighted the importance of effective communication with all stakeholders, including customers and regulatory bodies.

Lesson: Develop a comprehensive communication strategy. Clear, transparent communication about new technologies' benefits and potential challenges is crucial for stakeholder buy-in and trust.

8. Realistic Project Planning

All three cases demonstrated instances where project complexity was underestimated, leading to delays, cost overruns, or project failure.

Lesson: Conduct thorough project planning using realistic timelines and resource allocations. Organizations should also carefully assess potential challenges and build contingencies.

These case studies underscore the complex, multifaceted nature of digital EHS transformations. Success requires technological expertise and careful consideration of human factors, organizational processes, data management, and safety protocols. By learning from these experiences, organizations can better navigate the challenges of digital EHS initiatives and increase their chances of successful implementation.

Based on the insights from the case studies and cross-case analysis, here are critical recommendations for successful Digital EHS Transformation:

1. Phased Implementation Strategy

o   Begin with pilot projects to identify and address issues early.

o   Scale gradually, allowing for adjustments based on real-world performance.

o   Example: Start with a single facility or department before company-wide rollout.

2. Comprehensive System Integration Planning

- o Conduct thorough assessments of existing systems before integration attempts.

- o Develop detailed integration plans that account for legacy systems.

- o Allocate sufficient resources for integration challenges.

3. Prioritize Data Quality and Governance

- o Establish clear data governance policies and procedures.

- o Implement data cleansing and standardization processes before integration.

- o Assign clear ownership and responsibility for data quality maintenance.

4. User-Centered Design and Change Management

- o Involve end-users in the design process to ensure intuitive, valuable systems.

- o Develop comprehensive training programs for all affected employees.

- o Implement a robust change management strategy to address resistance and ensure adoption.

5. Enhanced Safety Protocols for New Technologies

- o Develop specific safety protocols for new digital systems, especially in mixed environments.

- o Conduct thorough risk assessments for all new technological implementations.

- o Ensure new systems enhance rather than compromise existing safety measures.

6. Robust Testing Procedures

- o Implement rigorous testing under various real-world conditions before deployment.

- o User acceptance testing should be a critical step before the full rollout.

o   Continuously monitor and test system performance post-implementation.

7. Scalable and Adaptable System Design

o   Design systems that can function effectively across different operational scales.

o   Ensure adaptability to varying environmental and operational conditions.

o   Build flexibility to accommodate future technological advancements.

8. Transparent Stakeholder Communication

o   Develop a comprehensive communication strategy for all stakeholders.

o   Articulate benefits, potential challenges, and impacts of new technologies.

o   Maintain open channels for feedback and address concerns promptly.

9. Realistic Project Planning and Resource Allocation

o   Carefully assess project complexity and potential challenges.

o   Set realistic timelines and budgets, including contingencies.

o   Ensure adequate allocation of both technical and human resources.

10. Continuous Improvement and Learning

o   Establish mechanisms for ongoing evaluation of system performance.

o   Foster a culture of continuous learning and improvement.

o   Regularly reassess and update digital strategies based on emerging technologies and lessons learned.

11. Cybersecurity and Data Privacy Focus

o   Implement robust cybersecurity measures to protect sensitive EHS data.

o   Ensure compliance with data privacy regulations.

o   Regularly update security protocols to address evolving threats.

12. Cross-Functional Collaboration

o   Foster collaboration between EHS, IT, operations, and other relevant departments.

o   Ensure alignment of digital EHS initiatives with broader organizational goals.

o   Leverage diverse expertise for comprehensive solution development.

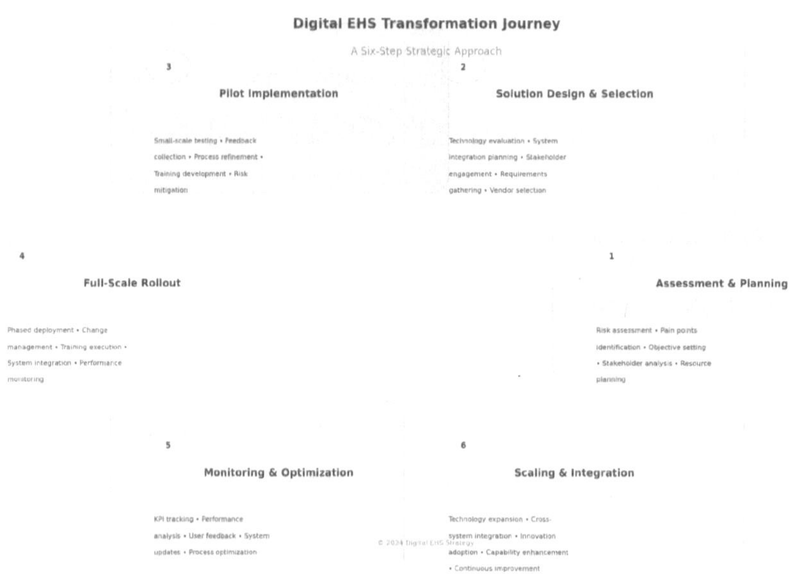

Figure 6.1: Digital EHS Transformation Journey

By following these recommendations, organizations can significantly improve their chances of successful digital EHS transformation. They can avoid the pitfalls illustrated in the case studies while capitalizing on the potential benefits of new technologies in EHS management.

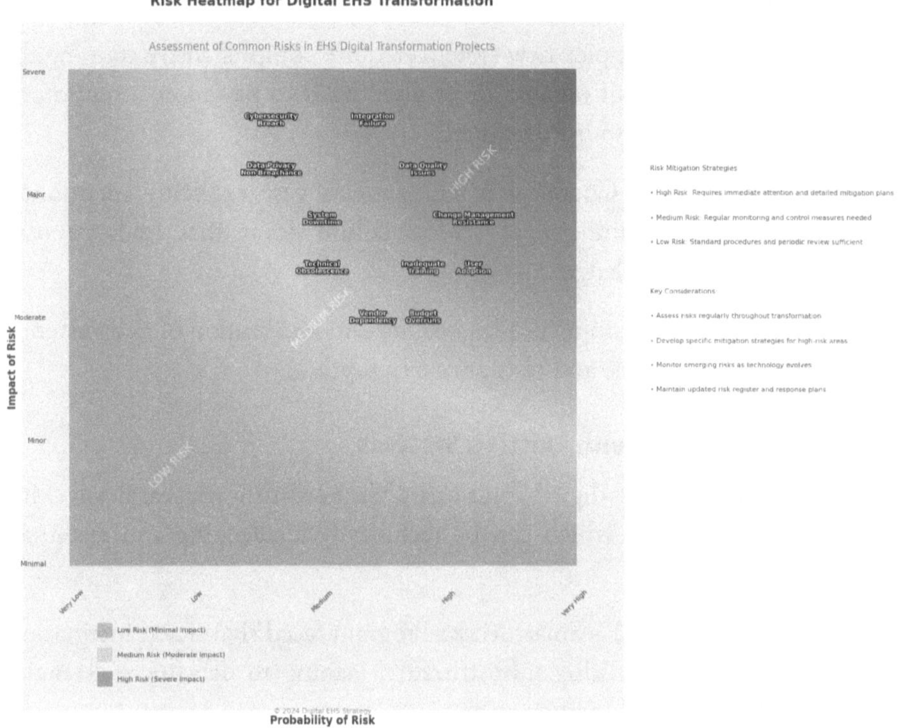

Figure 6.2: Risk heatmap for digital EHS Transformation

Common pitfalls in Digital EHS transformation

Common pitfalls in digital EHS transformation, drawing insights from the case studies and broader research:

1. Lack of Leadership Buy-in

   o   Challenge: Without solid support from top management, digital EHS initiatives often struggle to get necessary resources and organizational priorities.

   o   Example: In the Chemical Manufacturer's EHS Data Integration case, the lack of an apparent data governance framework suggests insufficient leadership engagement in the project.

   o   Impact: This can lead to underfunded projects, inconsistent implementation, and a lack of organization-wide commitment to change.

2. Insufficient Employee Training

o Challenge: Complex new systems require comprehensive training for practical use, but organizations often need to pay more attention to the time and resources required.

o Example: The Chemical Manufacturer's case explicitly mentioned inadequate training as a critical failure point that leads to user adaptation challenges.

o Impact: Poor training can lead to the underutilization of new systems, data entry errors, and resistance to adoption.

3. Poor Integration with Existing Systems

o Challenge: New digital solutions often need to work seamlessly with legacy systems, which can be technically challenging and resource-intensive.

o Example: PG&E's Smart Meter Program faced significant integration failures with existing infrastructure, leading to data inconsistencies and operational inefficiencies.

o Impact: Failed integration can cause data silos, duplicate work, and reduced efficiency – the opposite of what digital transformation aims to achieve.

4. Data Privacy and Security Concerns

o Challenge: As EHS processes become digitized, ensuring the security and privacy of sensitive data becomes increasingly complex.

o Example: PG&E's program raised concerns about data privacy and grid vulnerability, highlighting the importance of robust cybersecurity measures.

o Impact: Inadequate data protection can lead to regulatory non-compliance, loss of trust from employees and stakeholders, and potential safety risks if systems are compromised.

5. Resistance to Change from Workers

o   Challenge: Employees often resist new technologies that significantly alter their work processes, especially if they need help understanding the benefits.

o   Example: In Rio Tinto's case, introducing autonomous vehicles required significant changes in how human workers interacted with and worked alongside these systems.

o   Impact: Resistance can slow down implementation, reduce the effectiveness of new systems, and create a hostile work environment.

6. Overambitious Scope and Timeline

o   Challenge: Organizations often need to pay more attention to the complexity of digital transformation, setting unrealistic goals and timelines.

o   Example: The Chemical Manufacturer's project team underestimated the complexity of integrating diverse EHS systems, leading to delays and cost overruns.

o   Impact: This can result in rushed implementations, inadequate testing, and project failure.

7. Inadequate Risk Assessment

o   Challenge: Failing to thoroughly assess potential risks of new digital systems, especially in safety-critical environments.

o   Example: Rio Tinto's autonomous haulage system faced unexpected challenges adapting to dynamic mining environments, suggesting incomplete risk assessment.

o   Impact: Unforeseen risks can lead to safety incidents, operational disruptions, and loss of confidence in digital initiatives.

8. Neglecting Change Management

o   Challenge: Organizations often focus on technical aspects while underestimating the importance of managing the human side of change.

- o Example: The Chemical Manufacturer's case highlighted the need for more effective change management strategies, contributing to user adoption issues.

- o Impact: Poor change management can lead to low adoption rates, resistance, and failure to realize the benefits of new systems.

9. Data Quality Issues

- o Challenge: Digital systems rely on high-quality data, but organizations often need more consistent, complete, and accurate data.

- o Example: The Chemical Manufacturer's integration process revealed significant data quality problems in legacy systems.

- o Impact: Poor data quality can lead to incorrect analytics, faulty decision-making, and loss of trust in the new systems.

10. Lack of Clear Metrics and Evaluation

- o Challenge: Without clear success metrics, it isn't easy to evaluate the effectiveness of digital initiatives and justify continued investment.

- o Example: While not explicitly mentioned in the cases, the lack of clear evaluation criteria can be inferred from the difficulties in assessing project success.

- o Impact: This can lead to continued investment in ineffective systems or prematurely abandoning potentially valuable initiatives.

Organizations can significantly improve their chances of successful digital EHS transformation by understanding and proactively addressing these common pitfalls.

The Importance of Change Management in EHS Digital Transformation

While technological solutions are crucial in digital EHS transformation, the human element often determines the success or failure of these initiatives. Change management is a critical yet frequently underestimated component of digital transformation. Here's why it's essential and how organizations can effectively manage the cultural shift required:

1. The Human Factor in Digital Transformation

Digital EHS transformation isn't just about implementing new technologies and changing how people work. Employees at all levels must adapt to new processes, learn new skills, and often shift their mindsets about safety and environmental management. Even the most advanced technological solutions can only deliver the expected benefits with proper change management.

2. Strategies for Effective Change Management

a) Clear Communication

- Articulate the vision and benefits of the digital transformation clearly and consistently.

- Use multiple channels to reach all employees, from frontline workers to executives.

- For example, PG&E could have mitigated public backlash by better communicating the benefits and addressing concerns about its innovative meter program.

b) Leadership Engagement

- Ensure visible support and engagement from top management.

- Train middle managers to be change champions who can address concerns and motivate their teams.

c) Employee Involvement

- Involve employees in the design and implementation process to increase buy-in.

- Create feedback mechanisms to capture and address employee concerns.

- Example: Rio Tinto could have benefited from more extensive collaboration with human operators in designing their autonomous haulage system interfaces.

d) Comprehensive Training Programs

- Develop tailored training programs that address different learning styles and technological proficiencies.

- Provide ongoing support and resources beyond initial implementation.

- Example: The Chemical Manufacturer case highlighted how inadequate training led to user adoption challenges.

Figure 6.3: Digital EHS Transformation – Success Vs Failure Factors

e) Phased Implementation

- Start with pilot programs to identify and address issues before full-scale rollout.

- Use early successes to build momentum and demonstrate benefits.

f) Addressing Resistance

- Anticipate and proactively address sources of resistance.

- Create a safe environment for employees to express concerns and ask questions.

g) Cultural Alignment

- Align the digital transformation with existing organizational values and culture.

- If necessary, work on shifting the organizational culture to be more receptive to technological change.

3. Managing the Cultural Shift

a) Fostering a Digital Culture

- Encourage a mindset of continuous learning and adaptation.

- Reward innovation and willingness to embrace new technologies.

b) Balancing Technology and Human Expertise

- Emphasize that digital tools are meant to enhance, not replace, human expertise in EHS.

- Demonstrate how technology can empower employees to make better decisions and work more efficiently.

c) Building Trust in New Systems

- Be transparent about data usage and privacy protection.

- Showcase early wins and improvements in safety outcomes to build confidence.

d) Encouraging Collaboration

- Use digital tools to facilitate better communication and collaboration across departments.

- Break down silos between EHS, IT, and operations teams.

4. Measuring Change Management Success

a) Employee Adoption Metrics

- Track usage rates of new systems.

- Measure employee satisfaction and comfort with new technologies.

b) Cultural Indicators

- Assess changes in safety culture and risk awareness.

- Monitor improvements in cross-functional collaboration.

c) Performance Outcomes

- Link change management efforts to improvements in crucial EHS performance indicators.

5. Case Study Example: Successful Change Management in EHS Digital Transformation

While our previous case studies highlighted challenges, let's consider a hypothetical success story:

A large manufacturing company implemented a new digital EHS management system. They:

- Involved employees at all levels in the design phase.

- Conducted extensive pilot testing and gathered feedback.

- Developed a comprehensive communication plan, clearly articulating benefits.

- Provided tailored training programs and ongoing support.

- Celebrated early successes and addressed challenges transparently.

Result: High adoption rates, improved safety metrics, and positive employee feedback on the new system.

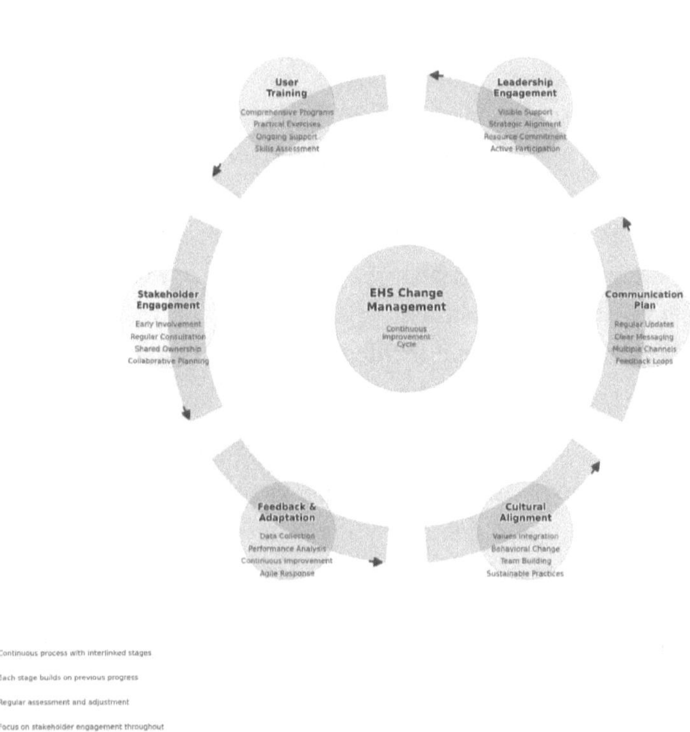

Figure 6.4: Change Management Process in EHS Digital Transformation

Effective change management is not just a supporting element but a critical success factor in digital EHS transformation. By focusing on the human side of change – through clear communication, employee involvement, comprehensive training, and cultural alignment – organizations can significantly increase the chances of successful digital EHS initiatives. Remember, digital transformation is as much about people as technology.

Power of Digital Technologies

As the world becomes increasingly digitized, environment, Health, and Safety (EHS) systems are embracing the transformative power of digital sensors, IoT, AR/VR, Big Data, and mobile technologies. From real-time monitoring of workplace conditions to incident management and environmental compliance tracking, many enterprises are embedding sensors in critical EHS infrastructure, such as manufacturing equipment, air quality monitors, or worker safety gear. The challenge remains: How will these enterprises monetize and fully capitalize on the value created by these connected systems?

In the EHS context, mobile devices can now act as control centers for managing safety, environmental data, and compliance processes. Workers can use smartphones to receive alerts about potential hazards, track safety protocols, and manage equipment maintenance schedules. Simultaneously, the IoT can provide real-time data on everything from gas emissions to machine performance, giving EHS managers and frontline workers unprecedented control and visibility over their environments. This connectivity enables more efficient monitoring and incident prevention while ensuring regulatory compliance.

As these technologies converge, the IoT and mobile devices are unlocking a world of data-driven decision-making. For example, wearable sensors that track a worker's vital signs can immediately alert a safety officer if a worker is exposed to dangerous levels of heat or toxins. Similarly, real-time environmental data can be integrated into an organization's EHS platform, providing decision-makers with a complete view of potential risks and enabling quicker responses to mitigate those risks.

Integrating mobile and IoT in EHS management creates a powerful overlap between worker safety and organizational efficiency. It gives workers more control over their safety by tracking real-time risks and enables organizations to reduce incidents, streamline reporting, and enhance compliance efforts. This level of connectivity promises significant cost savings by preventing accidents and ensuring that businesses remain compliant with evolving EHS regulations.

Through my career spanning many industries, I've found that this intersection of mobile and digital technologies can redefine how enterprises approach EHS management. The combination of connectivity, real-time monitoring, and data integration allows companies to move up and to the right on the EHS competitive framework (toward becoming ecosystem leaders). This connectivity empowers innovation, enabling companies to deliver proactive risk management solutions and quickly adapt to emerging regulations.

However, as with any technological evolution, the path forward is with risk. Failures and setbacks will occur as enterprises attempt to master this new frontier, but the potential rewards are immense. Enterprises that successfully integrate IoT and mobile technology into their EHS strategy will dominate the space, driving better safety outcomes, operational efficiencies, and regulatory compliance.

This chapter will explore how your EHS enterprise can develop a mobile strategy and commit to the IoT, helping you find your sweet spot in this powerful overlap. As leaders consolidate their EHS platforms and dominate the ecosystem through smart connectivity, those who fail to adopt these technologies may need to catch up and be forced to play a commodity role in more advanced players' safety and compliance ecosystems.

I'll illustrate these concepts with examples from industries that have mastered this connectivity, demonstrating how mobile and IoT can be leveraged to create real value in the EHS space. Let's start by understanding mobile's role in EHS management's future.

What's Your Mobile Strategy in EHS?

In Environment, Health, and Safety (EHS), mobile devices transform how organizations engage with workers, monitor risks, and ensure compliance. Smartphones, with their sensors, cameras, and location tracking, are pivotal in making workplaces safer and more efficient. These devices, always within reach, offer real-time alerts, incident reporting, safety checklists, and compliance tracking, making mobile engagement a vital strategy for modern EHS systems.

As mobile technologies have evolved and become ubiquitous in personal and professional spaces, the importance of mobile devices in EHS has grown significantly. Just as consumers spend more time on mobile devices—66% of the digitally connected time in 2022—EHS professionals also increasingly rely on mobile platforms to conduct inspections, monitor conditions, and manage real-time incidents.

Imagine the traditional process of workplace safety inspections or incident reporting. In the past, it required manual logging, filling out forms, and submitting reports, often leading to delays in addressing potential hazards.

With mobile devices, safety officers can snap a photo, record a hazard, and submit reports instantly, leading to faster issue resolution and better compliance management. Mobile devices allow for faster, more efficient handling of critical EHS activities, cutting down response times and enabling real-time monitoring of risks.

Just as mobile has revolutionized industries like travel, where booking vacations has shifted from a multi-step process to a single mobile experience, the same shift is happening in EHS. Workers and managers no longer rely on paper-based systems or multiple steps to record safety incidents or monitor environmental conditions. With EHS mobile platforms, they can manage everything—from reporting hazards to tracking emissions—all on one device.

The Role of Mobile in EHS Engagement

Mobile strategies in EHS must focus on consolidating services and providing a seamless experience for employees, safety officers, and executives. Companies can keep workers engaged by creating EHS-specific apps or mobile-friendly dashboards that allow them to:

- Monitor environmental conditions in real-time, such as air quality or noise levels.

- Receive alerts on potential safety risks, like hazardous chemical exposure or machine malfunctions.

- Log incidents or near misses quickly through easy-to-use forms and photo uploads.

- Access safety protocols and checklists instantly, ensuring compliance during inspections or audits.

- Review historical data and performance metrics for continuous improvement of safety measures.

For instance, mobile EHS apps can be customized for specific industries or environments, such as construction or manufacturing. These apps allow workers to track potential hazards and receive safety alerts based on their GPS location. This improves safety and proactively engages workers, helping them feel more in control of their work environment.

Example: EHS Mobile Strategy

Take the example of a chemical manufacturing company that wanted to improve its incident response times and compliance tracking. They developed a mobile app for workers and managers that allowed for:

- Real-time incident reporting: Workers could quickly log safety incidents using voice commands or taking photos, automatically triggering management alerts.

- Mobile audits and inspections: Safety officers could conduct audits using digital checklists that are updated in real-time, ensuring that any compliance gaps are addressed immediately.

- Geo-tagged hazard alerts: The app used GPS data to notify workers when they entered high-risk zones, prompting them to take precautionary actions.

By adopting a mobile-first approach, the company reduced its incident reporting times by 30% and improved overall compliance by ensuring that audits were completed on time. All data was stored centrally for easy access during inspections.

Five Mobile Strategies for EHS

When developing your EHS mobile strategy, consider the following approaches:

1. **Safety Engagement:** Increase worker engagement by providing a helpful, free mobile service, such as an app that allows workers to check air quality levels or monitor noise exposure in real-time.

2. **Integrated safety channel:** To improve the EHS experience, mobile apps can be integrated with other platforms, such as incident management systems or environmental monitoring platforms, to provide a seamless workflow for employees.

3. **Worker Safety Connection:** Connect directly to end-users (such as workers) via mobile apps that provide immediate access to compliance checklists, incident reporting, and emergency protocols, ensuring that workers always comply with safety regulations.

4. **Industry-specific solutions:** Create a unique mobile app tailored for specific high-risk industries like mining, oil and gas, or construction, where real-time hazard alerts and location-based safety notifications can significantly improve safety outcomes.

5. **Mobile first EHS Innovation:** Launch all EHS innovations on the mobile channel. For example, prioritize developing mobile apps for conducting safety inspections, reporting environmental violations, or monitoring worker health data through wearables.

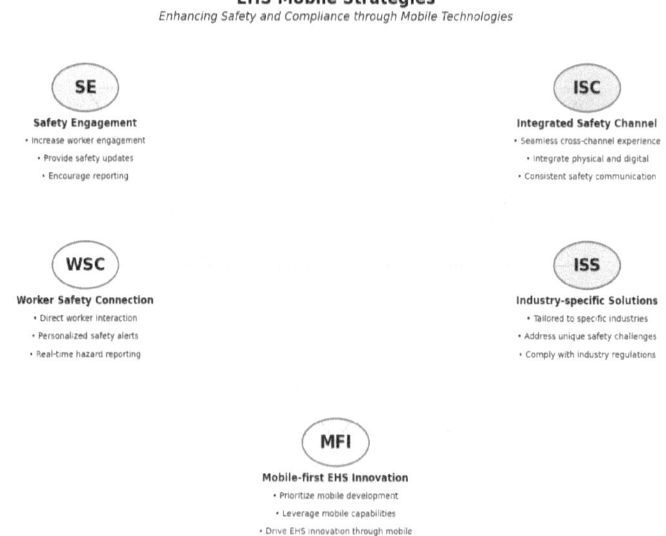

Figure 6.5: EHS Mobile Strategies

Incorporating a solid mobile strategy into your EHS program is crucial to improving safety outcomes, ensuring regulatory compliance, and engaging workers. As I elaborate in the next section, mobile combined with IoT offers an even more powerful opportunity for EHS leaders to innovate and create value in the connected workplace. Now is the time to define your EHS mobile strategy, as it will shape the future of safety management and your ability to compete in the digital era.

Safety Engagement in EHS

A Safety Engagement mobile app strategy in the Environment, Health, and Safety (EHS) domain focuses on increasing worker and stakeholder engagement with an organization's safety and sustainability brand. Enterprises operating in EHS can be creative in using mobile apps to enhance their safety engagement, reinforce their commitment to safety and compliance, and promote sustainability efforts. Typically, an enterprise deploys a mobile app or platform that complements its core safety, health, and environmental management services.

Here are a few examples of how EHS-focused organizations might implement safety engagement mobile apps:

- iAuditor: is a leading safety management app that allows workers to log incidents, conduct inspections, and report near-misses in real-time. It also offers checklists and daily reminders to help workers stay safe.

- Virgin Pulse: Virgin Pulse is a well-being platform designed to help employees track personal health metrics (e.g., heart rate, sleep, activity levels), set wellness goals, and receive mental health support. The app also provides reminders for healthy habits such as stretching and hydration.

- Sphera Sustainability Platform: Sphera is a sustainability-focused platform for tracking environmental metrics such as carbon emissions, water usage, and waste generation. It provides personalized sustainability insights and allows users to monitor their environmental impact.

- iNaturalist: iNaturalist encourages users to take photos of plants, animals, and environmental conservation efforts. It is a social network for sharing biodiversity observations and is often used for environmental awareness and conservation efforts.

Why Safety Engagement Is Critical in EHS

In EHS, enterprises must often enhance their brand to show commitment to employee safety, regulatory compliance, and sustainable practices. Unlike direct product sales or customer engagement strategies, these apps aim to build trust and strengthen the company's reputation in the EHS domain while aligning the workforce with safety and environmental priorities.

For example, a company specializing in industrial safety equipment might launch a safety-engaging mobile app that provides workers with safety training videos, incident-reporting tools, and real-time hazard alerts. This app helps reinforce the company's commitment to workplace safety while encouraging better compliance and proactive safety behaviors.

Integrated safety Channel in EHS

An Integrated safety Channel mobile strategy in the Environment, Health, and Safety (EHS) domain focuses on enhancing the overall relationship with employees, safety managers, and stakeholders by providing a seamless cross-channel experience. Like retail, EHS enterprises must create consistent, connected experiences across physical and digital platforms to ensure efficient communication, reporting, and safety management.

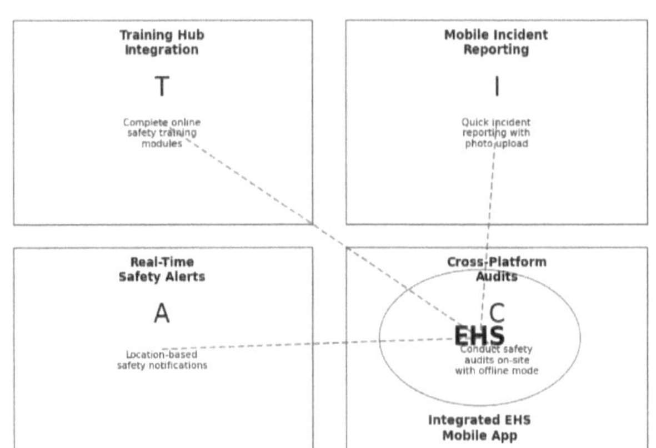

Impact of an Integrated Safety Channel Approach

Integrated safety Channel strategy can achieve significant improvements in engagement and compliance via:

- Increased Engagement: Workers who use in-person and digital training channels are 30% more likely to complete safety certifications than those who rely on physical channels alone.

- Faster Incident Reporting: With mobile integration, incident reporting times have decreased by 40%, allowing safety managers to address real-time risks.

- Higher Compliance Rates: Integrated safety Channel training and audits have contributed to 15% higher compliance rates across sites, reducing the number of workplace accidents and fines for non-compliance.

These results highlight the power of cross-channel safety management, where digital platforms enhance physical processes, creating better safety outcomes.

Lessons for EHS Enterprises

EHS companies can invest in mobile platforms that complement physical safety efforts. By ensuring that employees and managers can access safety tools, training materials, and reporting systems across multiple platforms (desktop, mobile, and physical sites), EHS companies can ensure greater engagement, compliance, and safety outcomes.

The competitive environment in EHS, like in retail, requires constant innovation. As digital safety tools evolve, companies like SHE Software Assure must continuously enhance their mobile applications, incorporating features such as predictive safety analytics, AI-driven hazard identification, and automated compliance updates to stay ahead of the competition.

In the EHS domain, an Integrated safety Channel strategy can significantly enhance safety engagement and compliance by integrating mobile apps with physical safety processes. By allowing workers and managers to move seamlessly between platforms, enterprises can improve the overall safety experience, increase compliance rates, and ensure critical safety information is always accessible, on-site or on the go.

Worker Safety Connection in EHS

In an Environment, Health, and Safety (EHS) context, the Worker Safety Connection model can bridge the gap between an EHS service provider and the end-users (employees or contractors) by creating direct connections via mobile apps and platforms. Historically, EHS service providers primarily dealt with businesses(employers) to manage compliance, safety protocols, and environmental health standards. The workers, who are the end consumers of the safety tools and training, often lack the need for more direct interaction with the safety provider. However, the rise of mobile technology presents a unique opportunity for EHS providers to engage directly with employees, ensuring that safety tools, guidelines, and training are more accessible and personalized.

For example, consider a company that provides workplace safety equipment or hazardous material handling training to large corporations. Traditionally, the employer mediated the connection between the safety equipment provider and the worker who uses the gear. In a Worker Safety Connection model, the EHS provider could now develop a mobile app or platform that connects directly with the end-user, ensuring more immediate access to safety guidelines, training materials, and incident reporting tools.

Benefits in EHS

An EHS provider can leverage mobile platforms to communicate with workers across multiple worksites. For instance, an EHS company working with various construction firms can create a unified safety management app used by all site contractors. Workers from multiple employers can benefit from a standardized and customized safety platform, while the EHS provider gains access to data across various projects, enhancing the overall safety strategy.

A B2B2C or Worker Safety Integration model in the EHS space allows safety providers to engage directly with end-users, creating better safety outcomes and deeper customer relationships. By providing workers with mobile-enabled tools for training, incident reporting, and safety protocols, EHS providers can ensure compliance is met and workers are more engaged in their safety practices. This creates a win-win situation, where the business and end-user are better served through seamless connectivity and direct communication.

Mobile First in EHS

In Environment, Health, and Safety (EHS), a mobile-first strategy can revolutionize how organizations handle workplace safety, environmental compliance, and health management. As workplaces adopt digital tools, a mobile-first approach ensures that safety solutions are accessible directly from workers' pockets, empowering them to manage EHS issues instantly and efficiently.

Results and Benefits of a Mobile-First EHS Strategy:

A mobile-first EHS platform would:

- Increase Engagement: With safety tools readily available on workers' mobile devices, adoption rates would improve, and workers would engage more regularly with safety processes.

- Boost Compliance: The ability to quickly and easily document incidents and complete compliance tasks would increase adherence to safety protocols and regulations.

- Fast Feedback Loops: As in the banking sector, a mobile-first strategy in EHS can capture real-time feedback from the workforce, which would be critical in identifying potential risks and responding effectively.

- Enhanced Safety Culture: When EHS management becomes an integral part of daily work facilitated by mobile technology, it fosters a stronger safety-first mindset across the organization.

Reimagining Physical Channels

EHS organizations would need to reimagine physical safety processes. Traditional safety audits, compliance checks, and manual reporting must be integrated into a digital framework that centers on mobile use, ensuring that all physical processes are digitally supported and instantly actionable.

Focusing on mobile-first EHS can enhance safety management and compliance by making real-time reporting and immediate action a seamless part of the workday, driving more robust engagement, safer workplaces, and better outcomes.

Whatever strategy your EHS enterprise chooses, developing mobile engagement with your employees and stakeholders can provide significant benefits. Initial successes in mobile adoption often encourage more widespread use of mobile platforms, with enterprises making more significant investments and more substantial organizational commitments. This virtuous cycle—where success in mobile channels drives further engagement and investment—applies equally to the EHS industry. For instance, implementing mobile platforms for real-time incident reporting, safety audits, and compliance tracking can significantly improve employee safety and regulatory compliance.

Critical Considerations for Mobile in EHS

As you reflect on the role mobile can play in your EHS enterprise's overall strategy, consider the following key questions:

1. **Is Your EHS Business a Leader or a Follower in Mobile?**

   o   Leading EHS organizations leverage mobile technology to enhance safety, boost compliance, and engage employees on-site and remotely. Mobile technology helps digitize manual processes, allowing faster responses to safety issues and better incident tracking.

2. **Are You Seeing Bottom-Line Benefits?**

   o   The ROI from mobile EHS platforms includes reductions in incident rates, fewer workplace injuries, and improved regulatory compliance, which ultimately translate into cost savings and improved worker productivity.

3. **Who Drives Mobile Success in Your Organization?**

   o   EHS managers, safety officers, and compliance teams must champion mobile adoption. The key to success is ensuring that employees at all levels—especially on the ground—use mobile platforms effectively.

4. **How Can Young Employees Help Lead Mobile Innovation?**

   o   Younger employees, who are often more tech-savvy, can drive mobile innovation in EHS by contributing fresh ideas for improving mobile safety solutions and engagement strategies.

By answering these questions and reflecting on your current mobile strategy, your EHS enterprise can take meaningful steps toward becoming a leader in mobile safety management. As you advance up the Digital EHS Strategy, leveraging mobile tools will be crucial in helping your organization become an ecosystem driver in the EHS space, where real-time data, automation, and mobile connectivity play critical roles in ensuring workplace safety and compliance.

EHS: How Strong Is Your Commitment to the IoT?

The Internet of Things (IoT) promises to transform the EHS (Environment, Health, and Safety) landscape by connecting systems, equipment, people, and processes into an integrated real-time data network, creating enhanced safety, efficiency, and compliance opportunities. In this connected world, IoT-enabled devices like sensors, wearables, and intelligent machinery will allow organizations to monitor workplace conditions, predict hazards, and respond to incidents before they escalate.

For EHS enterprises, IoT represents a crucial shift in managing workplace safety and environmental monitoring. IoT technology will enable the creation of intelligent workplaces where real-time data can optimize both safety outcomes and operational efficiency. The question is: How committed is your EHS organization to leveraging IoT technologies, and are you positioned to lead or participate in this connected ecosystem?

The IoT Opportunity in EHS

The potential market for IoT solutions is enormous. Globally, companies are expected to invest $6 trillion in IoT technologies over the next five years, and by 2025, IoT could generate up to $11.1 trillion in economic value. In the EHS space, this will translate into advanced systems monitoring air quality, machine health, worker location, noise levels, and other critical factors, feeding real-time data into centralized platforms.

Successful EHS enterprises will use these technologies to improve risk management, ensure regulatory compliance, and create safer working environments. For instance, predictive analytics powered by IoT devices could anticipate equipment failure before it happens, preventing accidents and reducing downtime. Additionally, wearable technology, like intelligent helmets and connected sensors, can monitor worker fatigue, alert supervisors to dangerous situations, and enhance emergency response times.

Shifting Business Models in EHS

One of the most significant shifts the IoT will bring is the transformation from product-centric to service-centric business models. EHS organizations will no longer focus solely on selling equipment or software but will instead provide real-time safety solutions as services. For example, a company could give continuous air quality monitoring services instead of just selling a gas detection device with real-time alerts sent to managers and workers.

This shift requires a strong organizational commitment to IoT. Embracing IoT means investing in smart devices and building the data infrastructure needed to analyze the massive amounts of information these devices will produce. The ability to respond automatically to potential hazards—such as shutting down unsafe machinery or evacuating an area—will distinguish the leaders from the followers in this IoT-driven landscape.

Commitment to IoT: Leading vs. Following

The degree of your enterprise's commitment to IoT will determine whether you lead or follow in the coming hyperconnected world. Leaders will develop sophisticated IoT ecosystems integrating sensors, data analytics, and automated systems to proactively manage safety risks and improve regulatory compliance. Conversely, followers may rely on basic IoT implementations, such as monitoring and reporting, without using the data to drive real-time decision-making.

The IoT can potentially revolutionize EHS management, but only for those organizations that make a concerted effort to build and fully integrate these technologies into their operational models. Now is the time for EHS leaders to assess their IoT strategy, invest in the right tools, and move toward an ecosystem-based approach to enhance workplace safety and environmental sustainability.

The following sections explore how various organizations implement IoT solutions to create value and drive safety improvements.

Challenges and Considerations in Digital EHS Implementation

Managing Data Overload in IoT-Enabled EHS Systems

The proliferation of IoT devices in EHS management has led to an unprecedented influx of data. While this wealth of information offers immense potential for improving safety, environmental performance, and operational efficiency, it also presents significant data management and utilization challenges. Here's how organizations can effectively handle the data deluge:

1. The Data Overload Challenge

IoT devices in EHS contexts can generate massive volumes of data, including:

- Real-time environmental readings (air quality, noise levels, temperature)

- Equipment performance metrics

- Worker safety indicators (from wearable devices)

- Compliance-related data points

This data's sheer volume, velocity, and variety can overwhelm traditional data management systems and processes.

2. Strategies for Effective Data Management

a) Implement a Robust Data Architecture

- Design a scalable data infrastructure capable of handling large volumes of real-time data.

- Utilize cloud-based solutions for flexible storage and processing capabilities.

- Implement data lakes or data warehouses to centralize and organize diverse data types.

b) Prioritize Data Quality

- Establish data quality standards and validation processes.

- Implement automated data cleansing and error detection mechanisms.

- Regularly audit data quality to ensure reliability for decision-making.

c) Data Governance

- Develop transparent data governance policies defining data ownership, access rights, and usage guidelines.

- Create a data catalog to provide a clear overview of available data assets.

- Establish data retention and archiving policies to manage historical data effectively.

3. Practical Data Analysis Techniques

a) Advanced Analytics and AI

- Leverage machine learning algorithms to identify patterns and anomalies in large datasets.

- Use predictive analytics to forecast potential safety or environmental issues.

- Implement AI-driven systems for real-time risk assessment and alert generation.

b) Data Visualization

- Develop intuitive dashboards that present vital EHS metrics in an easily digestible format.

- Use interactive visualizations to allow users to explore data at various levels of granularity.

- Implement geospatial visualizations for location-based EHS data.

c) Edge Computing

- Process data at the source (IoT devices) to reduce the volume of data transmitted and stored centrally.

- Use edge analytics for immediate, localized decision-making in time-critical situations.

4. Actionable Insights and Decision Support

a) Establish Clear KPIs and Thresholds

- Define key performance indicators aligned with EHS objectives.

- Set clear thresholds for alerts and automated actions.

b) Implement Decision Support Systems

- Develop systems that present data and suggest actions based on predefined rules and AI-driven insights.

- Create automated workflows for routine decisions and escalation processes for complex issues.

c) Contextual Analysis

- Integrate EHS data with other business data (e.g., production schedules and maintenance records) for more comprehensive insights.

- Consider external factors (e.g., weather data, regulatory changes) in data analysis.

5. Training and Skill Development

a) Data Literacy Programs

- Implement training programs to improve data literacy across the organization.

- Develop specialized training for EHS professionals in data analysis and interpretation.

b) Cross-functional Collaboration

- Foster collaboration between EHS, IT, and data science teams.

- Create roles like 'EHS Data Analyst' to bridge the gap between EHS expertise and data analytics.

6. Continuous Improvement and Feedback Loops

a) Regular Review and Optimization

- Continuously assess the effectiveness of data collection, analysis, and action processes.

- Regularly update data models and algorithms to improve accuracy and relevance.

b) User Feedback

- Establish mechanisms for end-users to provide feedback on the usefulness and accuracy of data-driven insights.

- Use this feedback to refine data collection and analysis processes.

7. Case Study Example: Effective EHS Data Management

Consider a large chemical manufacturing plant that implemented an IoT-based EHS monitoring system:

- Challenge: The system generated terabytes of data daily from thousands of sensors monitoring air quality, equipment performance, and worker safety.

- Solution:

  o We implemented a cloud-based data lake for centralized storage.

  o We utilized edge computing to process non-critical data locally, reducing central data volume.

  o She developed AI-driven analytics to identify potential safety risks and environmental compliance issues.

  o They created role-specific dashboards providing actionable insights for different user groups.

- Result: Improved response time to potential hazards, 30% reduction in safety incidents, and more efficient environmental compliance reporting.

Conclusion:

Effectively managing the data influx from IoT devices in EHS is crucial for realizing the benefits of digital transformation. By implementing robust data management strategies, leveraging advanced analytics, and focusing on actionable insights, organizations can turn data overload into a powerful asset for improving EHS performance. Remember, the goal is not just to collect data but to transform it into meaningful actions that enhance safety, environmental stewardship, and operational excellence.

Cybersecurity Risks in Connected EHS Systems: Threats and Mitigation Strategies

As EHS systems become increasingly digitized and interconnected, they become more vulnerable to cyber threats. These risks can compromise data integrity, physical safety, and environmental protection. Here's an in-depth look at the cybersecurity challenges in EHS and strategies to mitigate them:

1. Understanding the Cybersecurity Landscape in EHS

Unique Vulnerabilities in EHS Systems:

- Direct impact on physical safety and environmental protection

- Integration of IT (Information Technology) and OT (Operational Technology) systems

- Legacy systems with limited security features

- Remote access requirements for monitoring and management

Common Cyber Threats in EHS:

- Data breaches exposing sensitive safety and environmental data

- Ransomware attacks disrupting critical safety systems

- Industrial espionage targeting proprietary environmental technologies

- Manipulation of sensor data leading to false safety alarms or missed hazards

- Unauthorized access to control systems, potentially causing physical harm or environmental damage

2. Key Cybersecurity Risks in Connected EHS Systems

a) Compromised Sensor Data

- Risk: Hackers manipulating sensor readings, leading to incorrect safety or environmental assessments

- Impact: Potential safety incidents, environmental non-compliance, or unnecessary shutdowns

b) Control System Vulnerabilities

- Risk: Unauthorized access to control systems (e.g., emissions control, safety shutoffs)

- Impact: Potential for sabotage leading to safety hazards or environmental releases

c) **Data Privacy Breaches**

- Risk: Theft of sensitive EHS data, including personal health information of employees

- Impact: Regulatory non-compliance, legal liabilities, loss of trust

d) **Disruption of EHS Monitoring Systems**

- Risk: Denial-of-service attacks on monitoring platforms

- Impact: Inability to detect and respond to safety or environmental incidents in real-time

e) **Supply Chain Vulnerabilities**

- Risk: Compromised third-party software or hardware components in EHS systems

- Impact: Backdoor access for attackers, compromised system integrity

3. **Strategies for Mitigating Cybersecurity Risks in EHS**

a) **Implement a Comprehensive Cybersecurity Framework**

- Adopt frameworks like the NIST Cybersecurity Framework or ISO 27001

- Develop EHS-specific cybersecurity policies and procedures

- Regularly conduct cybersecurity risk assessments specific to EHS systems

b) **Secure Network Architecture**

- Implement network segmentation to isolate critical EHS systems

- Use firewalls and intrusion detection/prevention systems (IDS/IPS)

- Employ virtual private networks (VPNs) for remote access

c) **Robust Access Control**

- Implement strong authentication methods (e.g., multi-factor authentication)

- Apply the principle of least privilege for system access

- Regularly review and update access rights

d) Data Encryption and Protection

- Encrypt sensitive EHS data both in transit and at rest

- Implement secure data backup and recovery procedures

- Use data loss prevention (DLP) tools to prevent unauthorized data exfiltration

e) Continuous Monitoring and Incident Response

- Implement 24/7 monitoring of EHS systems for unusual activities

- Develop and regularly test incident response plans specific to EHS cybersecurity events

- Establish a security operations center (SOC) with EHS-specific expertise

f) Supply Chain Security

- Conduct security assessments of third-party vendors and partners

- Implement secure procurement practices for EHS hardware and software

- Regularly audit and update third-party systems and integrations

g) Employee Training and Awareness

- Conduct regular cybersecurity awareness training for all employees

- Provide specialized training for EHS personnel on system-specific security practices

- Foster a culture of cybersecurity awareness in EHS operations

h) Secure Software Development and Patching

- Implement secure coding practices for in-house EHS software development

- Establish a rigorous patching and update process for all EHS systems

- Conduct regular vulnerability assessments and penetration testing

i) Physical Security Integration

- Integrate physical security measures with cybersecurity practices

- Secure physical access to critical EHS infrastructure and control systems

j) Compliance and Regulatory Adherence

- Stay informed about and compliant with relevant cybersecurity regulations (e.g., GDPR, CCPA for data privacy)

- Participate in industry-specific information sharing and analysis centers (ISACs) for threat intelligence

4. Case Study: Cybersecurity in Action

Consider a petrochemical company that implemented a comprehensive cybersecurity program for its EHS systems:

- Challenge: Increasing cyber threats to its interconnected environmental monitoring and process safety systems.

- Solution:

    o Implemented network segmentation, isolating critical control systems

    o Deployed AI-powered anomaly detection for early threat identification

    o Conducted regular cybersecurity drills involving both IT and OT teams

    o Implemented end-to-end encryption for all sensor data

    o Established a dedicated EHS cybersecurity team within their SOC

- Result: Successfully thwarted several attempted cyber-attacks, maintained continuous operation of critical EHS systems, and improved overall security posture.

5. Future Trends and Considerations

- Increasing use of AI and machine learning for threat detection and response

- Growing importance of IoT security as more devices are connected to EHS networks

- Rising focus on cyber-physical systems security to protect against attacks that could cause physical harm

- Emerging regulations specifically addressing cybersecurity in critical infrastructure and EHS systems.

Conclusion:

Cybersecurity must be a top priority as EHS systems become more connected and digitized. By implementing comprehensive cybersecurity strategies tailored to the unique needs of EHS operations, organizations can protect against threats that could compromise safety, environmental integrity, and operational continuity. Remember, cybersecurity in EHS is not just about protecting data – it's about safeguarding human lives and the environment. Continuous vigilance, regular updates to security measures, and a culture of security awareness are essential in this ever-evolving landscape of cyber threats.

Implementing Successful Digital EHS Initiatives

Phase 1: Assessment and Planning

1. Conduct a Comprehensive Needs Assessment

- o Identify current EHS pain points and inefficiencies

- o Evaluate existing EHS processes and technologies

- o Gather input from all levels of the organization, from frontline workers to executives.

2. Define Clear Objectives and Success Metrics

- o Set specific, measurable goals for the digital EHS initiative

- o Align objectives with overall business strategy

- o Establish key performance indicators (KPIs) to measure success

3. Perform a Readiness Assessment

o   Evaluate organizational culture and openness to change

o   Assess current technological infrastructure and capabilities

o   Identify potential barriers to implementation

4. Develop a Detailed Implementation Strategy

o   Create a phased implementation plan

o   Define timelines, milestones, and resource requirements

o   Establish a governance structure for the initiative

Phase 2: Solution Design and Selection

5. Define System Requirements

o   Develop detailed functional and technical requirements

o   Consider scalability, integration capabilities, and future needs

o   Involve end-users in the requirements gathering process

6. Evaluate and Select Technology Solutions

o   Research available EHS technology solutions

o   Conduct vendor assessments and demos

o   Consider factors like user-friendliness, support, and total cost of ownership

7. Design the Solution Architecture

o   Plan for integration with existing systems

o   Ensure compatibility with current IT infrastructure

o   Address data security and privacy requirements

Phase 3: Preparation and Risk Mitigation

8. Develop a Change Management Strategy

o   Create a comprehensive communication plan

o   Design training programs for different user groups

o   Identify and engage change champions across the organization

9. Conduct a Risk Assessment

o   Identify potential implementation risks (technical, operational, cultural)

o   Develop risk mitigation strategies

o   Create contingency plans for high-impact risks

10. Establish Data Governance Framework

o   Define data ownership and access rights

o   Establish data quality standards and processes

o   Develop data retention and archiving policies

Phase 4: Pilot Implementation

11. Select a Pilot Site or Department

o   Choose a representative area of the organization for initial implementation

o   Ensure the pilot scope is manageable but meaningful

12. Implement the Pilot Project

o   Deploy the selected technology solution in the pilot area

o   Provide intensive support and training during this phase

o   Closely monitor system performance and user adoption

13. Gather and Analyze Feedback

o   Collect user feedback through surveys, interviews, and observation

o   Analyze system data to assess performance against KPIs

o   Identify areas for improvement and necessary adjustments

Phase 5: Full-Scale Implementation

14. Refine the Implementation Plan

o   Incorporate lessons learned from the pilot phase

o   Adjust timelines and resource allocation as needed

o   Update training materials and support processes

15. Phased Rollout

o   Implement the solution in phases across the organization

o   Prioritize high-impact areas or those most ready for change

o   Allow time between phases for adjustment and learning

16. Provide Ongoing Training and Support

o   Offer continuous training opportunities for all users

o   Establish a dedicated support team or helpdesk

o   Create user guides and FAQs for common issues

Phase 6: Monitoring and Optimization

17. Continuous Monitoring and Evaluation

o   Regularly assess system performance against established KPIs

o   Gather ongoing user feedback

o   Monitor for emerging risks or issues

18. Iterative Improvement

o   Implement regular system updates and enhancements

o   Continuously refine processes based on user feedback and performance data

o   Stay updated on new EHS technologies and best practices

19. Conduct Post-Implementation Review

- o Evaluate the overall success of the implementation

- o Identify lessons learned for future initiatives

- o Celebrate successes and recognize key contributors

Phase 7: Scaling and Integration

20. Expand Functionality

- o Gradually introduce advanced features (e.g., predictive analytics, AI)

- o Integrate with other business systems (e.g., ERP, HR)

- o Explore new use cases for the technology

21. Foster a Culture of Continuous Improvement

- o Encourage ongoing innovation in EHS practices

- o Implement a system for employees to suggest improvements

- o Regularly benchmark against industry best practices

Key Considerations Throughout Implementation:

- Maintain strong executive sponsorship and visible leadership support

- Ensure clear and frequent communication with all stakeholders

- Prioritize data quality and integrity at every stage

- Remain flexible and ready to adapt to changing needs or unforeseen challenges

- Keep cybersecurity and data privacy at the forefront of all decisions

- Regularly review and adjust to changing regulatory requirements

- Foster cross-functional collaboration, especially between EHS, IT, and operations teams

By following this roadmap and remaining attentive to the lessons learned from past failures, organizations can significantly increase their chances of successfully implementing digital EHS technologies. Remember, digital transformation is an ongoing journey rather than a destination, requiring continuous attention, adaptation, and improvement.

Measuring Success in Digital EHS Initiatives: A Comprehensive Metrics Framework

1. Safety Performance Metrics

a) Incident Rate Reduction

- Measure: Percentage decrease in recordable incident rates

- Goal: Quantify improvements in overall safety performance

b) Near-Miss Reporting

- Measure: Increase in near-miss reports

- Goal: Assess effectiveness of the system in capturing potential hazards

c) Time to Incident Resolution

- Measure: Average time from incident report to resolution

- Goal: Evaluate efficiency improvements in incident management

d) Proactive vs. Reactive Actions

- Measure: Ratio of proactive safety measures to reactive responses

- Goal: Gauge shift towards preventive safety culture

2. Environmental Impact Metrics

a) Emissions Reduction

- Measure: Percentage decrease in greenhouse gas emissions or other pollutants

- Goal: Quantify environmental performance improvements

b) Resource Efficiency

- Measure: Reduction in energy or water consumption per unit of production

- Goal: Assess improvements in resource management

c) Waste Reduction

- Measure: Decrease in waste generation or increase in recycling rates

- Goal: Evaluate progress in waste management initiatives

d) Environmental Compliance Rate

- Measure: Percentage of time in full environmental compliance

- Goal: Assess effectiveness in meeting regulatory requirements

3. Operational Efficiency Metrics

a) Process Automation Level

- Measure: Percentage of EHS processes automated

- Goal: Evaluate the extent of digital transformation

b) Data Collection Efficiency

- Measure: Time saved in data collection and reporting

- Goal: Quantify improvements in data management processes

c) Decision-Making Speed

- Measure: Average time to make EHS-related decisions

- Goal: Assess improvements in data-driven decision-making

d) Predictive Maintenance Effectiveness

- Measure: Reduction in unplanned downtime due to equipment failure

- Goal: Evaluate the impact of predictive analytics on maintenance

4. User Adoption and Engagement Metrics

a) System Usage Rate

- Measure: Percentage of employees regularly using the digital EHS system

- Goal: Assess the level of adoption across the organization

b) User Satisfaction Score

- Measure: Employee satisfaction ratings with the new system

- Goal: Gauge user acceptance and identify areas for improvement

c) Training Completion Rate

- Measure: Percentage of employees who have completed EHS system training

- Goal: Ensure workforce readiness for digital EHS initiatives

d) Employee Feedback Volume

- Measure: Number of suggestions or improvement ideas submitted by employees

- Goal: Assess employee engagement with the new system

5. Data Quality and Integrity Metrics

a) Data Accuracy Rate

- Measure: Percentage of data entries that meet quality standards

- Goal: Ensure the reliability of EHS data

b) Real-Time Data Availability

- Measure: Percentage of EHS data available in real-time

- Goal: Assess improvements in data timeliness

c) Data Integration Level

- Measure: Percentage of EHS data integrated with other business systems

- Goal: Evaluate the comprehensiveness of data integration

d) Data Utilization Rate

- Measure: Frequency of data access and use in decision-making processes

- Goal: Assess how effectively data is being leveraged

6. Compliance and Risk Management Metrics

a) Audit Performance

- Measure: Improvement in internal and external audit scores
- Goal: Evaluate enhanced compliance capabilities

b) Regulatory Violation Reduction

- Measure: Decrease in the number of regulatory violations
- Goal: Assess effectiveness in maintaining compliance

c) Risk Identification Rate

- Measure: Increase in proactively identified potential risks
- Goal: Evaluate improvements in risk assessment capabilities

d) Insurance Premium Reduction

- Measure: Decrease in insurance premiums due to improved risk profile
- Goal: Quantify risk reduction from an external perspective

7. Innovation and Continuous Improvement Metrics

a) Feature Adoption Rate

- Measure: Percentage of new system features actively used
- Goal: Assess the organization's ability to leverage advanced capabilities

b) Continuous Improvement Initiatives

- Measure: Number of EHS process improvements implemented post-digital transformation
- Goal: Evaluate ongoing optimization efforts

c) Technology Integration Rate

- Measure: Speed of adopting and integrating new EHS technologies
- Goal: Assess organizational agility in tech adoption

d) Cross-Functional Collaboration

- Measure: Increase in collaborative projects between EHS and other departments

- Goal: Evaluate the breaking down of silos

8. Financial Impact Metrics

a) Cost Savings

- Measure: Total cost savings from improved efficiency and reduced incidents

- Goal: Quantify financial benefits beyond initial ROI calculations

b) Productivity Gains

- Measure: Increase in output per employee hour in EHS-related activities

- Goal: Assess efficiency improvements in monetary terms

c) Avoided Costs

- Measure: Estimated costs avoided due to prevented incidents or compliance violations

- Goal: Quantify the value of risk mitigation

d) Revenue Impact

- Measure: Increase in revenue attributed to improved EHS performance (e.g., winning new contracts due to better safety records)

- Goal: Assess the broader business impact of EHS improvements

Implementation of Metrics:

1. Establish Baselines: Before implementing new digital EHS systems, measure current performance across all relevant metrics.

2. Set Realistic Targets: Define achievable goals for each metric based on industry benchmarks and organizational objectives.

3. Regular Reporting: Implement a system for regular (monthly or quarterly) reporting on these metrics.

4. Dashboard Creation: Develop visual dashboards that provide real-time updates on key metrics.

5. Continuous Review: Regularly review the relevance and effectiveness of metrics, adjusting as needed.

6. Balanced Scorecard Approach: Use a balanced scorecard that includes metrics from all categories to get a holistic view of success.

Conclusion:

Implementing a comprehensive set of metrics beyond traditional ROI calculations can help organizations gain a more nuanced and complete understanding of the impact of their digital EHS initiatives. This multifaceted approach allows for a balanced assessment of technological, operational, and cultural changes, providing valuable insights for continuous improvement and strategic decision-making in EHS management.

EHS: Commitment: The Ultimate Driver of Your Success in the IoT

The Internet of Things (IoT) promises a transformative future for EHS (Environment, Health, and Safety) management, offering real-time data, predictive insights, and improved safety systems. As organizations explore IoT adoption, the degree of their commitment to these technologies will ultimately determine their success. The IoT can fundamentally change how EHS enterprises operate, monitor risks, and ensure compliance, but that change requires a significant commitment of resources and strategic alignment.

In the world of EHS, this means embedding IoT sensors in machinery, personal protective equipment (PPE), and work environments to collect crucial data on worker health, environmental conditions, and equipment status. Such systems can prevent incidents before they happen, ensure compliance with safety standards, and optimize operational performance. However, realizing these benefits hinges on your enterprise's commitment to integrating IoT technologies into its core EHS strategy.

The IoT Promise in EHS

The EHS sector is facing unprecedented disruption. IoT is set to create a connected ecosystem that integrates people, processes, and systems for proactive safety management. The global IoT market is projected to increase, and enterprises that commit to these technologies will likely outperform their peers.

Commitment Drives Growth

In the EHS context, the correlation between IoT commitment and reduction in recordable injuries is stark. Enterprises that invested robustly in IoT technologies—implementing connected systems for real-time environmental monitoring and worker safety—generated 60 to 90 percent of their revenues from new products or services introduced in the last three years. By contrast, companies with low IoT commitment generated as little as 10 percent of revenues from new products during the same period. The more an organization commits to IoT, the greater its growth from innovation—a crucial factor for EHS enterprises striving to remain competitive and relevant in the rapidly evolving digital landscape.

Four Key Drivers of IoT Commitment in EHS

Based on market assessment, four key components can be identified that enable EHS enterprises to commit successfully to IoT:

1. Threat from Disruption: EHS organizations facing significant risks from digital disruption—such as increasing regulatory requirements or new industry standards—are more motivated to commit to IoT as a strategy for growth and survival.

2. Vision: Leadership teams that spend time analyzing digital disruption and the opportunities that IoT presents are likelier to develop a solid commitment to safety innovations driven by IoT technologies.

3. New IoT Capabilities: EHS enterprises committed to IoT tend to develop open APIs for internal and external use, enabling seamless integration of IoT devices into broader safety and compliance ecosystems.

4. Organizational Readiness: Successful EHS organizations invest in building leadership, governance, and resources to facilitate the significant changes required to shift their business models toward IoT-based ecosystems.

Strategic Choices for IoT in EHS

The differences in IoT commitment became apparent during a workshop with a safety manager. One safety director of an energy enterprise expressed a goal of designing and leading an IoT ecosystem for comprehensive energy management solutions. This level of commitment positions the company to become an ecosystem driver in the IoT landscape. Conversely, another company's safety leader manufacturing industrial motors expressed a more modest goal: participating in as many IoT networks as necessary to ensure their motors are connected across different ecosystems. This approach positions the company as a modular producer, focusing on plugging into existing networks rather than leading one.

For EHS enterprises, the choice is clear: Some will aim to lead an IoT network, focusing on workplace safety management and environmental compliance, while others will participate in existing IoT networks, contributing specialized services like predictive maintenance or hazard detection. Most organizations will likely adopt a hybrid approach, leading in areas where they have expertise and participating in others.

Commitment to the IoT is the ultimate driver of success for EHS organizations. Whether your goal is to lead an IoT ecosystem or participate in multiple networks, your commitment to integrating IoT technologies into your EHS strategy will determine your organization's competitive edge. Those enterprises that make bold moves and invest in IoT capabilities today will be better positioned to revolutionize safety practices and lead the future of EHS management.

EHS: Three Company Journeys to the IoT

The following three case studies explore how enterprises leverage IoT technologies to transform their EHS (Environment, Health, and Safety) strategies and operational models. Each organization takes a unique approach to utilizing IoT to move up the Digital EHS Strategy framework and drive change in the EHS domain.

Return to the Digital EHS Strategy

Now, let's return to the Digital EHS Strategy with the EHS context in mind, drawing on the examples of the company, Safety Solution Major, and Electric Major. EU Chemical Major's leadership in developing IoT-driven safety and environmental solutions, Safety Solution Major's Connected Worker platform, and Electric Major's vision of providing sustainable energy and automation solutions highlight enterprises striving to lead IoT networks and become ecosystem drivers in the EHS space. These companies are not just focusing on compliance and risk management but aiming to transform how organizations monitor and manage EHS risks, worker safety, and environmental impacts.

In contrast, enterprises like Safety Solution Major empower other companies through IoT-enabled safety solutions like Connected Worker, helping those enterprises become ecosystem drivers in their industries. Modular producers in this context, like Safety Solution Major's scalable IoT platforms, contribute to broader EHS ecosystems without necessarily leading them. These enterprises offer connectable assets, sensors, and analytics platforms that enable others to optimize safety and environmental management—but they may not control the IoT network itself.

Ecosystem Driver Aspirations in EHS

Leading an IoT network within the EHS realm, like the EU chemical major's efforts to digitize safety management or the Electric major's efforts to automate energy management and sustainability, seamlessly integrates connected sensors, predictive analytics, and real-time data. These enterprises don't just focus on their internal operations—they aim to influence entire industries by providing solutions that other companies rely on to enhance their EHS performance.

For example:

- EU chemical major's Connected Plants focuses on real-time safety and environmental monitoring across global facilities.

- Electric primary drives sustainable energy and resource management, helping organizations improve operational efficiency while reducing their environmental footprint.

- Safety Solution Major enables industries to monitor and protect workers in hazardous environments with wearable technology and real-time health and safety data.

By leading IoT-driven ecosystems, these companies aim to be the go-to platforms for safety, environmental sustainability, and operational excellence. As ecosystem drivers, they create value within their enterprises and the wider EHS industry, offering platforms that improve overall safety and sustainability outcomes.

Modular Producers in EHS

On the other hand, enterprises like Safety Solution Major can also be seen as modular producers. They provide essential EHS IoT platforms integrated into larger ecosystems led by different enterprises. For instance, Safety Solution Major's Connected Worker technology is a modular solution that integrates seamlessly with broader safety and environmental management systems run by other organizations. This ensures that Safety Solution Major's technology can be plugged into different EHS ecosystems, enabling organizations to meet compliance standards and monitor safety performance across various industries.

However, the modular producer model comes with its own set of challenges. Suppose an enterprise leads the market in providing essential EHS technologies or IoT-enabled safety platforms. In that case, it will enjoy healthy profits, high market share, and strong partnerships with leading ecosystem drivers. However, for those modular producers that hold less market share, the competitive landscape can become a race to the bottom, where price competition erodes profitability. To remain competitive, these companies must continuously innovate and provide value-added services beyond just offering the essential components of an IoT-enabled safety system.

Envisioning EHS in the IoT-Driven Future

The critical question for your enterprise is: Will you become a leader in driving IoT-enabled EHS ecosystems, or will you participate as a modular producer providing essential components to more extensive networks? Both models offer growth opportunities, but the degree of success will depend on your market position, level of IoT commitment, and ability to innovate.

- Suppose your company aims to lead the EHS industry, driving safety and environmental solutions across sectors. In that case, the goal is to become an ecosystem driver—providing integrated IoT solutions that other companies depend on.

- If your company's strengths lie in providing connectable assets or modular platforms, you'll still play a vital role but may face greater competition and the risk of commoditization.

Ultimately, the IoT presents vast opportunities in the EHS realm, transforming enterprises' risk, compliance, and worker safety management. As a driver or modular producer, your role in this ecosystem will depend on your strategy and willingness to invest in next-generation EHS technologies.

A Powerful Combination: Mobile and the IoT in EHS

My assessment of the rapidly evolving mobile landscape and the vast potential of the Internet of Things (IoT) reveals an incredible opportunity for EHS (Environment, Health, and Safety): a world where mobile-only users, integrated with expansive IoT networks, lead to highly efficient, proactive, and responsive safety and environmental solutions. This powerful combination presents a unique value proposition for EHS enterprises aiming to improve worker safety, environmental monitoring, and regulatory compliance by advancing through the Digital EHS Strategy framework.

At the intersection of mobile and IoT, EHS professionals can use mobile devices to manage real-time sensor data, monitor safety hazards, track emissions, and automate alerts for immediate action. Enterprises leveraging this combination can offer proactive solutions through IoT-enabled networks, improving compliance, worker well-being, environmental sustainability, and operational efficiency. Competitive advantages will go to those enterprises that can harness this real-time data, understand how safety equipment and systems are used, and provide actionable insights.

Many EHS functions will become automated as enterprises engage workers and management through mobile platforms. Algorithms and AI will act based on predefined safety rules or regulatory requirements. For example, if air quality levels in a factory exceed safe thresholds, an automated response could trigger ventilation systems, send alerts to workers' mobile devices, and initiate shutdown procedures for specific equipment.

Through mobile and IoT integration, enterprises will gain better data on environmental conditions, worker health, and equipment performance, enabling a higher level of predictive maintenance and incident prevention. These data-driven insights will help enterprises take corrective actions before incidents occur, significantly reducing risks and improving compliance with EHS regulations. Additionally, customers will benefit from better information on compliance metrics, sustainability performance, and worker safety, allowing them to make informed decisions about their business partners and suppliers.

The overlapping area between mobile and IoT will become a strategic battleground for enterprises in the EHS sector. Companies that can successfully lead an IoT-enabled EHS network—enabling real-time monitoring of air quality, noise levels, worker conditions, and machinery safety—will secure significant growth and a competitive edge. Those who fall behind in mobile integration and IoT adoption may struggle to meet modern EHS requirements and deliver value to stakeholders.

Data Privacy in EHS IoT Networks

As more data becomes available from IoT-enabled EHS systems, enterprises must navigate the challenges of data privacy and ethical data use. Workers and customers must trust that their data—whether health metrics from wearable devices or environmental data from sensors—will be used responsibly. This means building internal policies around acceptable data practices and meeting regulatory data security and privacy requirements.

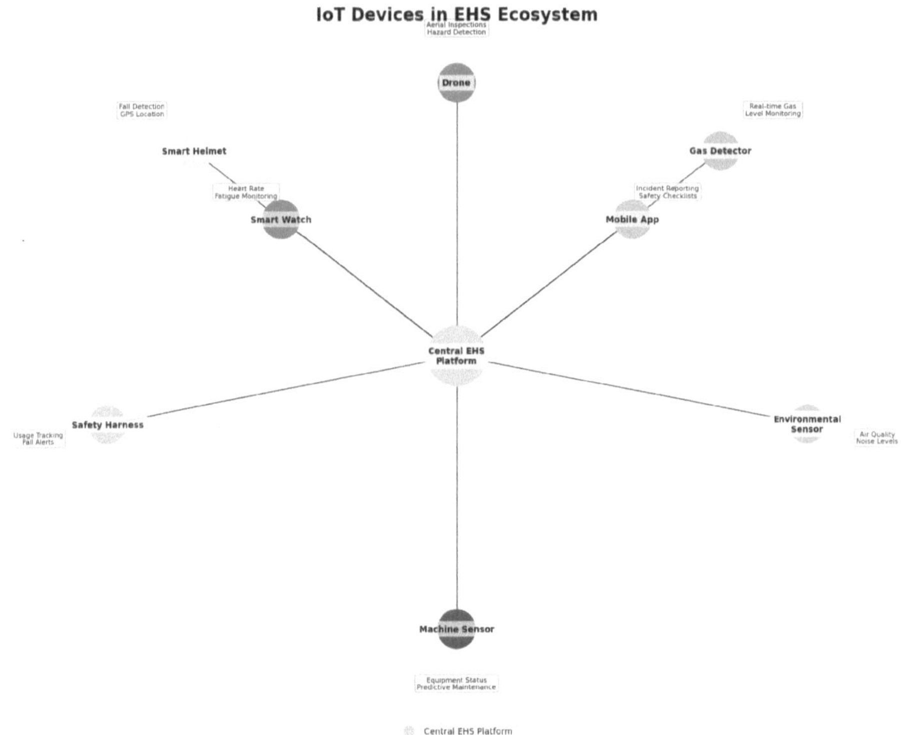

Figure 6.7: IoT devices in the EHS Ecosystem

For EHS enterprises, the focus should be on:

- They ensure IoT data delivers tangible safety improvements or environmental benefits.

- Being transparent with workers and stakeholders about how EHS data is collected, used, and shared.

- Offering clear value in return for data sharing, such as improved safety outcomes or reduced environmental impact.

EHS in the Mobile-IoT Ecosystem

As the mobile IoT combination transforms EHS, the question for enterprises becomes: Will you be the one to lead an EHS IoT network, or will you participate as a modular producer in a network led by others? The answer to this question will define your position in the EHS digital ecosystem and determine whether you can drive innovation in environmental protection and workplace safety or respond to it.

Ultimately, the companies that master mobile and IoT integration in the EHS sector can offer real-time solutions that protect workers, preserve the environment, and ensure regulatory compliance—all while staying ahead of the competition.

The Digital EHS Strategy: Bringing All the Pieces Together

As we explore the future of mobile and IoT in the Environment, Health, and Safety (EHS) sector, it's essential to understand how enterprises can successfully operate in this evolving landscape. The Digital EHS Strategy provides a strategic tool for identifying where an enterprise fits in this mobile IoT world and how it can move toward becoming an ecosystem driver. Let's look at how EHS companies can apply these strategies.

For instance, in a smart factory where various environmental monitoring and safety systems are integrated, the ecosystem driver could be a company like Safety Solution Major, managing the IoT network for air quality, temperature, and worker safety through its connected devices. Other companies, such as sensor manufacturers or software providers offering specialized services, would act as modular producers, plugging into the IoT network led by Safety Solution Major.

IoT Strategy in EHS: Leading vs. Participating

Enterprises have two options when it comes to their IoT strategy:

1. Lead an IoT network: In this case, the enterprise manages and coordinates the entire IoT ecosystem, including sensors, data analytics, compliance monitoring, and safety management.

2. Participate in IoT networks: Alternatively, enterprises can focus on participating in those led by others, contributing their specialized expertise, such as providing wearable safety devices or environmental data services.

Mobile Strategy in EHS

As mobile devices become increasingly central to operations, particularly in EHS, enterprises must decide how to leverage mobile technology effectively. Consider a scenario where EHS managers use mobile apps to monitor real-time emissions, worker health, or equipment safety. These apps could be built with geolocation capabilities, sensor integration, and automated reporting features that deliver real-time compliance data to field and remote teams.

The mobile strategy will likely encompass several approaches:

- Safety Engagement: Use mobile apps to increase customer engagement by offering real-time safety updates or compliance reminders.

- Multichannel: Provide a seamless experience across devices and channels, where safety data can be accessed from desktops, mobile phones, or tablets.

- B2B2C: Facilitate direct interaction with employees and contractors using mobile platforms to ensure safety protocols are followed and incidents are reported.

- Targeted segment: Create mobile apps to address the unique safety needs of sectors with high-risk environments (e.g., construction, and manufacturing).

- Mobile-first: Lead with mobile innovation, ensuring all EHS services and tools are first developed for mobile use, making it the primary interface for safety and environmental management.

Why Move Fast?

In their EHS transformations, many enterprises rely on strategic partnerships to move quickly, access new skills, and build capabilities they don't possess. Moving swiftly and adopting new technologies in a rapidly evolving industry can provide a significant competitive advantage—improving compliance, reducing risks, and enhancing overall performance.

Ask yourself:

- How fast do you need to move?

- Do you have the right partnerships in place?

- Are you prepared to commit to a mobile and IoT strategy that will transform your EHS operations?

Now is the time to evaluate your readiness and take steps to ensure your enterprise is well-positioned to benefit from the mobile and IoT revolution in the EHS space

Business Models, EHS Framework, and Digital Strategy in EHS

Digital EHS Strategy Framework: Evolution of Mobile, IoT, and Digital Strategies

The journey from Basic Compliance Seeker to Digital EHS Leader represents a transformative progression in how organizations approach Environment, Health, and Safety management. The increasing sophistication and integration of mobile, IoT, and digital strategies characterize this evolution. Let's explore this journey in detail, examining how these strategies evolve and intertwine across each EHS Knowledge vs. Business Design matrix quadrant.

1. Basic Compliance Seekers

Organizations in this quadrant are at the beginning of their digital EHS journey. Their primary focus is meeting regulatory requirements with minimal investment in digital technologies.

The mobile strategy at this stage needs to be revised. Organizations typically rely on essential communication tools like email and text messages for EHS-related communications. They might have simple, standalone mobile apps for conducting safety inspections or reporting incidents, but these are often little more than digital versions of paper forms. The apps need more integration with other systems, requiring manual data entry and limiting utility.

The IoT strategy for Basic Compliance Seekers is minimal or nonexistent. If IoT devices are used at all, they are likely to be basic sensors for critical parameters such as gas detection or temperature monitoring in high-risk areas. Data from these sensors is often collected manually or with minimal automation, primarily serving as a safeguard against immediate dangers rather than as a tool for proactive risk management.

The digital strategy at this stage focuses primarily on digitizing paper-based processes. Organizations implement basic digital record-keeping systems to maintain compliance documentation, incident reports, and training records. However, these systems are often siloed and have limited capabilities for data analysis or integration with other business processes.

2. Traditional Operators

As organizations evolve into traditional operators, they begin to recognize the value of digital tools in enhancing EHS management efficiency and effectiveness.

The mobile strategy becomes more defined and purposeful. Organizations have started adopting mobile devices more widely for field operations. They implement more sophisticated mobile apps beyond basic reporting, including tasks like task management, real-time communication, and access to safety procedures. These apps integrate with central EHS management systems, allowing for more streamlined data flow and reducing duplicate data entry.

IoT strategy sees significant advancement in this quadrant. Organizations start implementing IoT devices more systematically across critical processes. Automated data collection has become more widespread, covering a broader range of EHS parameters. While real-time monitoring capabilities are still limited, the groundwork is laid for more advanced IoT applications. For instance, automated alerts might be set up when specific parameters exceed predefined thresholds.

The digital strategy expands to include the implementation of dedicated EHS management software. These systems centralize data collection, storage, and fundamental analysis, providing a holistic view of EHS performance. Organizations begin to conduct fundamental trend analysis, identifying recurring issues or high-risk areas. Digital training modules and e-learning platforms are introduced, enhancing the efficiency and effectiveness of EHS training programs.

3. Reactive Performers

Reactive Performers demonstrate a significant leap in their approach to EHS management, leveraging digital technologies to respond more effectively to EHS challenges.

Mobile strategy at this stage is characterized by the widespread adoption of mobile devices across all levels of the organization. Advanced mobile apps with offline capabilities ensure that EHS processes can continue uninterrupted, even in areas with poor connectivity. Real-time incident reporting and investigation tools enable faster response times and more accurate data collection. Mobile access to EHS dashboards and KPIs empowers field workers and managers with up-to-date decision-making information.

The IoT strategy has become much more sophisticated. An extensive network of IoT sensors is deployed across facilities, enabling real-time monitoring of multiple EHS parameters simultaneously. This might include environmental conditions, equipment performance, and even personal safety by integrating wearable devices. The IoT system can now generate automated alerts and notifications based on complex algorithms, allowing for more proactive risk management.

Digital strategy at this stage leverages advanced EHS software with predictive analytics capabilities. These systems can forecast potential incidents based on historical data and current conditions, allowing for preventive actions. Integrating EHS data with other business systems like ERP and HR provides a more comprehensive view of how EHS performance impacts overall business operations. Digital platforms for stakeholder engagement and reporting enhance transparency and communication.

4. Digital EHS Leaders

Organizations in this quadrant are at the forefront of digital EHS innovation, fully leveraging the power of mobile, IoT, and digital technologies to drive EHS excellence.

The mobile strategy adopts a mobile-first approach to EHS management. A comprehensive suite of mobile apps covers all aspects of EHS, from risk assessment and incident management to compliance monitoring and performance reporting. Augmented reality (AR) applications are introduced for training and risk assessment, providing immersive and context-specific guidance to workers. AI-powered mobile assistants offer real-time decision support, helping workers navigate complex EHS scenarios with expert advice at their fingertips.

IoT strategy evolves into a fully connected ecosystem of smart devices. Advanced sensors with edge computing capabilities process data locally, reducing latency and enabling faster responses to changing conditions. Predictive maintenance based on IoT data helps prevent equipment failures that could lead to safety incidents or environmental releases. Digital twins of facilities or processes allow for sophisticated simulations, optimizing EHS processes, and testing improvement strategies in a risk-free virtual environment.

The digital strategy at this stage is characterized by the use of cutting-edge technologies to drive EHS performance. AI and machine learning algorithms analyze vast amounts of EHS data to identify subtle patterns and predict potential risks before they materialize. Blockchain technology is employed to ensure the integrity and traceability of EHS data, particularly useful for complex supply chain management and regulatory compliance. Advanced analytics capabilities enable continuous improvement and benchmarking against industry best practices. Importantly, EHS is no longer seen as a standalone function but is fully integrated into broader digital transformation initiatives, influencing and being influenced by overall business strategy.

As organizations progress through these quadrants, they enhance their EHS capabilities and fundamentally transform how EHS is perceived and managed. The journey from Basic Compliance Seekers to Digital EHS Leaders represents a shift from viewing EHS as a necessary cost of doing business to recognizing it as a source of competitive advantage and a driver of business value.

By leveraging mobile, IoT, and digital technologies, organizations can create safer workplaces, reduce environmental impacts, enhance regulatory compliance, and ultimately contribute to improved business performance. This evolution requires technological investment and a cultural shift towards embracing innovation, data-driven decision-making, and integrating EHS principles into every aspect of business operations.

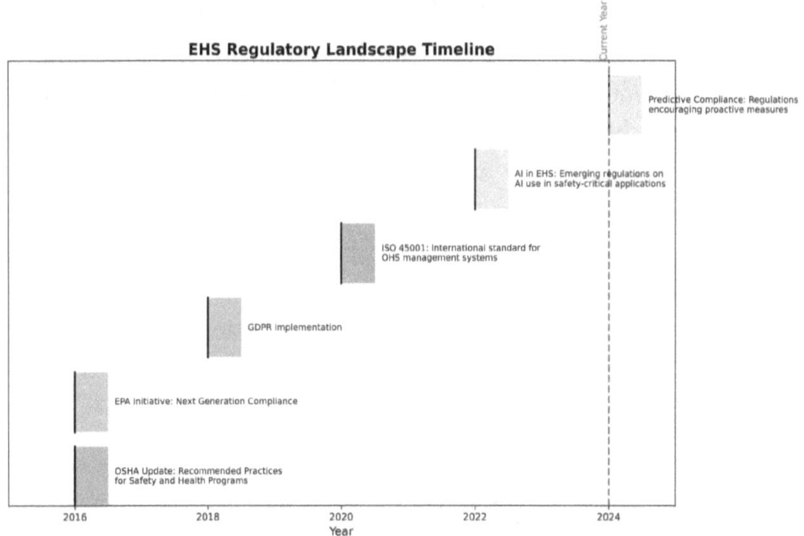

Figure 6.8: EHS Regulatory Landscape Timeline

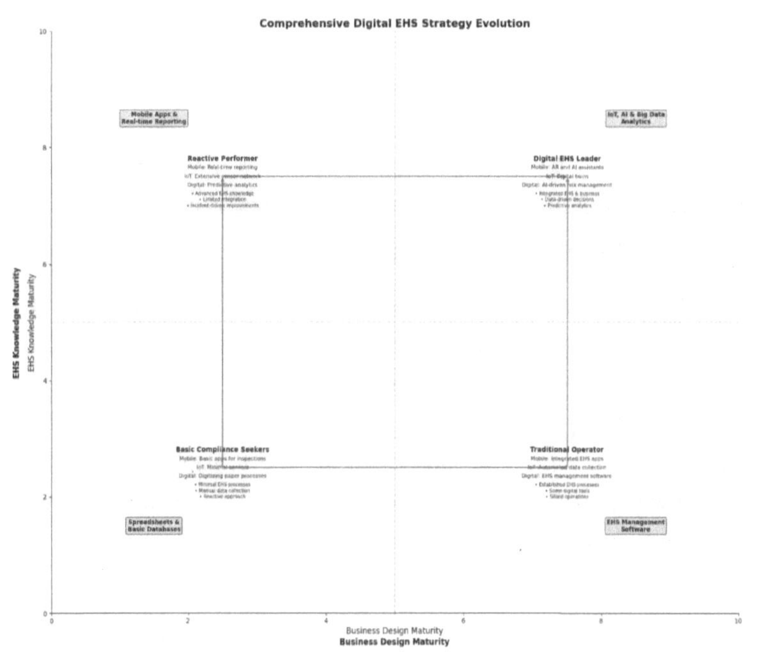

Figure 6.9: Comprehensive Digital EHS Strategy Evolution

Business Models, EHS Framework, and Digital Strategy in EHS

In the rapidly evolving landscape of Environment, Health, and Safety (EHS) management, organizations are developing their internal capabilities and positioning themselves strategically in the market. This positioning is increasingly influenced by and dependent on their digital strategy. The EHS Knowledge vs Business Design framework provides a structure for understanding an organization's internal EHS maturity. At the same time, the concepts of suppliers, modular producers, omnichannel, and ecosystem drivers describe different business models and market positions. These perspectives are closely interrelated and often align as organizations progress in their EHS journey and digital transformation.

1. Suppliers generally correspond to Basic Compliance Seekers in the EHS framework. These organizations typically need higher EHS knowledge and essential business design. They focus on providing fundamental EHS products or services, often with minimal digital integration. Their digital strategy is usually limited to primary data collection and reporting tools.

2. Modular Producers align with Traditional Operators. With moderate EHS knowledge and improved business design, these organizations offer more specialized EHS solutions that can integrate with other systems. Their digital strategy often involves developing specific EHS software modules or IoT-enabled devices that can plug into larger EHS management systems.

3. Omnichannel businesses share characteristics with Reactive Performers. These organizations have developed significant EHS knowledge and more advanced business designs. They provide comprehensive EHS solutions across multiple channels and are responsive to market needs. Their digital strategy typically includes advanced analytics, mobile applications, and integrated platforms that allow real-time monitoring and reporting across various touchpoints.

4. Ecosystem Drivers correlate strongly with Digital EHS Leaders. These organizations demonstrate high levels of both EHS knowledge and business design maturity. They lead the creation of integrated EHS platforms, driving innovation in the industry. Their digital strategy is at the forefront of technological adoption, often incorporating AI, machine

learning, IoT, digital twins, and blockchain to create comprehensive EHS ecosystems.

In the upcoming discussions, we will explore how these business models and their corresponding levels in the EHS Knowledge vs Business Design framework influence and are influenced by digital strategy. We'll examine:

- How digital technologies are reshaping EHS management at each level

- The role of mobile and IoT technologies in advancing EHS capabilities

- How data analytics and AI are transforming decision-making processes in EHS

- The challenges and opportunities of digital transformation in EHS

- Strategies for organizations to progress from one level to the next, leveraging digital technologies

Understanding these relationships helps organizations align their EHS strategy with broader business goals and digital transformation initiatives. As companies progress in their EHS knowledge and business design, they often find opportunities to evolve their market position from suppliers to ecosystem drivers. This evolution reflects not just an improvement in EHS performance but a fundamental shift in how EHS is integrated into business strategy, value creation, and digital innovation.

By exploring these interconnected perspectives, we aim to provide a comprehensive view of how organizations can navigate the digital landscape in EHS, enhancing their capabilities, market position, and overall performance.

Digital EHS Strategy

EHS enterprises can evolve into ecosystem drivers in the next-generation digital environment by integrating mobile-first strategies with IoT networks. The combination of mobile apps that connect to IoT-enabled safety devices and environmental sensors allows enterprises to deliver real-time, actionable insights for safer, more sustainable operations. Enterprises that seize this opportunity will lead the future of EHS management, offering predictive solutions that protect workers and the environment and create lasting value for stakeholders.

Ecosystem Drivers in EHS

Being an ecosystem driver in the EHS (Environment, Health, and Safety) space means leading a comprehensive, branded IoT network that integrates data from various environmental and safety monitoring systems. This network coordinates the efforts of multiple companies, suppliers, and partners, all working within the ecosystem you manage. As the ecosystem driver, your enterprise controls critical aspects like regulatory compliance, data ownership, pricing models, and service quality while ensuring that all participants adhere to the necessary safety and environmental regulations.

The potential benefits of being an ecosystem driver in EHS are vast. By integrating IoT sensors, compliance management platforms, and real-time monitoring, your company could be the go-to destination for organizations needing comprehensive safety monitoring, environmental tracking, and compliance reporting. You will have access to massive amounts of data from air quality sensors, hazardous material trackers, worker safety wearables, and facility management systems. This data can be analyzed to offer predictive insights and automated responses, making your platform indispensable.

Control and Responsibilities as an EHS Ecosystem Driver

As an ecosystem driver in EHS, you will manage all critical decisions, such as:

- Regulatory Compliance: Ensuring the IoT network adheres to local, national, and international safety and environmental standards, including OSHA, EPA, and other regulatory bodies.

- Data Ownership: Defining who owns and can access the data collected from IoT devices is essential for maintaining trust and transparency among participants.

- Pricing Models: Establishing how pricing is structured for access to the ecosystem, including services like predictive analytics, environmental monitoring, and compliance reporting.

- Intellectual Property: Deciding who owns the proprietary technologies and insights generated from the network, especially critical in sectors like chemical production or hazardous material handling, where innovation is vital.

The ecosystem driver must also take responsibility for security and privacy, ensuring that the network is protected from cyber threats, data breaches, and unauthorized access. Security will be paramount given the sensitive nature of EHS data—such as employee health records, exposure to hazardous materials, and real-time incident reports.

Upfront Investment and Potential Challenges

An ecosystem driver requires a significant upfront investment in developing a branded IoT network, including recruiting EHS platform participants, such as sensor manufacturers, data analytics companies, and regulatory agencies. This may involve building an integrated platform that connects wearable devices for worker safety, environmental sensors for air and water quality, and automated compliance systems for reporting and auditing.

While the benefits of leading such a network are high, the risks include the possibility that the platform may need to attract more participants or generate sufficient data to provide valuable insights. Additionally, balancing the cost of maintaining compliance and security within the network can strain resources, especially in industries with fast-evolving regulatory environments.

Mobile-First Strategy for Ecosystem Drivers in EHS

A critical aspect of leading an EHS IoT ecosystem is a mobile-first strategy. In today's connected world, safety officers, environmental managers, and compliance teams increasingly rely on mobile devices to access real-time data, monitor incidents, and report compliance metrics. As an ecosystem driver, your branded mobile app or mobile-friendly platform will be the central hub for users to access everything they need—from incident reports and safety checks to environmental metrics and regulatory updates.

By integrating IoT data streams from various sources into a mobile app, you offer a seamless user experience where EHS professionals can:

- Monitor real-time safety alerts (e.g., gas leaks, fire hazards).

- Track compliance requirements and deadlines.

- Receive automated reports on air quality or waste management.

- Coordinate incident response with other network participants.

Ultimately, the mobile-first strategy enables faster decision-making, real-time monitoring, and a user-friendly interface that encourages continuous engagement with the IoT network.

The Destination of Choice for EHS

As an EHS ecosystem driver, you aim to become the destination of choice for enterprises and regulatory bodies seeking comprehensive environmental and safety solutions. Whether managing energy consumption in a manufacturing plant or monitoring worker exposure in a hazardous environment, your IoT-enabled network will be the platform they turn to.

By leveraging mobile connectivity and IoT integration, you provide value that other platforms cannot, ensuring long-term dominance in the EHS digital ecosystem.

Omnichannel in EHS

In the EHS (Environment, Health, and Safety) domain, the omnichannel enterprise aims to provide seamless service across multiple channels, allowing customers to engage through mobile apps, web platforms, or IoT-enabled devices, depending on their preferences. EHS enterprises can adopt similar strategies, leveraging an Integrated safety Channel mobile approach to provide comprehensive environmental and safety services across platforms.

Leveraging IoT Networks

The IoT plays a pivotal role in omnichannel strategies for EHS enterprises. For example, by participating in relevant IoT networks, an EHS company can:

- Monitor real-time environmental conditions (e.g., air quality, water pollution) using sensors installed across facilities.

- Track workplace safety metrics, such as employee exposure to hazardous substances, through wearables.

- Automate compliance reporting by connecting devices that monitor emissions and energy consumption to a centralized platform.

At a basic level, EHS companies must participate in industry-wide IoT networks that connect assets, infrastructure, and workplaces to improve safety and compliance. For instance, these networks could link factories, construction sites, or mining operations, collecting and sharing data that helps companies meet regulatory standards and prevent accidents.

Customer-Centric Omnichannel Strategies

EHS customers—who might be safety officers, environmental managers, or regulatory authorities—increasingly expect the flexibility to interact with systems through their preferred channels, whether it's a mobile app for monitoring real-time data, a desktop dashboard for creating reports, or direct IoT device integration for immediate alerts.

For example, a safety manager could use a mobile app to:

- Get real-time alerts about hazardous gas levels in a facility.

- Monitor incident reports and take immediate action on the go.

- Access compliance checklists or submit regulatory forms instantly from a mobile device.

On the other hand, the desktop platform might generate in-depth trend analysis reports on worker injuries or create visual dashboards that monitor multiple sites across different regions. This Integrated safety Channel strategy enhances user experience, ensuring EHS professionals can seamlessly transition between devices depending on their immediate needs.

Becoming an IoT Network Leader

While many EHS companies will participate in IoT networks led by other enterprises, such as regulatory bodies or technology providers, some may aspire to lead their own branded IoT network. For example, a company specializing in safety monitoring systems could create an IoT network that integrates wearables, sensors, and compliance software to provide end-to-end safety and environmental solutions. This would allow customers to:

- Connect and manage all safety devices in one platform.

- Receive automated alerts for any environmental or safety violations.

- Integrate with third-party compliance systems to generate real-time reports.

By leading the network, the EHS enterprise controls the data flow, standards, and platform governance, giving it a competitive edge. The company can determine who participates in the network, how pricing models are set, and how data insights are leveraged for internal and customer benefits.

Pros and Cons of Leading an EHS IoT Network

Leading a branded EHS IoT network has advantages and challenges. On the pro side, the enterprise gains substantial influence over the ecosystem, allowing it to differentiate its offerings, innovate faster, and secure customer loyalty by controlling the entire service stack—from data collection to actionable insights.

However, the downside involves significant investment in infrastructure, security, and governance and the ongoing challenge of recruiting partners and customers to adopt the network. Additionally, questions about data ownership, privacy, and compliance with evolving environmental and safety regulations require constant attention, especially in industries with strict oversight, such as oil and gas, chemical manufacturing, or mining.

The Future of Omnichannel EHS Services

As more EHS enterprises adopt an omnichannel approach, we will see tighter integration between mobile platforms, IoT devices, and traditional systems. This evolution could lead to safety and environmental management systems that entirely automate tasks like:

- Accident prevention through real-time monitoring of hazardous environments.

- Predictive maintenance by identifying faulty equipment or safety risks before they occur.

- Compliance automation, ensuring regulatory adherence with minimal human intervention.

In conclusion, EHS omnichannel enterprises that embrace mobile technology and IoT integration will offer their customers the flexibility and control they demand. Whether participating in more extensive IoT networks or leading their own branded ecosystems, these companies are poised to drive innovation and improve safety and environmental outcomes across industries.

Suppliers in EHS

The overlap between mobile and IoT presents challenges and opportunities for suppliers of EHS (environment, health, and safety). Whether they provide safety equipment, environmental sensors, or compliance software, EHS suppliers must adapt their strategies to stay relevant in a connected world. Moving up the Digital EHS Strategy, suppliers can use mobile strategies to gain deeper insights into their end customers' needs while leveraging IoT networks to enhance the value they provide.

Mobile Strategy for EHS Suppliers

A solid mobile strategy can help EHS suppliers build stronger customer relationships and increase engagement. EHS suppliers can begin with a brand-enhancement strategy, offering useful mobile apps or services that improve customer interactions. For example:

- Safety gear suppliers could develop a mobile app that helps users track the condition and usage of personal protective equipment (PPE) and reminds them when it's time for replacements.

- Environmental monitoring suppliers might offer mobile tools that allow users to track real-time air or water quality data from sensors deployed across facilities.

As these strategies mature, EHS suppliers could evolve to a B2B2C model, offering mobile apps that connect end customers directly to their services. For instance:

- A waste management supplier could develop a mobile app that lets companies monitor their waste disposal services, schedule pickups, and receive compliance reports, bridging the gap between the supplier and end user.

IoT Networks and EHS Suppliers

Suppliers in the EHS sector will likely need to participate in multiple IoT networks. These networks could be managed by traditional customers like large industrial manufacturers or construction firms that rely on EHS suppliers for safety and environmental compliance. Alternatively, IoT networks might be led by tech companies offering integrated industrial IoT (IIoT) platforms or even by new entrants focused on providing holistic EHS services.

For EHS suppliers, the critical question is: Which IoT networks will be most beneficial?

- Traditional customers (e.g., large manufacturers) may lead networks that focus on integrating safety data and compliance metrics across facilities, providing EHS suppliers with opportunities to offer sensor data, monitoring tools, and safety solutions.

- New digital platforms like Amazon or Alibaba, or emerging EHS-focused tech providers, may lead IoT networks that aggregate data from multiple industries, allowing suppliers to offer products and services tailored to a broad range of EHS needs.

Participating in Multiple IoT Networks

EHS suppliers must be agile enough to participate in competing IoT networks, as some may be led by long-standing clients and others by newer tech companies. For example:

- Industrial safety equipment suppliers must integrate with construction industry IoT platforms to provide data on equipment usage and worker safety.

- Environmental sensor providers could connect to multiple IoT networks led by companies in industries like oil and gas, mining, or manufacturing, providing real-time environmental monitoring and compliance data.

This ability to integrate with various networks while maintaining direct mobile engagement with end users will enable suppliers to thrive in an increasingly digital and connected world.

Mobile Interaction for EHS Suppliers

Besides participating in IoT networks, suppliers must offer their customers mobile solutions to interact with their products and services. This could involve:

- Mobile apps that provide real-time insights on safety gear usage, allowing customers to see when equipment needs replacement.

- Tools that enable compliance officers to track sensor performance and receive alerts directly on their mobile devices when environmental limits are exceeded.

By combining mobile engagement with IoT integration, EHS suppliers can provide higher value to their customers, differentiate their offerings, and ensure they remain competitive in an evolving market.

In the EHS industry, suppliers have a significant opportunity to leverage the convergence of mobile technology and the IoT to move up the Digital EHS Strategy. By adopting a mobile-first strategy that enhances customer engagement and participating in multiple IoT networks, EHS suppliers can position themselves as indispensable partners in creating safer, more compliant, and environmentally sound operations for their customers. Whether they are working with traditional industrial giants or tech-driven IoT networks, agility and innovation will be crucial to success.

Modular Producers in EHS

Mobile strategies present both a challenge and an opportunity for modular producers in the EHS (Environment, Health, and Safety) sector. Modular producers provide products or services that seamlessly integrate with broader EHS ecosystems. They also supply critical components or services—such as compliance software, sensor data management, or safety systems—that must be compatible with multiple EHS platforms and IoT networks.

Mobile Engagement for EHS Modular Producers

EHS stakeholders—like compliance officers, safety managers, and environmental engineers—may only interact with a modular EHS app when something goes wrong, such as a compliance breach, equipment malfunction, or environmental hazard. This limited interaction challenges EHS modular producers, who must develop a mobile engagement strategy to keep their solutions relevant and valuable.

One approach could be to target specific segments within the EHS industry, such as:

- Compliance officers who need real-time data on environmental regulations, allowing them to manage compliance reports and data submissions from their mobile devices.

- Safety managers who monitor real-time alerts on workplace incidents or safety gear usage from a mobile dashboard, allowing for rapid response to emergencies.

- Environmental engineers track sensor performance and environmental data, such as air quality or wastewater levels, and need immediate access to performance analytics through mobile devices.

EHS modular producers can increase user engagement and build deeper customer relationships by offering targeted mobile apps that provide specific value-added services.

Plug-and-Play with IoT Networks

A critical aspect of being a successful EHS modular producer is the ability to integrate seamlessly with multiple IoT networks. EHS modular producers must ensure their solutions can easily fit into various EHS management systems and IoT-enabled environments.

For instance:

- Environmental monitoring sensors must integrate with IoT platforms for waste management, air quality control, and water treatment, feeding real-time data into larger systems that track environmental compliance.

- Safety gear providers, such as those offering smart helmets or wearable sensors, must ensure their products work across different safety management platforms in construction, manufacturing, or oil and gas industries.

- Compliance software providers must ensure their tools are interoperable with broader corporate governance platforms, enabling seamless communication of EHS data with internal enterprise systems and external regulatory bodies.

Opportunities to Become Ecosystem Drivers

While modular producers traditionally operate within the ecosystems of other businesses, mobile strategies and IoT integration present an opportunity to evolve into ecosystem drivers within EHS. For example:

- A safety equipment provider could expand its offerings to include real-time data monitoring, analytics, and compliance reporting, positioning itself as a platform that integrates with multiple safety tools and platforms. Thus, it would become indispensable to industries that need comprehensive workplace safety solutions.

- A compliance software producer could transform into a hub integrating data from environmental sensors, regulatory reporting systems, and legal frameworks, becoming the go-to platform for EHS compliance across industries.

To move from a modular producer to an ecosystem driver, EHS companies must provide solutions within existing platforms and aggregate, analyze, and optimize the data from these platforms, creating new value for end users.

Modular producers in the EHS industry can harness mobile technology and IoT compatibility to stay competitive and relevant. They can maintain their position in the value chain by developing targeted mobile strategies and ensuring their products seamlessly integrate with various EHS networks. More ambitiously, modular producers can evolve into ecosystem drivers by creating comprehensive platforms that combine data, services, and insights across industries, leading to enhanced customer engagement, improved compliance outcomes, and a safer, more sustainable environment for all stakeholders.

EHS: Seizing the Opportunity in Mobile and IoT Integration

This chapter explored how the dramatic rise of mobile technology and the Internet of Things (IoT) presents a transformative opportunity for enterprises to enhance their strategic positions—particularly within the EHS (Environment,

Health, and Safety) sector. However, with this opportunity comes the risk of falling behind if the transition is not managed effectively. The concurrent rise of mobile and IoT technologies can either strengthen your EHS platform's position or weaken it if not adopted strategically.

Mobile and IoT technologies offer the chance to digitally transform how EHS enterprises monitor, manage, and respond to environmental and safety conditions. This could mean using real-time sensor data to track air quality, monitor safety compliance in industrial settings, or assess the ecological impact of business operations. EHS platforms must now adopt mobile and IoT strategies to survive and thrive in an increasingly connected and data-driven world.

Assessment for EHS Enterprises

As you consider your next steps, the end of the chapter assessment will help you evaluate how well your EHS enterprise is positioned to leverage mobile and IoT technologies. This assessment will compare your capabilities with top performers and help you identify areas where you need to strengthen your mobile and IoT strategies.

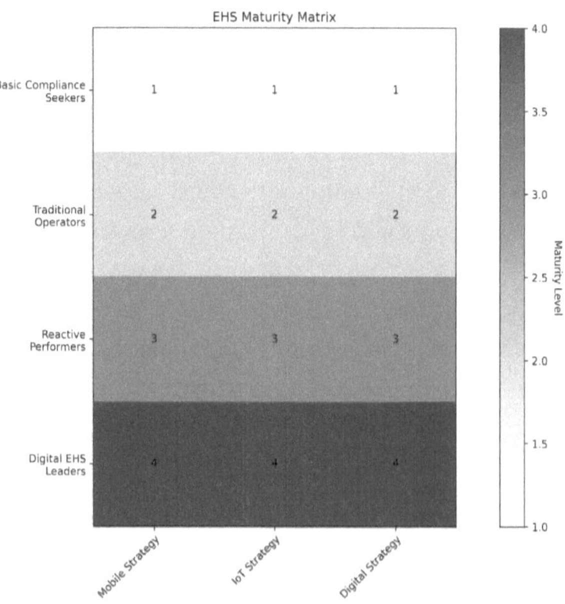

Figure 6.10: EHS Maturity vs Mobile, IoT, and Digital Strategy

High Stakes: Leaders vs. Followers

Statistical analysis of mobile and IoT success shows high stakes. As in other sectors, leaders and followers will also be quickly established in the EHS industry. Enterprises that adopt these technologies successfully will emerge as ecosystem drivers. At the same time, those who lag may find themselves relegated to modular producers, operating within others' ecosystems rather than controlling their own.

Strategic Path: Experiment or Commit?

There are two primary paths for EHS enterprises to pursue:

1. Safe Strategy: Conduct experiments with mobile and IoT technologies to identify future business opportunities. This allows enterprises to explore where they fit into the Digital EHS Strategy, whether as suppliers, modular producers, omnichannel businesses, or ecosystem drivers.

2. Ambitious and Risky Strategy: Recognize that the EHS industry is undergoing rapid transformation, and boldly move to reshape your enterprise fundamentally for the future. Like GE's strategy with Predix, your EHS enterprise could evolve into a platform that leads IoT networks and delivers cutting-edge mobile capabilities.

Moving Forward in EHS

In the EHS industry, this shift toward mobile and IoT-driven solutions will change how businesses manage compliance, safety, and environmental monitoring. Enterprises that successfully integrate these technologies can gather more accurate and timely data, streamline processes, and improve EHS performance.

In the next chapter, we will focus on building the capabilities needed to move your business up and to the right on the Digital EHS Strategy, ensuring your enterprise is prepared for the next generation of EHS digital transformation. Whether your enterprise aims to be a leader in mobile and IoT technologies or a participant in an ecosystem led by others, your choices will determine your future success in the evolving EHS landscape.

Regulatory Considerations in Mobile and IoT Adoption for EHS

As mobile and IoT technologies transform the EHS landscape, regulatory bodies worldwide are adapting their frameworks to address these new capabilities and challenges. Understanding the evolving regulatory environment is crucial for organizations that want to leverage these technologies effectively while maintaining compliance.

Evolving Regulatory Landscape

Regulatory bodies such as the Occupational Safety and Health Administration (OSHA) in the United States and the European Agency for Safety and Health at Work (EU-OSHA) are updating their guidelines to account for integrating mobile and IoT technologies in workplace safety practices.

For instance, OSHA has begun to recognize the value of real-time monitoring enabled by IoT devices. In its 2016 update to the "Recommended Practices for Safety and Health Programs," OSHA emphasized the importance of utilizing technology to enhance hazard identification and assessment processes. This shift signals a growing acceptance of IoT-enabled safety solutions among regulatory bodies.

Similarly, the Environmental Protection Agency (EPA) has started encouraging the use of advanced monitoring technologies for environmental compliance. The EPA's Next Generation Compliance initiative promotes innovative tools for real-time emissions monitoring, which aligns well with the capabilities of IoT sensors and mobile reporting systems.

Data Privacy and Security Regulations

Adopting mobile and IoT technologies in EHS brings new data privacy and security challenges. Regulations like the General Data Protection Regulation (GDPR) in Europe and the California Consumer Privacy Act (CCPA) in the United States significantly affect how companies collect, store, and use personal data gathered through IoT devices and mobile applications.

For example, wearable safety devices that monitor worker health and location must comply with these data protection regulations. Companies must also ensure proper consent mechanisms and provide transparency about data use. Failure to comply can result in severe penalties—up to €20 million or 4% of global annual turnover under GDPR.

Compliance Reporting

Mobile and IoT technologies are revolutionizing compliance reporting in EHS. Regulatory bodies are beginning to expect more frequent, accurate, and detailed reporting, which these technologies can facilitate.

For instance, the EPA's Electronic Reporting Rule requires submitting specific environmental data electronically. This shift towards digital reporting aligns with the capabilities of IoT sensors and mobile apps, which can automatically collect and transmit compliance data in real-time.

Industry-Specific Regulations

Different industries are seeing regulatory changes that specifically address or encourage the use of IoT and mobile technologies for safety and environmental monitoring.

The Bureau of Safety and Environmental Enforcement (BSEE) has promoted real-time monitoring systems for offshore drilling operations in the oil and gas industry. Their 2016 Well Control Rule explicitly mentions enhancing this technology's safety and environmental protection.

In the manufacturing sector, OSHA's emphasis on Process Safety Management (PSM) has led to increased adoption of IoT sensors for continuous monitoring of critical processes and potential hazards.

Predictive Compliance

The concept of "predictive compliance" is gaining traction as IoT and mobile technologies enable companies to anticipate and prepare for regulatory changes proactively. By analyzing trends in data collected through IoT devices, companies can identify potential compliance issues before they become problems.

For example, a chemical manufacturing plant using IoT sensors to monitor air quality can detect trends that might lead to non-compliance with emissions standards. This early warning allows the company to take corrective action before a violation occurs, potentially avoiding fines and reputational damage.

Regulatory Technology (RegTech)

The emergence of Regulatory Technology, or RegTech, is helping companies navigate the complex and changing regulatory landscape in EHS. RegTech solutions often leverage AI and machine learning to interpret vast amounts of regulatory data, assisting companies to stay compliant with minimal manual effort.

For instance, companies like Enablon and Cority offer EHS compliance management platforms integrating IoT devices and mobile apps to provide real-time compliance monitoring and reporting. These platforms can automatically update their rules engines when regulations change, ensuring companies have the most up-to-date compliance requirements.

Global Regulatory Harmonization

Mobile and IoT technologies facilitate greater harmonization of EHS regulations across different countries and regions. As these technologies enable more consistent data collection and reporting methods, it becomes easier for multinational companies to standardize their EHS practices globally.

The International Organization for Standardization (ISO) has recognized this trend. ISO 45001, the international standard for occupational health and safety management systems, encourages the use of technology for hazard identification and risk assessment, aligning well with the capabilities of mobile and IoT technologies.

Regulatory Challenges

Regions need help keeping pace with rapidly evolving technologies despite the opportunities. There often needs to be more clarity between emerging new technologies and developing appropriate regulations to govern their use in EHS contexts.

For example, the use of drones for safety inspections in industries like construction and oil and gas has outpaced regulatory frameworks. The FAA in the United States has been working to develop comprehensive regulations for commercial drone use, but the process has been complex and time-consuming.

Future Regulatory Trends

We expect more regulations mandating real-time monitoring and reporting technologies in high-risk industries. There may also be an increased focus on the cybersecurity aspects of IoT devices used in safety-critical applications.

Furthermore, as artificial intelligence and machine learning become more prevalent in EHS applications, regulations may address their use in safety-critical decision-making processes.

In conclusion, while mobile and IoT technologies offer tremendous opportunities for enhancing EHS performance, companies must navigate a complex and evolving regulatory landscape. Organizations can turn regulatory challenges into opportunities for improved safety, environmental performance, and operational efficiency by staying informed about regulatory trends and leveraging technologies that enable agile compliance management.

EHS Self-Assessment: How Ready Are You for Mobile and IoT?

Is your EHS enterprise prepared to take full advantage of mobile technologies and the Internet of Things (IoT) to move up and to the right on the Digital EHS Strategy? By conducting a self-assessment, you can measure your enterprise's readiness for the digital transformation that mobile and IoT technologies bring to the EHS landscape.

Mobile Readiness and IoT Commitment

Take the Chapter 5 Self-Assessment to evaluate where your enterprise stands in terms of mobile readiness and IoT commitment. Across various industries, the average scores for enterprises are:

- 30 out of a 50-point scale for mobile readiness

- 18 for IoT commitment

Top-performing enterprises score higher, with 35 for mobile readiness and 29 for IoT commitment.

How Does Your EHS Enterprise Compare?

Suppose your EHS enterprise plans to adopt mobile and IoT technologies to improve safety compliance, environmental monitoring, or operational efficiency. In that case, you should aim to score above average on both assessments. High scores indicate that your enterprise is well-equipped to integrate mobile and IoT technologies into its processes, enhancing your ability to monitor, manage, and predict EHS-related risks.

If your enterprise's scores are average or below, assessing whether you have the in-house capabilities to increase your mobile technology integration and IoT commitment is essential. If you lack these capabilities, consider partnering with technology providers specializing in mobile and IoT solutions to accelerate your digital transformation.

1. To what extent is your senior management involved in your enterprise's EHS mobile and digital transformation initiatives? (1 = Not at all, 10 = Very involved)

2. To what extent are your customers or facility stakeholders involved in your EHS mobile design and development efforts? (1 = Not at all, 10 = Very involved)

3. What percentage of your EHS program engagement or reporting comes from the mobile channel? (1 = None, 10 = All of them)

4. To what extent does your EHS mobile initiative rely on API-enabled enterprise capabilities, such as integrating incident reporting, compliance tracking, or environmental monitoring? (1 = Not at all, 10 = We rely on APIs)

5. To what extent are you capturing and using customer or facility data from your EHS mobile initiatives, such as incident reports, compliance logs, or sensor data? (1 = Not at all, 10 = We capture and use all the data)

6. How important is a well-developed IoT initiative for monitoring and improving EHS performance to your enterprise's success? (1 = Not important, 10 = Critical to our success)

7. What percentage of your EHS-related assets (e.g., environmental sensors, safety equipment) are IoT-enabled and IP-addressable now? (1 = None, 10 = Most of them)

8. How involved is your CIO in your enterprise's EHS innovation and technology transformation initiatives? (1 = Not at all involved, 10 = Critical to the success of all our innovation efforts)

9. How involved is your executive team in developing the digital strategy for EHS programs and technologies? (1 = Not at all involved, 10 = Critical to the development of the strategy)

10. How can your organization adapt and leverage IoT and digital solutions to improve EHS management and outcomes? (1 = Not at all ready, 10 = Very ready)

Return on Investment: The Business Case for Mobile and IoT in EHS

While the potential benefits of mobile and IoT technologies in Environment, Health, and Safety (EHS) are clear, organizations often need to justify the significant investment these technologies require. Understanding the Return on Investment (ROI) is crucial for decision-makers when considering the adoption of these transformative technologies.

Quantifying the ROI of EHS Technology Investments

The ROI for mobile and IoT technologies in EHS can be substantial, but it's essential to consider both tangible and intangible returns. Here's a breakdown of key areas where organizations can expect to see returns:

1. Incident Reduction and Associated Cost Savings

Mobile and IoT technologies can significantly reduce workplace incidents through real-time monitoring and early warning systems.

For example, a study by the American Society of Safety Professionals found that companies implementing IoT-based safety solutions saw a 30-50% reduction in workplace incidents within the first year of implementation.

Calculation example:

- Average cost per incident: $50,000

- Annual incidents before implementation: 20

- Reduction in incidents: 40%

- Incidents avoided: 8

- Yearly savings: $400,000

2. Improved Operational Efficiency

Automating data collection and reporting through mobile and IoT technologies can save time and increase productivity.

A Verdantix case study showed that companies adopting mobile EHS solutions reduce the time spent on compliance reporting by 25-30%.

Calculation example:

- EHS staff hours per year: 10,000

- Average hourly rate: $50

- Time saved on reporting: 25%

- Annual labor cost savings: $125,000

3. Reduced Insurance Premiums

Improved safety performance through IoT and mobile technologies can reduce insurance premiums.

The National Safety Council reports that companies with solid safety programs can see insurance premium reductions of up to 25%.

Calculation example:

- Annual insurance premium: $1,000,000

- Reduction in premium: 15%

- Yearly savings: $150,000

4. Energy and Resource Efficiency

IoT sensors can optimize resource usage, leading to significant cost savings.

According to the Department of Energy, intelligent building technologies can reduce energy consumption by 20-30%.

Calculation example:

- Annual energy costs: $500,000

- Energy savings: 20%

- Yearly savings: $100,000

5. Regulatory Compliance and Avoided Penalties

Real-time monitoring and automated reporting can help avoid costly regulatory violations.

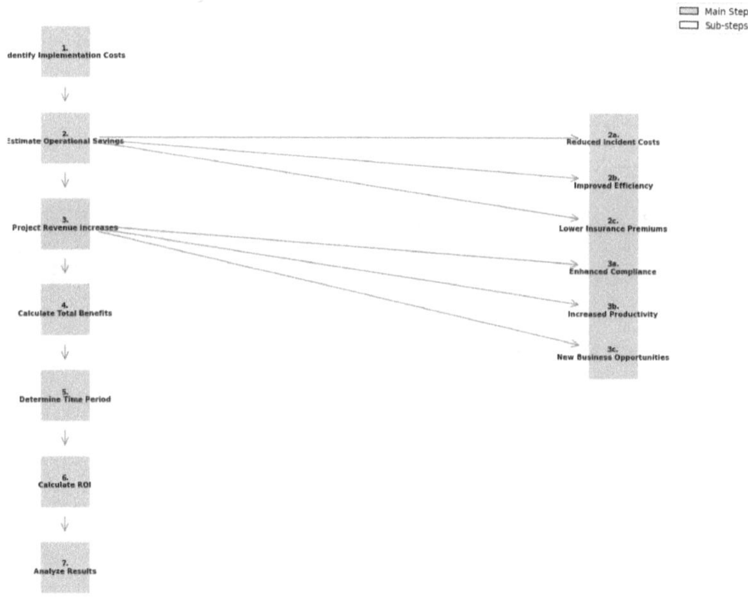

Figure 6.11: ROI Calculation framework

OSHA reports that the average cost of a safety violation is $13,260, with repeat violations costing up to $132,598.

Calculation example:

- Average cost per violation: $13,260

- Violations avoided per year: 5

- Annual savings: $66,300

Intangible Benefits

While more challenging to quantify, intangible benefits contribute significantly to the overall ROI:

1. **Enhanced Brand Reputation**: Demonstrating a commitment to safety and sustainability can improve stakeholder perceptions and increase market share.

2. **Improved Employee Satisfaction and Retention**: A safer workplace leads to higher employee satisfaction and lower turnover rates.

3. **Competitive Advantage**: Early adopters of these technologies may gain a significant edge over competitors in efficiency and safety performance.

Case Study: ROI in Action

Let's consider a real-world example from the oil and gas industry:

A major oil company implemented an IoT-based safety monitoring system across its refining operations. The initial investment was $5 million.

Results after one year:

- 35% reduction in safety incidents

- 20% improvement in operational efficiency

- 10% reduction in insurance premiums

- 15% reduction in energy consumption

Total quantifiable savings: $12 million

ROI calculation: (Net Profit / Cost of Investment) x 100 = ($12 million - $5 million) / $5 million x 100 = 140% ROI in the first year.

Considerations for Calculating ROI

When assessing the ROI of mobile and IoT technologies in EHS, consider the following:

1. **Implementation Costs should include** the cost of hardware and software and training, integration, and potential disruptions during implementation.

2. **Maintenance and Upgrade Costs**: Factor in ongoing costs for system maintenance, updates, and potential scalability.

3. **Time to Value**: Some benefits may take time. Consider the timeline for realizing different types of returns.

4. **Risk Mitigation**: While more challenging to quantify, the value of avoiding a significant incident or regulatory penalty can be substantial.

Conclusion

The ROI for implementing mobile and IoT technologies in EHS can be significant, often exceeding 100% within the first few years of implementation. While the initial investment may be substantial, the long-term benefits of improved safety, efficiency, and compliance often outweigh the costs.

However, conducting a thorough analysis based on your organization's specific circumstances is crucial. Factors such as industry, current safety performance, regulatory environment, and existing technology infrastructure will all impact the potential ROI.

By carefully considering the quantifiable and intangible returns, organizations can build a compelling business case for investing in these transformative technologies, positioning themselves for improved EHS performance and long-term success.

Chapter 6 References

1. Verdantix. (2022). Green Quadrant EHS Software 2022. Retrieved from https://www.verdantix.com/report/green-quadrant-ehs-software-2022

2. Occupational Safety and Health Administration. (2016). Recommended Practices for Safety and Health Programs. Retrieved from https://www.osha.gov/safety-management

3. Environmental Protection Agency. (2015). Next Generation Compliance. Retrieved from https://www.epa.gov/compliance/next-generation-compliance

4. European Union. (2018). General Data Protection Regulation (GDPR). Retrieved from https://gdpr-info.eu/

5. California State Legislature. (2018). California Consumer Privacy Act (CCPA). Retrieved from https://oag.ca.gov/privacy/ccpa

6. Bureau of Safety and Environmental Enforcement. (2016). Oil and Gas and Sulphur Operations in the Outer Continental Shelf-Blowout Preventer Systems and Well Control. Retrieved from https://www.bsee.gov/guidance-and-regulations/regulations/well-control-rule

7. International Organization for Standardization. (2018). ISO 45001:2018 Occupational health and safety management systems Requirements with guidance for use. Retrieved from https://www.iso.org/standard/63787.html

8. American Society of Safety Professionals. (2021). The ROI of Safety: A Look at the Costs and Benefits of Occupational Safety and Health. Professional Safety Journal, 66(5), 22-28.

9. Verdantix. (2021). The Business Case For Investing In EHS Software. Retrieved from https://www.verdantix.com/report/the-business-case-for-investing-in-ehs-software

10. National Safety Council. (2022). Safety Management Systems. Retrieved from https://www.nsc.org/workplace/safety-topics/safety-management-systems

11. U.S. Department of Energy. (2021). Smart Buildings. Retrieved from https://www.energy.gov/eere/buildings/smart-buildings

12. Occupational Safety and Health Administration. (2022). OSHA Penalties. Retrieved from https://www.osha.gov/penalties

13. Gartner. (2021). Market Guide for Environment, Health and Safety Software. Retrieved from https://www.gartner.com/en/documents/4001459

14. McKinsey & Company. (2020). The Internet of Things: Capturing the Accelerated Opportunity. Retrieved from https://www.mckinsey.com/business-functions/mckinsey-digital/our-insights/the-internet-of-things-capturing-the-accelerated-opportunity

15. Deloitte. (2021). The Fourth Industrial Revolution and its Impact on EHS. Retrieved from https://www2.deloitte.com/us/en/pages/advisory/articles/fourth-industrial-revolution-impact-on-ehs.html

16. Safety+Health Magazine. (2022). The ROI of safety: Making the business case. Retrieved from https://www.safetyandhealthmagazine.com/articles/21609-the-roi-of-safety-making-the-business-case

17. Journal of Occupational and Environmental Hygiene. (2019). The Fourth Industrial Revolution and Its Impact on Occupational Health and Safety, Worker's Compensation and Labor Conditions. 16(9), 614-619.

18. Environmental Health and Safety Today. (2022). The Future of EHS: Embracing Digital Transformation. Retrieved from https://ehstoday.com/safety-technology/article/21920177/the-future-of-ehs-embracing-digital-transformation

19. Harvard Business Review. (2020). A Manager's Guide to the Internet of Things. Retrieved from https://hbr.org/2020/07/a-managers-guide-to-the-internet-of-things

20. MIT Sloan Management Review. (2021). The New Elements of Digital Transformation. Retrieved from https://sloanreview.mit.edu/article/the-new-elements-of-digital-transformation/

Crucial Capabilities for the Future of EHS

07

In the modern business landscape, enterprises are challenged to meet regulatory requirements and integrate **safety** as a core component of their **strategic business design**. Reinventing an enterprise through the lens of **EHS (Environmental Health and Safety) knowledge** and **business design** requires more than compliance—it demands a shift toward proactive, innovative safety cultures that align with broader operational and strategic goals.

This chapter delves into the **EHS Knowledge and Business Design Framework**, illustrating the journey from **Basic Compliance Seekers** to **Digital Leaders**. Each quadrant in the framework reflects a different level of EHS maturity and business innovation. As companies move through the quadrants, they must develop and master several **crucial capabilities** to succeed:

1. **Proactive Leadership**: Leadership must shift from reactive, compliance-driven actions to a proactive approach, viewing safety as an integral part of long-term business success.

2. **Digital Transformation**: The adoption and integration of **digital tools**—such as IoT, AI, and predictive analytics—into safety programs is key to improving outcomes, reducing incidents, and driving operational efficiency.

3. **Balancing Safety Innovation with Cost Control**: Successful companies innovate in safety while maintaining cost-effectiveness, ensuring that safety investments contribute to **operational improvements** and financial stability.

4. **Creating a Digital Safety Culture**: To be effective, the organization must fully embrace safety technologies. Building a **robust digital culture**

ensures employees are trained, engaged, and empowered to use digital tools to enhance safety outcomes.

5. **Embedding Safety in Business Strategy**: Safety must be integrated into the company's **strategic vision**, not treated as an isolated function. Digital leaders use safety innovation as a competitive advantage, turning compliance into an opportunity for differentiation.

These capabilities are essential for any company moving from **basic compliance** to **digital leadership**. As the chapter progresses, we will explore how these areas contribute to organizational success and how leadership can steer a company toward becoming an industry leader in safety.

The chapter includes a comprehensive **self-assessment checklist** to help guide this transformation. This tool will enable you to evaluate your organization's current capabilities and pinpoint the areas needing improvement to move forward in the **EHS Knowledge and Business Design Framework**. Whether you're operating as a **Basic Compliance Seeker**, **Traditional Operator**, **Reactive Performer**, or **Digital Leader**, this assessment will provide a clear picture of your company's strengths and areas for growth.

Ultimately, this chapter offers insights and actionable guidance on developing the **crucial capabilities** that will enable your enterprise to stay competitive, innovative, and safe—paving the way for **long-term success**.

Leadership perspectives:

Analyzing each leadership facet from the EHS Knowledge and the Business Design Framework perspective allows us to explore how various companies navigate these domains to drive safety, compliance, and operational efficiency. We'll break this down into detailed sections based on key leadership traits, emphasizing EHS Knowledge (technical and regulatory mastery) and Business Design (strategic integration of safety into business operations).

1. Proactive Innovation and Safety Integration

In my years as a consultant, I've seen how leaders who integrate EHS knowledge deeply into their business design gain substantial competitive advantages. They understand that safety isn't just a compliance obligation; it's a core driver of innovation and a crucial differentiator in the market. These leaders don't separate safety from their broader strategy—they treat it as a critical enabler that drives operational excellence and customer trust.

From an **EHS Knowledge** perspective, I've observed companies pioneering the use of safety regulations and advanced technologies to innovate. One company developed **connected safety solutions** using **IoT**, real-time **data analytics**, and strict adherence to safety standards. Their approach allows them to minimize hazards in real time while leveraging predictive analytics to identify and mitigate risks before they escalate. By staying within compliance frameworks, they've turned safety into a powerful tool for innovation.

From a **Business Design** perspective, this same company aligned its safety innovations with its overall strategy, positioning safety as a compliance requirement and a differentiating feature in the marketplace. They integrated safety technologies into their product offerings, such as **IoT wearables** that monitor worker safety. This shift enhances safety and creates new revenue streams, proving that safety can be a marketable product feature.

Another company I've worked with has focused on **autonomous industrial equipment**. Here, safety is viewed as a core business objective. By reducing human risk and improving operational efficiency through automation, they've demonstrated how safety can simultaneously address compliance and drive operational innovation.

The lesson is clear: companies that view EHS not just as a regulatory necessity but as an integral part of their business strategy stand to gain a significant competitive edge. They innovate within compliance frameworks and position safety as a value-adding element, enhancing product offerings and creating safer, more efficient operations. In this way, safety transforms from a cost center into a source of growth and differentiation.

2. Strategic Vision and Digital Transformation

In my experience as a consultant, I've observed that **EHS Knowledge** is essential but only truly impactful when strategically aligned with a company's overall business design. In organizations with solid safety knowledge but evolving business models, the focus tends to remain on compliance-driven leadership, with emerging innovations that have yet to be fully integrated.

For example, I worked with a healthcare company with impeccable EHS processes due to the high-risk nature of its operations. The leadership emphasizes **real-time compliance monitoring** to ensure all safety protocols meet global standards. However, despite their robust focus on regulatory alignment, the company still needs to transition to using safety as a strategic differentiator. Safety is necessary to avoid risks and fines rather than a lever for business growth or innovation.

In contrast, another global energy company I advised had significant EHS knowledge, particularly in high-risk environments. While the organization made strides in using **AI to predict and mitigate risks**, its overall safety approach remained reactive rather than proactive. Despite efforts to leverage advanced technologies, safety needed to be fully embedded into its broader business strategy. The digital transformation strategy was fragmented, and while their leadership was aware of the importance of safety, they still needed to align it with their core business objectives in a way that drives innovation or adds value.

In both cases, the challenge lies in moving from a compliance-first mindset to viewing **EHS** as an integral part of **strategic business design**. Companies must make this shift to take advantage of the opportunity to leverage safety for competitive advantage. However, the companies that can combine their EHS knowledge with forward-thinking business strategies—using safety as an asset rather than a mere regulatory obligation—are the ones that set themselves apart in the marketplace.

The critical insight here is that **EHS Knowledge** must evolve into **strategic alignment** with the business model. Leaders who proactively integrate safety into their strategic goals, embed digital solutions and view safety as a core aspect of business design is the ones who ultimately transform safety from a compliance necessity into a market differentiator.

3. Ambidextrous Leadership: Innovating and Cutting Costs

In my experience as a consultant, I've seen how **ambidextrous leadership**—balancing innovation with cost optimization—is a hallmark of companies that excel in both **EHS knowledge** and robust business design. One example is a steel manufacturing company I worked with that successfully incorporated **sustainable processes** using recycled materials in production while investing in

digital platforms to monitor workplace safety. This organization has mastered embedding sustainability and safety within its cost structure, ensuring its safety innovations don't undermine its operational efficiency. They've created a model where safety improvements, such as real-time hazard monitoring and predictive analytics, seamlessly align with cost-saving measures, allowing them to innovate without compromising their bottom line.

On the other hand, I've also seen companies still navigating the complexities of balancing **safety innovation** with cost efficiency. One automotive company I advised had invested heavily in **predictive analytics** to monitor safety risks, making impressive strides in safety technology. However, they needed help fully integrating these innovations into a broader business model emphasizing **cost control** and safety excellence. This left them in a middle ground where they had the tools for innovation but needed to optimize these advancements to ensure they were financially sustainable. As a result, they should have made safety an integral part of their operational success.

The key takeaway is that thriving companies can achieve this **balance of innovation and cost efficiency**. They use their EHS expertise to drive safety improvements while focusing on cost optimization, ensuring that safety is a compliance requirement and a driver of business success. Conversely, companies that need help finding this balance often find themselves in situations where innovation comes at unsustainable costs or misses opportunities for **cost-effective safety solutions**. It's this ability to balance the two that sets industry leaders apart.

4. Reactive vs. Proactive Leadership in Safety

As a consultant, I've often encountered companies operating with a **reactive safety leadership model**, where safety measures are only introduced in response to incidents. These organizations focus on compliance and avoiding penalties rather than fostering a **proactive risk management culture**. I've seen how frequent violations and incidents occur in these environments, revealing a gap in their ability to translate **EHS knowledge** into an effective, integrated business design. In these companies, safety is viewed as something that must be managed to avoid fines, not as a strategic business driver.

One example I recall is a manufacturing company that would only tighten safety measures after an incident. This reactive approach led to repeated violations and worker injuries, demonstrating that their safety model needed more sustainability. Their leadership was focused on short-term fixes and compliance audits rather than embedding safety into the fabric of their business.

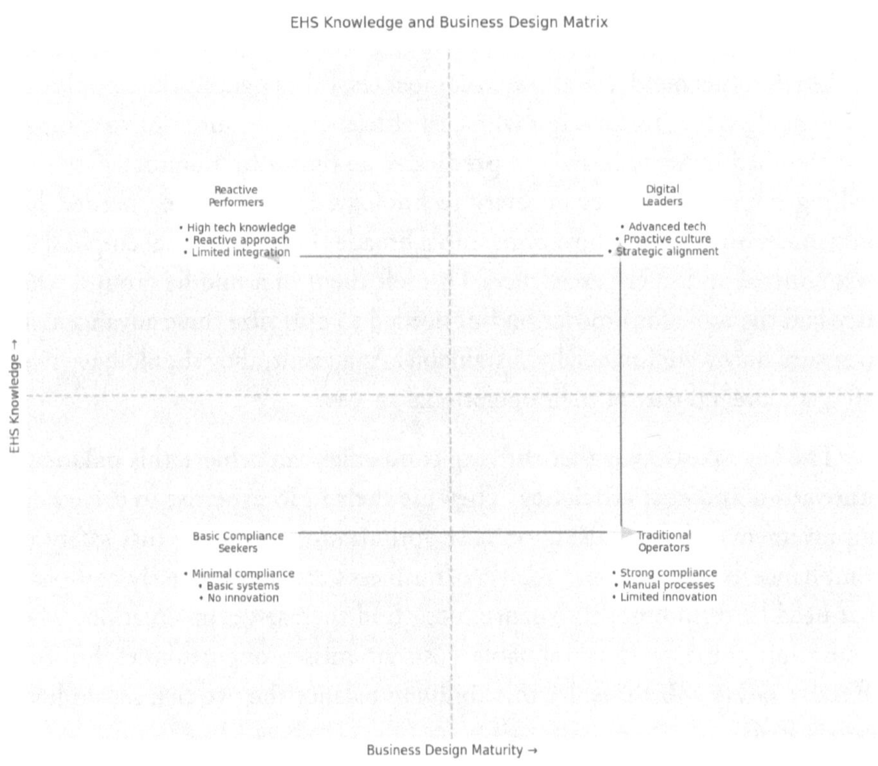

Figure 7.1: EHS Knowledge and Business Design Matrix

In contrast, I've also worked with organizations that exemplify **proactive leadership**. These companies consider safety integral to their operations, embedding it at every level. For instance, companies developing **autonomous machinery** have made worker safety a key feature of their products. By integrating **digital tools** like IoT and predictive analytics, they can pre-empt incidents before they happen. One client in the industrial sector used real-time data to identify potential hazards, allowing them to address issues before they escalated. This approach protected workers and positioned safety as a differentiating feature in their products.

From my experience, the companies that thrive shift from a **reactive** model to a **proactive** one. When safety becomes a central part of the business strategy, it drives innovation, reduces violations, and creates long-term cost savings. It's clear that proactive safety leadership improves outcomes and turns safety into a strategic asset that enhances operations and product offerings.

5. Building a Digital EHS Culture

In my work as a consultant guiding companies through **EHS digital transformation**, I've seen that a critical leadership trait is the ability to foster a **digital culture** where safety technologies are implemented and fully embraced by the workforce. Some organizations I've worked with have introduced **digital tools** for real-time safety reporting, but technical issues—like mobile app glitches or poor user interfaces—have slowed their progress. These challenges underscore a common problem: a gap between having strong **EHS knowledge** and successfully integrating it into a business model, prioritizing seamless technology and employee engagement.

I've also witnessed companies that have taken a different path, successfully building a **digital EHS culture**. One company I worked with used digital tools to integrate **real-time compliance tracking** across its global operations, ensuring safety is maintained at every level. Their leadership focused not just on deploying technology but on making sure it fit smoothly into day-to-day operations. By providing reliable and easy-to-use technology, they achieved widespread adoption and, as a result, improved safety performance across the board.

I've learned that successful **EHS digital transformation** comes down to leadership's ability to align safety technology with **operational needs** and employee engagement. It's not enough to introduce digital tools; they must be designed for the workforce to use effortlessly, with a strong focus on overcoming technical barriers. This is where companies can move from just deploying tools to building a robust digital safety culture that transforms how they manage risks and compliance.

6. Problematic Leadership: Short-Term Focus and Resistance to Change

From my experience working with various industries, I've often seen that when safety is viewed as an added expense rather than a core value, it leads to **problematic leadership** and frequent safety violations. Companies usually possess strong **EHS knowledge**, but that knowledge needs to be more utilized, focusing more on **short-term cost savings** and minimal compliance to meet regulatory standards. This mindset typically results in recurring safety incidents, as the emphasis is on cutting corners rather than embedding safety into the business's long-term vision.

In contrast, I've worked with companies that take a different approach—ones that integrate **EHS knowledge** into their **long-term business strategy**. Their leadership sees safety not as an expense but as an **investment** that enhances operational efficiency, reduces risk, and even serves as a market differentiator. One example comes from a manufacturing firm that shifted its perspective on safety from a regulatory obligation to a core part of its innovation and efficiency model. This approach reduced the frequency of incidents, improved overall productivity, and strengthened their brand reputation.

What I've learned is that companies with a **long-term vision**—where safety is seen as a critical driver of **sustainable success**—are the ones that manage to innovate, reduce safety violations, and outperform their competitors. Their investment in safety creates a foundation for **operational excellence** and positions them for long-term profitability, far outweighing any short-term cost savings.

Now, we will assess leadership in detail using our **EHS Knowledge and Business Design Framework**. This approach will help us understand how leadership in different organizations integrates **EHS knowledge** into their broader business models to foster proactive, innovative safety cultures. By doing so, we can differentiate between those companies that excel at turning safety into a **competitive advantage** and those that remain stuck in reactive modes of operation.

In companies where EHS knowledge is deeply aligned with strategic business design, safety isn't just about compliance—it becomes a core driver of innovation. These companies demonstrate an apparent ability to embed safety into their long-term goals, ensuring integration across all operational levels. Their leadership champions safety as a tool for **innovation**, leveraging digital technologies and data analytics to meet regulatory requirements and push the boundaries of operational excellence. By doing this, they reduce the frequency of safety incidents, enhance worker morale, and ultimately drive higher profitability through **efficiency gains** and reduced disruptions.

On the other hand, we find that companies with a **reactive mindset** often need help to make this transition. These organizations focus heavily on short-term compliance, dealing with safety as an expense rather than an investment. Their leadership needs to pay more attention to the value that safety innovation can bring. As a result, they miss out on the competitive benefits of integrating safety into their broader business goals. Moreover, there is often resistance to embracing **digital tools**, which hinders their ability to proactively manage risks and optimize safety processes. This leads to frequent violations, operational inefficiencies, and higher long-term costs.

As we delve deeper into this analysis, it will become evident which leadership teams are effectively using EHS as a strategic advantage and which are still playing catch-up, stuck in a cycle of reactive safety management and short-term thinking. Through this lens, we can clearly see how companies are positioning themselves for safety compliance and **long-term success** driven by innovative safety leadership.

Observation based on EHS Knowledge and Business Design Framework:

Basic Compliance Seeker

1. Proactive Innovation and Safety Integration

In my experience working with **primary compliance seekers**, I've seen how companies in this quadrant focus on doing the bare minimum to meet regulatory standards. Their approach to **EHS knowledge** is often limited to avoiding fines and penalties, and they rarely invest in the in-depth technical knowledge needed to drive real innovation in safety practices. These organizations must explore advanced safety systems or technologies that could prevent hazards or improve operational efficiency, missing out on opportunities to create safer, more effective workplaces.

From a **business design** perspective, these companies don't view safety as a strategic advantage. Safety is treated as a necessary cost rather than something that can be integrated into the core of the business to create value. Safety measures are often reactive—implemented only after external pressures such as regulatory inspections or incidents force action. There's no proactive planning to embed safety into daily operations, and the long-term benefits of a robust safety culture are often overlooked.

I've worked with **small and medium-sized construction firms** that perfectly fit this description. They meet basic regulatory requirements but don't invest in the technologies or processes that would allow them to innovate in safety. Their leadership focuses more on short-term cost-saving measures than building a sustainable, safety-oriented business model. As a result, these companies often face operational inefficiencies and higher safety risks, which could be avoided with a more integrated and proactive approach.

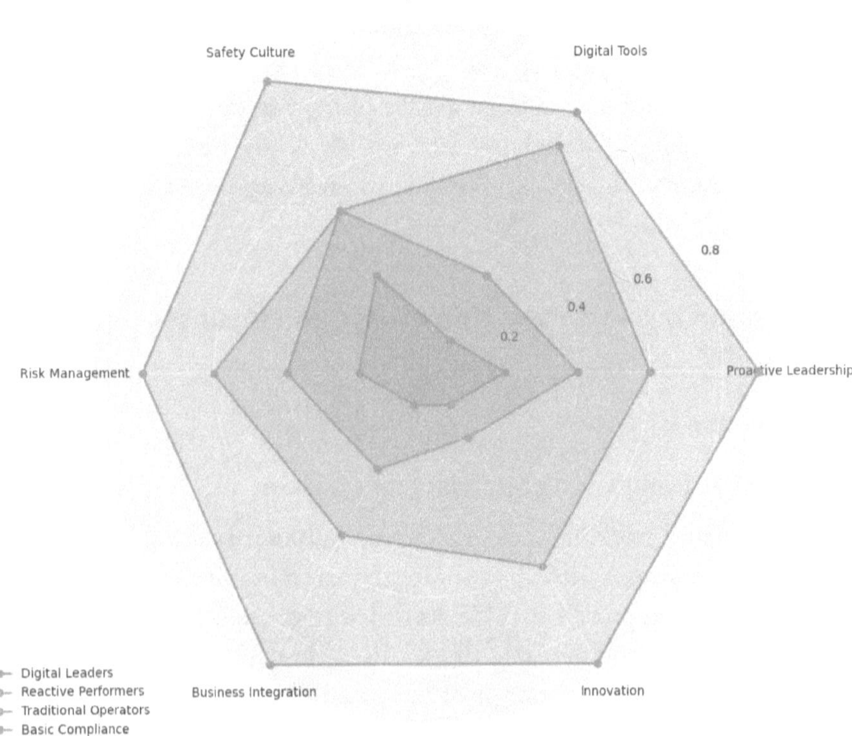

Figure 7.2: EHS Crucial Capabilities assessment

This lack of investment in **EHS knowledge** and the absence of safety as part of their **business design** keep these organizations from realizing the full potential of safety as a competitive advantage. This short-sighted approach often leads to recurring safety issues and higher long-term costs without ever truly optimizing operational efficiency or protecting their workforce.

2. Strategic Vision and Digital Transformation

I've noticed a recurring challenge in my firsthand experience working with companies with minimal digital integration in their EHS systems. These organizations often need more vision to leverage **safety as a competitive differentiator**. Their safety processes remain largely **traditional and manual**, with minimal investment in **digital tools** or real-time monitoring systems. This leaves them stuck in outdated methods, unable to capitalize on the potential of modern safety technologies to drive innovation or efficiency.

From a **business design** perspective, these companies need more **digital transformation** regarding safety. Digital tools are often limited to essential compliance rather than being strategically aligned with long-term business goals. As a result, safety remains siloed, disconnected from **operational efficiency** and risk mitigation strategies that could boost their competitive edge.

I recall working with a **large food company** that exemplified this mindset. While maintaining compliance with all safety regulations, their approach was entirely **compliance-driven**. They still needed to fully integrate **digital safety systems** into their broader operations, relying instead on traditional methods. This created operational inefficiencies and missed opportunities to enhance safety performance and reduce risks. On the other hand, their competitors were investing in real-time data monitoring and predictive safety tools, making safety an asset that drove business success.

In my experience, companies that fail to embrace **digital transformation** in their EHS processes are often left behind, not just in terms of safety performance but in overall **business competitiveness**. Safety must be viewed as more than a regulatory checkbox to keep pace with industry leaders; it should be a **strategic component** of long-term operational success.

3. Ambidextrous Leadership

In my experience working with **Basic Compliance Seekers**, I've seen that these organizations often need help to balance **safety innovation** with **cost optimization**. Their approach to safety is typically reactive, driven by regulatory requirements rather than a proactive strategy. Safety measures are usually implemented only when necessary to meet compliance, and because of this, they miss out on opportunities to reduce costs and improve efficiency through advanced safety technologies.

One example that stands out involves a mid-sized manufacturing company. Leadership was focused on meeting the minimum safety standards required by regulators, and they were hesitant to invest in **new safety technologies**. Their EHS measures needed to be updated, and while they avoided fines, they could not **optimize costs** or achieve any significant operational efficiencies. Their reliance on manual safety processes often led to costly operational delays and higher risks of incidents, further increasing long-term costs.

From a **business design** perspective, these companies need a **proactive mindset**. Leadership tends to respond to safety issues only as they arise rather than using **innovation** to improve safety and operations. This reactive approach limits their ability to leverage safety as a driver for **cost savings** and operational excellence. Without integrating safety innovation into their business strategy, they consistently miss out on the efficiencies and cost benefits of adopting advanced technologies.

From working with these types of organizations, I've learned that their short-term approach to safety ultimately costs them more in the long run. By failing to invest in **innovative safety measures**, they forgo the opportunity to streamline operations, reduce risks, and drive long-term profitability. Instead, safety remains a compliance burden rather than an opportunity for **business improvement**.

4. Reactive vs. Proactive Leadership

In my firsthand experience working with **basic compliance seekers**, I've often encountered companies that operate in a **reactive mode** regarding safety. These organizations typically respond to **incidents and compliance violations** only after they've occurred, with their primary focus being on avoiding penalties rather than proactively managing risks. Their approach to **EHS knowledge** is driven more by the need to meet regulatory standards than by a desire to integrate safety into their everyday operations.

One notable example I've come across is a **large meat processing company**. This company frequently reacts to safety and environmental violations after the fact, resulting in penalties and operational downtime. Their leadership only addresses safety issues when external pressures force them to do so, demonstrating an apparent lack of **proactive safety management**. Because safety isn't embedded into their broader business strategy, they experience recurring violations, inefficiencies, and disruptions that could have been prevented with a more forward-thinking approach.

From a **business design** perspective, these companies must integrate safety into **strategic decision-making**. Instead of using safety as a foundation for operational efficiency and risk reduction, they treat it as an isolated compliance requirement. The result is frequent safety incidents that disrupt operations, cost them financial penalties, and lost productivity.

Through these experiences, I've learned that **reactive safety leadership** leads to more than just penalties—it causes **long-term operational disruptions** and missed opportunities for **growth**. Companies that view safety as merely a compliance burden struggle with inefficiencies. In contrast, those who proactively integrate safety into their business can use it to drive **operational success** and **competitive advantage**.

5. Building a Digital EHS Culture

In my firsthand experience working with companies that have yet to embrace **digital EHS culture**, I've noticed a significant gap in how safety is integrated into their broader business operations. These companies typically **need more investment** in creating a digital EHS framework. If they implement **digital tools**, it's usually in response to **external regulatory pressures** rather than internal initiatives to improve safety performance.

From an **EHS knowledge** perspective, these companies don't see the value in using digital technologies to enhance safety, relying instead on outdated, manual processes. This lack of foresight limits their ability to identify risks early and optimize real-time safety measures. The leadership implemented a basic safety reporting app in one case I encountered. However, because it was driven solely by compliance requirements, the workforce needed to embrace it thoroughly, and its potential went largely untapped.

Regarding **business design**, these digital tools must be fully integrated into day-to-day operations, leaving safety isolated from other aspects of the business. Employees are often not **empowered** or trained to use technology to improve safety outcomes, so the potential for **operational efficiencies** or meaningful improvements in **worker safety** is rarely realized.

By building a **digital safety culture**, companies can take advantage of opportunities to turn safety into a driver of **efficiency** and **innovation**. Instead, safety remains an isolated function, detached from the broader business strategy. In my experience, when companies finally begin to align their safety culture with digital tools and integrate them across their operations, they see immediate improvements in safety and operational performance.

6. Problematic Leadership

In my firsthand experience, **leadership** in Basic Compliance Seeker companies often focuses on **short-term gains**, avoiding deeper investments in safety that could drive long-term benefits. These leaders prioritize immediate compliance needs, reacting to violations when they occur rather than proactively integrating **EHS knowledge** into their business strategy. This short-sighted approach prevents them from realizing the full potential of **safety innovation**.

I've worked with companies where leadership needed to be more open to investing in **advanced safety technologies** or comprehensive safety programs. They focused on ticking off the compliance boxes to avoid fines rather than using safety to improve efficiency and reduce risks. For example, one organization I consulted for consistently postponed investing in digital safety tools, opting instead to handle incidents manually and reactively. This led to **frequent violations**, operational disruptions, and an overall resistance to change.

From a **business design** perspective, these companies resist change, sticking to outdated safety practices instead of incorporating safety into their long-term **strategic vision**. They view safety as an operational cost rather than an investment that could lead to **business growth**. This resistance to change and failure to integrate safety into their business goals limits their potential to innovate and improve operational efficiency.

I've seen that problematic leadership in this quadrant not only results in repeated violations but also prevents these companies from unlocking the **full benefits** of safety innovation. With a proactive, forward-thinking approach, they can avoid a reactive cycle, missing out on the long-term advantages of embedding safety into their broader **business strategy**.

Traditional Performer

1. Proactive Innovation and Safety Integration

In my firsthand experience working with **Traditional Performers**, I've seen that while these companies have a solid grasp of **EHS regulations**, they tend to rely on **conventional methods** to meet safety standards. Their focus is predominantly on compliance, with little exploration of new technologies that could drive **innovation** or enhance **operational efficiency**. These organizations understand the importance of safety but often stick to what has worked in the past, needing more opportunities to leverage **advanced safety tools** like predictive analytics or real-time monitoring systems.

From a **business design** perspective, safety is well-integrated into their operations but managed through **traditional, manual processes**. I've worked with companies with solid safety compliance frameworks but were reluctant to shift away from outdated systems. While their safety measures effectively met regulatory requirements, they weren't using safety as a **competitive advantage** or a driver of innovation. For example, safety was deeply embedded in one manufacturing company in daily operations, but the processes were entirely manual. Adopting digital safety tools or automation is needed to enhance safety and productivity.

I've observed that these companies do a great job **maintaining compliance**, but they miss out on the potential **operational and strategic benefits** that come from integrating innovation into their safety programs. By not embracing new safety technologies or innovative approaches, they limit their ability to **optimize efficiency** and reduce long-term risks, keeping safety as a compliance-focused function rather than a strategic tool for business growth.

2. Strategic Vision and Digital Transformation

In my firsthand experience working with **Traditional Operators**, I've seen that while these companies have a solid understanding of **safety management**, they need to catch up when adopting **digital tools** that could further optimize their safety processes. They excel at compliance, ensuring they meet all regulatory requirements, but they miss the opportunity to integrate **technology** that could enhance efficiency, improve real-time monitoring, and reduce risks.

From a **business design** perspective, leadership in these companies maintains a strong focus on compliance. Still, **digital transformation** is viewed as something other than an essential component of their long-term safety strategy. I worked with a manufacturing firm with well-established safety protocols but relied entirely on manual processes for incident reporting and safety audits. While they were compliant, they weren't leveraging tools like **predictive analytics** or **IoT-enabled safety systems** that could have helped them prevent incidents before they occurred.

This approach creates a gap between where they are and where their competitors are heading. The need for **digital integration** in their safety strategy keeps them reactive, addressing safety issues after they happen rather than proactively preventing them. In contrast, competitors investing in digital tools improve safety outcomes and drive **operational efficiencies** that traditional operators can only match by embracing these innovations.

In my experience, these companies risk being left behind as **digital transformation** becomes more central to **EHS management**. While they remain strong in compliance, their reluctance to innovate keeps them from achieving the **long-term benefits** of using technology to enhance safety and optimize their operations.

3. Ambidextrous Leadership

In my firsthand experience working with **Traditional Performers**, I've observed that these companies often need help to balance **innovation with cost**. Their safety processes are typically built around **tried-and-tested methods** that, while effective in maintaining compliance, don't continually optimize safety or reduce costs. These companies tend to stick with what has worked in the past rather than exploring new technologies that could make their operations safer and more efficient.

From a **business design** perspective, leadership in these organizations tends to focus primarily on **compliance-driven safety processes** and needs to be faster to adopt new technologies. I've seen this mindset in a manufacturing company that relied heavily on manual safety checks and audits. While these processes kept them compliant with regulations, they needed to be optimized to proactively reduce long-term costs or prevent incidents. Leadership was hesitant to invest in **digital tools** or safety innovations that could streamline processes and enhance both safety and operational efficiency.

This reluctance to embrace **innovation** prevents these companies from gaining the full benefits of modern safety strategies. While maintaining compliance, they miss opportunities to **optimize costs** and **drive operational improvements** through innovation. In my experience, their over-reliance on traditional methods keeps them from gaining the **competitive edge** that comes from integrating cutting-edge safety technologies into their business operations. Without a shift in focus toward balancing cost and innovation, these companies will continue to face challenges in improving safety outcomes and operational efficiency in the long run.

4. Reactive vs. Proactive Leadership

In my firsthand experience with **Traditional Operators**, I've seen that these companies often exhibit **reactive leadership** when it comes to safety. They have well-established safety processes, but any improvements are typically driven by **regulatory changes** or in response to past incidents, rather than through **proactive safety planning**. This approach means that while maintaining compliance, they exploit opportunities to avoid potential risks and optimize their safety practices.

One example that stands out involves a manufacturing company I worked with. They had a solid compliance history, and their safety management systems were functional, but leadership primarily viewed safety as a **compliance function**. Any significant updates or improvements were only made when new regulations required them to act or after an incident. While proud of their track record, they should have invested in more forward-thinking safety measures, such as **predictive analytics** or **real-time safety monitoring**. This lack of **proactive planning** meant they were often caught off guard by preventable issues that could have been addressed sooner with more innovative safety approaches.

From a **business design** perspective, these companies tend to act only when there is external pressure to meet new safety regulations or address immediate safety concerns. Leadership is primarily concerned with staying compliant rather than using safety as an opportunity for **operational efficiency** or a way to drive **innovation** in their processes.

I've learned that while these companies manage safety well on a surface level, they take advantage of long-term benefits. Without proactive safety planning, they limit their ability to **streamline operations** and prevent incidents before they arise. This reactive approach ultimately prevents them from achieving greater efficiency and safety outcomes.

5. Building a Digital EHS Culture

In my firsthand experience working with **Traditional Performers**, I've observed that while some investment is made in **digital safety tools**, their adoption is often slow, and **manual processes** still dominate. These companies recognize the need for digital transformation but need help to fully integrate these tools into their daily operations, relying heavily on traditional methods to manage safety.

I remember working with a **manufacturing company** that had started adopting digital safety platforms, but they were using them primarily for **compliance** rather than for driving operational improvements. The leadership had purchased safety monitoring software to track incidents and ensure regulatory adherence, but the tools needed to be fully utilized beyond that. Much of their safety management was still manually, and the digital systems required integration into their broader **strategic vision** for the company.

Because the tools were not embedded in the core of their operations, they missed opportunities to use data analytics and real-time monitoring to **optimize efficiency** and **reduce risks**. Digital systems needed to be more utilized, and safety was treated as a compliance task rather than an area for **continuous improvement**.

From what I've seen, these companies need to shift their focus from using digital tools solely for compliance to integrating them into their operational strategy. They must fully embrace **digital transformation** before they can continue to rely on outdated processes, which will limit their ability to stay competitive and realize the full potential of these technologies.

6. Problematic Leadership

In my firsthand experience working with **Traditional Performers**, I've noticed that **leadership's resistance to innovation** is one of the critical factors holding these companies back from evolving into more advanced safety leaders. While their **EHS knowledge** is solid, with a clear focus on maintaining compliance, their leadership tends to shy away from adopting new technologies or methods that could significantly improve safety outcomes.

For example, I worked with a manufacturing company whose leadership was highly focused on **compliance**, ensuring that all safety regulations were met. However, any suggestions to implement **new safety technologies**—such as real-time monitoring systems or data-driven safety analytics—were met with reluctance. The leadership prioritized maintaining the **status quo** and relied on tried-and-tested methods that, while sufficient for compliance, limited their ability to innovate and proactively manage risks.

This **resistance to change** often prevents these companies from realizing the full potential of their safety programs. Instead of viewing safety as an area ripe for **continuous improvement** and operational enhancement, leaders in these organizations see it as a regulatory box to check. Over time, this mindset leads to **organizational stagnation**, where safety processes remain reactive and focused on compliance rather than evolving into strategic assets that can drive **efficiency and competitive advantage**.

These companies must embrace **innovation** and integrate new safety methods into their broader **business design** to ensure they get the opportunity to become true **EHS leaders**. I've seen that this leadership hesitation ultimately hinders their growth, preventing them from leveraging **safety technologies** to streamline operations, reduce incidents, and stay ahead of competitors who are more willing to innovate.

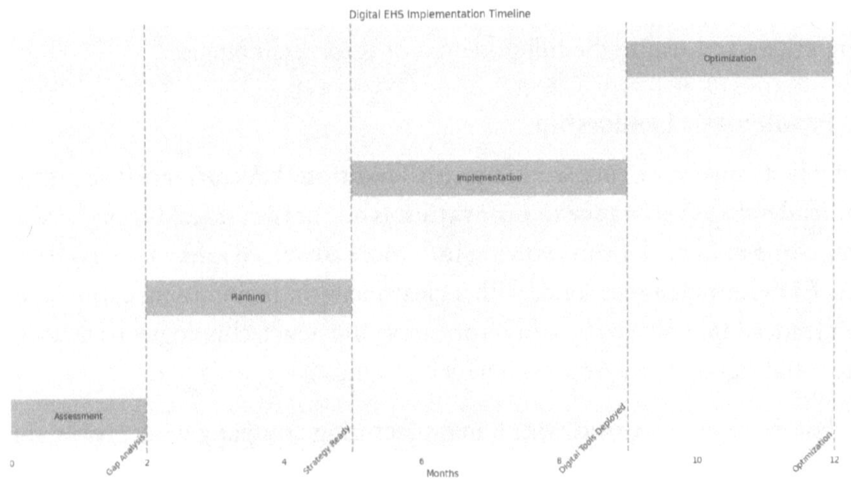

Figure 7.3: Digital EHS Implementation timeline

Reactive Performer

1. Proactive Innovation and Safety Integration

In my firsthand experience working with **Reactive Performers**, I've often seen companies that possess strong **technical and regulatory EHS knowledge** but apply it reactively. They tend to respond to safety problems as they arise, addressing issues only when forced by circumstances like violations or regulatory scrutiny. Instead of proactively leveraging their safety knowledge to prevent incidents, these companies wait for problems to happen before making changes.

One example that stands out is a **large energy company** I worked with. Despite repeated fines for **environmental and safety violations**, their leadership approached safety reactively. Rather than integrating **safety innovation** into their long-term strategy, they would implement improvements only in response to penalties or external pressure. For them, safety was viewed as a **necessary cost**—an overhead expense to be minimized, not as a strategic advantage that could help streamline operations or boost their market standing.

From a **business design** perspective, these companies see safety as a compliance requirement rather than something that could drive operational efficiency or differentiate them in the marketplace. This short-term, reactive mindset leads to missed opportunities for **proactive risk management** and innovation. Competitors who invest in **safety innovation**—utilizing digital tools and forward-thinking practices—often outperform them in reducing incidents and positioning themselves as **industry leaders** in safety.

Through my experiences with these companies, I've learned that they need to see the **long-term strategic value of safety** to avoid a reactive cycle, limiting their ability to **improve operations** and capitalize on safety as a growth driver. Without a proactive shift, they continue to face recurring safety challenges, missing the chance to turn safety into a **market differentiator** that enhances their brand and bottom line.

2. Strategic Vision and Digital Transformation

I've observed a recurring pattern in my firsthand experience working with **Reactive Performers**—those in the **third quadrant** of our **EHS Knowledge and Business Design Framework**. These companies often possess the **EHS knowledge** needed to comply with regulations but struggle to integrate it into a broader **digital transformation strategy**. While they may adopt new technologies like **AI for predictive risk management**, their implementations are often **piecemeal**, reactive solutions rather than part of a cohesive, long-term strategy.

I worked with a **global corporation** that had invested in digital tools like AI to identify potential safety risks. However, their safety measures were still deployed reactively in response to past violations rather than as part of a forward-thinking, proactive approach. Their leadership focused more on addressing immediate regulatory needs than embedding safety into their **strategic vision**. As a result, while their digital tools helped them meet compliance standards, they needed to be used to their full potential in delivering **operational efficiency** or comprehensive **risk mitigation**.

From a **business design** perspective, companies like these adopt **digital tools** late in the game, usually when meeting compliance requirements is necessary. This reactive approach means they miss out on the broader value that these technologies could offer if fully integrated into their operations. They don't use safety as a driver for **efficiency** or a tool to enhance their competitive advantage; instead, they view it as a cost to be managed when problems arise.

I've learned that **Reactive Performers** can only fully benefit from their **EHS knowledge** once they align their safety strategies with their **business goals**. Taking a more **proactive** approach and fully integrating **digital safety tools** could significantly improve safety outcomes and operational performance. But as long as they continue to treat safety as a reactive, compliance-driven function, they remain stuck in a cycle of inefficiency and missed opportunities for **growth** and **innovation**.

3. Ambidextrous Leadership: Innovating and Cutting Costs

In my firsthand experience working with **reactive companies**, I've often observed that while these organizations have a solid grasp of **safety regulations**, they need help to **innovate cost-effectively**. Their investments in safety tend to be **reactive and expensive**, usually made after incidents occur or regulatory violations are detected. Leadership in these companies faces ongoing challenges in finding the right balance between **safety innovation** and **cost control**.

I remember working with a manufacturing company whose leadership viewed **safety innovation** as costly and inefficient. They were reluctant to invest in proactive measures, believing the expense wouldn't justify the results. Instead, they focused on addressing safety issues after incidents, which ultimately led to **higher costs**—not just from fines and penalties but also from the operational downtime and disruptions that came with these incidents.

Their approach to **business design** was centered around reacting to problems rather than preventing them. Leadership needed help to see how **preventative safety measures** could **optimize safety costs** by reducing the likelihood of incidents in the first place. As a result, they kept pouring resources into reactive solutions, which were far more expensive than upfront investments in **proactive safety tools** like real-time monitoring or predictive analytics.

What I've seen time and again is that this approach leads to an **inefficient cost structure**. Reactive companies spend more on post-incident responses and safety violations than they would if they integrated **proactive safety measures** into their broader business strategy. Leadership in these organizations often views safety innovation as a financial burden. Still, the failure to innovate and prevent incidents costs them far more in the long run.

4. Reactive vs. Proactive Leadership in Safety

My experience working with **reactive companies has** consistently seen how they implement **safety measures** only after incidents or violations occur. While these organizations possess the necessary **EHS knowledge**, they fail to apply it proactively, waiting until problems arise before taking action. This approach results in repeated **safety violations** and increased costs due to fines and operational disruptions.

One example is a company in the **food industry** that has faced multiple **safety and environmental violations**. Their response was always reactive, addressing the issues only after they had become significant problems. Leadership viewed safety as a **damage control** function rather than a critical element of **risk prevention**, which led to **operational inefficiencies** and recurring violations. Rather than investing in **safety technology** or proactive measures, they would implement temporary fixes to meet compliance standards after an incident.

Regarding **business design**, these companies often see safety as something that needs attention only when external pressures—like fines or regulatory audits—force them to act. This mindset keeps them trapped in a cycle of **reactive leadership**, where safety is more about managing incidents after the fact than preventing them from happening in the first place.

From what I've experienced, this leads to **higher costs** over time. By failing to integrate **proactive planning** and investment in **safety technology**, these companies continually face the financial and operational consequences of their reactive approach. If they shifted toward **preventative safety measures**, they could reduce violations and improve operational efficiency. Still, with that strategic change, they can move forward in an efficient, costly cycle of **reactive management**.

5. Building a Digital EHS Culture

In my firsthand experience working with **Reactive Performers**, I've seen that while these companies may invest in **digital tools** for safety management, their **adoption** could be faster and more effective. Rather than being integrated into a cohesive **EHS strategy**, these tools are viewed as temporary fixes, implemented only after incidents occur. This reactive mindset keeps them from realizing the full potential of the technology they have at their disposal.

I worked with a logistics company that had invested in **digital safety tools**, but the technology needed to be embedded into their day-to-day operations. The tools were used sporadically, often in response to specific safety incidents or compliance audits. Employees weren't **empowered** to use these digital solutions effectively, and leadership needed to provide support to integrate the tools into their overall safety strategy. The result was **disjointed safety measures**—there were systems in place, but they weren't used consistently or strategically to prevent incidents.

From a **business design** perspective, these companies need a robust **digital culture**. Employees must be trained and encouraged to fully utilize digital safety tools, which can lead to fragmented safety processes and ongoing compliance challenges. Without a comprehensive, integrated approach to **digital transformation**, these organizations struggle with the same safety issues, reacting to incidents rather than preventing them.

In my experience, this **reactive approach** prevents them from improving safety outcomes or optimizing operational efficiency. By fully integrating digital tools into a **proactive EHS strategy**, they could reduce safety incidents and compliance risks. However, they will continue facing these persistent challenges until they develop a more robust digital culture.

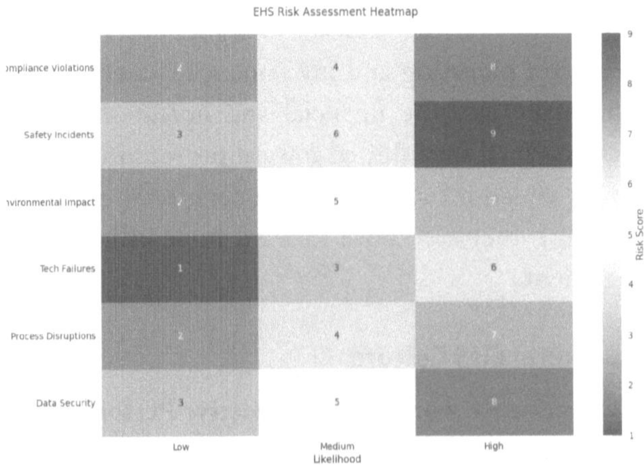

Figure 7.4: EHS Risk assessment Heatmap

Digital Leader

1. Proactive Innovation and Safety Integration

In my firsthand experience working with **Digital Leaders**, I've seen how these companies, with their **advanced EHS knowledge**, are at the forefront of integrating cutting-edge technologies like **IoT**, **AI**, and **predictive analytics** into their safety programs. They don't just react to incidents—they **anticipate risks** before they escalate, creating safer, more efficient workplaces.

One **industrial company** I worked with was a prime example of this. They fully embraced **IoT** and **real-time data** monitoring data monitoring to manage safety risks proactively. This wasn't just about meeting compliance; they integrated safety into their **product offerings**, using these innovations to secure a significant **competitive edge** in their market. By incorporating safety as part of their value proposition, they didn't just protect their workforce—they also leveraged safety as a **market differentiator**.

From a **business design** perspective, safety is viewed in these organizations as a **core part of the business model**, not just a regulatory obligation. **Safety innovation** drives **operational improvements** and helps set them apart from competitors. These companies understand that investing in safety technologies enhances their operations, creates **new revenue streams**, and ensures they maintain the highest **compliance standards**.

I've observed that **Digital Leaders** use safety to their advantage, transforming it from a cost burden into a **strategic asset** that fuels both **efficiency** and **market growth**. Their ability to integrate advanced technologies into their EHS systems sets them apart and allows them to stay ahead of their competitors.

2. Strategic Vision and Digital Transformation

In my firsthand experience working with **Digital Leaders**, I've seen how a clear **strategic vision** paired with **digital transformation** enables these companies to excel in **safety management** while outperforming their competitors in safety and business outcomes. These organizations don't just integrate safety technologies—they weave them into the very fabric of their business strategy, ensuring that **safety innovation** becomes a key driver for growth.

One industrial company I worked closely with had fully embraced **digital transformation** across their operations. By implementing **IoT** devices, **AI-driven analytics**, and **real-time risk monitoring**, they could predict and prevent safety incidents before they even occurred. This proactive approach allowed them not only to improve workplace safety dramatically but also to achieve a level of **operational efficiency** that set them apart in the market. Their leadership had a **long-term vision** that recognized safety as a cost and a **competitive advantage**—an integral part of their business model that directly contributed to **market differentiation** and **profitability**.

What stands out to me in these companies is how **safety innovation** integrates into their overall business design. They leverage their **advanced EHS knowledge** and digital tools to enhance **risk management**, optimize processes, and deliver better safety outcomes than their competitors. This approach positions them as industry leaders, capable of protecting their workforce and driving **sustained business success** through **safety excellence**.

EHS Digital Technology Stack

Data Collection	IoT Sensors Mobile Apps Wearables SCADA Systems
Data Processing	Edge Computing Cloud Processing Real-time Analytics
Analysis	AI/ML Models Predictive Analytics Risk Assessment
Integration	ERP Systems Safety Management Compliance Tools
Presentation	Dashboards Alert Systems Reporting Tools

Figure 7.5: EHS Digital Technology Stack

In my experience, companies that combine a **strategic vision** with **digital transformation** truly thrive, outperforming their competitors not just in safety performance but also in overall business outcomes. They recognize that safety isn't just about compliance—it's about creating a safer, more efficient, and more successful business.

3. Ambidextrous Leadership: Innovating and Cutting Costs

In my firsthand experience working with **Digital Leaders**, I've seen how companies that effectively balance **safety innovation** with **cost control** set themselves up for long-term success, both in safety and overall business performance. These organizations understand that safety isn't just a cost center but an opportunity to drive efficiency, reduce risks, and improve operational outcomes.

I worked with a technology-driven company in the energy sector that had fully integrated **real-time safety monitoring** and **predictive analytics** into their operations. They weren't just focused on compliance; they approached safety as an opportunity for continuous improvement. By carefully managing costs while adopting cutting-edge safety technologies, they significantly reduced workplace incidents and improved productivity simultaneously. Their leadership understood that investing in **safety innovation** could lead to immediate cost savings and long-term gains in operational efficiency.

From a **business design** standpoint, companies that find this balance benefit from improved **operational performance** and **safety outcomes** without overspending on new technologies. The key to their success lies in integrating **innovative safety solutions** with smart, controlled investments that deliver tangible results.

In my experience, those companies that strike the right balance between **innovation** and **cost control** improve their safety performance and create a strong foundation for sustained **business success**. They ensure long-term competitiveness and efficiency by making **strategic safety investments** without overextending resources.

4. Reactive vs. Proactive Leadership in Safety

In my firsthand experience working with **Digital Leaders**, I've seen that these companies take a **proactive approach** to safety, leveraging advanced technologies like **AI**, **IoT**, and **predictive analytics** to anticipate risks and prevent incidents before they occur. Their use of **real-time data** and **autonomous technologies** reduces the number of safety violations and leads to improved **compliance** and a more robust safety culture across the organization.

One company I worked with—a major industrial machinery manufacturer—stood out for how it integrated **autonomous technology** into its operations to enhance safety. By using automated systems to monitor hazardous environments and real-time data to predict potential issues, they significantly reduced safety incidents. This **proactive safety leadership** helped them boost **operational efficiency** while maintaining a strong compliance record. It was clear that their approach to safety wasn't just about meeting regulations and using safety to drive **business performance**.

From a **business design** perspective, the leadership in these companies ensures that safety is fully integrated into all functions, allowing them to stay ahead of **regulatory changes** and industry trends. Safety isn't siloed—it's woven into the fabric of their operations, keeping them compliant and **competitive**.

I've learned that **proactive safety leadership** leads to **long-term cost savings**, fewer safety incidents, and a clear **competitive advantage**. By staying ahead of risks and ensuring safety innovation is part of the company's strategic goals, these companies drive both safety excellence and operational success.

5. Building a Digital EHS Culture

In my firsthand experience working with **Digital Leaders**, I've seen how a strong **digital EHS culture** enables companies to improve safety outcomes while consistently driving **operational efficiencies**. These companies implement safety technologies for compliance and integrate them deeply into their daily operations, creating a proactive environment where safety risks are anticipated and managed before they escalate.

I worked closely with a manufacturing company that had built a **robust digital EHS framework**. They used **real-time monitoring systems**, **predictive analytics**, and **automated safety checks** to minimize safety risks at every step. This was about more than just preventing accidents and driving continuous improvement across their operations. With these systems in place, they were able to reduce downtime caused by safety incidents, improve compliance, and optimize resource allocation—all while maintaining a solid safety record.

I've learned that companies with a solid **digital safety culture** can **continuously improve** safety and **operational efficiency**. By embedding digital tools across all functions, they create a system that protects workers and helps streamline operations, reduce costs, and increase productivity. These companies show that when safety is integrated as a core element of the business, it becomes a driver for **long-term success.**

Conclusion: Quadrant Comparison and Leadership Insights

Across the four quadrants—Basic Compliance Seeker, Traditional Performer, Reactive Performer, and Digital Leader—the critical leadership traits of EHS Knowledge and Business Design vary significantly:

- Basic Compliance Seekers integrate safety minimally into their business designs, viewing safety as a cost center rather than a strategic asset.

- Traditional performers focus on compliance and regulatory adherence but must adopt digital tools and safety innovations faster.

- Reactive Performers have strong EHS knowledge but must apply it reactively, missing opportunities for proactive risk management and cost optimization.

- Digital Leaders use EHS knowledge to drive safety innovation and operational efficiency, integrating safety into their core business strategies.

Key Takeaway

Summary, across the four quadrants—Basic Compliance Seeker, Traditional Performer, Reactive Performer, and Digital Leader—we see stark differences in how companies manage EHS Knowledge and Business Design. Let's reflect on the critical leadership insights for each quadrant:

Basic Compliance Seeker

- EHS Knowledge: Minimal focus, basic compliance.

- Business Design: Safety is viewed as a cost, with minimal integration into strategy.

Critical Insight: These companies are focused on regulatory minimums, and their lack of innovation leads to high risks and operational inefficiencies. Leadership here is typically reactive and compliance-driven, with no vision for safety as a strategic advantage.

Traditional Performer

- EHS Knowledge: Moderate; good at meeting regulatory standards.

- Business Design: Focuses on compliance but needs full digital integration.

Key Insight: Traditional performers manage safety well within existing frameworks but miss opportunities for innovation. Leadership often emphasizes manual processes, making it hard to transition to a more agile, technology-driven safety model.

Reactive Performer

- EHS Knowledge: High, but applied reactively.

- Business Design: Safety improvements are driven by incidents rather than proactive measures.

Key Insight: Reactive companies know safety but fail to apply it strategically, resulting in costly and inefficient post-incident fixes. Leadership needs to work on viewing safety as a strategic advantage instead of treating it as damage control after violations occur.

Digital Leader

- EHS Knowledge: High, focusing on proactive innovation and digital transformation.

- Business Design: Safety is integrated into the business model, seen as a differentiator and an operational efficiency driver.

Key Insight: Digital leaders like Honeywell and Nucor embed safety into their business strategies to enhance both safety outcomes and business performance. These companies balance innovation and cost, proactively leveraging technology to manage safety and drive competitive advantages.

Final Takeaway: The most successful companies move beyond compliance to embrace safety as a strategic business function. Digital Leaders excel by combining EHS Knowledge with forward-thinking Business Design, embedding safety into their long-term goals. In contrast, companies stuck in Reactive or Basic Compliance Seeker quadrants are more likely to face ongoing operational challenges, regulatory penalties, and inefficiencies due to their lack of proactive safety management.

By understanding these leadership traits and aligning EHS Knowledge with strategic business goals, companies can drive safety performance, reduce risks, and unlock significant competitive advantages.

Moving Up and Forward in EHS Digital Reinvention: A Holistic Approach Based on EHS Knowledge and Business Design Framework

To achieve successful digital transformation in Environment, Health, and Safety (EHS), companies must simultaneously enhance their technical knowledge of safety (EHS Knowledge) and strategically integrate safety into their overall business operations (Business Design Framework). Moving both "up" and "forward" on the digital EHS strategy is critical to transforming safety from a regulatory burden into a strategic asset that drives operational efficiency, compliance, and market differentiation.

Moving Up: Strengthening Core EHS Capabilities

1. Gathering and Using Critical Information about Compliance and Safety Goals

   The first step in moving up involves gathering and managing data from IoT sensors, safety inspections, and compliance audits. Companies must leverage this data to understand safety risks in real-time, anticipate potential hazards, and reduce environmental impacts. A robust data infrastructure allows organizations to be proactive, transforming safety from reactive risk management to a forward-thinking approach. For example, organizations implementing predictive analytics in their safety operations can forecast potential incidents, leading to better prevention strategies.

Critical Insight: Real-time data collection and analytics empower companies to anticipate safety risks, ensuring regulatory compliance and proactive hazard mitigation.

2. Amplifying the Voice of the Workforce and Stakeholders in Safety Initiatives

A crucial component of effective EHS management is involving employees and stakeholders directly in the safety process. Workers can provide immediate feedback on safety issues, incidents, and hazards using mobile apps and digital reporting platforms. Companies can implement immediate corrective measures when the workforce is empowered to report problems in real-time, thereby enhancing safety culture. This feedback loop integrates safety into the decision-making processes at every level of the organization.

Key Insight: Giving workers a platform to voice safety concerns helps build a proactive safety culture, reducing the time between identifying and addressing hazards.

3. Creating a Culture of Evidence-Based Decision-Making in EHS

EHS leaders must foster a culture where decisions are based on data rather than instinct or tradition. By utilizing IoT and big data, companies can deploy predictive analytics to foresee potential safety issues, minimizing risks before they escalate. This shift from reactive to proactive decision-making enables companies to avoid safety risks while optimizing operations.

Critical Insight: Embedding data-driven decision-making into the fabric of EHS management enhances operational efficiency, reduces safety violations, and improves compliance.

4. Providing an Integrated, Multi-Department, Multichannel Safety and Compliance Experience

Seamless integration across departments is essential for consistent safety compliance. When EHS systems communicate across departments—from HR and operations to legal—safety protocols can be enforced universally. A digital platform integrating real-time reporting, compliance tracking, and operational management fosters collaboration and streamlines safety procedures.

Critical Insight: Cross-departmental digital integration drives unified safety practices, ensuring that compliance efforts are consistent and efficient across the organization.

Moving Forward: Leveraging Strategic Business Design in EHS Leadership

1. Becoming the First Choice for EHS Compliance Solutions

   To establish leadership in EHS, companies need to offer reliable and easy-to-use safety and compliance solutions. Companies that become the go-to providers for EHS compliance solutions position safety as a strategic advantage, offering comprehensive services that integrate seamlessly into existing enterprise systems. Organizations with cloud-based EHS platforms assure clients that safety is always maintained while simplifying compliance processes.

   Critical Insight: Becoming a trusted EHS solution provider differentiates companies, helping them leverage safety for market differentiation and competitive advantage.

2. Identifying and Developing Strategic Partnerships in the EHS Ecosystem

   Companies must address only some aspects of safety and environmental compliance. Establishing partnerships with technology providers, regulators, and industry experts enhances EHS capabilities, from real-time incident reporting to safety training. For example, collaborating with an IoT provider for real-time safety monitoring can significantly expand a company's operational capabilities.

   Critical Insight: Strategic partnerships in the EHS ecosystem expand companies' reach and capabilities, positioning them as holistic solution providers.

3. Service-Enabling EHS Management Systems with Exposed APIs

   Open APIs allow companies to integrate safety data across departments and with third-party providers. This capability makes safety management systems more accessible and flexible, enabling organizations to benefit from real-time data sharing. For example, service-enabling APIs allow external auditors or regulators to access compliance data directly, ensuring transparency and building stakeholder trust.

Critical Insight: Open APIs enhance the flexibility and scalability of EHS systems, making it easier to integrate safety data across the organization and with external partners.

4. Developing Efficiency, Security, and Compliance as Core Competencies

Developing security, compliance, and operational efficiency as core competencies becomes vital as companies progress. Regulatory compliance, data integrity, and cybersecurity must be prioritized to maintain operational resilience. Organizations that excel in these areas meet regulatory standards and build trust with customers, regulators, and stakeholders, positioning safety as a core business function.

Critical Insight: Mastering security, compliance, and operational efficiency allows companies to run seamless, transparent EHS operations while maintaining stakeholder confidence.

Conclusion: Moving Up and Forward on the EHS Knowledge and Business Design Framework

For companies to lead in EHS digital transformation, they must not only master core safety practices (moving up) but also strategically embed safety into their business models (moving forward). Moving up focuses on building capabilities such as real-time data collection, cross-functional integration, and evidence-based decision-making. Moving forward emphasizes becoming an industry leader through strategic partnerships, service-enabled platforms, and developing efficiency and compliance as competitive strengths.

Aligning EHS knowledge with strategic business design transforms safety from a reactive function into a core driver of business success. This dual approach ensures that safety is a regulatory requirement and a powerful tool for driving innovation, reducing risks, and enhancing market differentiation.

EHS Transformation of an Aerospace and Defense Major: A Digital Journey

An Aerospace and Defense major offers a compelling case study of a company that transitioned from a traditional, product-focused enterprise into a leader in environmental, health, and safety (EHS), utilizing the principles of EHS Knowledge and the Business Design Framework. Through strategic use of cutting-edge technologies like IoT, AI, and cloud-based solutions, the company elevated its EHS systems to meet compliance and drive operational efficiency and safety innovation.

Real-Time Safety and Risk Management through IoT and AI

This Aerospace and Defense leader employed IoT-enabled devices and sensors to move from a reactive to a proactive safety management approach. These systems continuously monitor worker safety, environmental conditions, and operational risks, delivering real-time alerts to management whenever safety thresholds are exceeded. This technological integration allows for immediate interventions, significantly reducing on-site incidents. For example, workers with wearables can instantly report hazards, while safety teams track environmental and worker health metrics in real time through mobile devices.

Critical Insight: Integrating IoT for real-time monitoring ensures a rapid response to potential hazards and facilitates the collection of long-term data, enabling predictive safety measures that reduce future risks.

Amplifying the Workforce's Voice through Digital Platforms

A significant component of this transformation was amplifying the voice of the workforce through digital platforms. The company deployed mobile apps that allowed workers to report real-time incidents, near-misses, and unsafe conditions. This worker-centered approach empowered the workforce to participate in creating a safer environment, fostering a culture of safety deeply embedded in the company's daily operations.

Critical Insight: Empowering employees with digital tools for real-time safety reporting improves engagement and helps build a proactive safety culture. This creates an environment where employees actively contribute to upholding safety standards.

Strategic Partnerships and Ecosystem Development

To reinforce its position as a leader in EHS, the company forged strategic partnerships with regulators, technology providers, and data analytics companies. These alliances enabled the company to develop a holistic EHS solution, integrating compliance management with real-time analytics to ensure safety across various industries. This collaborative approach helped the company become the go-to provider for comprehensive EHS solutions.

Key Insight: Strategic partnerships enhance the breadth and effectiveness of EHS solutions. By integrating technologies and regulatory expertise, companies can offer multi-departmental and multi-industry safety systems that are both compliant and efficient.

Service-Enabling EHS Systems with Open APIs

The Aerospace and Defense primary service enabled its EHS systems using open APIs to ensure scalability and cross-industry adaptability. This allowed various departments and external partners to access and share critical safety data in real time. The company expanded its ecosystem role by integrating its systems with other enterprise platforms, ensuring its solutions are flexible and scalable for diverse industry needs.

Critical Insight: Exposing APIs enables seamless data sharing and enhances customization, making EHS systems adaptable to different industries while maintaining their core safety functions.

Developing Core Competencies in Compliance, Efficiency, and Security

The company's transformation was rooted in building core competencies around data security, operational efficiency, and regulatory compliance. Given the stringent regulations in the aerospace and defense industry, the company invested heavily in ensuring its safety systems complied with the latest global safety standards while streamlining operational processes to maintain a competitive edge.

Critical Insight: Mastering compliance, security, and operational efficiency builds trust with regulators and customers, positioning the company as a market leader in industrial safety.

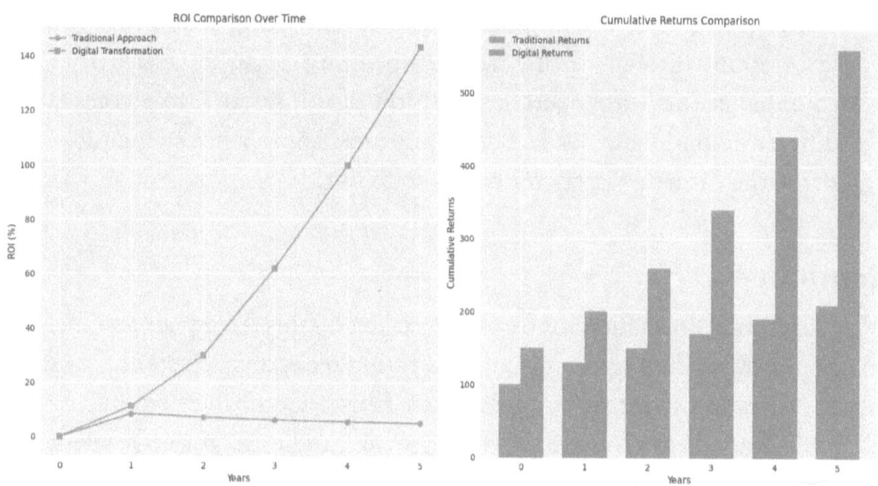

Figure 7.6: ROI comparison and Cumulative benefit comparison

The Path to Becoming an EHS Digital Leader

By mastering these core capabilities, the Aerospace and Défense major transitioned from a product manufacturer to an ecosystem driver in the EHS space. Through its ability to integrate advanced technologies, foster strategic partnerships, and adapt its services across industries, the company set new standards for safety, operational efficiency, and environmental responsibility.

Next Steps for EHS Leaders

For EHS leaders in other industries, this Aerospace and defense major's journey serves as a blueprint for success. Assessing current capabilities in data management, worker engagement, and digital integration is essential. By investing in the right technologies and partnerships, companies can move up and forward on their EHS transformation journey, turning safety and compliance into a competitive advantage.

Moving Up and Forward: The Digital EHS Strategy

- Moving Up: Companies must focus on improving data collection, increasing worker engagement, and adopting evidence-based decision-making to manage safety proactively. With real-time data, EHS leaders can anticipate risks and ensure that safety is deeply integrated into all operations.

- Moving Forward: Developing strategic partnerships, enabling service integration through APIs, and embedding security, efficiency, and compliance into core operations can transform safety into a competitive differentiator. Digital leaders don't just meet compliance standards—they shape the future of safety for others to follow.

Conclusion

The digital transformation journey undertaken by this Aerospace and Defense major illustrates the importance of integrating technology, fostering a safety-first culture, and building strategic partnerships. Companies embracing this path will find themselves better equipped to handle the modern safety and compliance challenges, turning EHS into a critical driver of operational success and market leadership.

Creating a Culture of Evidence-Based Decision-Making in EHS: A Reimagined Approach

Traditionally, Environment, Health, and Safety (EHS) decision-making was often guided by managerial intuition, experience, and anecdotal information. However, with the rise of big data, real-time analytics, and IoT technologies, this approach no longer delivers the competitive advantage or safety outcomes that modern organizations require. Today's EHS culture must shift toward evidence-based decision-making, relying on data-driven insights to enhance safety and operational efficiency. This transition requires a cultural and technological shift grounded in EHS Knowledge and the Business Design Framework.

A Data-Driven Transformation in Aerospace and Defense

A major aerospace and defense company demonstrates a notable example of this transformation. The company transitioned from reactive safety protocols to proactive risk management by implementing IoT-enabled sensors across operations, machinery, and workers. These sensors continuously track critical safety metrics, such as air quality, worker fatigue, and potential hazardous conditions. The data is aggregated into Key Performance Indicators (KPIs), which are displayed on real-time dashboards. This enables managers to monitor safety conditions, mitigate risks before they escalate, and make decisions based on solid data rather than instinct.

Critical Insight: Real-time safety data enables organizations to anticipate risks and act proactively, minimizing reliance on reactive safety responses. This approach ensures that comprehensive, data-backed insights support decision-making.

Breaking Down Silos: Transforming EHS Decision-Making Across Departments

In many organizations, EHS management operates in silos, where various departments handle safety independently. This fragmentation can result in inconsistent decision-making, as each department relies on localized data that may reflect only some of the scope of the organization's safety environment. To foster a culture of evidence-based decision-making, EHS leaders must break down these silos and centralize safety data, integrating it across departments.

For example, imagine a manufacturing company where safety protocols vary across different locations. An integrated EHS platform would consolidate data from incident reports, environmental sensors, and worker feedback into a single system. Managers across different facilities could access the same data, facilitating collaboration and enabling a unified strategy that aligns with the company's safety objectives.

Critical Insight: Centralizing and integrating safety data across departments allows decision-makers to gain a holistic view of risks, leading to better alignment and more effective safety outcomes.

Benefits of a Data-Driven EHS Culture

Adopting an evidence-based EHS culture goes beyond just achieving compliance. It brings significant benefits, including reduced incidents, fewer workplace injuries, and an agile response to emerging risks. By leveraging predictive analytics, organizations can detect patterns in unsafe behaviors or equipment malfunctions before they escalate into significant safety concerns.

In the aerospace and defense industry, for example, predictive safety tools powered by real-time analytics have enabled organizations to not only meet regulatory requirements but also enhance their operational efficiency. This proactive approach to safety has reduced workplace injuries and created a more resilient safety culture.

Key Insight: A culture of evidence-based decision-making strengthens an organization's ability to manage risks proactively, improving overall safety outcomes and operational efficiency.

Providing an Integrated, Multichannel EHS Experience

To create a truly proactive EHS model, organizations must integrate safety measures into their operational strategy. This involves connecting physical inspections, digital monitoring systems, and mobile platforms into one cohesive system, allowing seamless and multichannel safety management.

Overcoming the Challenge of EHS Integration

Many organizations still need to work on fragmented EHS systems. For instance, physical safety inspectors might report hazards through separate systems that don't sync with the real-time digital monitoring platforms that track environmental data. Organizations must combine these systems into a unified platform to stay competitive in today's data-driven landscape.

Consider a scenario where a manufacturing company's safety inspectors use mobile apps to report hazards. These reports would feed into the same platform as the data from IoT devices monitoring equipment health, creating an integrated system where human and machine-generated data work to identify and mitigate risks.

Key Insight: Integrating digital tools and real-time data enables a shift from reactive safety management to proactive risk identification and mitigation.

Conclusion: Building an Evidence-Based EHS Future

Creating a culture of evidence-based decision-making in EHS requires more than simply implementing digital tools. It demands an organizational commitment to integrating data into every aspect of safety management. Organizations can transform their safety culture from reactive compliance to proactive risk management by leveraging IoT, real-time data, and analytics. The aerospace and defense industry provides a clear example of how embracing these principles can improve safety outcomes and enhance operational efficiency.

Safety Culture:

In my 20 years of experience working with various organizations on EHS (Environmental, Health, and Safety) integration, I've witnessed firsthand how safety culture shapes the behaviors of leadership, employee engagement, and overall organizational outcomes. Based on these observations, I've grouped companies into four categories reflecting their EHS maturity and business innovation.

Quadrant: Basic Compliance Seekers

Organizations: Companies focused on compliance without much innovation

Safety Culture at Leadership and Employee Level:

Organizations in this quadrant focus on compliance, ensuring that safety standards are met to avoid regulatory issues. However, leadership views safety as a box to check rather than an opportunity for innovation. Employees follow strict protocols, but the organization needs more resources or the drive to go beyond these basic requirements.

One example is a company in a traditional industry that maintains basic safety measures but still needs to integrate safety into its broader strategic vision. Similarly, smaller firms in construction and resource-driven sectors often focus on risk management and regulatory compliance, but they need more resources to innovate in safety.

Critical Insight: Leadership in these organizations needs to shift from viewing safety as a compliance issue to recognizing it as a potential area for innovation. Employees should be given the tools and encouragement to improve safety rather than just following pre-set rules.

Quadrant: Traditional Operators

Organizations: Companies with mature safety systems but slower innovation

Safety Culture at Leadership and Employee Level:

These organizations are vital in safety compliance and have well-established systems for maintaining safe work environments. However, their leadership tends to focus more on maintaining these systems than innovating or transforming their business models. One company in this category, known for its stringent safety practices, uses a system that ensures every operational decision considers safety risks. However, their approach to integrating safety with business innovation must catch up.

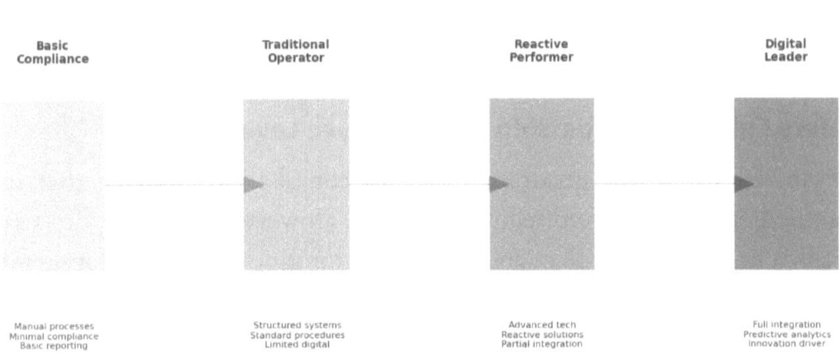

Figure 7.8: Safety Culture evolution Journey

In another example, the leadership is heavily invested in safety compliance but slower in integrating digital tools and innovative safety measures. Employees here follow strict protocols, but there needs to be more opportunity for them to drive safety improvements. Compliance is prioritized, and while safety is undoubtedly respected, it needs to be seen as an area ripe for innovation.

Critical Insight: These organizations excel in safety compliance but must shift from simply maintaining safety systems to innovating within those frameworks. Leaders should encourage employees to take more active roles in driving safety improvements and aligning them with business innovation.

Quadrant: Reactive Knowledge Holders

Organizations: Companies with high innovation but reactive safety practices

Safety Culture at Leadership and Employee Level:

In this group, leadership aggressively drives business innovation, but safety practices are often reactive. For example, one company has led innovations in automation and supply chains, but its safety practices have come under scrutiny. Injuries and safety incidents often spark reactive changes rather than proactive improvements. Another organization in this category is a leader in its industry but faces significant safety challenges due to its high-risk environments.

Here, employees tend to see safety as secondary to operational efficiency. Safety incidents are often handled after the fact, leading to a reactive culture. Leadership in these organizations needs to take a more proactive approach, ensuring that safety measures evolve alongside business innovations.

Key Insight: Companies in this quadrant must work on integrating safety with their innovation strategies. Leadership should foster a culture where safety is not an afterthought but a core element of operational success.

Quadrant: EHS Digital Leaders

Organizations: Companies that lead in both safety and innovation

Safety Culture at Leadership and Employee Level:

In these organizations, safety is deeply embedded in every aspect of operations. Leadership actively promotes a culture where safety is part of the organization's DNA, leading the charge by ensuring that every employee—from the top executives to the front-line workers—understands and participates in creating a safe environment. For example, one company has implemented a "Zero Harm Culture," combining safety with digital tools like IoT and automation. Leadership doesn't just pay lip service to safety; they make it a priority. Employees are empowered to raise safety concerns and collaborate to make the workplace safer through predictive analytics and real-time monitoring tools.

Another company in this category has restructured its entire business model around sustainability, with safety at the core. Leaders here are committed to long-term sustainability goals, seeing safety as key to achieving them. Across all these organizations, the leadership is deeply engaged in safety practices, ensuring that employees are compliant and proactive in improving safety.

Critical Insight: In these companies, safety is seen as an integral part of the innovation strategy. Leadership champions safety initiatives, while employees are encouraged to participate in the continuous improvement of safety systems.

Strategic Recommendations for Each Quadrant:

1. **EHS Digital Leaders**: Continue advancing safety technologies and aligning safety with sustainability initiatives. These companies should focus on maintaining their leadership roles by continually evolving safety practices alongside technological innovations.

2. **Traditional Operators**: Leadership should explore new ways to integrate digital safety solutions and foster a more active role for employees in shaping safety practices. Encouraging innovation in safety will help these companies stay competitive.

3. **Reactive Knowledge Holders**: Leadership needs to embed safety more deeply into their business strategies. Employees should be empowered to take proactive safety measures, and innovation should include safety as a core consideration.

4. **Basic Compliance Seekers**: These organizations need to invest in safety innovations to move beyond basic compliance. Leadership should focus on adopting best practices and exploring digital tools to enhance safety in an increasingly regulated market.

In my experience, companies that effectively integrate safety into their innovation strategies are better positioned for long-term success. Leadership engagement, employee involvement, and a proactive approach to safety are key to building resilient and competitive organizations.

Moving from Basic Compliance Seeker to Traditional Operator

In a **Basic Compliance Seeker** organization, safety is viewed primarily as a legal obligation to check off to avoid penalties. Becoming a **Traditional Operator** involves shifting from a reactive, compliance-only mindset to embedding safety more thoroughly into daily operations, focusing on structured and mature systems.

1. **Shift in Leadership Mindset**: Leaders need to see safety as a regulatory necessity and a fundamental aspect of operational success. This requires

investing in safety systems and treating EHS as part of the company's core mission, not just a cost center. Leaders should actively promote safety during executive meetings and ensure it is aligned with business goals.

2. **Establish a Strong Safety Framework**: The next step is implementing formalized safety management systems like ISO 45001 or OHSAS 18001. These frameworks standardize safety practices across the organization, ensuring consistent application of safety protocols. The goal is to move from ad-hoc safety measures to a structured, organization-wide commitment to safety excellence.

3. **Employee Training and Engagement**: Employees must be trained on compliance and safety best practices that go beyond the basics. Engaging workers in regular safety drills, training, and workshops promotes a safety-first culture that involves more than just following checklists.

Moving from Traditional Operator to Reactive Knowledge Holder

Once a company has established a mature safety system, it can evolve into a **Reactive Knowledge Holder** by integrating innovation into its safety practices. This phase is characterized by a more profound recognition that safety and business success are linked and that innovation can enhance safety outcomes.

1. **Encouraging Safety-Driven Innovation**: Leadership must start to see safety as a driver of innovation. This might involve investing in wearable safety devices, real-time monitoring systems, or predictive analytics to anticipate and prevent safety incidents better. Leaders should also encourage employees to participate in safety innovation efforts.

2. **Proactive Risk Management**: Companies should adopt a proactive risk management approach rather than simply reacting to safety incidents. This involves using data and insights from past incidents to predict and mitigate future risks. Companies should start leveraging tools like AI and machine learning to analyze safety data and identify patterns that can inform better decisions.

3. **Employee Ownership of Safety**: Employees in a **Traditional Operator** environment often follow protocols but don't take ownership of safety. Moving to the next level requires fostering a culture where employees are empowered to take the lead on safety initiatives. This could be done by forming safety committees or offering rewards for innovative safety solutions.

Moving from Reactive Knowledge Holder to EHS Digital Leader

Organizations already innovative but reactive in their safety practices can evolve into **EHS Digital Leaders** by embedding safety deeply into their business strategy and fully integrating technology into safety practices.

1. **Fully Integrating Safety with Business Strategy**: Leaders must ensure that safety is considered a strategic business priority, not just a reactive measure. This means integrating safety into key performance indicators (KPIs) and business metrics. For example, reducing workplace incidents should be a core business goal alongside profitability and growth.

2. **Advanced Use of Digital Tools**: Becoming an EHS Digital Leader involves utilizing advanced technology such as IoT, AI, and big data analytics to monitor and improve real-time safety. Predictive analytics can help identify potential hazards before they result in incidents, while AI can offer insights into optimizing safety protocols.

3. **Continuous Improvement and Learning**: EHS Digital Leaders are characterized by a continuous learning culture. Employees are not only empowered to contribute to safety initiatives but also encouraged to use digital tools to suggest improvements. Safety is no longer reactive but constantly evolving based on new data, insights, and technologies.

4. **Leadership as Safety Champions**: In this phase, leadership actively champions safety innovation, ensuring it is integrated into all aspects of business operations. Leaders set the tone by continuously exploring how new technologies or processes can improve safety and business outcomes.

Summary of the Transition Process:

1. **Basic Compliance Seeker → Traditional Operator**: Shift leadership mindset to prioritize structured safety management, implement formal systems, and engage employees in safety practices.

2. **Traditional Operator → Reactive Knowledge Holder**: Foster a culture of safety-driven innovation, adopt proactive risk management, and encourage employees to take ownership of safety.

3. **Reactive Knowledge Holder → EHS Digital Leader**: Fully integrate safety into business strategy, leverage advanced digital tools, foster continuous improvement, and ensure leadership actively champions safety initiatives.

This progression highlights the steps organizations must take, from merely meeting safety regulations to becoming industry leaders in safety and innovation. Each phase builds on the previous one, creating a culture where safety is a core business driver, not just a regulatory obligation.

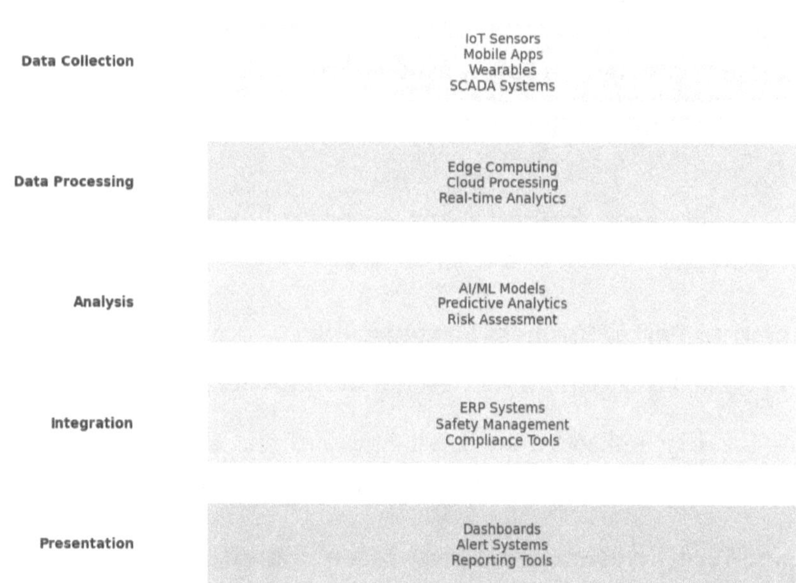

Figure 7.9: EHS Digital technology Stack

Self-Assessment: Do You Have the Crucial Capabilities to Reinvent Your Enterprise through EHS Knowledge and Business Design?

Evaluate how effectively your organization integrates **EHS Knowledge** and **Business Design** into its operations to reinvent and thrive in today's competitive environment (1 = Not effective, 6 = Very effective).

1. Proactive Safety Risk Management:

How effectively does your company **anticipate and prevent safety risks** before they escalate?

   o   Are you implementing proactive safety measures using your EHS knowledge or primarily reactive to incidents?

2. Integration of Digital Tools in Safety Programs:

How well are **digital tools** (IoT, AI, real-time monitoring) integrated into your safety programs?

   o   Is digital transformation part of your safety strategy, or are tools adopted piecemeal only to meet compliance?

3. Leadership's View on Safety Innovation:

How does your leadership view **safety**—as a **strategic asset** or a **necessary cost**?

   o   Is safety innovation used to drive operational efficiency and competitive advantage, or is it seen as an overhead cost?

4. Safety as Part of Business Strategy:

How integrated is safety into your **overall business design**?

   o   Is safety embedded across all functions and aligned with strategic goals, or is it a siloed function driven by compliance?

5. Long-Term Investment in Safety Technologies:

How well does your organization **invest in safety innovations** (predictive analytics, real-time data) for long-term success?

o   Are these tools fully used to prevent incidents and reduce operational costs, or is investment driven by short-term regulatory needs?

6. Balancing Safety Innovation with Cost Control:

How effectively does your company balance the **costs** of safety innovation with the long-term **benefits**?

o   Do you invest in the right technologies while maintaining cost control or struggle to balance safety with budget concerns?

7. Developing a Digital EHS Culture

How well-developed is your **digital safety culture**, and how empowered are your employees to use digital tools?

o   Are employees trained and engaged with digital safety technologies, or are tools that need to be more utilized and better integrated?

8. Proactive Leadership and Continuous Improvement:

How effective is your leadership in promoting **continuous improvement** in safety through **proactive planning**?

o   Does leadership consistently push for innovation in safety measures, or do they react only after incidents or violations?

9. Leveraging Safety as a Market Differentiator:

To what extent does your organization use **safety innovation** to differentiate in the marketplace?

o   Is safety used to strengthen your brand and competitive positioning, or is it simply a compliance function?

10. Staying Ahead of Regulatory Changes:

How well does your company stay ahead of **regulatory changes** through proactive EHS management?

o   Are you leading the industry by adopting innovative safety practices or frequently reacting to new regulations?

11. Using Data and Predictive Analytics for Risk Management:

How frequently does your company use **data analytics** and **predictive tools** to improve safety outcomes?

- o   Are you preventing risks through data-driven decisions or addressing problems after they arise?

12. Operational Efficiency and Cost Optimization through Safety:

13. How effectively is your organization using safety innovations to optimize operational efficiency and reduce costs?

- o   Are safety measures contributing to leaner operations and improved productivity?

Total Score (out of 72)

Multiply your total score by **1.33** to calculate your score out of 96. This score helps assess whether your organization is positioned as a **Basic Compliance Seeker**, **Traditional Operator**, **Reactive Performer**, or **Digital Leader** based on how well it integrates **EHS Knowledge** and **Business Design** into its overall strategy for safety and operational excellence.

A Summary on EHS Transformation

08

The growing wave of digital disruption presents a critical opportunity for you as a leader to help reinvent your enterprise's Environmental, Health, and Safety (EHS) practices. As we've discussed throughout, the question is no longer if your organization will transform but rather when and how it will make the necessary changes to survive and thrive in the digital era. The most successful enterprises in EHS must be ambidextrous: innovating to improve safety and compliance while simultaneously reducing costs through automation and process optimization.

Successful EHS enterprises will focus on learning more about their operational risks and safety data, opening up their systems to integrate with external partners, and becoming more efficient by continuously simplifying and automating processes. With this ambidexterity, your enterprise can stay caught up while more agile competitors and startups slice bits off your business, innovating with real-time safety monitoring, AI-driven risk assessments, and connected systems until there is little left for the slower-moving companies.

As you move forward with your EHS digital transformation, asking the right questions and guiding your company through each process step is essential. The self-assessments in each chapter serve as a powerful tool to spark discussion, identify areas that need attention, and drive action.

Take a moment to reflect on the critical questions for each phase of your EHS transformation and consider your actions to move your organization forward. The journey may require rethinking your safety processes, investing in digital tools, and fostering a culture of innovation. However, the rewards—safer workplaces, enhanced compliance, and reduced costs—will be worth the effort.

Key Steps for EHS Transformation:

1. **Understanding organisation challenges:** Where does your organization stand today regarding safety data collection, risk analysis, and compliance monitoring?

2. **Vision for EHS Transformation:** What does success look like for your EHS transformation? What are the key safety goals and outcomes?

3. **Technology Integration:** How effectively is your enterprise integrating digital tools like IoT, AI, and predictive analytics into safety and compliance operations?

4. **Efficiency and Cost Reduction:** How will you ensure that your EHS processes become more efficient and cost-effective through automation and simplification?

5. **Collaboration and Partnerships:** What role do external partnerships play in enhancing your EHS capabilities? How will you leverage external innovations to stay ahead of emerging risks?

6. **Leadership and Culture:** How can you foster a culture of safety innovation, empowering your workforce to embrace digital tools and data-driven decision-making?

As you move forward with your EHS digital transformation, these steps will help guide your enterprise through the challenges and opportunities of the digital era. With the right strategy, leadership, and technology, your organization can become a model of safety and operational excellence in the years to come.

1. What Is the Digital Threat—and Opportunity for EHS?

The first step in transforming your enterprise's Environmental, Health, and Safety (EHS) practices is identifying the digital threats and opportunities in your industry. This question sets the foundation for the conversation and helps align your leadership team on the case for action. Often, different stakeholders in EHS, including safety managers, compliance officers, and operational leaders, will have varying perspectives on the digital threat. Engaging in this discussion allows you to define the terms clearly and helps to quantify the risks and opportunities presented by digital transformation, especially in areas like safety automation, predictive analytics, and real-time compliance monitoring.

In EHS, some enterprises may still rely heavily on manual processes, paper-based reporting, and reactive safety management, which leaves them vulnerable to digital disruption. For instance, the rise of AI-driven risk assessment, IoT-enabled safety monitoring, and automated compliance tracking are creating new standards for proactive safety management. If your leadership team determines that a significant percentage of your safety and compliance operations are vulnerable to digital disruption, the urgency to act increases.

This stage often requires developing new business models to integrate digital tools into safety and compliance processes. It may also entail major organizational shifts to ensure that safety is embedded into the broader business operations and culture. During this process, clear communication is key—senior leaders must articulate to the entire organization the digital threats, the opportunities they aim to capitalize on, and the changes to decision-making structures and culture. This alignment is essential to build the consensus and momentum needed for successful transformation.

In summary, recognizing the digital threats and opportunities in EHS helps create a shared understanding of the risks, sets the stage for action, and lays the groundwork for reinventing your organization's approach to safety and compliance.

2. Which Business Model Is Best for Your Enterprise's EHS Future?

The second step is determining the most suitable business model for your enterprise's EHS transformation. In the digital economy, various models can help your organization generate value, especially in EHS management. These include transitioning from manual, reactive safety processes to proactive, predictive safety models integrating real-time data and advanced technologies like IoT, AI, and automated compliance tools.

Many large enterprises find their EHS revenue opportunities from multiple business models. For example, you may currently operate as a basic or traditional compliance operator, but your future lies in adopting an ecosystem-driven approach where safety and compliance are integrated seamlessly across all business operations. Start by assessing where your EHS capabilities stand today, whether you're reactive or proactive in addressing safety risks, and where you'd like to be. For many companies, the path to the future involves building an integrated platform that offers predictive safety insights, automates reporting, and ties safety performance to broader business outcomes.

If your current EHS capabilities are lagging, this might be the moment to reevaluate your entire approach radically. This may sometimes require creating a new business unit dedicated to leading the EHS digital transformation. Engaging the board in these discussions is crucial. Digital transformation in EHS, like other areas, requires significant investment in technology, people, and processes, and board members will be key allies in securing the necessary resources and support.

By defining your target EHS business model, whether it's moving towards an EHS ecosystem or becoming a digital leader in safety, you'll create a common language for your leadership team and employees. This shared understanding will be vital as your enterprise navigates its transformation, helping everyone align on the future direction and strategy.

3. What Is Your Digital Competitive Advantage in EHS?

Now that you've identified where you want to position your enterprise on the DBM framework for EHS, it's time to assess your competitive advantage in the digital realm. In the digital economy, competitive advantage often stems from three key areas: **content**, **customer experience**, and **platforms**. For an EHS-focused enterprise, this means evaluating how well you leverage safety data (content), provide a seamless safety and compliance experience for employees and partners (customer experience), and integrate your EHS processes into scalable, interoperable systems (platforms).

If your company is vulnerable to digital disruption, it's likely that one of these areas is lacking. You may not be collecting or using real-time safety data effectively, or your compliance management may be disjointed, preventing you from offering a seamless experience. Additionally, your EHS platforms might not be fully integrated across your operations, limiting your ability to scale digital safety initiatives.

Your task Is to determine Ih areas can become your digital competitive advantage In EHS. Will it be your ability to deliver predictive safety insights and compliance automation (content)? Or the creation of a unified, user-friendly EHS platform that integrates across all business units (platform)? Or may your focus be on revolutionizing how employees engage with safety tools and processes, creating a proactive safety culture (customer experience)?

Once you've identified the area where you'll build your competitive advantage, create a road map to strengthen it. This strategic focus will align your leadership team and employees, helping everyone work toward the same goal of transforming your EHS capabilities for the digital era.

4. How Will You Connect Using Mobile and the Internet of Things (IoT) in EHS?

Digital technologies like **mobile** and the **Internet of Things (IoT)** are critical enablers for transforming EHS operations. Mobile technology lets your company stay connected with employees, contractors, and stakeholders in real time, enabling instant communication and action on safety and compliance matters. IoT, on the other hand, provides continuous data on how your equipment, environment, and workforce are performing, allowing for proactive safety management and enhanced decision-making.

You'll need to connect these technologies to your business model and competitive advantage to effectively harness them. For instance, if your competitive edge lies in **predictive safety** or **compliance automation**, IoT sensors can monitor conditions in real time and predict potential hazards before they happen, while mobile platforms can notify employees of risks and collect incident reports instantly. This integration can transform your safety culture from reactive to proactive.

The challenge lies In embedding mobile and IoT technology into your EHS capabilities. You must first ensure that these tools are interoperable with your current systems, providing seamless integration across all business units. Once done, these technologies will enable you to deliver better services, foster a safer work environment, and gain deeper insights into your operations.

5. Do You Have the Crucial Capabilities to Reinvent EHS?

After defining the need for transformation and identifying your future EHS business models, the next step is to ensure that your organization has the necessary capabilities to execute this vision. Eight key capabilities are required to reinvent your EHS operations and succeed in the digital age.

The first task is to have an honest discussion among senior leadership about the company's strengths and weaknesses in these eight areas, specifically as they relate to EHS. This conversation will identify where your organization already excels and where substantial investments are needed. After this, you can build capability programs focusing on **skills, technology, culture**, and **partnerships**.

Senior management must communicate the chosen EHS business model and define how capabilities like **predictive analytics, IoT-driven safety monitoring**, and **automated compliance tracking** fit into the overall strategy. These choices will dictate the scope of your investment, including upskilling staff, implementing new technologies, and building partnerships to support continuous improvement.

The challenge is that becoming world-class in any of these capabilities—**real-time safety management** or **global compliance integration**—is a long-term commitment. Continuous focus and investment will be required across the organization to sustain success, but the payoff will be a safer, more compliant, and proactive EHS culture.

6. Do You Have the Leadership to Make Your EHS Transformation Happen?

Leadership is vital for driving any transformation, and in the case of **EHS digital transformation**, leaders must focus on two primary tasks: **(1) Aligning the organization with new EHS models** (e.g., proactive safety management) and **(2) Shaping the culture** so that the company not only reaches its targets but continues to evolve as technology advances.

Leaders must guide the transformation by **setting clear goals** and continuously **tracking progress** toward achieving new EHS standards, such as real-time compliance tracking or integrating IoT-driven safety monitoring. A key method to ensure progress is to set specific, measurable **revenue targets,**

operational improvements, or safety metrics that align with your chosen EHS business model. Leaders should avoid a common pitfall—scattering resources across too many initiatives without focusing innovation efforts on the strategic EHS decisions that have already been made.

Cultural change is also crucial. EHS leaders can foster a **data-driven culture** where safety decisions are based on predictive analytics and real-time monitoring, thus embedding an evidence-based approach. Engaging **more employees in innovation** (e.g., enabling them to contribute to EHS improvements) is another critical goal. Building strong **partnerships**, internally through cross-functional collaboration and externally with EHS solution providers, is essential for maintaining safety leadership in the digital era.

Finally, it's essential to have the right leader guiding the EHS transformation. For example:

- **CIOs** are well-positioned to lead when **platforms and technology** are central to transformation (e.g., IoT integration).

- **Chief EHS Officers** can lead when **safety culture and compliance** are the primary focus.

- For enterprises focusing on **integrated ecosystems**, the **COO or CEO** might need to drive the transformation to align all aspects of EHS into a unified, proactive framework.

Ensuring that the right person is in charge of transformation will significantly contribute to achieving long-term success in EHS.

The research and writing we've undertaken for this book have been an incredibly rewarding journey. First, we understand what is crucial for leaders in **EHS transformation,** and then we observe how they implement these findings, providing invaluable feedback on what works and what doesn't.

None of the leaders we studied had **EHS transformations** that came quickly. Transforming safety and environmental management practices in a digital age is challenging work. Successful transformations require leaders to build a shared understanding of the **risks and opportunities**, articulate where the company is headed, and communicate that vision clearly across the organization. They must make hard decisions about **roles, responsibilities**, and **organizational restructuring**. It's also critical to ensure that the company's

safety capabilities and **innovation** investments align with decisions about EHS goals, competitive advantages, and operational needs. All of this must happen while developing the leadership and talent needed to implement these changes. Additionally, leaders must foster a culture that supports **proactive safety management**—aligning incentives, training, and investments with this vision, and holding people accountable for results.

These steps represent a formidable challenge, but the rewards are immense, both for the leaders themselves and for the entire enterprise. The digital era offers a unique and thrilling opportunity—it's not often that leaders have the chance to **reinvent safety management** in such a transformative way. Now it's your turn. What actions will you take today to ensure your enterprise is positioned for a safer, more sustainable future?

Digital Leadership

Introduction to Leadership's Role in EHS Digital Transformation

In Environment, Health, and Safety (EHS), digital transformation represents far more than simply implementing new technologies. It is a strategic evolution that requires a fundamental shift in organizational culture. This transformation is spearheaded by visionary leadership, as highlighted in *"Leading Digital: Turning Technology into Business Transformation"* by George Westerman, Didier Bonnet, and Andrew McAfee. The book emphasizes that successful digital transformation hinges on leaders who can articulate a clear vision, guide the organization through change, and foster a digital-first culture.

At its core, digital transformation in EHS involves rethinking how the organization approaches risk management, compliance, and sustainability through technology. Leaders play a pivotal role in this process by ensuring that digital initiatives are not isolated technical upgrades but are integrated into the company's long-term strategic goals. They must communicate a compelling vision highlighting the efficiency and safety improvements digital tools can bring and emphasize how these technologies align with broader corporate objectives like sustainability and operational excellence.

Leadership is particularly critical in driving **cultural change**. A digital-first culture requires a mindset shift from all employees, encouraging collaboration, innovation, and the adoption of new technologies across departments. As Westerman et al. point out, fostering this type of culture involves more than just implementing tools; it requires leaders to engage their teams, encourage experimentation, and create an environment where learning from failures is acceptable. Without this cultural foundation, even the most advanced digital tools will likely fall short of their potential.

Moreover, leaders in EHS must work to break down silos that traditionally exist between departments like IT, operations, and safety. They must ensure that digital transformation is a cross-functional effort that involves stakeholders from all levels. According to LNS Research, a *Connected Workforce* strategy is essential for EHS leaders to integrate technology into everyday operations, ensuring that digital tools like IoT, data analytics, and real-time risk management systems are used effectively to enhance safety and compliance.

The role of leadership In EHS digital transformation Is not limited to technical oversight; it involves championing **change management** and continuously reinforcing the importance of digital tools in everyday safety practices. Leaders must model the behavior they want to see, demonstrating an openness to innovation and encouraging their teams to engage with new technologies. As a result, organizations can cultivate a safety culture that is proactive, data-driven, and aligned with the organization's overall digital strategy.

In conclusion, leadership is the driving force behind successful EHS digital transformation. By creating a clear vision, fostering a digital-first culture, and aligning technology initiatives with broader strategic goals, leaders can ensure that digital tools significantly enhance safety, compliance, and operational efficiency across the organization. With committed leadership, EHS digital transformation risks becoming a cohesive effort rather than a sustained and integrated cultural shift.

Transformational Leadership for EHS

Transformational leadership is critical in driving successful digital transformation within the Environment, Health, and Safety (EHS) space. According to *"The Role of Leadership in Organizational Culture and EHS Performance"* (Journal of Safety Research, 2019), transformational leadership is not just about managing day-to-day operations; it's about inspiring and motivating employees to go beyond compliance and embrace digital tools and innovative practices that enhance safety outcomes and ensure sustainability.

7. Inspiring Vision and Motivation

Transformational leaders in EHS play a crucial role in creating and communicating a clear and compelling vision for digital transformation. This vision includes the adoption of cutting-edge tools such as AI-driven analytics, IoT for real-time monitoring, and digital dashboards for tracking compliance and how these tools align with the organization's mission of ensuring safety and environmental sustainability. By providing this vision, leaders inspire employees to see the broader impact of their work, fostering a sense of ownership and purpose.

A compelling vision also acts as a motivational force. Employees are more likely to embrace digital tools and new practices when they understand their role in achieving overarching goals, such as reducing workplace incidents, minimizing environmental impacts, and improving regulatory compliance. Transformational leaders use this vision to generate excitement and commitment across all levels of the organization.

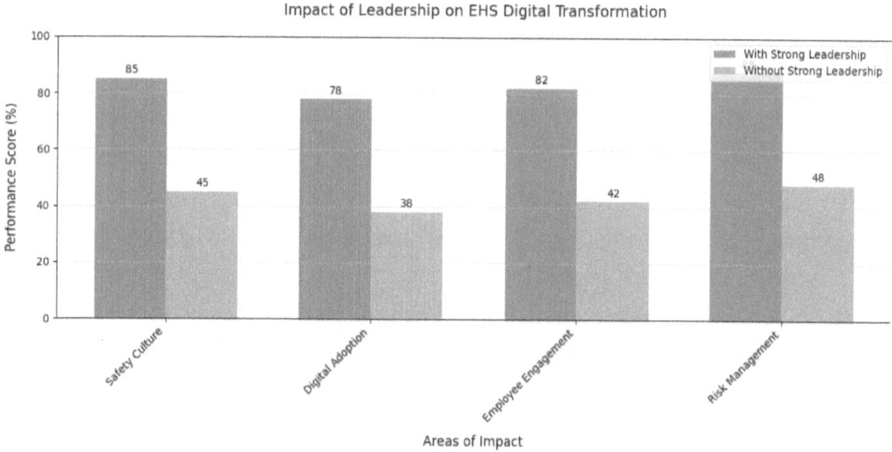

Figure 9.1: Impact of leadership on EHS Digital Transformation

2. Fostering a Culture of Innovation

One of the hallmarks of transformational leadership is the ability to create an environment where innovation is encouraged, and employees are not afraid to take risks and experiment with new ideas. This is particularly important in the context of EHS digital transformation, where leaders need to promote the adoption of new technologies, such as predictive analytics for risk management or virtual reality for safety training.

According to the *Journal of Safety Research* (2019), transformational leaders foster a culture of continuous improvement by encouraging their teams to seek innovative solutions to traditional EHS challenges. Instead of relying on reactive safety measures, employees are empowered to use data analytics and IoT sensors to predict potential hazards and take preventative action. This culture of innovation is vital for staying ahead of regulatory changes and improving safety and compliance outcomes.

3. Leading by Example and Building Trust

A Transformational leader models the behaviors they wish to see in their teams. By being early adopters of digital tools and technologies, they demonstrate the value of these innovations in enhancing EHS processes. For instance, a leader who actively engages with digital safety dashboards and data analytics tools signals to their team that these technologies are essential for achieving the organization's safety goals.

Building trust is another critical aspect of transformational leadership. Employees are more likely to follow a leader who is transparent and trustworthy. In the context of EHS, this means being open about the challenges and benefits of digital transformation, acknowledging potential risks, and involving employees in the decision-making process. By cultivating trust, leaders create a safe environment where employees feel empowered to embrace digital solutions without fear of failure.

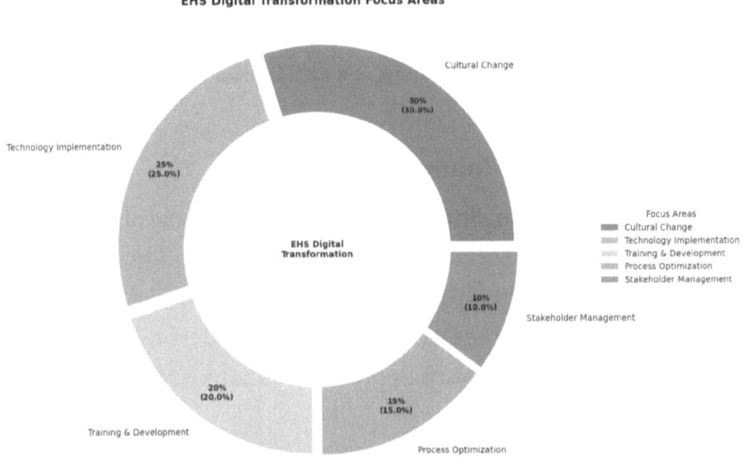

Figure 9.2: EHS Digital transformation focus areas

4. Personalizing Support and Development

Transformational leaders recognize their employees' individual needs and potential. In EHS, digital transformation means offering personalized support to help employees develop the skills to use digital tools effectively. For example, some employees may require more training in data analysis, while others may need support using real-time monitoring systems or AI-based predictive tools.

By offering tailored training and development opportunities, transformational leaders ensure that employees are not just using digital tools but are using them effectively. This personalized approach leads to higher engagement, better safety outcomes, and a more prosperous digital transformation overall.

5. Encouraging Collaboration and Teamwork

Transformational leadership in EHS also focuses on breaking down silos and encouraging cross-functional collaboration. Digital transformation often requires input and coordination between various departments, such as IT, operations, and safety teams. Leaders who promote collaboration foster an environment where different teams can share knowledge and collaborate to implement digital solutions that benefit the organization.

For example, when implementing IoT for real-time safety monitoring, collaboration between IT specialists and EHS professionals ensures that the technology is both technically sound and practically helpful in identifying and mitigating risks on the ground. This collaborative approach ensures that digital transformation efforts are holistic and integrated across the organization.

Conclusion

In summary, transformational leadership is essential for successful digital transformation in EHS. Leaders who can inspire a compelling vision, foster a culture of innovation, build trust, offer personalized support, and encourage collaboration will be more effective in motivating their teams to embrace digital tools and practices. This, in turn, leads to better safety outcomes, enhanced compliance, and a more sustainable organization. As EHS continues to evolve with the integration of advanced technologies, transformational leadership will remain a key driver for organizational success in this critical area.

Embedding Safety Culture in High-Reliability Organizations (HROs)

High-reliability organizations (HROs) operate in high-risk environments where the potential for error can have catastrophic consequences, yet they maintain exceptionally high safety records. Industries such as aviation, nuclear power, and healthcare are often cited as examples of HROs, where safety is ingrained into every level of the organization. Leadership is critical in fostering this pervasive culture of safety, as outlined in *"Building a Culture of Safety: Leadership Lessons from High-Reliability Organizations"* (Safety Science, 2020). The leadership practices in these organizations provide valuable lessons that can be directly applied to **EHS's digital transformation**.

1. Leadership Commitment to Safety

HROs prioritize safety above all else, and this is a direct reflection of leadership's commitment. Leaders in HROs do more than implement policies and procedures; they actively promote safety as a core organizational value. This is achieved through continuous communication, regular engagement with frontline employees, and leading by example. Safety is integrated into every business decision, and leaders consistently reinforce its importance.

In the context of **EHS digital transformation**, this leadership commitment translates to embedding safety considerations into every journey phase. When adopting digital tools such as IoT sensors for real-time monitoring or AI-based risk management systems, leaders must ensure that safety is a non-negotiable factor. Leadership must visibly champion the use of digital technologies to enhance safety, showing employees that digital transformation is not just about operational efficiency but about elevating safety standards across the organization.

2. Fostering a Preoccupation with Failure

One of the critical traits of HROs is their preoccupation with failure. Rather than assuming that everything will go as planned, these organizations operate with the mindset that errors can happen at any time and must be anticipated. Leadership encourages constant vigilance where employees are trained to look for minor, early warning signs of potential problems before they escalate into significant risks. This mentality helps prevent incidents from occurring by proactively identifying risks.

In an EHS digital transformation context, this preoccupation with failure can be supported by digital tools such as predictive analytics, which use data to anticipate safety incidents before they happen. Leadership can drive the implementation of these tools and ensure they are used effectively by training employees to interpret the data and act on potential risks early. For instance, by using predictive maintenance technology in hazardous environments, companies can predict equipment failures and take corrective action before accidents occur.

3. Reluctance to Simplify Interpretations

Leaders in HROs avoid oversimplifying complex safety issues. They recognize that safety is multi-dimensional and requires a nuanced understanding of various factors, including human behavior, technological systems, and environmental conditions. As a result, they encourage open dialogue, diverse perspectives, and cross-functional collaboration to ensure that safety issues are fully understood before decisions are made.

In the EHS domain, digital transformation often involves complex technologies, such as advanced data analytics and machine learning models. Leaders must ensure that employees are equipped with the knowledge to handle these complexities and that safety issues are accurate. For example, when using data analytics for safety monitoring, leadership should encourage teams to dive deeply into the data and identify subtle patterns indicating underlying safety risks rather than relying on surface-level interpretations.

4. Deference to Expertise

HROs strongly emphasize deferring to the expertise of individuals closest to the work. Leaders in HROs understand that frontline employees often have the most direct experience with safety risks, and therefore, their input is invaluable when making decisions. By empowering these employees to take the lead in identifying and addressing safety issues, HROs ensure that decision-making is informed by practical, real-time knowledge.

In the context of EHS digital transformation, leaders should create a culture where frontline workers are empowered to use digital tools and provide feedback on their effectiveness. For instance, workers using wearable devices to monitor air quality in real-time should be encouraged to share their insights and suggest improvements to how the technology is used. By fostering this deference to expertise, leadership ensures that the digital tools implemented align with the actual needs and challenges employees face on the ground.

5. A Commitment to Resilience

HROs are characterized by their ability to adapt and respond to unexpected events. Leadership in these organizations ensures that systems and processes are designed to be resilient, meaning that when disruptions occur, the organization can quickly recover without compromising safety. This is achieved through thorough training, well-defined contingency plans, and real-time data to inform decision-making.

Digital transformation in EHS can enhance resilience by providing real-time data, enabling organizations to respond swiftly to safety incidents. Leaders must ensure that their teams are trained to use these tools effectively and that contingency plans are in place for potential digital system failures. For example, in an IoT sensor malfunction, employees should be trained on manual procedures to maintain safety. Leadership's focus on resilience ensures that digital tools enhance rather than detract from the organization's ability to respond to risks.

Applying HRO Lessons to EHS Digital Transformation

The leadership practices from HROs can be directly applied to the digital transformation of EHS. As organizations adopt digital tools, leadership must foster a culture where safety is prioritized, failure is anticipated, and employees are empowered to take an active role in maintaining safety. Digital transformation provides new tools to enhance safety, but without strong leadership that embeds these principles into the organization's culture, the benefits of these tools may not be fully realized.

In conclusion, HROs offer a wealth of knowledge on building and sustaining a pervasive safety culture. These lessons are especially relevant as organizations look to transform their EHS practices through digital innovation. Leaders who adopt these practices will be well-positioned to guide their organizations through successful and sustainable EHS digital transformation.

Driving Cultural Change through Digital Leadership

Leadership's role in driving cultural change is essential for a successful EHS digital transformation. A digital-first culture supports implementing new technologies and fosters an environment where innovation, collaboration, and continuous learning thrive. Leaders are responsible for embedding these values into the organization's DNA and ensuring digital tools are fully embraced and optimized across all workforce levels.

1. Creating a Culture of Innovation

Leaders must foster a culture encouraging experimentation and risk-taking, which is essential for driving innovation in EHS's digital transformation. According to *"Digital Transformation in EHS: Leadership and Culture,"* Deloitte Insights (2021), companies that have successfully integrated digital tools into their EHS practices are those where leadership promotes a culture of continuous improvement and innovation. These organizations empower employees to experiment with new technologies, like predictive analytics and AI, without fear of failure. Leaders set the tone by emphasizing that innovation is an iterative process, where setbacks are learning opportunities rather than obstacles.

To cultivate this culture, leaders should:

- **Encourage experimentation**: Employees should feel comfortable trying new digital tools and proposing innovative solutions to EHS challenges. Leaders can create an environment that nurtures creative problem-solving by celebrating small wins and allowing room for failure.

- **Provide innovation resources: Investing** in training programs and cutting-edge technologies, such as IoT, for real-time monitoring or AI-driven risk management is essential. This equips employees with the tools they need and signals leadership's commitment to staying at the forefront of innovation.

2. Promoting Cross-Functional Collaboration

Digital transformation often requires breaking down organizational silos, and leadership plays a crucial role in fostering collaboration between departments. For EHS to fully leverage digital tools, close cooperation is needed between departments such as IT, operations, and safety teams. Leaders must actively promote an open culture where cross-functional teams work together to implement and maintain digital solutions, ensuring these technologies are optimized for EHS applications.

Deloitte's report highlights how companies that successfully transform their EHS functions through digital initiatives often have leaders who prioritize cross-functional collaboration.

For example, IT teams might handle the technical setup when implementing IoT for workplace safety, while EHS professionals interpret the data and ensure compliance with safety standards. By encouraging teamwork and knowledge-sharing across departments, leaders ensure that digital tools are applied effectively and holistically across the organization.

3. Embedding Continuous Learning

A digital-first culture requires continuous learning, where employees constantly update their skills and stay abreast of new technologies and practices. In the fast-evolving digital landscape, EHS teams must continuously improve their knowledge to keep up with new technologies like advanced data analytics, machine learning models for risk assessment, and automated compliance tools.

Leadership can drive continuous learning by:

- **Providing ongoing training**: Organizations should offer training and development programs that equip employees with the skills to navigate new digital tools. This includes technical training and soft skills like data interpretation and digital communication.

- **Promoting a growth mindset**: Leaders should encourage a growth mindset, where employees view challenges as opportunities to learn and grow. This mindset supports the adoption of digital tools and processes as employees become more adaptable to technological changes

4. Leveraging Digital-First Strategies

A digital-first approach means integrating digital tools into the very fabric of EHS processes. Leadership must champion digital initiatives by ensuring that these tools are used to improve efficiency and enhance safety outcomes and compliance. This means adopting a strategic approach where digital technologies are aligned with broader EHS goals and objectives.

For instance, implementing predictive analytics can shift the EHS focus from reactive to proactive risk management. Leaders must communicate the value of these tools and guide their teams in using them effectively to prevent incidents before they occur. This also involves integrating digital dashboards for real-time monitoring, ensuring that employees at all levels have access to critical safety data and insights

5. Encouraging Employee Engagement with Digital Tools

For digital transformation to succeed, leaders must ensure employees fully engage with the new digital tools. This involves more than just training; it requires creating a sense of ownership and accountability among employees. Leaders should encourage employees to actively participate in the digital transformation process, providing feedback on the tools' effectiveness and suggesting improvements.

By involving employees in the decision-making process, leadership can foster a sense of empowerment and ensure that digital tools are tailored to meet the organization's unique needs. This also promotes a culture where digital tools are not seen as external impositions but as integral parts of daily operations that enhance safety and productivity

Conclusion

Driving cultural change through digital leadership is a multi-faceted effort that requires a strong focus on innovation, collaboration, continuous learning, and employee engagement. Leaders in EHS must champion digital-first strategies, ensuring that digital tools are implemented and embedded into the organization's culture. Leaders can create an environment where digital transformation thrives by promoting a growth mindset, encouraging experimentation, and fostering cross-functional collaboration, leading to enhanced safety, compliance, and operational excellence.

The insights from Deloitte's *"Digital Transformation in EHS: Leadership and Culture"* offer a roadmap for how leaders can effectively guide their teams through this cultural shift and ensure that digital initiatives result in meaningful and lasting improvements.

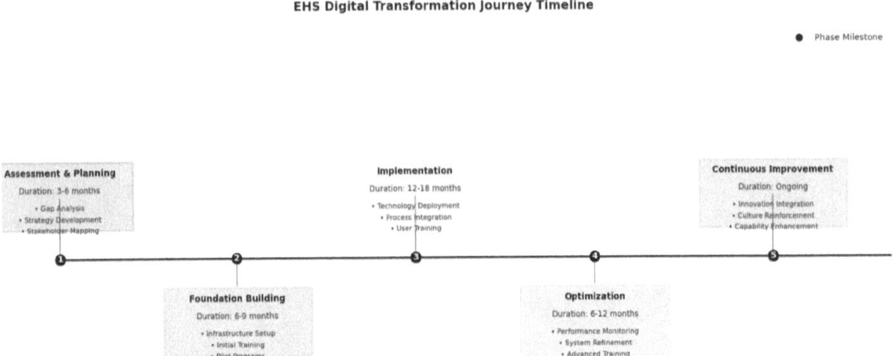

Figure 9.3: EHS Digital Transformation Journey timeline

Leadership Strategies for a Digital-First Safety Culture

A **digital-first safety culture** in the Environment, Health, and Safety (EHS) domain is one in which technology is fully integrated into safety processes, decision-making, and employee behaviors. Leadership is crucial in building this culture, especially in setting clear strategic goals, engaging stakeholders, and managing change. According to McKinsey & Company's *"The Future of EHS: Leadership Strategies for Digital Transformation,"* there are key strategies that leaders can adopt to ensure a thriving digital-first safety culture.

1. Setting Clear and Aligned Goals

To build a digital-first safety culture, leaders must start by setting clear, strategic goals aligning with EHS objectives and broader organizational priorities. These goals should articulate how digital tools will improve safety outcomes, reduce incidents, and ensure regulatory compliance. Leadership must communicate these goals effectively throughout the organization, ensuring employees understand how adopting digital tools contributes to safer working environments.

Key Actions:

- Define measurable EHS outcomes that digital transformation will support (e.g., reducing workplace injuries by leveraging predictive analytics).

- Align these goals with the organization's long-term sustainability or operational excellence objectives.

- Create roadmaps that identify critical milestones for digital adoption across different EHS functions.

2. Ensuring Continuous Training and Skill Development

Digital transformation often introduces new technologies that employees may need to become more familiar with, such as AI-based safety tools, IoT devices for real-time monitoring, or advanced data analytics for risk management. Leaders must ensure employees receive continuous training and development opportunities to use these tools effectively. This involves technical training and fostering digital literacy and comfort with data-driven decision-making across the organization.

Key Actions:

- Develop training programs focusing on the technical and strategic aspects of digital tools in EHS.

- Provide ongoing workshops and hands-on sessions for employees to familiarize themselves with new technologies, such as wearable devices for real-time hazard detection or digital dashboards for compliance tracking(

- Encourage cross-functional learning, where IT and EHS professionals collaborate to enhance their digital capabilities.

3. Fostering Employee Engagement with Digital Tools

Building a digital-first safety culture requires active engagement from employees at all levels. Leadership should create an environment where employees feel empowered to use digital tools and are encouraged to provide feedback on their effectiveness. Engaged employees are more likely to adopt and optimize digital safety tools, improving safety outcomes. Leaders can promote engagement by involving employees in selecting and implementing these tools and ensuring they understand the tangible benefits of their day-to-day roles.

Key Actions:

- Establish feedback loops where employees can share their experiences and suggestions regarding the digital tools in place.

- Involve employees in pilot programs for new technologies to ensure their input is considered in broader adoption.

- Use success stories and real-life examples to demonstrate the impact of digital tools on workplace safety, motivating employees to engage with the technology.

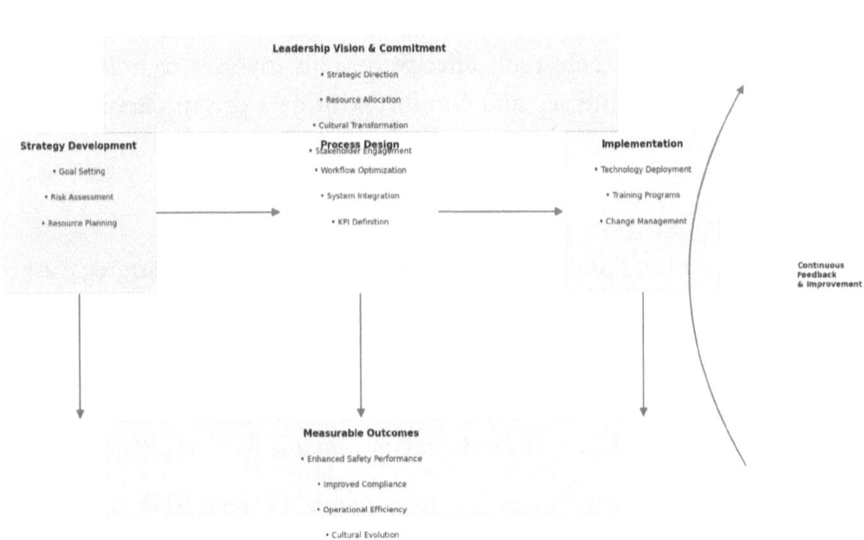

Figure 9.4: Leadership influence on EHS Digital Transformation

4. Promoting Stakeholder Engagement

Leaders must focus on internal teams and ensure that external stakeholders are engaged in the EHS digital transformation process. This includes collaborating with regulatory bodies, external auditors, and technology partners to ensure compliance and successfully implement digital tools. Engaging stakeholders early and frequently helps identify potential challenges and ensures alignment across all parties.

Key Actions:

- Hold regular meetings with key stakeholders to align on safety and compliance goals and discuss the progress of digital initiatives.

- Work closely with technology providers to customize digital solutions that meet the unique needs of the organization's EHS function.

- Engage with external experts to validate the effectiveness of digital tools in improving safety and regulatory compliance(

5. Leading Change Management

Adopting digital tools in EHS is not just a technical change but a cultural shift requiring effective change management. Leaders must manage this change by actively guiding their teams through the transformation, addressing resistance, and ensuring the new digital processes are integrated into the EHS function's daily operations. This involves clear communication, managing expectations, and providing employees with an understanding of how digital tools enhance safety and make their jobs easier.

Key Actions:

- Communicate the benefits of digital transformation regularly and clearly, emphasizing how these tools improve safety and compliance while reducing operational risks.

- Create change champions within teams—employees who can advocate for digital tools and help colleagues adapt to new processes.

- Monitor the adoption of digital tools closely, using data to track the effectiveness and identify areas where further support may be needed(

Conclusion

Leadership is central to building a digital-first safety culture in EHS. Leaders can create an environment where digital tools are fully integrated into safety practices by setting clear goals, ensuring continuous training, fostering employee engagement, promoting stakeholder involvement, and effectively managing change. This results in improved safety outcomes, more effective compliance, and a culture prepared for the challenges and opportunities of the digital age. As outlined in McKinsey's *"The Future of EHS: Leadership Strategies for Digital Transformation,"* these leadership strategies are vital to ensuring the success of EHS digital transformation(

Case Study: Leadership-Driven EHS Digital Transformation at DuPont

DuPont is widely recognized as a leader in safety innovation. Its approach to EHS digital transformation is a benchmark for organizations seeking to improve safety outcomes through leadership commitment and the adoption of advanced technologies. DuPont's leadership has played a critical role in driving this transformation by setting clear strategic goals, fostering a safety-first culture, and leveraging digital tools like safety analytics and IoT (Internet of Things) for real-time monitoring.

1. Leadership's Role in Setting Clear Goals

DuPont's leadership prioritized safety as a core strategic objective. They understood that integrating digital tools into their safety practices would enhance compliance, improve operational efficiency, and reduce incidents. The leadership team set clear, measurable goals focused on reducing safety risks through technology to achieve this. This vision was communicated effectively across the organization, ensuring every employee understood digital transformation's importance in improving safety outcomes.

Key Actions:

- Leadership defined **safety performance metrics** that would be tracked through digital systems.

- Clear targets were set for reducing workplace incidents and leveraging digital tools to anticipate and prevent risks.

- The leadership team regularly communicated the importance of safety and technology adoption in achieving these goals, embedding digital transformation into the organization's long-term strategy.

2. Adoption of Digital Safety Analytics and IoT

One of the cornerstones of DuPont's digital transformation in EHS was the implementation of **safety analytics** and **IoT** technologies. These tools provided real-time data on workplace conditions, allowing the company to monitor potential risks and respond proactively. For example, IoT sensors were installed in high-risk environments to detect changes in air quality, temperature, and machinery performance, all of which could indicate potential safety hazards.

DuPont's leadership ensured these technologies were integrated into the company's operations rather than siloed as standalone systems. By doing so, safety data became a vital part of the decision-making process, empowering employees and managers alike to act on real-time insights to prevent incidents before they occur.

Key Actions:

- DuPont invested in **real-time monitoring systems** powered by IoT, enabling continuous surveillance of workplace environments.

- The leadership promoted using **data analytics** to identify trends and predict safety risks based on historical and real-time data.

- Employees were trained extensively on how to interpret the data and respond to potential risks, ensuring that digital tools were fully integrated into the safety culture(

3. Leadership Commitment to Training and Development

DuPont's digital transformation was not just about technology but also about people. Leadership recognized that successfully adopting digital tools required well-versed employees at all levels. Therefore, they implemented comprehensive **training programs** to ensure employees were equipped with the skills to use IoT devices, interpret safety data, and make data-driven decisions.

These training programs were designed to build digital literacy within the workforce and create a culture of **continuous learning**. Leadership ensured that employees understood how to use the tools and why they were necessary for safety and operational excellence. This commitment to training created a workforce engaged with the digital transformation process and motivated to improve safety outcomes.

Key Actions:

- Leadership launched **extensive training programs** for employees to build their digital and analytical skills.

- Employees were encouraged to participate in **ongoing learning opportunities** to stay updated on the latest EHS technologies.

- Leadership reinforced the importance of digital tools through regular workshops, safety briefings, and feedback sessions, creating a culture of embracing digital transformation at all levels.

4. Cultural Shift Towards a Safety-First Mindset

At DuPont, leadership also played a pivotal role in driving a cultural shift towards a **safety-first mindset**. This shift was critical for ensuring the long-term success of the company's EHS digital transformation efforts. The leadership team worked to embed safety into every aspect of the company's operations, ensuring that safety was prioritized in high-risk areas and across all departments and functions.

Digital tools that provided greater transparency into safety performance supported this cultural transformation. Digital dashboards and analytics tools allow managers and employees to track safety metrics in real-time, making safety a visible and measurable part of daily operations. This transparency helped foster accountability and encouraged employees to take ownership of safety in their roles.

Key Actions:
- Leadership **prioritized safety** in all operational and strategic decisions, ensuring it was treated as a core value rather than an afterthought.

- Digital dashboards and real-time data tools were used to track safety metrics, fostering a culture of **transparency and accountability**.

- Leadership reinforced the safety-first mindset through **employee recognition programs**, celebrating teams that made significant contributions to improving safety using digital tools(

Key Outcomes
- Due to its leadership-driven digital transformation, DuPont saw significant improvements in **safety performance**. Workplace incidents were reduced, and the company achieved higher compliance with safety regulations.

- **Employee engagement** with safety initiatives increased as workers were empowered by the real-time data provided by IoT sensors and analytics tools.

- The company developed a **proactive safety culture**, where potential risks were identified and addressed before incidents could occur, thanks to the predictive capabilities of digital tools(

Conclusion

DuPont's leadership-driven approach to EHS digital transformation offers a powerful example of how commitment to clear goals, technology adoption, and cultural shifts can drive safety improvements. DuPont's leadership ensured that digital tools were implemented and embraced by setting a vision for digital transformation, investing in training, and embedding safety into the company's culture. This case demonstrates the transformative power of leadership in making EHS a digital-first function that enhances safety, compliance, and operational excellence.

This example can be a model for other organizations looking to lead their EHS digital transformation efforts. Through strong leadership and a focus on continuous improvement, companies can leverage digital technologies to create safer, more resilient operations.

Case Study: BAF's Leadership in Fostering Continuous Improvement and Digital Twin Integration

BASF, one of the world's largest chemical companies, has long been recognized for its innovative approach to sustainability and safety. The company's leadership has been pivotal in driving continuous improvement through digital transformation, particularly by aligning its **EHS (Environment, Health, and Safety) goals with sustainability** and leveraging cutting-edge technologies like **digital twins** for real-time monitoring and risk management. This integration of digital tools has allowed BASF to achieve more efficient and safer operations while meeting stringent sustainability targets.

1. Leadership Commitment to Continuous Improvement

BASF's leadership has consistently emphasized the importance of continuous safety and operational efficiency improvement. They recognize that maintaining the highest safety standards is a dynamic process that requires constant adaptation and refinement. Through regular assessments and goal-setting, BASF's leadership ensures that the company remains at the forefront of safety innovation, using data-driven insights to enhance performance.

Key Actions:

- **Strategic Planning**: BASF leadership regularly revisits its EHS strategy, aligning it with global sustainability goals such as reducing greenhouse gas emissions and improving energy efficiency. This ensures that safety and sustainability are integrated rather than treated as separate initiatives.

- **Performance Metrics**: By setting clear performance metrics and benchmarks, BASF's leadership encourages a culture of continuous improvement embedded in daily operations. These metrics are tied directly to the company's sustainability goals and monitored using digital technologies.

2. Integration of Digital Twin Technology

One of the key technological innovations embraced by BASF's leadership is the implementation of **digital twin technology**. A digital twin is a virtual replica of physical assets, processes, or systems that allows real-time monitoring and predictive analysis. Using digital twins, BASF can simulate various safety and operational scenarios, identify potential risks, and proactively adjust to improve performance.

Key Actions:

- **Real-Time Monitoring**: BASF's digital twin technology allows for real-time tracking of critical plant operations, providing insights into equipment performance, environmental conditions, and safety risks. Sensors installed throughout their plants feed data into digital twin models, allowing operators to monitor real-time conditions like temperature, pressure, and emissions.

- **Predictive Maintenance**: By integrating IoT sensors and digital twin technology, BASF can predict equipment failures before they occur. This reduces downtime, minimizes safety risks, and ensures smoother operations. For example, the system can alert operators when a machine is likely to fail, allowing them to conduct maintenance proactively rather than reactively.

- **Scenario Planning**: Digital twins enable BASF to simulate "what-if" scenarios, such as potential equipment malfunctions or environmental changes, to assess how these factors might impact safety and sustainability. This predictive capability enhances decision-making, allowing the company to mitigate risks before they manifest.

3. Strategic Alignment of EHS and Sustainability Goals

BASF's leadership has successfully aligned its EHS initiatives with broader sustainability goals. The company's **sustainability strategy** focuses on minimizing environmental impact, improving energy efficiency, and enhancing operational safety, all of which are closely linked to its EHS digital transformation efforts.

Key Actions:

- **Sustainability and Safety Integration**: BASF's leadership ensures that safety is not viewed in isolation but is tightly integrated with the company's sustainability initiatives. For instance, reducing emissions and minimizing resource use are both safety and sustainability objectives. Through digital twins, BASF can track energy usage and emissions in real time, making adjustments to optimize safety and environmental performance.

- **Data-Driven Decision-Making**: BASF uses real-time data to make informed decisions that improve safety and support sustainability goals. For example, real-time monitoring through digital twins helps the company ensure that production processes remain safe while reducing its environmental footprint by optimizing resource use.

- **Cross-Functional Collaboration**: Leadership fosters collaboration between EHS, sustainability, and operations teams to ensure that digital tools like the digital twin are used effectively across departments. This holistic approach strengthens BASF's commitment to operational safety and environmental sustainability.

4. Building a Culture of Innovation and Collaboration

BASF leadership actively promotes a culture of innovation and cross-departmental collaboration to encourage the adoption of digital tools. Employees are empowered to embrace technology and contribute to the company's continuous improvement efforts by leveraging digital platforms.

Key Actions:

- **Employee Engagement**: BASF's leadership encourages employees to engage with digital tools by providing training and development opportunities. Employees are given the resources and support needed to work with digital twins and other technologies, ensuring they can actively contribute to safety and sustainability initiatives.

- **Collaborative Platforms**: Leadership promotes using collaborative platforms where teams can share insights and data generated from digital twins, fostering greater collaboration across departments like EHS, IT, and operations.

Key Outcomes

- **Improved Safety and Efficiency**: By integrating digital twin technology, BASF has significantly enhanced the safety and efficiency of its operations. Real-time monitoring and predictive analytics have reduced the likelihood of equipment failures and safety incidents while optimizing resource use and energy efficiency.

- **Sustainability Performance**: BASF's leadership has successfully aligned its safety goals with sustainability objectives, using digital tools to minimize environmental impact while maintaining high safety standards. This alignment has improved compliance and bolstered the company's reputation as a leader in sustainable manufacturing.

- **Continuous Improvement Culture**: BASF has fostered a culture of constant improvement, where innovation and collaboration are central to safety and sustainability efforts. By empowering employees and using real-time data, BASF ensures that its operations are constantly evolving to meet the highest safety and environmental standards(

Conclusion

BASF's leadership in driving continuous improvement and integrating digital twin technology is a model for organizations looking to enhance their EHS performance through digital transformation. By strategically aligning safety with sustainability goals, investing in digital tools, and fostering a culture of innovation, BASF has improved safety outcomes while advancing its sustainability agenda. This case study highlights leadership's critical role in ensuring that digital transformation delivers meaningful and measurable results across safety, operations, and sustainability.

Case Study: Shell's Leadership in Promoting a Digital Safety Culture

Shell has been at the forefront of integrating digital tools into its Environment, Health, and Safety (EHS) practices, focusing on empowering employees through real-time data access and transparent safety reporting. The company's leadership has been critical in driving this transformation, mainly by adopting **mobile safety apps and digital dashboards** for continuous monitoring, reporting, and enhanced decision-making across their global operations. Shell's strategy revolves around creating a **digital-first safety culture** that empowers employees, increases transparency, and ultimately enhances operational safety.

1. Leadership Commitment to Digital Safety

Shell's leadership has long recognized the importance of safety in its high-risk energy sector. It has been proactive in adopting digital technologies to enhance safety processes. By embracing mobile apps and dashboards, Shell's leaders have enabled real-time access to critical safety data, improving decision-making at all levels of the organization. The leadership's commitment to digital safety is reflected in its investments in cutting-edge technologies that allow for more efficient monitoring and reporting of safety metrics.

Key Actions:

- **Adoption of Mobile Apps**: Shell deployed mobile applications that instantly enable employees to report safety incidents, hazards, and near misses. This shift from paper-based systems to mobile apps ensures that safety data is captured in real-time, allowing for quicker responses and data-driven decisions.

- **Use of Digital Dashboards**: Leadership implemented digital dashboards that aggregate safety data from various sources, giving managers and executives a real-time overview of safety performance across multiple locations. These dashboards are accessible to all levels of the organization, increasing transparency and fostering a culture of accountability(

2. Transparent Safety Reporting

Shell's leadership understood that building trust and accountability in safety requires a high level of **transparency**. Using mobile apps and digital dashboards, the company has created a system where safety data is available to everyone, from field workers to executives. This transparency ensures that safety incidents are not hidden or downplayed and that all stakeholders know current safety performance metrics.

Key Actions:

- **Real-Time Reporting**: Shell's mobile apps enable employees to report incidents quickly, providing immediate visibility into safety issues. This data is fed into digital dashboards, which track safety performance continuously. By allowing safety information to be reported and viewed instantly, Shell promotes a transparent safety culture in which employees are encouraged to maintain safety standards actively.

- **Accessible Dashboards**: Shell's digital dashboards are designed to be user-friendly and accessible to many employees, ensuring that safety metrics are easily understood and actionable. This transparency enables Shell's workforce to understand how their daily activities contribute to the overall safety performance of the organization(

3. Empowering Employees Through Digital Tools

A significant aspect of Shell's digital transformation in EHS is empowering employees through mobile apps and digital tools. By equipping employees with these tools, leadership encourages proactive engagement with safety initiatives, ensuring safety is embedded into the company's daily operations.

Key Actions:

- **Employee-Driven Reporting**: The introduction of mobile apps allows employees to take ownership of safety in their work environment. Employees can quickly report unsafe conditions or near-miss incidents without bureaucratic delays, empowering them to play a direct role in preventing accidents. This decentralized approach to safety reporting creates a sense of responsibility among workers.

- **Data-Driven Decision Making**: Shell's leadership ensures that employees can access the safety data they need to make informed decisions in real-time. Whether it's managing risks in the field or ensuring compliance with safety regulations, employees are empowered to act quickly and confidently using the data provided by mobile apps and dashboards(

4. Enhancing Accountability and Compliance

Shell's use of digital tools empowers employees and enhances **accountability** across all levels of the organization. Leadership uses digital dashboards to track safety metrics and ensure compliance with safety regulations is consistently met. With these tools, Shell's leadership can quickly identify trends, track performance, and intervene when necessary, creating a more proactive approach to safety management.

Key Actions:

- **Tracking Compliance Metrics**: Leadership monitors compliance through digital dashboards, which provide real-time insights into whether safety standards and regulatory requirements are being met. This approach allows Shell to avoid potential compliance issues and swiftly take corrective action.

- **Leadership Oversight**: Digital tools provide Shell's leadership with comprehensive oversight of safety performance. Regular reports generated from the dashboards are used to review progress, identify areas for improvement, and ensure accountability at all levels. This ensures that safety remains a top priority for the organization(

Key Outcomes

- **Improved Safety Performance**: Shell has reduced safety incidents by ensuring employees actively report hazards and incidents in real time through mobile apps and dashboards.

- **Increased Employee Engagement**: Shell's leadership-driven focus on digital safety tools has empowered employees to maintain safety standards proactively. The ease of reporting and access to data has resulted in higher employee participation in safety initiatives.

- **Enhanced Transparency and Accountability**: The transparent reporting of safety metrics has created a culture of accountability across Shell's global operations. Employees and managers alike have a clear view of safety performance, ensuring that issues are addressed promptly and effectively(

Conclusion

Shell's leadership has successfully promoted a **digital safety culture** by integrating mobile apps and digital dashboards into their EHS processes. These tools have empowered employees, increased transparency, and enhanced accountability, resulting in a more proactive and data-driven approach to safety. Shell's leadership commitment to digital safety serves as a model for organizations looking to harness technology to improve their safety performance and foster a culture of continuous improvement. By investing in real-time reporting and accessible safety data, Shell has positioned itself as a leader in EHS digital transformation, achieving operational safety and regulatory compliance at scale.

Figure 9.5: Organisational structure for EHS Digital transformation

Frameworks for Leading Cultural Change in EHS

Leading cultural change in EHS (Environment, Health, and Safety) during digital transformation is a complex process that requires structured approaches to ensure the change is successful and sustainable. One of the most well-regarded frameworks for managing organizational change is **Kotter's 8-Step Change Model**, which offers a clear, actionable roadmap that leaders can adopt to drive cultural change in EHS, particularly during the transition to digital systems and practices. This framework is highly relevant to EHS digital transformation, focusing on building urgency, collaboration, and anchoring new practices into the organization's culture.

Kotter's 8-Step Change Model Applied to EHS Transformation

1. Create a Sense of Urgency

The first step in Kotter's model is establishing a sense of urgency around the need for change. For EHS digital transformation, leaders must emphasize adopting digital tools to enhance safety, compliance, and sustainability. By demonstrating the risks of sticking to outdated practices (such as increased incidents or failure to comply with regulations), leaders can motivate employees to embrace new technologies.

Actions for EHS:

- Communicate the risks of inaction, such as workplace incidents and regulatory fines.

- Highlight the benefits of digital transformation, including improved safety outcomes, real-time monitoring, and predictive analytics.

- Share industry benchmarks showing how competitors have successfully implemented digital EHS solutions(

2. Build a Guiding Coalition

Kotter emphasizes the need to build a coalition of influential individuals who will support and drive the change. In EHS transformation, this coalition could include EHS managers, IT professionals, safety officers, and executives committed to implementing digital tools and practices.

Actions for EHS:

- Assemble a team of change champions across various departments to promote digital adoption.

- To create a comprehensive approach, ensure the coalition includes leaders at all levels, from executives to frontline workers.

- Assign roles and responsibilities for leading specific areas of digital transformation, such as implementing IoT sensors or training programs(

3. Form a Strategic Vision and Initiatives

Leaders must craft a clear vision for what the digital EHS transformation will achieve, including specific initiatives aligning with the broader organizational goals. The vision should include how digital tools improve safety performance, regulatory compliance, and operational efficiency.

Actions for EHS:

- Define the specific outcomes of the digital transformation, such as reducing incident rates or improving hazard identification through AI-powered tools.

- Align the EHS digital transformation with broader corporate sustainability goals to ensure long-term support.

- Break the vision into actionable initiatives, such as the deployment of mobile apps for safety reporting or predictive analytics for risk assessment(

4. Communicate the Vision

The vision must be communicated clearly and frequently for cultural change to take root. Leaders should use every available communication channel to share the benefits of digital transformation and how it will enhance safety practices in the organization.

Actions for EHS:

- Hold town halls, team meetings, and workshops to explain the EHS digital transformation vision.

- Use digital dashboards to demonstrate how real-time data improves safety outcomes.

- Provide regular updates on the progress of digital initiatives, ensuring transparency and reinforcing the urgency of the change(

5. Empower Employees for Broad-Based Action

To successfully implement digital tools in EHS, employees must feel empowered to change their roles. This involves removing obstacles, such as outdated processes or resistance to new technologies, and providing employees with the necessary tools, resources, and training.

Actions for EHS:

- Provide extensive training programs on new digital tools, such as mobile safety apps or IoT sensors.

- Encourage frontline workers to report safety issues using real-time digital platforms, making acting on potential hazards easier.

- Address cultural resistance by emphasizing the personal and organizational benefits of digital transformation(

6. Generate Short-Term Wins

Digital transformation can take a long time, so achieving and celebrating short-term wins is essential. These early successes help build momentum and keep employees motivated.

Actions for EHS:

- Identify small, achievable goals, such as implementing a digital dashboard or reducing incident reporting time through mobile apps.

- Celebrate early wins through company-wide announcements, highlighting teams that have successfully adopted new technologies.

- Use data from short-term wins to demonstrate the tangible benefits of digital transformation, such as improvements in safety performance metrics(

7. Sustain Acceleration

Even after early successes, leaders must keep the momentum and continue driving the transformation forward. This involves revisiting the goals, refining the strategies, and encouraging employees to keep pushing for improvement.

Actions for EHS:

- Continuously update digital systems and tools based on employee feedback and technological advancements.

- Set new, more challenging goals after each success to keep employees engaged and committed to continuous improvement.

- Maintain a strong leadership presence to ensure that digital transformation remains a priority(

8. Anchor New Approaches in the Culture

The final step in Kotter's model is ensuring the changes become embedded in the organization's culture. Digital tools and practices should become a standard part of EHS's operations, with continuous improvement ingrained in daily work processes.

Actions for EHS:

- Incorporate digital tools into performance evaluations, training programs, and safety procedures.

- Recognize and reward employees who exemplify the digital-first safety culture.

- Continuously reinforce the importance of digital tools in improving safety outcomes through leadership communication and company policies(

Conclusion

Kotter's 8-Step Change Model provides a structured framework for leading cultural change during EHS digital transformation. By creating urgency, building coalitions, communicating a clear vision, and empowering employees, leaders can drive a successful transformation that embeds digital tools into the safety culture. The model also emphasizes celebrating short-term wins and sustaining the momentum needed for long-term change. As EHS leaders guide their organizations through this journey, Kotter's framework offers a clear path to follow, ensuring that the transformation not only succeeds but also becomes a permanent part of the organizational culture(

ADKAR Model for Guiding Individual and Organizational Change in EHS

The **ADKAR Model** is a widely used change management framework that guides individual and organizational transformation. Developed by Prosci, it stands for **Awareness, Desire, Knowledge, Ability, and Reinforcement. The model** is beneficial in navigating complex transformations like those in the EHS (Environment, Health, and Safety) domain during digital transitions. It helps organizations break down the change process into manageable steps, ensuring employees are engaged and empowered throughout the journey.

1. Awareness of the Need for Change

The first step in the ADKAR model is building **awareness** about why the change is necessary. For EHS digital transformation, this involves explaining the reasons behind adopting digital tools—improving safety performance, ensuring compliance with new regulations, or enhancing operational efficiency. Leadership must communicate the risks of not evolving, such as missed opportunities for incident prevention or non-compliance penalties.

Actions for EHS:

- Highlight the increasing regulatory pressure and the role of digital tools in meeting safety and compliance requirements.

- Share incidents that could have been prevented with real-time data from IoT sensors or predictive analytics.

- Create a sense of urgency by discussing the competitive advantages of adopting EHS digital technologies.

2. Desire to Support the Change

Next, leaders must foster an employee desire to embrace change. This is one of the most challenging steps, requiring alignment of personal motivations with organizational goals. Employees need to understand how adopting digital tools will benefit them directly through improved safety, streamlined processes, or reduced workloads.

Actions for EHS:

- Show employees how digital tools can make their jobs easier, safer, and more efficient (e.g., using mobile apps to report incidents).

- Involve employees in the decision-making process for selecting and implementing new digital systems.

- Recognize and reward employees who engage early with digital tools, fostering a positive attitude toward the transformation.

3. Knowledge of How to Change

Knowledge refers to providing employees with the training and skills to use digital tools and technologies effectively. Without the proper knowledge, even the most willing employees can feel lost during a digital transformation. This step involves creating structured learning programs that help employees understand both the technology and the processes that will change.

Actions for EHS:

- Offer training programs tailored to the specific needs of different employee groups, such as managers, field workers, or EHS professionals.

- Use hands-on workshops and simulations (e.g., training with IoT sensors, AI-based predictive analytics, or digital dashboards) to build competency in the new tools.

- Access online resources, manuals, and support channels to ensure employees can learn independently.

4. Ability to Implement the Change

The **ability** step concerns ensuring employees can successfully apply the knowledge they've gained to their day-to-day tasks. This means leaders must provide training and create an environment where employees can practice using the new tools without fear of failure. Leaders should also provide ongoing support to help employees overcome challenges as they integrate digital tools into their work.

Actions for EHS:

- Offer mentoring programs where more experienced employees or early adopters of digital tools can help others.

- Provide real-time feedback through digital dashboards to show employees how effectively they use new tools.

- Encourage experimentation with new systems and show tolerance for mistakes during the transition phase to establish a safe environment for learning.

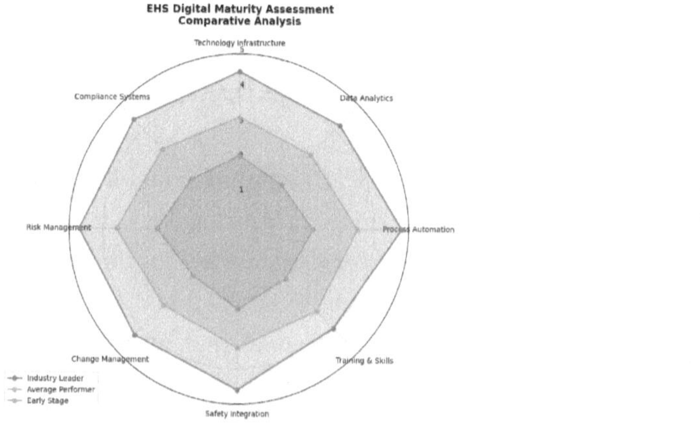

5. Reinforcement to Sustain the Change

The final step in the ADKAR model is **reinforcement**, which ensures that the change sticks and becomes a permanent part of the organizational culture. Leaders play a crucial role in embedding digital-first behaviors into daily practices and rewarding employees who continue to support and use the new systems.

Actions for EHS:

- Continue to measure the impact of digital tools on safety outcomes and operational efficiency through ongoing data analysis.

- Recognize and reward individuals or teams who have successfully adopted and championed digital tools.

- Use regular check-ins, surveys, and feedback loops to identify areas for reinforcement and adjust accordingly.

Conclusion

The ADKAR model is a robust framework for guiding cultural and organizational change, particularly in EHS digital transformation. By breaking down the change process into clear steps—awareness, desire, knowledge, ability, and reinforcement—leaders can ensure that their employees are prepared, motivated, and supported throughout the transformation journey. This structured approach helps foster the long-term adoption of digital tools, ensuring that safety and compliance are enhanced through new technologies. As EHS organizations increasingly adopt digital solutions, applying the ADKAR model can ensure a smoother and more successful transition.

Conclusion: Leadership as the Catalyst for EHS Digital Transformation

Leadership plays a pivotal role in the success of **EHS's digital transformation**. In this journey, visionary leadership acts as the catalyst, ensuring that integrating digital tools like predictive analytics, IoT, and real-time monitoring systems improves safety outcomes and aligns with broader organizational goals such as sustainability and operational efficiency. **EHS transformation** is far more than a technological shift—it is a cultural transformation that requires strong leadership to drive changes in mindset, behavior, and organizational processes.

The key to success lies in leadership's clear vision of how digital tools will enhance EHS practices. Leaders must inspire employees to embrace these technologies by showing how they will make workplaces safer, more compliant, and more efficient. As shown in case studies from industry leaders like **DuPont, BASF, and Shell**, leadership that sets clear goals, invests in continuous learning, and promotes transparent reporting is critical in ensuring that digital tools are not only implemented but fully integrated into everyday operations(

A successful EHS digital transformation also requires **a solid commitment to culture change**. Leaders must create an environment where innovation, collaboration, and continuous improvement are the norm. Using frameworks such as **Kotter's 8-Step Change Model** and the **ADKAR Model**, leadership can guide the organization through the cultural shifts necessary to make digital tools an integral part of safety and compliance processes. This involves empowering employees to take ownership of safety, providing them with the tools and training they need, and recognizing and rewarding their contributions to the transformation(

Finally, **continuous engagement with new technologies** is essential. Leaders must drive the initial adoption of digital tools and ensure that these technologies evolve alongside the organization's needs. This requires ongoing investment in training, data analysis, and system upgrades to ensure that the digital transformation remains relevant and effective over time.

In conclusion, the success of EHS digital transformation rests on leadership's ability to champion both technological innovation and cultural change. Visionary leaders who can set a strategic direction, foster a culture of continuous learning, and engage employees with digital tools will ensure that their organizations remain at the forefront of safety and compliance in an increasingly digital world.